The Peasantry in the
French Revolution

The Peasantry in the
French Revolution

P. M. JONES

Lecturer in Modern History
University of Birmingham

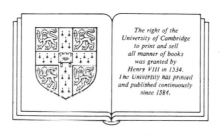

The right of the
University of Cambridge
to print and sell
all manner of books
was granted by
Henry VIII in 1534.
The University has printed
and published continuously
since 1584.

CAMBRIDGE UNIVERSITY PRESS

Cambridge
New York   New Rochelle
Melbourne   Sydney

Published by the Press Syndicate of the University of Cambridge
The Pitt Building, Trumpington Street, Cambridge CB2 1RP
32 East 57th Street, New York, NY 10022, USA
10 Stamford Road, Oakleigh, Melbourne 3166, Australia

First published 1988

Printed in Great Britain at Redwood Burn Ltd, Trowbridge, Wiltshire

British Library cataloguing in publication data
Jones, P. M.
The peasantry in the French Revolution.
1. French Revolution, 1789–1799. Role of peasants
I. Title
944.04

Library of Congress cataloguing in publication data applied for

ISBN 0 521 33070 X hard covers
ISBN 0 521 33716 X paperback

For Carolyn, Nicholas and Anna

Contents

Illustrations

Plates

Maps

Tables

Preface

This book fills a gap in the literature available to scholars and students on the social history of the French Revolution. As such it is a work of synthesis which contains little in the way of original research, and offers rather an up-to-date account of the part played by the peasantry in the events unfolding in France between 1787 and 1800. The extent to which I have relied upon research undertaken or inspired by Georges Lefebvre will be apparent to all but the most cursory reader. Rural historians owe an especially profound debt to Lefebvre, for it was he who set the terms of the debate over the relationship between the peasantry and the revolution. Fifty years after the publication of his *Paysans du Nord pendant la Révolution française* in 1924, Lefebvre's pioneering analysis of the revolutionary process still enjoyed widespread support. Only in comparatively recent times have scholars begun to examine the role of the peasantry from a different perspective.

Research into the origins of France's peasant revolution had been in progress for nearly two decades when Lefebvre's book came out. Yet the fruits of that research had not filtered into the standard textbooks. They depicted a drama in which the bourgeoisie hogged the stage. Neither the peasantry, nor, for that matter, the nobility played much more than 'walk on' parts. Lefebvre's unique contribution was to rescue the peasantry from the myth of their passivity. Not even the standard authorities, it is true, could overlook the role played by country dwellers in 1789, but Lefebvre formulated a vision of peasant activism which transcended 1789 and the struggle over feudalism. By uncovering clear signs of a pre-revolutionary agrarian crisis, by dislocating the rural insurrections from the fulcrum of 14 July, and by detailing a whole programme of socio-economic reforms which country dwellers expected their legislators to implement, he made the case for a separate, autonomous and intermittently antagonistic peasant revolution locked within the bosom of the bourgeois revolution portrayed in contemporary historiography.

⌈Their relationship was antagonistic because bourgeois and peasant did not see eye to eye on many of the issues brought to the boil by the revolution⌋ The question of common rights over field and fallow divided them, as did that of enclosure, of compulsory crop rotation and of common land partition. Indeed, Lefebvre goes so far as to argue that bourgeois and peasant juxtaposed rival conceptions of property. The former expected the revolution to vindicate absolute or freehold property rights, whereas the latter attached more significance to use or access rights. Even the vaunted joint offensive against the trappings of the feudal regime was not without tension and ambiguity: bourgeois proprietors were content to watch peasant insurgents destroying seigneurial rent rolls, but they were no less eager to form punitive militias when popular violence got out of hand. Would the revolutionary bourgeoisie ever have taken the decision to clear away unredeemed dues, had it not been for the persistent and unremitting pressure of country dwellers? The question is a nice one and serves to remind us that the peasantry should not be excluded from the historical stage.

Lefebvre's singular vision of an autonomous (and largely anti-capitalist) peasant revolution may be found in embryo in his monumental *Paysans du Nord*. Subsequently, he fleshed it out in a series of articles, culminating with a succinct statement of his views entitled: 'La Révolution française et les paysans' which appeared in 1933.[1] Curiously, this enormously influential article did not lead on to a comprehensive study of the peasantry during the revolution, yet no one was better qualified than Georges Lefebvre to write such an account. In the course of a long career as a working historian, he produced a daunting number of textbooks, but only one, *La Grande Peur de 1789* (1932), addressed the central idea of a distinctive peasant revolution. A collection of documents published with a commentary in the same year gives some indication as to how he might have set about drafting a synthetic history of the peasantry during the revolution,[2] but that is all. In a sense, therefore, the present endeavour may be regarded as the book which Lefebvre never wrote. What seems odd, in retrospect, is that no one has thought to write such a book before. True, Edmond Soreau published in 1936 a masterly survey of the urban and rural proletariat during the French Revolution, but his account of events stops abruptly with the deposition of Louis XVI.[3] More recently, Anatoli Ado, the Soviet historian, has mounted a challenge to the interpretation pioneered by Lefebvre in an impressive full-length study of the peasant revolution.[4] Yet his work remains inaccessible to the majority of French and English scholars since it remains untranslated from the Russian, and consequently difficult to use.

Whilst acknowledging Ado's attempt to instil fresh life into the debate over how the peasantry apprehended the revolution, the present book substantially endorses the viewpoint formulated by Georges Lefebvre. His work may be criticised on grounds of emphasis and omission; otherwise it has withstood the passage of time and the accretions of scholarship remarkably well. Nobody would today dispute the notion that the peasantry waged their own revolution which imperfectly coincided with that of the bourgeoisie. Perhaps he exaggerates the gulf in order to express his dissent from the prevailing orthodoxies of the late nineteenth century. And it may be that the distinction between peasant and bourgeois conceptions of property is too sharply drawn. Nevertheless, Lefebvre is surely correct in stressing the role of custom and customary agricultural practices in determining collective behaviour at the grass-roots. Whether this equates with a scenario pitting anti-capitalist poor peasants against resolutely modernising legislators has been questioned, by Ado among others. I would not quarrel with Lefebvre's depiction of the peasantry, but I find the capitalist thrust of successive revolutionary Assemblies to be overstated. To be sure, the revolutionary bourgeoisie wanted to press the agrarian reforms of the old monarchy to a successful conclusion. Yet what strikes the modern historian is their relative failure, not their relative success. In the face of massive popular resistance, the revolutionaries eschewed prescriptive legislation: collective rights and communal land holding survived, in consequence, as did much of the fabric of the rural community.

By contrast, the omissions are more glaring, although it would be anachronistic to condemn Lefebvre for failing to answer questions that historians had yet to pose. His is a socio-economic interpretation of peasant responses to the revolution, an interpretation, moreover, which bears the marks of debates current among intellectuals in the early decades of the twentieth century. Implied in the detailed attention which he pays to land ownership and social structure is a comparison between the serf economies of the East and the more settled and differentiated peasant societies of Western Europe. While he was preparing *Les Paysans du Nord*, revolution broke out in the Russian Empire and peasant political parties emerged in several of the successor states of Eastern Europe. Not surprisingly, such events helped to clarify, but also, perhaps, to narrow his understanding of the processes which predisposed country dwellers to collective action. It was feudalism, he believed, which impelled the peasantry into the political arena in the first place, and it was fear of feudalism which kept them there – united and watchful – until the summer of 1792. In marked contrast, the non-economic facets of peasant politicisation receive short shrift. The cultural impact of the French Revolution at the grass-roots goes by default; religion rates scarcely a mention; and the integrative function of electoral democracy remains unexplored. As for counter-revolution, Lefebvre was smitten with the myopia common among republican historians of his generation and appears never to have entertained the possibility of a peasant-based movement of opposition to the new regime.

Much new material bearing upon the peasantry has been published in recent decades and this study exploits it to amplify the thesis first laid before the public by Georges Lefebvre in 1924. Every effort has been made to extend that thesis to the cultural and political areas of current concern among historians, as well. Readers will find that the book consists of a series of thematic chapters arranged within a loose chronological format. Chapter 1 identifies the many different types of French peasant and places them in an agrarian context. The second chapter examines the rural dimensions of the malaise afflicting society and government at the end of the *ancien régime*. In chapter 3 chronology is paramount: the peasantry make their debut on the political stage. The illusory gains of that hot summer of peasant activism form the subject matter of chapter 4, while chapter 5 endeavours to elucidate the non-feudal agrarian issues on which bourgeois and peasant were unable to reach agreement. Chapter 6 looks at some of the topics which Lefebvre skates over, notably the impact of dramatic administrative and ecclesiastical reforms on the lives of ordinary country dwellers. The growing sense of exasperation at the invasiveness of the revolution forms the nub of chapter 7, which explores the social under-pinnings of both the Terror and counter-revolution. Finally, chapter 8 attempts an answer to the question: 'what had the peasantry learned from the revolutionary experience?'

As befits a textbook, scholarly appendages in the form of notes and references have been used sparingly. The attentive reader who wishes to pursue matters in greater depth will find a full list of manuscript and printed sources at the end of the book. All translations from the French are mine.

Acknowledgements

Works of synthesis generate many debts which I have tried to acknowledge in the endnotes and the bibliography. However, several historians played a more active role and deserve particular mention. Alan Forrest, Hilton L. Root, Pierre Lévêque and Donald Sutherland all offered helpful suggestions or advice, whilst Colin Lucas provided both advice and an opportunity to test my views on the French History Graduate Seminar in Balliol College, Oxford. I am indebted to Tim Tackett and to Princeton University Press for their help in drawing up map 12, and to the Centre Départemental de Documentation Pédagogique of Tarbes for permission to reproduce the cover illustration and plates 1, 2 and 5. Funds for basic research in the libraries and archives of France were generously supplied by the British Academy, by the Faculty of Arts Research Grants Committee of Birmingham University and by the School of History (Birmingham University). As for the typescript, it was prepared by Sue Offley with her usual care and efficiency.

Abbreviations

A.D.	Archives Départementales
A.N.	Archives Nationales
Amer. Hist. Rev.	*American Historical Review*
Annales E.S.C.	*Annales, Economies, Sociétés, Civilisations*
Ann. hist. Rév. fran.	*Annales historiques de la Révolution française*
C.D.D.P. Tarbes	Centre Départemental de Documentation Pédagogique de Tarbes
Rev. d'hist mod. et contemp.	*Revue d'histoire moderne et contemporaine*

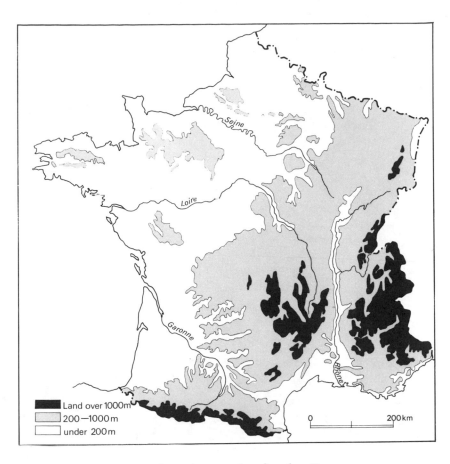

Map 1. Physical geography of modern France

Chapter 1

Rural France in the eighteenth century

France, it has often been remarked, is an aggregate which should be studied piece by piece. Nowhere is the truth of this dictum more evident than in the field of rural history. Many of the topics examined in this chapter resist analysis in global terms. The 'country dweller', 'patterns of land ownership', 'agrarian structures', 'common rights' and so forth are convenient portmanteau phrases which few historians would choose to be without. But they are meaningful only in a context of time and place. Rural history is perforce local history — the history of villages, peasants and peasantries conflated into an intelligible whole. Nevertheless, the lives of all country dwellers were shaped by biological rhythms, and these rhythms controlled the fortunes of the poor to a considerable degree. Beneath the surface of late *ancien régime* society an important demographic transition was taking place.

Demographic recovery

What was the population of France in 1789? The answer partly depends on which of France's several frontiers is adopted as the basis for calculation. Notwithstanding these adjustments, however, population historians have revised their estimates upwards in recent years. In place of the traditional estimate of 25 or 26 millions, it is now suggested that the hexagon numbered within its borders (those of 1861, admittedly) some 28 million inhabitants on the eve of the revolution. This revision has implications for the way in which we conceptualise population growth across the century, as well. The Institut National d'Etudes Démographiques has computed a figure of 24.6 millions for 1740 which is at least 2 millions higher than previous best estimates. Such a figure calls into question the so-called watershed decade of the 1750s when population growth in France is said to have begun in earnest. Instead we are left with a gentler profile of growth. From a threshold of 21.5 millions at the turn of the century, an increase of roughly 14 per cent had been registered by 1750. Thereafter the rate of growth gathered momentum to yield a 19 per cent increase by 1800. Even so, the contrast between the first half of the century and the second is scarcely dramatic. Nor does an overall growth rate of 33 per cent across the century appear impressive when compared with equivalent indicators for England (+61 per cent), Sweden (+67 per cent), Spain (+72 per cent) and European Russia (+80 per cent). As a description of crude population increase, the contention that France experienced a 'demographic revolution' in the course of the eighteenth century is misplaced.

Nevertheless, the population of France *did* increase across the century and that increase was sustained into the next (+25 per cent between 1800 and 1850). This contrasts with the mediocre profile of growth during the seventeenth century (+10 per cent at best), and it calls for an explanation. One approach is to assume within a given population a natural capacity for growth which is realised to a greater or lesser degree as a result of the interplay of several external 'regulators'. According to this theory recurrent bouts of warfare, epidemic disease and, above all, famine depressed reproductive capacity during the final decades of the seventeenth century. Thereafter, the virulence and frequency of these 'regulators' eased and population growth resumed. Initially, this growth simply took up the slack in the rural economy, but ultimately it risked a repetition of the cycle, unless, that is, the food supply kept pace with demand. Such a neo-Malthusian model of population change still has explanatory potential provided that we do not apply it too mechanically. It focuses attention on the role of the harvest, and more especially of harvest failure or a succession of poor harvests, in triggering demographic crises. Pierre Goubert succinctly describes the price of corn as the 'barometer' of short-term population change and suggests that we confine the term 'demographic crisis' to those years in which the usual death rate doubled and conceptions plunged by a third or more.[1] When such harvest crises occurred at frequent intervals, as happened in the late seventeenth and early eighteenth centuries, population levels dropped or stagnated. The pool of marriageable women was reduced in size and the losses of one generation were passed on to the next. When, on the other hand, the intervals between catastrophic crop failures lengthened, as happened in the second half of the eighteenth century, reproductive capacity remained buoyant and losses were soon made good. Epidemic disease and warfare could, of course, take their own toll, but deaths from the plague virtually ceased after the 1720–2 outbreak in Provence.

The neo-Malthusian model provides a pleasingly balanced and global explanation of demographic fluctuations, but it simplifies the processes involved to an unacceptable degree. The scenario of an even growth in population pressing uniformly against finite food resources with evenly distributed consequences cannot be demonstrated in practice. Some localities and regions undoubtedly experienced over-population in relation to available resources, but there was no generalised crisis of over-population in France at the end of the *ancien régime*. As Jacques Dupâquier has pointed out, emigration – the classic symptom of an over-populated countryside – was negligible in either the seventeenth or the eighteenth century.[2] Moreover, acute food shortages and outbreaks of epidemic disease were by no means restricted to densely populated areas. The point is surely that no single, monolithic demographic regime ever existed: rural France was divided into numerous petty demographic regimes with highly individual characteristics.

A further objection levelled against the neo-Malthusian approach is that it emphasises mortality at the expense of fertility. Whilst a modest decline in mortality, especially infant mortality, is beyond question in this period, research has shown that fertility can no longer be ignored as if it were a constant impervious to short-term fluctuation. From this has followed the realisation that the rural population actively contrived to limit or promote fertility and that different social groups practised different types of demographic behaviour. To take the first point, it seems clear that mortality and fertility should not be viewed in isolation, for Dupâquier has demonstrated how periods of demographic crisis could be followed by periods of high fertility (expressed in terms of a lowering of mean age at first marriage), which more than compensated for earlier losses.[3] His findings suggest that a small decline in the pool of marriageable women would *not* necessarily reduce the childbearing potential of the next generation.

The second point is more controversial and concerns the likely impact of different patterns of demographic behaviour on overall population growth. 'Was there a demographic regime for the rich and a demographic regime for the poor?', asks Bernard Derouet.[4] He provides an unambiguous answer in a case study of four villages on the cereal plains to the west of Paris. In common with other researchers, he draws attention to the technique of controlling fertility by varying the age at first marriage. Thus, the decade 1710–19 marked a population nadir and the period of lowest age at first marriage, whereas age at first marriage was adjusted upwards as population pressure rose in subsequent decades. More important, however, he introduces a socio-economic variable and shows how the reproductive cycle of the well-to-do peasant household and that of the agricultural labourer differed in important respects. For example, when the average age at first marriage dropped, that of labourers (men as well as women) dropped even lower. By contrast, the fertility of landed households remained fairly stable. Far-reaching conclusions flow from this line of argument for it appears that the profile of population shifts can be explained in terms of the expansion or contraction in the numbers of agricultural labourers within the rural community. On the other hand, many rural communities did not contain a substantial percentage of peasant proletarians. And in any case we should allow for the possibility that differential levels of fertility were counteracted by differential levels of mortality. Derouet seems to acknowledge as much when he likens the category of day labourers to 'shock absorbers'[5] which acted to limit the damage caused by periodic demographic crises.

Whether this pioneer research into the social and economic dimension of reproductive behaviour will result in a new vision of *ancien régime* demography is not yet clear, but it has already undermined the global assumptions of the neo-Malthusian model. We must now take this process a stage further and distinguish between the total population and the rural population and, if possible, between the rural population and that population actively engaged in agriculture. The crude totals proposed by historians can be ignored because they are based on divergent computations of global population, but this does not alter the validity of proportional estimates. According to the Institut National de la Statistique et des Etudes Economiques, 83 per cent of the population of France were country dwellers in 1700, compared with 78 per cent in 1789 and 77 per cent in 1801.[6] In a pre-statistical age, these figures should be regarded as approximations, but it is reassuring to note that they do not fundamentally depart from those suggested by E. Le Roy Ladurie (1660 = 85 per cent; 1789 = 81.5 per cent).[7] Estimating the agricultural population of *ancien régime* France is a more hazardous exercise which has rarely been attempted, but the I.N.S.E.E. statisticians put it at 79 per cent in 1700 (93 per cent of the rural population) and 67 per cent in 1789 (87 per cent of the rural population). Le Roy Ladurie opts for a slightly lower figure and describes 82 per cent of country dwellers as peasants in 1789. So the urban population of France grew in the course of the eighteenth century, but that growth was uneven and unspectacular. Most of the excess served to swell the ranks of village society.

Population growth was also exceedingly patchy. In parts of Flanders the population doubled between 1750 and the revolution, and growth was especially rapid in the eastern provinces of Lorraine, Alsace and the Franche-Comté, too. These were all regions which had suffered badly from the effects of warfare during the seventeenth century. In the Massif Central, the Centre and the Ile-de-France demographic recovery was more measured. Sometimes the expansion was steady and cumulative, at least until the 1770s (Toulouse region; Vivarais), sometimes it occurred late and in the form of headlong spurts (Normandy; southern Champagne) and sometimes it made a timid appearance only to be cut back by waves of epidemic disease. This was the situation in the western provinces of France (Brittany, Anjou, Maine, Touraine). Brittany registered only a small net population increase over the century after outbreaks of dysentery and pneumonia arrested and then reversed the trend in the 1770s and 1780s. Population growth was imperceptible in Anjou, too. Indeed, the province may have counted fewer inhabitants in 1789 than in 1720.

The differential impact of dearth and disease can be held principally responsible for these unevennesses. However, another factor seems to have been in play: the conscious and deliberate limitation of fertility within marriage. Historians have long been aware that France's demographic vitality began to ebb towards the end of the eighteenth century; the problem has lain in ascribing a cause or causes to the phenomenon which was manifested nowhere else in Europe at this time. The obvious answer is to point to the wholesale revision of social habits unleashed by the revolution, but, unfortunately, the available documentation does not permit such a neat compartmentalisation of the problem. Two facts stand out: birth control was not unfamiliar to the peasants of the late *ancien régime*, and the birth rate actually went up during the revolution, not down. It has been suggested that modern methods of family planning were pioneered in two regions of the country: the South West and Normandy.[8] Derouet agrees and points out that raising the age at first marriage – the traditional response to increasing population pressure – could not be pushed beyond a certain point.[9] Thereafter, alternative stratagems were called for. By the 1770s that threshold had been reached in the villages along the southern borders of Normandy, or so he believes.

Nevertheless, the evidence to underpin this fundamental shift in popular behaviour is mainly inferential. In an attempt to introduce some rigour to the whole question of demographic transition, Dupâquier and Berg-Hamon pieced together all the fragmentary census data relating to the period 1784–1801.[10] The first hard fact to emerge was a graph of the marriage rate showing a slump coinciding with the onset of the pre-revolutionary crisis (1787–9), a marked recovery between 1790 and 1792, and a peak in 1793–4 which surely reflected the efforts of young peasants seeking to avoid conscription. More marrying spelt more children: after a downturn consequent upon the postponement of many marriages at the very end of the *ancien régime*, a buoyant birth rate was quickly restored. From 1793 until 1800 it held steady at a record level of about a million a year. Notwithstanding wartime losses, the total population of France increased by 1.3 million during the revolutionary decade. So it seems that the most immediate impact of the political crisis of 1789 lay in the encouragement it gave to marriage. The decline in the annual tally of births only set in during the Consulate. The year 1804 witnessed 933,700 births – the lowest level since 1748.

This puzzling development is the starting point from which historians have inferred the resort to birth control. Dupâquier and Berg-Hamon contrived to obtain a clearer picture of what was happening by conducting a region-by-region comparison of total births in the periods 1780–9 and 1800–9. This rough and ready method of analysis revealed the major areas of declining vitality to have been the Centre and the West. The presence of Brittany and the western provinces in this category holds no surprises, for here a depressed birth rate can be attributed to the crises of the 1770s and 1780s. The altered pattern of fertility in the Centre (in reality an amorphous region embracing Burgundy and the Franche-Comté as well as the Loire Country and the Massif Central) is less easily explained, however. Perhaps the 'dark secrets' of birth control, against which the church fulminated so forcefully, had begun to make headway among the peasantry, but there is a perplexing randomness about the areas which were first to register declining levels of fertility. In Normandy and the provinces of the South West contraceptive practices made a precocious appearance among the peasantry, or so we are told, and yet the birth rate remained remarkably stable in both regions between the late eighteenth and early nineteenth centuries. None the less, it cannot be denied that, nationwide, the birth rate plummeted from 38.8 per thousand to 32.9 per thousand between the end of the *ancien régime* and the end of the Consulate. Nor should we underestimate the impact of the revolution on demographic behaviour. If the freer social atmosphere prevailing after 1789 removed some of the traditional constraints on marriage, there is a *prima facie* case for arguing that – sooner or later – it also undermined the old taboos on the subject of procreation.

We return, then, to the disputed notion of 'demographic revolution'. Applied to the annual incremental increase in population registered in the course of the eighteenth century such a term is surely excessive. Applied to the forms of demographic behaviour uncovered as a result of family reconstitution studies it has greater validity. Sophisticated and efficient techniques of family limitation reached the masses during the second half of the eighteenth century. Moreover, they reached the rural masses before the urban masses, or so it would seem. Dupâquier likens the progress of birth control to an ink stain: limited to western and central Normandy around 1770, it quickly spread outwards towards the Paris basin, the Massif Central and the East.[11] He salutes the new posture as a victory for peasant individualism over the moral doctrines of the church, a victory which the revolution could only reinforce.

The peasantry

But who were the peasantry in 1789? The vast class of the wronged, retorted the revolutionaries: those who had shouldered the entire burden of the state while deprived of their rights. Even the term smacked of degradation: in 1802 the historian Amans-Alexis Monteil noted that the word *paysan* had gone out of use and had been replaced by the neutral-sounding *cultivateur*.[12] Such rhetorical definitions were designed to obscure social and economic realities, however. Our task must be to uncover them. In one sense the peasantry have already been identified: they were that portion of the population engaged in agricultural pursuits and who, by virtue of their close links to the soil, shared a common lifestyle and a common outlook. This could be termed the maximalist definition of the peasantry, for it embraces in a single category both owner-exploiters and those who worked the land of others for a wage. The minimalist definition invites an altogether more precise use of terms. It confines the label 'peasant' to self-sufficient farmers whose interests and outlook were sometimes opposed to those of other denizens of the countryside (landless labourers, rural artisans). Each definition has its merits, as the pages that follow will attempt to show. Sometimes the peasantry, in the broadest sense, thought and acted *en masse*. In so doing, they demonstrated a formidable capacity to shape the course of the revolution. Sometimes they spoke with many voices, only to dissipate their energies in sterile in-fighting. First, however, we must weigh up the peasantry in generic terms and compare them with the other groups forming *ancien régime* society.

On the eve of the revolution peasant households accounted for roughly 67 per cent of the population and yet it is unlikely that they owned more than 33 per cent of the land. This figure has been arrived at by averaging the results of case studies into property structures and it compares tolerably with the estimates proposed by Georges Lefebvre in 1932–3.[13] The trend of peasant land ownership is wellnigh impossible to quantify. Some historians believe that the peasantry owned less land in 1789 than at the start of the century, but there seems no good reason to suppose that this might have been so. On the contrary, population growth unleashed a massive assault on abandoned, waste and even collectively owned land surfaces, and the peasantry were the principal beneficiaries. In general, therefore, we are dealing with a landed peasantry, compared with the semi-servile peasantries across the Rhine where land remained imprisoned within the manorial system, and the dispossessed yeomanry of England with a title to no more than 10 per cent of the land by the end of the century.

Possession was one thing, however; access to land was arguably more important. Virtually the entire arable surface of the kingdom was farmed by the peasantry, either as freeholders, or as tenants, or as squatters. But such distinctions have a limited value, for, prior to the revolution, ownership was an imprecise concept. At one extreme the king, as feudal overlord, laid claim to all the territory of France; at the other the peasantry nourished a deep-seated conviction that they 'owned' the land. The practice of renewing tenancies tacitly and the existence of a formidable array of collective rights (see pp. 128–37) served only to deepen that conviction. All peasant households shared one overriding ambition: to assemble, by inheritance, by marriage, by purchase or by renting, a holding which would enable them to live decently. In some regions this was easier to achieve than in others. Peasant holdings tended to be densest in upland and mountainous areas where soil fertility was low and competition for land from members of the privileged orders less intense. In the Béarn, Haute-Provence, the Dauphiné, the Auvergne and along the western flanks of the Massif Central over 50 per cent of the land used for agriculture had fallen into the hands of peasant proprietors. Few of these proprietors approached the threshold of self-sufficiency; on the other hand few peasant households had failed to acquire a plot of land of some description on which to grow vegetables or cereals. In the Auvergne perhaps 5 per cent of households could be included in this latter category. Around the cities and even quite small seats of local government, competition from the privileged orders and the professional bourgeoisie proved irresistible and, in consequence, peasant property remained scanty and fragmented. The rich cereal-growing plains of the Beauce to the south-west of Paris were entirely dominated by noble and bourgeois landlords, while the clergy possessed substantial estates in Picardy and around the towns of Laon and Cambrai. According to Lefebvre, whose memorable thesis on this north-eastern corner of France (the future department of the Nord) contains a painstaking analysis of property structures, ecclesiastical possessions covered 40 per cent of the land surface of the Cambrésis.[14] When this region was caught up in the first flush of agrarian revolt in April–May 1789, monasteries and monastic storehouses were the obvious targets for popular anger.

So against the picture of a deeply rooted peasantry with a considerable stake in the land, we must set that of a rootless and, at the lowest reaches, semi-proletarianised peasantry struggling to retain control over the land in the face of pressure from seigneurs and bourgeois purchasers. Nor did the challenge issue solely from outside the rural community: in the eyes of the poor, the rich peasant who sought to engross the holdings of his neighbours was every bit as much of a social menace as the *forain* or *horsain* –

the absentee landlord. These latent tensions were undoubtedly most acute in the wheat-growing belt around Paris. In eastern Normandy, in the Beauce, in the Brie, the peasantry rarely owned more than 25 per cent of the land surface, and often far less. In the hinterland of Versailles, their stake had dwindled to insignificance. Correspondingly, the ranks of agricultural labourers bulked large and it is principally from these districts that we hear the authentic voice of the landless poor during the revolution. Comparable statistics are hard to come by since some historians prefer to group the 'virtually landless' together with the 'literally landless' which introduces an element of arbitrariness and confuses the picture. None the less, a sampling of thirteen villages in the Beauce and Gâtinais (department of the Loiret) revealed 24 per cent of the peasantry to have been non-proprietors, compared with 55.5 per cent in the Versailles district.[15] Further to the north, in the district of Amiens (department of the Somme), Florence Gauthier defines the 'rural proletariat' as those without holdings save, perhaps, for a small garden and estimates that they totalled 21 per cent of the rural population.[16] To label this substantial section of the peasant community a 'rural proletariat' is unhelpful, however, for it implies a polarisation between the 'landed' and the 'landless' which is much too neat. Derouet's study of several villages in the Thimerais district between Chartres and Dreux, which has already been discussed in a different context, enables us to take the analysis a stage further. While he notes that 'literally landless' labourers were not uncommon, he finds that 50 per cent of such households owned their dwellings; between 60 and 70 per cent owned a small garden; 27 per cent owned a cow and 7 per cent owned some sheep. The presence of livestock spells out once again that access to land was often the crucial factor. Free-for-all grazing on wastes, commons and unenclosed meadows and arable after the removal of the harvest mitigated the condition of landlessness to no small degree. It is noteworthy that during the revolution the defence of common rights became a key issue, perhaps *the* key issue, in the political programme of the poor peasantry.

Described variously in the documents as *journaliers*, *brassiers*, *manœuvriers*, *locataires* or *travailleurs de terre*, the number of landless peasants was increasing rapidly in the final decades of the eighteenth century. Most were born into this precarious social station, but some were driven into it as a result of the economic malaise which developed in the 1770s and 1780s. The echelon of the peasantry most likely to be precipitated into the ranks of the wage earners in the event of a crisis was that of the petty proprietors whose ability to live independently turned on finding additional land to rent at a price within their means. Before the revolutionary sleight of hand homogenising all peasants under the title of *cultivateurs*, such households appeared in multiple guises. In southern Picardy and the Ile-de-France they were known as *haricotiers*, in the Vexin and the Thimerais as *sossons*, and in the South West as *bordiers*. The amount of land farmed by these individuals varied a good deal, as did the proportion of freehold to leasehold. Around Beauvais *haricotiers* generally owned about four hectares, but might easily rent as much again. The *sossons* of the Thimerais exploited five or six hectares on average, of which two-thirds might be rented, whereas the *bordiers* of Bas Poitou worked hold-ings of up to fifteen hectares, often on the basis of a share-crop lease. 'Holding' is something of a misnomer, however, for petty peasant proprietors rarely enjoyed the luxury of farming compact units. Theirs was a life of patient accumulation of disparate plots in the hope that one day they could be welded into a *domaine*, that is to say a balanced agricultural exploitation. It follows, then, that the claim of the small landed peasant to self-sufficiency was highly precarious. During periods of economic buoyancy when harvests were plentiful and the products of cottage indus-try found an easy outlet, he and his family managed to avoid the recourse to day labouring. The position of the *vigneron* or small winegrower was little different in this respect. But the true mark of self-sufficiency was the ownership of draught animals. When it came to ploughing the small peasant proprietor had to rely on the resources of his larger neighbour.

These larger neighbours with ploughs and oxen or horses were usually described as *laboureurs*. The term seems apt, but it is also elastic. In most eighteenth-century usage *laboureur* denoted a substantial peasant farmer who owned the land which he cultivated and lived comfortably thereon. However, it could also be used to refer to peasant proprietors of less exalted status. In the Soissonnais the label was applied indiscriminately to large tenant farmers *and* to those whom we have described as *haricotiers*. In the Lauragais and the area around Carcassonne *laboureurs* were a humble species not very far removed from agricultural wage earners. The term *ménager* presents a similar problem. For most purposes it can be regarded as a synonym for independent peasant proprietor or *laboureur*. Like *pagès* and *bientenant*, *ménager* was a word with a southern flavour, but, on the other hand, Lefebvre describes the *ménager* of Flanders as a poor peasant with little land.[17] Indeed, he lumps them with day labourers to form a somewhat generously defined rural proletariat.

Confusing nomenclature should not be allowed to cloud the overall picture, however. In nine cases out of ten *laboureurs* were peasant land-owners of independent means. They stood at the apex of the peasantry in southern France where the spectrum of wealth was more restrained and social differentiation less acute. In the North this coveted position was occupied by a higher echelon of large tenant farmers known as *gros fermiers*, but the *laboureurs* were men of considerable substance for all that. Owners of compact and well-balanced agricultural holdings, they could afford to regard the vagaries of the harvest cycle without undue anxiety. The accumulated grain surpluses of good years provided a cushion in times of dearth as well as a highly marketable asset. Ownership of expensive capital items such as ploughs and plough-teams made every lesser member of the rural community a potential client, and the ability to overwinter livestock ensured that well-to-do farmers derived a disproportionate benefit from the commons. Not surprisingly, the poor peasantry concluded that to him that hath, everything is given.

Laboureurs formed a tiny fraction of the agricultural population, however, while *gros fermiers* were rarer still. Goubert suggests that a typical village of several hundred inhabitants on the Picard plain would contain two *gros fermiers*; five or six *laboureurs*; twenty or so *haricotiers*; and between twenty and fifty households of day labourers or part-time artisans.[18] He adds that the day labourers would often possess a house, a garden, a small barn, a cow and three or four sheep. *Gros fermiers* were a phenomenon of the North and the East where the development of large-scale cereal farming had undermined the position of the 'middle' peasantry (*haricotiers* and *laboureurs*) and accentuated social divisions. As tenants of the larger noble and ecclesiastical estates, as proprietors in their own right, they constituted the most dynamic element in the late *ancien régime* countryside. When the government took steps to promote agricultural progress by exempting cleared land from taxation in 1763 and 1766 *gros fermiers* were the first to respond to the challenge. When, in the 1770s, royal intendants sought to persuade villagers to abandon collective exploitation of their commons, the local instigators were frequently *gros fermiers* and enriched *laboureurs* hoping to convert a *de facto* domination of village pastures into an exclusive freehold or leasehold right. On the intensively cultivated cereal plains, pasturage was worth its weight in gold.

The *gros fermiers* were also routinely accused of land engrossment, and with some justification. As grain prices spiralled inexorably upwards in the second half of the eighteenth century, landowners of all descriptions sought to cash in. Rents rose by leaps and bounds; seigneurial obligations were exacted with greater efficiency (see pp. 54–8); and the profits accruing from speculation in basic foodstuffs were employed to purchase more land, usually at the expense of the lesser peasantry. Two forms of engrossment caused particular dismay: proprietors stealthily enlarged their estates by absorbing adjacent holdings, either by purchase or foreclosure; or they acquired scattered farms one by one. Neither practice was conducive to good relations in the countryside: amalgamation reduced the stock of peasant tenures, while piecemeal acquisition was generally accompanied by the ousting of the original owners or tenants. The princi-

Plate 1. A village clogmaker depicted in the *terrier* of Esparros (Bigorre), 1773

pal beneficiaries, of course, were the enriched *laboureurs*, known henceforth as *gros fermiers*. Endowed with financial muscle and entrepreneurial
flair, they rose to prominence as specialists in the science of farm management. Sometimes they took the lease on a single property, but by the end
of the *ancien régime* it was not uncommon to find batches of a dozen or
more farms being managed by one individual (known in this instance as a
fermier-général). To judge from the complaints reaching the authorities
the practice of land engrossment was fairly widespread, but the consequences were most keenly felt in the Paris region and in the North East
where the peasantry feared for its survival as a landed force. Significantly,
Lefebvre notes that engrossment only became an issue within the rural
community after 1760, the decade in which grain prices began to spiral.[19]
By 1789 it had become a major grievance and was stigmatised repeatedly
in the *cahiers de doléances*. On the coastal plain of Flanders where the
peasantry were fighting a losing battle against the consolidators, the parish
of Lederzeele declared in favour of an upper limit of 50 *mesures* (roughly
18 hectares) on the size of farms.[20]

    With the *gros fermiers* we reach the very pinnacle of the peasantry in
northern France. Indeed, it is debatable whether such individuals should
be included among the peasantry at all. Their specialist role as middlemen

Plate 2. Village bourgeois wearing their Sunday best, as depicted in the *terrier* of Sadournin (Gascony), 1772

managing estates on behalf of absentee landlords, collecting dues on behalf of seigneurs and the tithe on behalf of the church, conferred on them many of the qualifications of bourgeois status. Admitting the force of this argument, Georges Lefebvre describes the upper echelons of the peasantry as a 'rural bourgeoisie' in his epoch-making study of the Nord department and ascribes to them a key role in aligning the peasantry for and against the revolution. Several other historians have followed suit, but Lefebvre's key concept lacks rigour and leads to confusion. Sometimes he refers to a rural bourgeoisie made up of *laboureurs* and *gros fermiers*, sometimes to a rural bourgeoisie consisting of village 'intellectuals' such as notaries and attorneys.[21] Both categories played a leading part during the revolution, that much is certain; and both categories describe a coherent social reality. But to lump them together is to obscure those realities. In eighteenth-century parlance the title 'bourgeois' presupposed, at the very least, emancipation from the world of physical toil. The *laboureur* worked on the land for his living; the case of the *gros fermier* is more problematic, but he, too, derived part of his income from working the land. Therefore, it is more appropriate to regard this top 2 or 3 per cent of the agricultural population as forming part of the peasantry.

The same logic can be applied to the artisan. Most artisans lived in the countryside, and most rural artisans were part-time peasants. Artisanal activity was something that was taken up or put down as the seasons and the demand for wage-labour dictated. It follows, then, that artisans should not be conceived of as a group with interests and ambitions distinct from those of the great mass of full-time agriculturalists. However, the specialist artisans – carpenters, coopers, coppersmiths, leather dressers and so forth – who congregated in the small towns or *bourgs* occupied a slightly different position. To start with, they were more affluent, and more educated than their rustic cousins. In the South where municipal traditions were stronger than in the North, they also possessed a ready appetite for collective action. Nevertheless, it is important to stress the dominant reality: the majority of artisans lived and worked within the narrow horizons of their parish of birth. When weighty matters appeared on the agenda of village life in 1789, their political reflexes tended to match those of the poorer peasantry.

In the words of the social anthropologist Robert Redfield, there is 'something generic'[22] about the peasantry. Internecine antagonisms notwithstanding, the French peasantry as we have defined them possessed an overall organic unity on the eve of the French Revolution. 'Organic' is, of course, an overworked term. Perhaps that unity was a product of circumstance, of decades of resistance to seigneurialism and the incursions of royal power. Perhaps it would crumble once the enforcing agents of degenerate feudalism and unbridled fiscal pressure were removed. Perhaps the revolutionary legislators would succeed in destroying the rural community – something which the timid physiocratic reforms of the old monarchy had conspicuously failed to achieve. All these themes will be explored in the chapters that follow. At this stage it is important to avoid narrowing the field of enquiry with an overly schematic approach. It is true that the peasantry contained consumers as well as producers. It is likewise

true that by 1789 they were riven by social tensions which had been building up for half a century and more. However, it is no less true that peasants
were capable of overcoming their differences in the interests of collective
action. And in so doing they acknowledged the existence of a common culture which had the power to gloss over objective inequalities of condition.

Agriculture

When drafting an article on tenant farmers for the *Encyclopédie*, the eminent physiocrat, François Quesnay, distinguished between what he termed
the regions of 'grande culture' and those of 'petite culture'. This division is
fundamental to an understanding of the rural economy of *ancien régime*
France. The 'pays de grande culture' were the openfield plains of the North
and North East where an intensive cereal-based husbandry had developed.
Most of the land was farmed in large units by tenants on behalf of absentee
landlords. Owner-exploitation was restrained and sharecropping virtually
non-existent. In these regions nearly all the land was used for arable purposes and crops were rotated on a three-year cycle. Woodland, waste and
common had been trimmed back to the absolute minimum and there were
no hedges or fences to demarcate individual holdings. Four-fifths of the
land surface of Picardy was under the plough in 1780, according to
Goubert,[23] and in all likelihood this situation had obtained since the mid-
seventeenth century. The 'pays de petite culture' offered a complete contrast. In the West 'petite culture', or small-scale mixed farming, commenced where the plains of the Beauce encountered the hills of the Perche;
in the South the transition was marked by the arc of the river Loire and the
enclosed landscape of the Sologne. It therefore embraced the better part of
western, central and southern France. Pockets of openfield tillage had
developed around Clermont-Ferrand and in Upper Languedoc, just as
pockets of intensive 'petite culture' had evolved on the Flanders plain in the
extreme North, but, for most purposes, it is possible to talk of two discrete
agricultural regions.

The 'pays de petite culture' were unsuited to cereal production on a large
scale and were farmed by sharecroppers and small peasant proprietors.
Grain still had to be grown, of course, for otherwise the population would
starve, but rye was planted in preference to wheat. In the South West maize
replaced rye as the staple. Even so, much of the land surface lay bare of
crops to produce a physical environment quite different from that of
Picardy or the Ile de France. In Brittany between a third and two-thirds of
the land produced nothing beyond rough pasture, and since biennial crop
rotation was the norm in most western and southern provinces, only
50 per cent of the arable carried a harvest at any one time. Land-use cal-

culations for the province of the Vivarais suggest that at the end of the *ancien régime* under 15 per cent of its potential agricultural territory was actually put under cereals each year. With the notable exception of Flanders, yields were much lower, too. In fact, the grain harvest was so unreliable in upland regions such as the Massif Central, that the rural population took the precaution of planting chestnut orchards to produce a stand-by crop. People rarely starved in the North and the East during the reign of Louis XVI, in the sense that even mediocre harvests produced a sufficient volume of grain to feed the indigenous population. The problem lay at one remove: in how to conciliate the needs of rural and urban consumers, for the peasantry of the cereal plains were expected to provision the markets of Paris, Rouen and Orléans. In the 'pays de petite culture' and more especially in the hinterland regions of the Centre, by contrast, the possibility of harvest failure remained all too real. That possibility materialised in the autumn of 1788 with a harvest shortfall approaching 30 per cent in some districts. Worse, it was followed by a winter of unprecedented cold which froze the autumn sowings and severely damaged the chestnut orchards.

The declining risk of famine in the northern and eastern sectors of the country from 1750 or thereabouts, notwithstanding a steady increase in the population, suggests strongly that agricultural production was rising. Some historians and economists have even hazarded the idea that France experienced an 'agricultural revolution' in the course of the eighteenth century. According to Toutain, agricultural production rose by 60 per cent during the period;[24] Le Roy Ladurie finds his estimate to be excessive and using as data reference points the decades 1700–9 and 1780–9 proposes instead an increase of between 25 and 40 per cent.[25] However, the same historian has also declared in favour of a rise of *at least* 40 per cent between 1715 and 1789. These figures are hopelessly confusing and until a more reliable method of computing global production is devised, they are better ignored. In any case they miss the point because the case for an agricultural revolution hinges not on changes in production volume, but on changes in productivity. Productivity, measured in terms of new crops, new techniques and improved yields per hectare, remained stable throughout the eighteenth century. The increases registered as a result of the substitution of maize for rye in the South West and as a result of the suppression of the fallow period in Flanders were mainly developments of the seventeenth or earlier centuries. Large-scale cultivation of the potato, on the other hand, awaited the revolutionary and Napoleonic decades. Agricultural production surely did rise, however. And it was pushed up by largely traditional means as the peasantry adjusted land-use to cater for a growing number of mouths.

The simplest short-term expedient was to adjust the balance between crops that could be used to make bread and those which could not. Anne Zink's detailed analysis of the village of Azereix in the Pyrenees demonstrates well the flexibility of peasant polyculture in the 'pays de petite culture'.[26] As the population of the village rose, its agricultural territory expanded and a reallocation of the space devoted to cereals, vines and meadows took place. A similar reassessment of needs and priorities can be inferred from the massive extension of chestnut cultivation in the Vivarais during the second half of the eighteenth century. Land reclamation followed naturally from such initiatives and it is likely that the boost to agricultural production derived principally from this source. In the order of 600,000 hectares were cleared after 1750, whether as a result of individual enterprise or in consequence of one or other of the government's incentive schemes. This represented an increase of 3 per cent in the arable surface of the kingdom, assuming that all the cleared land was destined for cereal cultivation. In the belt of cereal plains around Paris all the waste had long since been ploughed up, and a further extension of arable could only be achieved at the expense of village commons and roadside verges, but in the West, the South and the East vast tracts of heath and rough pasture awaited more systematic exploitation. The bruised and battered province of Burgundy which had suffered badly in the wars of the seventeenth century registered the most spectacular gains. Here, land reclamation increased the crop-bearing surface by between 8 and 10 per cent in the latter half of the eighteenth century. Substantial inroads into the heath were also made in Alsace, Poitou and the area around Alençon.[27]

Without a doubt, this mania for hacking fields out of what is rather inappropriately termed 'waste' land stored up problems for the future. It contributed in no small measure to the stock-raising crisis which affected much of the openfield region by the end of the *ancien régime*. As the amount of permanent grazing land for cattle, sheep and goats diminished the entire edifice of cereal husbandry was undermined. Most farmers relied on animal manure as a means of fertilising the soil. The quest for land on which to build or raise crops also focused attention on the commons – commons which were already overloaded with stock. As chance would have it, this pressure on the commons from below also coincided with a spasm of interest from above. In the late eighteenth century the royal government chose to make the commons an issue, indeed a test, in its bid to modernise agriculture. Since the struggles engendered by attempts to alter the status of commons mobilised large numbers of peasants before as well as after 1789, the story is worth relating in some detail.

The first signs of government preoccupation with the commons can be traced back to the 1750s and to the influence of a group of writers known collectively as the physiocrats. They argued that agriculture alone provided the sinews of the state and demanded that all constraints upon the productive capacity of the land be removed. Collective ownership was anathematised, for it impeded improvement, as evidenced by the existence throughout the kingdom of substantial tracts of under-exploited common land. The prevalence of customary rights which prevented proprietors from disposing of their land and crops as they saw fit also incurred their hostility. In short, the physiocrats repudiated the concept of property espoused by the poor peasantry, and by many middling peasants, too. Any government seeking to promote agricultural progress on these lines found itself in conflict with the great mass of the rural population. For the royal government of the *ancien régime* this was a problem, but for the revolutionary legislators it became a real dilemma. The Provincial Estates of Burgundy, Languedoc and the Béarn were the first to register acceptance of the new ideas, but the driving force emanated from royal bureaucrats at the very centre of affairs: Henri Bertin, controller-general between 1759 and 1763 and subsequently secretary of state; Daniel Trudaine, intendant of finances; and the Marquis d'Ormesson. These men initiated a series of enquiries which sought to ascertain the extent of common land in the provinces, the methods of exploitation currently being employed, and the likely consequences of partition. Pretty soon they realised that there was neither uniformity, nor unanimity in these matters. Between 1769 and 1781 enabling legislation was introduced which permitted the division of common land in the Trois Evêchés, Lorraine, Alsace, Burgundy, Artois, Flanders, the Cambrésis and several other regions. Elsewhere the reform initiative encountered insuperable obstacles: the sub-delegates of the *élections* of Brioude, St Flour and Aurillac in the Auvergne all warned that the existence of common land helped to stabilise the rural population. Without it the lowest tier of the peasantry would be driven into vagabondage.

In any case, the notion sedulously propagated by the physiocrats that common land was barren land failed to withstand scrutiny. As the reports of intendants, sub-delegates and local agricultural societies filtered through to Paris, royal bureaucrats were forced to acknowledge that the commons satisfied real social and economic needs. Even the charge that collective ownership inhibited individual exploitation and amelioration proved to be not entirely founded. Many rural communities tolerated some tillage of common pastures on an *ad hoc* basis, and in some regions this practice had hardened into a custom which admitted a temporary division, but within a context of continuing collective control. Such was the 'portion ménagère' system which the government promoted as a *faute de mieux* method of obtaining an end to indiscriminate exploitation, an increase in grain production and a growth in taxable capacity. This system appears to have been pioneered in Walloon Flanders where a number of villages progressively divided up their commons (usually marshes) into family-sized plots or *wardelles* on a leasehold basis. Newly arrived house-holds were accommodated by carrying out a fresh partition at intervals, although this might involve a long wait during which the new resident was effectively debarred from access to the commons. Nevertheless, the new mode of exploitation became widespread in the North East during the last two decades of the *ancien régime*. In 1777 it was extended to the whole of Flanders, in 1779 to Artois and in 1780 to the Cambrésis. Poor peasants with little or no land were the principal beneficiaries and Lefebvre declares that these relatively egalitarian edicts were unique as an example of legis-lation that materially improved the condition of the rural masses on the eve of the revolution.[28] An analysis of the application of the reform in the Artois shows that the acquisition of a 'portion ménagère' all but doubled the landholding of two-fifths of the peasants of the village of Hulleich, and benefited two-thirds of the households of the village of Biache-Saint-Vaast by a similar amount.[29]

In spite of the gratuitous advice proffered by armchair agricultural theorists, royal administrators pursued a sensitive and flexible policy towards the commons. This pragmatism also tempered their prejudice against collective rights. Collective or common rights were an essential lubricant of the rural economy: without them agriculture would have seized up with the poor plotholder falling first victim. Since the issue of collective rights, like that of the commons, became a battleground during the revolution, it is important to begin with a clear understanding of what these rights presupposed. The most valuable rights invoked by the com-munity were as follows: gleaning (*glanage*) in the wake of harvesters; grazing of stock on unenclosed fields (*droit de vaine pâture*, also known as the *droit de compascuité* in the South); reciprocal stubble and fallow grazing between neighbouring villages (*droit de parcours*); open access to meadows after haymaking (*droit au regain*) and wood cutting in forests (*affouages*). Restrictions of this order on freehold property rights prevailed to a greater or lesser degree throughout France. They outlived the revol-ution and they bedevilled attempts to modify agricultural routines for much of the nineteenth century. These points deserve emphasising for many historians have assumed that collective rights only held sway in the North and the Centre, that is to say in the regions governed by Customary Law which tended to defend the rights of the community to the detriment of those of the individual. In the South, by contrast, written or Roman Law prevailed, which admitted few restrictions on the rights of individuals. Such, at least, was the theory, and no less of an authority than Georges

Lefebvre concludes that property rights were absolute under the jurisdiction of Roman Law.[30] In practice, however, this distinction is impossible to draw. The full battery of collective rights could be found in much of the South as it could in much of the North and Centre. But in the South, the right of *vaine pâture*, for instance, was not enshrined in a body of law. Instead, it derived from private agreements between consenting parties. These private treaties were known as *servitudes* and over time they developed into a body of prescriptive rights which amplified and often contradicted the stipulations of written law.

The prevalence of collective rights helps to account for the tenacity with which they were defended. The reforming bureaucrats of the late *ancien régime* had quite a shock when they discovered how widespread and deeply entrenched was the practice of free grazing and they quickly abandoned the idea of introducing general legislation. No government, indeed, was prepared to take the risk of abolishing *vaine pâture* outright, whether in the eighteenth or the nineteenth century. Instead, a long war of attrition commenced in the 1760s with the object of promoting enclosures and thereby curtailing free grazing. Where enclosure was impracticable, attempts were made to restrict the size of the common flock (*troupeau commun*) by ensuring that the poor who possessed little land subject to *vaine pâture* contributed only a few head of stock. To judge from case studies such efforts enjoyed a mixed success. The institution of the common flock gave privileged access to the common as well as to the stubble and fallow, and it was being abused as much by the rich as by the poor on the eve of the revolution. Vineyards and olive groves had long been placed out of bounds to roving cattle and sheep, and chestnut orchards acquired a measure of protection in the course of the century, too. However, the major bone of contention was the meadow. The government edicts of 1767–77 which limited *vaine pâture* in much of eastern and north-eastern France sought above all to preserve unenclosed meadow land from random grazing after the removal of the first hay harvest. Proprietors resented the loss of the highly marketable 'secondes herbes' (the second growth of hay), particularly in years in which the first haying had produced a modest yield. There were also sound military arguments for husbanding the stock of animal fodder, as revolutionary legislators would shortly discover.

Whether these piecemeal efforts to alter the practice of centuries had much effect is debatable. The signs suggest that in the final years of the *ancien régime* the royal government repented of its doctrinaire enthusiasms of the 1760s and 1770s and returned to a posture of conservatism. Florence Gauthier has chronicled the mounting offensive against common rights in Picardy,[31] but her account leaves room for doubt as to what was actually achieved. On the other hand, the emanations of physiocracy undoubtedly rattled the peasantry and in some regions they suffered real reverses. The villagers of Venoy in Burgundy listed among their grievances in 1789 the fact that for the past fifteen years the landowners had retained their *regain* and in so doing deprived the poor of the ability to keep stock.[32] Not surprisingly, therefore, the poor peasantry interpreted the revolution first and foremost as an opportunity to arrest and then, hopefully, to turn the tide of agrarian individualism. Landowners, by contrast, looked to the revolution for a vindication of the so-called 'bourgeois' concept of property. The Comte de Rochefort complained in 1790 that the Constituent Assembly was pursuing a policy of double standards:[33] the peasantry were being offered the chance to buy out feudal dues, whereas proprietors waited in vain for the chance to redeem the rights of *vaine pâture*, *regain* and *affouages*. In the event the revolution satisfied neither group: bourgeois property rights emerged strengthened, but by no means vindicated as is so often assumed. Nor did the revolutionaries improve upon the agrarian legislation of the old monarchy to any appreciable degree. Theirs was a muddled legacy of cautious, empiricist reforms interspersed with bombastic ideological pronouncements which nearly always missed their mark.

The institutions of village life

The year 1789 marked a watershed in the tangled administrative history of the rural community. Within months of coming to power, the revolutionaries chopped down the seigneurial and fiscal institutions which had given shape and meaning to village life for centuries. And as if that was not enough, they announced their intention to embark on a major overhaul of the third institution of village life: the parish. Two novel principles underscored this unprecedented explosion of reforming zeal. Uniformity replaced diversity and the electoral sanction replaced nomination and co-option. Henceforth, rural France was to be equipped with local government bodies and judicial institutions which varied little from one end of the land to the other. Moreover, these bodies were to be staffed with officials elected by citizens qualified to vote. In the brave new world of the French Revolution, even parish priests had to seek a mandate from the people. These, then are the elements of discontinuity. The elements of continuity are less obvious, but no less important. For all their determination to turn over a new leaf, the revolutionaries *did* build on institutional precedents set during the *ancien régime*. Furthermore, they brought to a head trends which the royal intendants had done much to encourage. An unbiased observer would have found much that was familiar about the new

KEY
1	Brittany	12	Orléanais
2	Normandy	13	Nivernais
3	Picardy	14	Burgundy
4	Artois	15	Lorraine
5	Flanders and Hainaut	16	Alsace
6	Champagne	17	Franche-Comté
7	Ile-de-France	18	Lyonnais
8	Maine	19	Bourbonnais
9	Anjou	20	Berry
10	Poitou	21	Marche
11	Touraine	22	Saintonge and Angoumois

23	Aunis
24	Gascony and Guyenne
25	Limousin
26	Auvergne
27	Languedoc
28	Dauphiné
29	Comtat Venaissin
30	Provence
31	Roussillon
32	Foix
33	Béarn

Map 2. France in 1789 (showing approximate provincial boundaries and major administrative centres)

Map 3. The *départements* of France in 1790
Source: D. M. G. Sutherland, *France, 1789–1815: Revolution and Counter-Revolution* (London, 1985)

municipalities, especially in the South — not least the fact that the same old faces, names and families still seemed to be in charge of local affairs. In this sense, the renewal of 1789 could be described as an exercise for putting old wine into new bottles.

Viewed from the angle of the state, the rural community or, for the sake of argument, the village was primarily a fiscal unit: that is to say, a group of individuals who paid taxes in common. As such they had evolved a framework for managing local affairs which distinguished them from two much older entities: the parish and the seigneurie. That framework was known as the *communauté d'habitants*, but its precise organisation and attributes varied enormously. In northern and central France the *communauté d'habitants* was a pretty rudimentary corporate body consisting of an assembly of the more substantial householders who appointed one or two tax collectors and an executive agent called the *sindic*. In the South, by contrast, the *communauté d'habitants* had evolved a more formal organisation consisting of a semi-permanent committee of village notables known as the *conseil politique*, a clerk (*secrétaire-greffier*) and two or more *consuls* who were charged with wide-ranging administrative powers as well as the task of collecting taxes. Unlike the *sindics*, the *consuls* were magistrates with the authority to validate legally decisions taken on behalf of the community. Usually they stood for election each year, and in Languedoc and Provence, where the 'civic' character of the *communauté d'habitants* was highly developed, they were often flanked by lesser officials: a treasurer, several inspectors of accounts and marketplace overseers. These posts, too, were frequently elective and contemporaries not unreasonably described the whole as a municipal body (*corps municipal*).

This is not to imply that the *communauté d'habitants* was a sovereign entity, however. On the contrary, its seigneurial antecedents were all too apparent. In Provence seigneurs had lost their right to intervene in the election of *consuls*, but they retained a right of oversight which aroused considerable resentment, to judge from the *cahiers de doléances*. In Languedoc seigneurs, or more likely their representatives, continued to preside over meetings of the *conseil politique* and it was not unknown for them to intervene in consular elections. Moreover, the seigneurie continued to provide the territorial format for the *communauté d'habitants* in the Velay, the northerly extremity of the province of Languedoc. In Gascony the *consuls* (also known as *jurats* in this region) were in fact chosen by the seigneur, but from a list submitted by the community. A similar sharing of power occurred in the Dauphiné where the seigneur usually appointed to the post of clerk, a post second in importance only to that of *consul*.

Nevertheless, these were all southern provinces in which seigneurial authority was perceptibly weakening on a number of fronts (see pp. 45–8). Matters were more finely balanced in the Centre and parts of the East and North East where collective decision-making was closely supervised by the judicial personnel of the seigneurie. This was inevitable since the *sindic* had none of the powers of a notary. In the Berry and Champagne the *sindic* usually presided over village deliberations, but under the shadow of a seigneurial judge or attorney who reserved the right to authorise decisions concerning the choice of *sindic*, the appointment of a school master, the date of commencement of the grape harvest and so forth. Seigneurial vigilance was greater still in Burgundy where a *parlementaire* aristocracy endeavoured to intensify its control over the peasant community in the second half of the eighteenth century. In 1756, Loppin de Gemeaux, honorary procurator fiscal of the Parlement of Dijon took the villagers of Gemeaux to court for meeting without his permission in order to appoint a new school master.[34] The provinces of the North East provide the most flagrant examples of seigneurial domination of the *communauté d'habitants*, however. In Flanders, Artois and Hainaut the rich fabric of collective life which distinguished the Midi was largely absent. Village assemblies met infrequently and headmen (called *mayeurs* or *échevins*) were usually in the pockets of the seigneurs, so much so, that Lefebvre comments that 'the peasantry regarded their *échevins* as opponents rather than representatives'.[35]

In such circumstances the parish was pressed into service as the forum for secular as well as spiritual life. This blurring of functions occurred most notably in the so-called *bocage* regions of the West and the Centre where the population lived in a scatter of isolated hamlets rather than in substantial villages. Faced with a human habitat which defied neat compartmentalisation into fiscal units, the *communauté d'habitants* shaded imperceptibly into the community of the parish. Thus we find that in the Berry the post of *sindic* evolved out of that of vestry clerk (*fabricien*) or church warden (*marguillier*). In Brittany even this rudimentary separation of responsibilities was lacking. On the eve of the revolution the province possessed neither *consuls*, nor *sindics*, nor municipalities, except in the towns. Instead, church and all types of secular business were handled indiscriminately by bodies called *généraux de paroisse* answerable primarily to the Parlement in Rennes. Of course, the parish existed alongside the *communauté d'habitants* throughout the rest of France, as did the seigneurie in many cases. Villagers hovered uncertainly between all three institutions and it is no easy task to decide which of these institutions provided the elementary cell for their social existence. Some matters fell within the province of the parish priest (*curé*) or his curate (*vicaire*), some within that of the *sindic* or *consuls*, and some were obviously matters for the seigneurial judge. But, at the same time, a substantial degree of overlap must be allowed for. Priests doubled as pulpit propagandists for the government and would shortly become *ex officio* municipal officers as a result of the reforms of 1787 (see p. 27). *Sindics* were closely involved in all decisions regarding maintenance of the church fabric, while the responsibilities of seigneurial judges included fixing the agricultural calendar as well as trying petty offenders.

This overlap expressed little more than the current state of play of competing authorities at the village level. It had evolved over several centuries, but like all *de facto* situations was liable to revision at any time. In the eighteenth century, the principal challenge to the status quo came from the monarchy. With the intermittent encouragement of reforming ministers, the intendants stealthily enlarged royal administrative and judicial prerogatives at the local level. Two trends can be discerned in these spasmodic attempts to achieve a more favourable distribution of power in the villages: a growing desire for uniformity and also for oligarchy. Uniformity hit those who exploited the historic diversity of institutions in the provinces in order to dodge taxation, while oligarchy carried with it the suspicion that the government intended to do away with the three-tier society and to vest power in an undifferentiated elite of major taxpayers. Neither objective was clearly spelt out by the monarchy and neither was consistently pursued; nevertheless they formed the common ground between the reforming bureaucrats of the old regime and the revolutionary legislators of the new.

Seigneurs felt most threatened by the trends in government policy, and understandably so. When Charles Catherine Loppin took up the cudgels to defend his rights and prerogatives in the village of Gemeaux (Burgundy), the provincial intendant, Joly de Fleury, intervened on the side of the community and warned Loppin to abandon his pretensions. Ignoring this advice, the irate seigneur petitioned the Royal Council only to be told again that the government considered that a community had a perfect right to assemble without the consent of the seigneur. Other intendants pursued a similar line when disputes arose between *communautés d'habitants* and seigneurs, although none as forcefully as did Joly de Fleury. By 1770 seigneurial officials appear to have abandoned their right to attend village assemblies in Burgundy, and in 1776 an edict applicable to the province of Champagne reiterated that the *sindic* alone was empowered to convene and to preside over village assemblies. In fact, this edict expressed the entire philosophy of the government in the most unambiguous terms. The umbilical linking the *communauté d'habitants* to the seigneurie was to be cut, but only in order to increase the scope for supervision by the intendant. And in case the *sindic* should lack the authority to conduct the affairs of the community in the interests of its more substantial members, he was to be aided by a corps of well-to-do householders called *notables* and elected for a term of six years. The poor were not excluded from the ballot, but they were grossly under-represented. Thus, in the closing decades of the *ancien régime* parts of northern France were beginning to acquire municipal institutions broadly comparable with those existing in the South.

A more thoroughgoing transformation of the institutions of village life would have occurred if reformers such as Turgot had had their way. In a propagandist work entitled *Mémoire sur les municipalités* which was drafted by Dupont de Nemours in 1775, Turgot urged the creation of a uniform network of rural municipalities in which landowners would have a preponderant voice. The scheme was remarkable less for the suggestion that there should be a property qualification for the vote, than for the way in which it deliberately overlooked the distinctions between the three orders. Asking the privileged orders to consider themselves first and foremost as undifferentiated proprietors whose rights hinged on wealth alone was clearly too much, however. When Calonne tabled a comprehensive programme of local government reform in February 1787 he took care to preserve the social distance between the two privileged orders and the Third Estate.

Calonne's proposals for local government reform issued in an edict of June 1787 which provided for a tripartite system of provincial, district and municipal assemblies. Although the regions possessing Provincial Estates were specifically excluded from the scope of the reform, it was enforced in a total of seventeen *généralités* and represented the biggest administrative shake-up to have been undertaken by the monarchy in over a century. Ironically, it lasted just two and a half years. This is presumably the reason historians have devoted scant attention to the episode. Yet the municipal assemblies created by Calonne embodied several decades of thinking about how power should be exercised at the grass-roots, thinking which powerfully influenced the revolutionaries when they came to frame their own local government legislation. The first thing to note about Calonne's reform is that it sought to bolster rather than to undermine the intendant. The intendant remained the chief executive of absolute monarchy in the provinces and he continued to supervise the new assemblies just as he had the old. That said, it is also noteworthy that the censitary conception of government had come of age. The edict provided for the election of a 'municipal assembly' in each *communauté d'habitants* with all those paying at least 10 *livres* in direct taxes forming the electoral constituency (revealingly described in official documents as the 'parish assembly'). However, Calonne avoided a clean break with the established traditions of the *ancien régime* by stipulating that the new municipal body would contain two *ex officio* members: the parish priest and the seigneur. The seigneur, not the elected *sindic*, would normally preside over meetings. These latter provisions make for curious reading, for they call into question much that the intendants had fought for during the previous three decades. In all likelihood they were concessions forced on the minister as he tried to steer the measure through the Assembly of Notables.

The new municipal assemblies came into being in August and September 1787, that is to say a full two years before the revolutionaries' own system of representative local government based on the commune which is usually regarded as the corner-stone of municipal freedom in modern France. Attempts were made to limit the impact of the reform, but with mixed success, for it seems that the minister set the franchise threshold too low. In the *généralité* of Rouen approximately 50 per cent of taxpayers were qualified to vote; in the *élection* of Montreuil-Bellay up to 60 per cent; in the Sélestat and Haguenau districts of Alsace 70 per cent; while in the Auvergne critics objected that the 10 *livres* tax qualification effectively enfranchised even the humblest peasant proprietor.[36] As the long and complicated business of holding elections in the countryside drew to a close, the intendants anxiously scrutinised the results for signs of disaffection. In some districts the rural masses remained indifferent to this novel irruption of politics into their midst, but in others the reform unleashed the first signs of an awakening in the villages. The sub-delegate of the *élection* of St Flour in the Auvergne, for instance, reported that the hustings had triggered 'a terrible combustion in the parishes'.[37]

More insidious and no less dangerous to the regime was the way in which Calonne's edict promoted to leadership an elite of rural proprietors who were neither faithful retainers of the seigneurs nor dutiful employees of the intendant. This elite swiftly colonised the new organs of local government with gentleman farmers, lawyers, barristers and other professionals congregating in the provincial and district assemblies, while well-to-do peasant farmers, millers, skilled artisans, small traders and minor *rentiers* packed the municipal assemblies. The poor were excluded since the legislation imposed a tax qualification of 30 *livres* on all candidates for elective positions. Thus ensconced, the future revolutionary bourgeoisie, together with leading elements of the peasantry, commenced a discreet apprenticeship to the concept of political liberty just as the *ancien régime* slipped into terminal crisis. The first tangible signs that Calonne's local government reform had taken root in the countryside appeared as Frenchmen gathered for the elections to the Estates-General. In the province of the Touraine about 70 per cent of the individuals chosen to represent their parishes at the *bailliage* assemblies were drawn from the ranks of the municipal officers. In the *généralité* of Rouen 61 per cent of the parish delegates were municipal officers. Such figures reflect more than simply a restricted electorate choosing familiar faces, for the parish elections of March 1789 were conducted on the basis of universal manhood suffrage. They reflect, rather, the popular endorsement of an elite which had already achieved a measure of political recognition.

Calonne's package of last-minute reforms has long been cited as evidence that absolute monarchy was not incapable of mounting a challenge to vested interests and of modernising existing structures. And, indeed, it is instructive to view the famous municipal law of 14 December 1789 in the context of several decades of tinkering with the institutions of village life. Nevertheless, we should conclude with a view of the whole. In the sense that there was a substantial overlap of personnel between the pre- and post-1789 municipalities, the new law can certainly be described as an exercise for putting old wine into new bottles. Even the new bottles had a familiar shape to them. In the small villages of Languedoc the municipalities elected early in 1790 resembled nothing so much as the municipalities of the *ancien régime*. Two or three *consuls* gave way to three municipal officers including a mayor, while six *conseillers politiques* gave way to six *notables*. In the sense that it embodied a franchise restriction, the new law can also be said to have consummated the traditions of the late *ancien régime*. To be sure, the prerequisite for 'active' citizenship (payment of direct tax equivalent to three days' wages) was paltry compared with the franchise provisions of the 1787 legislation, but the intention was plain enough. On the other hand, the decree 'for the constitution of the municipalities', as the official record termed it, marked a new departure in several important respects. The measure was enforced throughout the kingdom, in every 'town, *bourg*, parish or community', irrespective of existing corporate bodies which were abolished outright. With the demise of the intendants and the failure to organise an effective alternative system of administrative supervision until Napoleon instituted the prefects, the new municipalities emerged as near-autonomous bodies: autonomous bodies, moreover, on which the legislature devolved wide-ranging and easily abused powers such as the right to call out the army or the National Guard, the right to suspend civil liberties by proclaiming martial law and the right to compile the tax rolls. Finally, the electoral principle was taken to its logical conclusion and members of the privileged orders lost all *ex officio* rights in the new municipal councils. And as if to prove the point, municipalities all over France set about vigorously contesting every manifestation of seigneurial privilege.

Chapter 2

The crisis of the late 'ancien régime'

No aspect of the French Revolution has engendered more debate than the question of its origins. Do we seek them in the sharp escalation of conflict between the monarchy and the Parlement of Paris which the presentation of Calonne's package of reforms unleashed in 1787? Do we seek them, rather, in a widespread dissatisfaction with the manifold social, economic and political incongruities of the *ancien régime* which had matured over several decades? For Georges Lefebvre there could be no doubt upon this issue: the revolution was first and foremost the product of a crisis of the rural economy.[1] This view came to be shared by virtually every scholar of his generation, and all the more when Ernest Labrousse uncovered the main phases of French economic development in the eighteenth century in a massive statistical treatise published before the Second World War.[2] Lefebvre died in 1959, but even before his death the interpretation which he had done so much to promote was showing signs of wear. Since that date the volume of research devoted to the origins of the revolution has grown substantially, and so have the criticisms. The fundamental point of disagreement concerns Lefebvre's conviction that long-maturing social and economic processes made the revolution, or something pretty like it, inevitable. It has been put most succinctly by the American historian G. V. Taylor who declares that 1789 was 'essentially a political revolution with social consequences and not a social revolution with political consequences'.[3]

Succinct though this definition of the problem may be, it is also rather extreme. Few of the historians who reject Lefebvre's emphasis would deny that the *ancien régime* was smitten with a socio-economic malaise. Instead they would query whether that malaise had much to do with the downfall of absolute monarchy between 1787 and 1789. Political squabbles within the educated elite wrecked the regime, not the pressures associated with headlong population growth, rampant seigneurialism, bourgeois frustrations or any other socio-economic factor: this is the position espoused by William Doyle, a noted English critic of the Lefebvre thesis.[4] He acknowledges that France experienced a sharp economic crisis after 1787 during which the revolution occurred, but questions whether the relationship between the two events was one of cause and effect. No one, it seems, is prepared to forego the concept of crisis altogether, but historians construe the term in different ways. For some 'crisis' implies the chronic failure of the *ancien régime* to adjust to socio-economic realities, while for others it describes the short-term fluctuation in the economy consequent upon the disastrous harvest of 1788 – a fluctuation which had serious repercussions for the monarchy only because it coincided with a political rebellion already in the making.

The question 'Was there a crisis of the late *ancien régime?*' can be answered in the affirmative, therefore. But was that crisis pathological? This chapter draws together the case-study evidence and offers an assessment of the condition of the peasantry on the eve of the revolution. Lefebvre's monumental study of the North East provides the obvious starting point. In that work (and in subsequent books and articles), he defines the crisis of the rural economy as essentially a product of rapid population growth in the second half of the eighteenth century. Its symptoms were social polarisation, heightened conflict over the commons and common rights, and an intensification of seigneurial obligations. He also argues that the burden of taxation borne by the poor peasantry was increasing in the final decades of the *ancien régime*. Social polarisation increased because the demand for land outstripped the supply, while at the same time pushing up the value of land and the fruits thereof. Population growth swelled the ranks of the landless proletariat and rich peasants made themselves richer by exploiting the high prices–low wages conjuncture to 'engross' the holdings of their less well-endowed neighbours. Hence the popular resentment of *gros fermiers* throughout the openfield region. Hence, too, the demands for some kind of 'agrarian law' limiting the size of farms which the poor peasantry voiced repeatedly during the revolution. The escalation of conflict over the commons and common rights can also be tied to the changed demographic outlook. Poor peasants sought land, any land, on which to grow foodstuffs, while the *laboureurs* preferred to keep the commons under pasture for their flocks. At the same time, rising grain and fodder prices nurtured a more egotistical attitude towards collective rights. Landowners resented having to share their crops with the rest of the community and sought ways of curtailing gleaning and free grazing. The capitalist instinct infected seigneurs (who were often landowners in their own right), too. As the price of corn and many basic commodities such as firewood spiralled upwards from the 1760s, they brought a new zeal and efficiency to the collection of seigneurial dues, especially harvest dues. The peasantry complained bitterly, and all the more when seigneurs repudiated traditional wood-cutting rights in their forests while insisting that the *droit de plantis* entitled them to plant trees in the commons, on roadside verges and in village squares.

These are the salient features of the late *ancien régime* rural economy as depicted by Georges Lefebvre and a generation of historians guided by his example. It might be objected that the picture applies best to the cereal plains of the Paris basin, the North East and the East where the land supply was static and standards of living could only be maintained by dint of a revolution in agricultural techniques. In the 'pays de petite culture' of the West and South, population densities were generally lower and the land supply still elastic in the late eighteenth century. All other factors being equal, therefore, the Malthusian dilemma seemed less inescapable. Nevertheless, Lefebvre's thesis received a general theoretical underpinning from the work of Ernest Labrousse. Using a statistical method, Labrousse set out to uncover the trend of prices, incomes and farm rents during the period 1726 to 1789. His labours enabled him to draw a picture of the domestic economy which, in its fundamental aspects, appears as valid today as it did fifty years ago. Between the early 1730s and 1770, or thereabouts, a series of good harvests and the retreat of dearth and disease-induced demographic crises enabled the economy to expand. Prices started to rise, slowly at first, and then briskly in the 1760s. The following decade brought an abrupt curtailment of this rising tide of prosperity, however, and there was no resumption of sustained growth in the 1780s either. On the contrary, the years before the revolution were marked by a prolonged recession in the textile industry (mainly a rural and cottage-based activity), periodic collapses in the market for wine, and sharp fluctuations in grain prices. The crisis ushered in by the disastrous harvest of 1788 was not a rogue cloud in an otherwise unblemished sky. The economic outlook had been unpromising for quite some time.

The detail of Labrousse's analysis provides a clearer picture of how these trends affected the peasant.[5] Much the most celebrated statistic of French revolutionary historiography concerns the purchasing power of the urban and rural poor. Taking the years 1726–41 as his baseline Labrousse calculates that the average price of essential consumer goods had risen by 45 per cent when compared with the period 1771–89. If we isolate the period 1785–9 the rise was 65 per cent. Nominal wages, by contrast, rose by only 22 per cent over the period 1726–41 to 1785–9. One of the key aspects of Lefebvre's crisis of the rural economy begins to emerge, therefore: in the course of five decades the purchasing power of wage earners declined by a quarter. Yet poor peasants reliant on wage work were not the only ones to suffer from the adverse economic conjuncture. Many tenant farmers had achieved a real improvement in living standards during the 1760s when agricultural prices rose faster than rents. But after 1776 the trend was reversed: commodity prices languished, while landowners endeavoured to recoup the losses of earlier years by raising rents. Over the long term some commodity prices rose more steeply than others, and the steepest rises affected the foodstuffs of the poor. Wheat, for example, increased in price by between 56 and 66 per cent over the period 1726–41 to 1785–9, whereas rye rose by between 60 and 71 per cent. Half a labourer's daily wage might be spent on the purchase of bread made from rye or a mixture of coarse grains in normal years, but the price spiral of 1788–9 pushed this proportion up to 88 per cent. Firewood also constituted an important item in the budget of the poor, especially in the cities, and its price all but doubled between 1726–41 and 1785–9. Small wonder that seigneurs and proprietors of forests came to regard timber and dead wood as a highly marketable asset. Thanks to Labrousse, we can also discern some of the forces at play in the widespread abuse of the conventions regulating free grazing at the end of the *ancien régime*. Unlike most other agricultural products, the price of meat continued to rise after 1776 and it stimulated considerable investment in stock-raising. All too often the rural community paid the price of this investment as proprietors and rich *laboureurs* fattened their stock on village commons, stubble and fallow.

So much, then, for the crisis of the rural economy. No one would doubt that the evidence adduced by Lefebvre and Labrousse amounts to an impressive catalogue of strains and tensions. Yet Lefebvre and Labrousse perceived the crisis in apocalyptic terms. It was not any old crisis, but *the* crisis of the old regime, and thus linked inextricably to the outbreak of revolution. The crisis, that is to say, was structural and could only be resolved by a total renovation of the social and economic fabric of the state. Here it is necessary to sound a note of caution, for two difficulties arise. If, as William Doyle observes, the crisis presupposed nothing less than 'the final breakdown of an economic structure riddled with fatal contradictions',[6] it is curious that the revolution bequeathed to nineteenth-century France an economic structure that bore more than a passing resemblance to that of the late *ancien régime*. Increasingly, historians are distinguishing between the 'political' *ancien régime* which reached its nemesis in 1789 and the 'economic' *ancien régime* which evinced unsuspected powers of resilience. It is an argument that Lefebvre himself would have recognised (notwithstanding his attachment to the concept of 'crisis'), and it is one which the present study can only endorse. The conservative economic legacy of the revolution and, indeed, the jumbled conservative and radical reflexes of the peasantry are themes which crop up repeatedly in the chapters that follow. The second objection that might be levelled at the theory of a general crisis as sketched in by Lefebvre and Labrousse is that there is nothing very specific about it. Crises of over-population, or at least of rapid population growth, had occurred many times before and, more important, had been resolved many times before without resort to the *deus ex machina* of revolution. The symptoms described by Lefebvre – land hunger, social polarisation, dissension over the commons and common rights, escalating hostility towards those who creamed off peasant surplus – are banal. What was so special about the strains and stresses of the second half of the eighteenth century, apart from the fact that a revolution broke out in 1789? The answer must be that agrarian discontent was compounded by two developments of the utmost significance: the escalating fiscal pressure of a monarchy which had for-gotten the lessons of the mid-seventeenth century, and growing peasant resistance to the institutions of seigneurialism.

Fiscal pressure

Lefebvre never doubted that the late *ancien régime* crisis was exacerbated by a revenue-hungry state and by lay and ecclesiastical seigneurs who were no less determined to squeeze the peasantry. Neither view enjoys the unqualified support of historians nowadays, however. Decades of case-study research have vastly increased our knowledge of the revolution and its antecedents, but more knowledge has not made generalisation any easier. Quite the reverse: Lefebvre reckons that direct taxes rose by between 25 and 30 per cent in Flanders, Hainaut and the Cambrésis during the two decades prior to 1789.[7] While conceding that per capita direct taxation was probably lower in this region than in the rest of the kingdom, he leaves us with the impression that the actual burden of taxation on the peasantry (and particularly on the poor peasantry) was growing, and that this trend was typical. Other historians have reached precisely the opposite conclusion. Either the rate of increase was much less rapid, or else taxes were increasing rapidly, but the exchange value of farm production was rising more rapidly still. Thus, the peasant proprietor with a grain surplus to market was insulated from the impact of heavier taxation. In fact, his fiscal burden declined in real terms. This is the line argued by Abel Poitrineau in his case study of Lower Auvergne.[8] Between 1730–9 and 1780–90 direct taxation increased by 60 per cent in this region, but rye prices increased by 71 per cent and wine prices doubled during the same period. No doubt substantial peasant proprietors and long-lease tenants made a killing out of the eighteenth-century price inflation, but how many peasants could offset rising costs by selling grain? Most peasants were intermittent buyers, rather than sellers of grain and were highly vulnerable to shifts in the rate of taxation.

Nevertheless, Emmanuel Le Roy Ladurie hazards the view that the real weight of direct taxation was slowly diminishing in the reigns of Louis XV and Louis XVI,[9] which is at odds with the picture of fiscal reaction sketched in by Georges Lefebvre. The trouble with both of these generalisations is that they are based on narrow case studies. Plausibly, Le Roy Ladurie maintains that the intense and arbitrary fiscal pressure which the peasantry suffered at the hands of Richelieu and Mazarin had no parallel in the eighteenth century. Between the 1630s and the 1660s royal taxes tripled to the accompaniment of widespread popular disorders. In 1643 a Croquand army marched into Villefranche-de-Rouergue demanding a reduction of the *taille* to pre-Richelieu levels. But the point at issue is not whether the French peasant of 1789 was better or worse off than his ancestors of the 1630s and 40s. Rather, we need to know how that peasant generation born in the 1750s and 60s was affected by fluctuations in the level of taxation. Here, Le Roy Ladurie can only invoke the findings of Poitrineau, bolstered by some evidence from Gascony, to support his contention that the weight of direct taxation declined in the eighteenth century.

The monarchy levied several direct taxes, but they were assessed and collected in different ways, and it is most unlikely that we shall ever be able to establish a complete picture of the incidence of taxation throughout the kingdom during the last few years of the *ancien régime*. However, in the midst of the confusion some points do stand out. Direct taxation on presumed wealth was not the only, nor, perhaps, the most substantial source of revenue available to the monarchy. Confronted by powerful vested interests determined to resist the extension of existing taxes, ministers relied increasingly on indirect taxes (levied on salt, tobacco, food and drink, and the movement of goods) in order to finance government expenditure. At the end of the *ancien régime* the province of the Berry paid about 8 million *livres* per annum in taxes, of which approximately 2.5 million *livres* (31 per cent) derived from direct levies (*taille, capitation* and *vingtièmes*). Taxes on items of daily consumption such as salt hit the poor hardest, and the Berry formed part of that region of northern and central France in which the salt tax (*gabelle*) was extremely onerous.

Fiscal pressure reached the peasant in different ways, therefore. It also varied in its intensity quite independently of variations in population density, levels of income, patterns of consumption and so forth. The point is often made that per capita taxation (direct and indirect) was heavier in the *pays d'élections* than in the *pays d'états*, on the grounds that those regions possessed of powerful Provincial Estates were able to deflect part of the burden on to their less well-endowed neighbours. In the *pays d'élec-tions*, the intendants brooked no opposition. Such crude attempts as have been made to quantify fiscal pressure do not entirely bear out this reason-ing, however. In practice, the differences between individual *généralités* and *élections*, and between individual *pays d'états* were almost as great as those between *pays d'élections* and *pays d'états* viewed en masse. Among the latter, Brittany and Provence were notoriously undertaxed, but the resistance offered by the Estates of Languedoc and Burgundy to the fiscal demands of state seems to have been nominal. By the same token, we find considerable discrepancies between the *élections* which cannot be accounted for by reference to population and standards of living alone. Brittany provides the best-documented example of a province in which the global burden of taxation eased in the course of the eighteenth century. The Provincial Estates successfully resisted attempts to introduce the *taille* (the major direct tax) and the *gabelle* (the major indirect tax) to the region, and between 1738 and 1789 direct taxation increased by just 31 per cent, whereas wheat and rye prices doubled or tripled during the same period. On the basis of a model peasant household budget compiled as rigorously as possible for the harvest year 1784/5, Donald Sutherland calculates that the payment of direct taxes took about 4 per cent of gross income.[10] The tithe, by contrast, accounted for 8 per cent, and seigneurial dues 2 per cent. This is the budget of a self-sufficient peasant household whose major out-lay was rent (about 20 per cent), however. It is by no means certain that poor peasants benefited from the conjuncture.

For well-to-do Breton tenant farmers the trend of royal fiscality on the eve of the revolution gave little cause for concern. Not so in Languedoc, where public opinion took the view that direct taxes had doubled in the final decades of the *ancien régime*. That view has been endorsed, in part at least, by Georges Frêche whose researches have done much to demolish the myth that the vaunted privileges of the Estates of Languedoc provided any degree of protection from fiscal pressures.[11] In this region the *taille* increased in three main spasms which delineated the successive crises of absolute monarchy: between 1600 and 1626; between 1638 and 1661; and between 1755 and 1789. As Le Roy Ladurie surmised, the sharpest increases accompanied the accession to power of Richelieu, the architect of absolute monarchy. Between 1631 and 1634 the burden of the *taille* in the civil diocese of Castres shot up by a punitive 236 per cent following the defeat of the Duc de Montmorency's rebellion. The rate of increase in the decades before the revolution was less spectacular (approximately 100 per cent in the civil diocese of Lavaur between 1751–6 and 1784–9), but it was unremitting and it elicited a growing volume of complaint, not least because the burden of royal taxation was unfairly distributed among the fiscal districts (known as civil dioceses) which made up the province. Ironically, Languedoc suffered from its reputation for being a well-run and enlightened province. Supposing that taxation was more judiciously apportioned here than elsewhere in the kingdom, the monarchy did not hesitate to increase the load. But the Estates used a formula for distributing that load which was devised in 1530 and never modified subsequently. All attempts to reform the provincial *compoix* of 1530 foundered on the resistance of those civil dioceses which knew themselves to be undertaxed. Consequently, the escalating fiscal demands of the monarchy during the latter half of the eighteenth century fell disproportionately on the districts of Upper Languedoc whose sixteenth-century prosperity had long since ebbed.

Underlying government calculations was the assumption that tax liability was more accurately determined in the regions of *taille réelle*; that is to say in the regions where the *taille* was based on the fixed and measurable criteria of land holding, as compared with the regions of *taille personnelle* where it was based on crude administrative estimations of wealth. Broadly speaking, the *taille* was *réelle* in the *pays d'états* and in the south-western provinces of Guyenne and Gascony. Elsewhere, it was *personnelle*. This assumption continues to be held by historians, but for no very good reason. The superiority of the *taille réelle* depended upon the maintenance of up-to-date registers of land holdings and values which were costly to draw up and difficult to revise subsequently. We have already seen how the tax matrix employed by the Estates of Languedoc took no account of the shift in the prosperity of the province from Upper to Lower Languedoc. The same criticism can be levelled at the subordinate diocesan *compoix* which determined the distribution of taxation between the *communautés d'habitants*. On the eve of the revolution the *communautés* of the civil diocese of Toulouse paid royal and provincial taxes on the basis of a sliding scale devised in 1551. At Castres the diocesan *compoix* was dated 1610. Only in the civil diocese of Narbonne had an attempt been made to revise assessments in the light of changing circumstances. Here an entirely new *compoix* was compiled between 1711 and 1730.

The peasantry felt these injustices keenly. When two villages of similar population, similar agricultural vocation and similar income levels paid out vastly differing sums in royal *taille* and *vingtièmes*, even the dullest minds realised that something was wrong. Taxation, in short, retained a formidable capacity to mobilise public opinion. Nowhere is this more apparent than in the *généralité* of Montauban which became the theatre for an ambitious programme of tax reform in the 1780s. The *généralité* of Montauban embraced the mountainous hinterland of the old province of

Guyenne which, although its Estates had long ago ceased to meet, remained a region of *taille réelle* for the most part. Here, as in Languedoc, the rate of taxation increased substantially during the eighteenth century (roughly 300 per cent between 1723 and 1780) and here, as elsewhere, it had a divisive effect.[12] Those able to profit from the growing demand for foodstuffs improved their position, at least until the 1770s, whereas the poor, with only their labour to sell, suffered. However, popular resentment focused less on the upward spiral of taxes (as in the 1640s), than on the system of tax assessment and collection which was riddled with incongruity and abuse. That system rested on the *cadastre*, a register identical to the *compoix* which purported to record the details of land holdings and values in a given community. Each *communauté d'habitants* possessed a *cadastre*, therefore, and each alteration in the fiscal valuation of the built and unbuilt properties situated within the confines of the community had also to be consigned to the register. This, at least, was the theory. In practice, nothing of the sort took place, and with the passing of time the *cadastres* became more and more unreliable. The government recognised the danger and in 1666 Colbert instructed the intendant of Montauban to set in motion a thorough revision of the *cadastres* of his *généralité*. In the social and political conditions of the *ancien régime*, 'thoroughness' was not within the powers of the intendants to command, however, and the resultant tinkering merely made matters worse.

With the blessing of Necker, the newly appointed Provincial Assembly of Upper Guyenne gripped the nettle once more in 1780. If few practical reforms followed, the Assembly did launch a full-scale enquiry into the problem of fiscal distortion and it is from this investigation that our knowledge of the functioning of the tax system at the grass-roots derives.[13] The well-to-do proprietors of the Provincial Assembly seem to have been of the opinion that the *taille* should amount to no more than one-sixth (17 per cent) of net income, whereas expert opinion estimated that the totality of royal direct taxes took a quarter (25 per cent) of peasant surplus, once the costs of cultivation had been deducted. Expressed in per capita terms, each inhabitant of Upper Guyenne paid 10 *livres* 12 *sols* 6 *deniers* in direct taxes on the eve of the revolution, that is to say four times as much as each inhabitant in a sample of fifteen parishes in the Fougères–Vitré area of Upper Brittany (2 *livres* 14 *sols*).[14] Averaging the tax burden per head of population may facilitate a rudimentary comparison between provinces, but it glosses over the problem confronting the peasantry of Upper Guyenne, however. Very few peasant households (the notion of per capita taxation is a convenient statistical fiction) actually paid an 'average' tax contribution. Such were the shortcomings of the *cadastres* that most paid too little or too much.

The first case to be presented to the Provincial Assembly left little room for doubt on this point. For decades the villagers of Lincou had petitioned for a reduction in their tax burden and finally, in 1783, the authorities approved the drawing up of a new *cadastre* to replace the one compiled in 1606.[15] It transpired from this exercise that the 184 inhabitants of the community had been paying 2,421 *livres* 10 *sols* 4 *deniers* of *taille* on a net income of 7,165 *livres* 19 *sols* 10 *deniers* – a rate of 34 per cent, or exactly double that which the Provincial Assembly deemed appropriate. The case of Lincou was exceptional only in the consistency with which its fields, vines and woodland had been over-assessed. Some plots of arable paid two or three times their annual net yield in *taille*, while none paid less than 50 per cent of their net yield. Elsewhere, however, comparable non-noble land holdings were assessed for as little as 1 per cent of their net yield. The village of Auriac-L'Eglise, for instance, was in the enviable position of paying out just 3 or 4 per cent of its net income in direct taxation.[16]

These, then, are some of the negative aspects of the *taille réelle* as it prevailed in the South. In practice, if not in theory, the assessment of tax liability on the basis of land values tended to institutionalise unfairness, both as between communities and as between individuals. In so doing it kindled a flame of popular exasperation with the regime which the growing demands of the royal exchequer could only fuel. That sense of exasperation and frustration was captured time after time by the commissioners sent out by the Provincial Assembly of Upper Guyenne to examine the condition of the *cadastres*. Their detailed and dispassionate reports make for ominous reading. They reveal a peasantry inured to coping with the vagaries of royal fiscality, but which was finally beginning to lose patience. When the commissioners arrived in the village of Belmont which straddled the border between Guyenne and Languedoc, they were treated to a tirade against the 'horrors of capriciousness' which governed the levying of taxes in the former province.[17] The peasants added that their land holdings in Languedoc attracted a third less tax than equivalent possessions in Guyenne. Not surprisingly, they divided their energies in proportion.

When the tax system lost all rhyme or reason only two solutions remained: the peasantry could move off the land or they could rebel. Land abandonment was a perennial worry to royal administrators in the regions of low soil fertility and heavy direct taxation such as Upper Guyenne and Upper Auvergne. It was also a source of apprehension to the rural community, for the tax burden was fixed and a peasant who abandoned his homestead simply transferred its liability on to those taxpayers remaining. Nevertheless, peasants did abandon their holdings, and occasionally entire communities collectively renounced their possession, too. On the eve of the revolution there were eighty-two abandoned farms in the vicinity of St Flour in Upper Auvergne.[18] Several large estates which had hitherto paid hundreds of *livres* in taxes figured on this list, and the minutes of the *élection* assembly of St Flour painted a dire picture of mass emigration and deserted villages steadily being engulfed by heather. Almost inevitably, heavy taxation brought in its train the threat of coercion as well. When peasants fell behind with their payments – and in the Brioude *élection* of Upper Auvergne arrears of tax for the years 1783, 1785 and 1786 were still outstanding in 1788[19] – the intendants activated a formidable apparatus of repression. Bailiffs and distraint officers (*porteurs de contrainte*) battened upon the rural community with a licence to behave like the free-billeting troops which had been the scourge of the countryside in the seventeenth century. Usually they arrived at harvest time, or on the eve of a local fair, when the pickings were richest. The abuse of *contrainte* was universal, but in the Auvergne and Guyenne it reached epic proportions. Defaulting tax-payers in the *élection* of Villefranche-de-Rouergue kept 106 *porteurs de contrainte* in full-time work at the end of the *ancien régime*.[20] The administrative costs of their activities were simply added to the total tax bill. In 1779 the intendant of Montauban estimated that the cost of *contrainte* increased the burden of direct taxation in the *généralité* by some 70,000 to 80,000 *livres*. The Provincial Assembly of Upper Guyenne considered this estimate much too conservative and proposed the figure of 150,000 *livres* per annum as a minimum.

Rebellion was an option which the peasantry of the South, South West and West had freely invoked in the seventeenth century. Yet the century prior to the revolution witnessed few outbreaks of collective violence, and none on the scale of the Croquandages of the 1630s and 1640s. The reason, suggests Le Roy Ladurie, is that the pressures of royal fiscality had eased, state subsidies were levied with more care and sophistication, prices were rising and both the church and central government exercised a constant surveillance over every aspect of village life. 'Rural society', he claims, 'had become more docile, better policed and less wretched.'[21] This picture is altogether too bland. It rules out of court the fiscal animus behind the widespread peasant mobilisations of the winter and spring of 1789 – immortalised in Arthur Young's famous encounter with a peasant woman on the road to Metz;[22] it presents a fettered and lifeless image of the rural community which no historian of the revolutionary epoch would recognise, and it makes no allowance for the possibility that the form in which collective anger was expressed changed over time. The eighteenth century pioneered an elaborate array of popular sanctions which stopped short of atavistic violence.

The boycott, the masked assault on moneylenders (as in the Masques

Armés 'revolt' of 1783 in the Vivarais), the contrived riot against agents of the fisc, social banditry, and above all collective ill will (*mauvais gré*) and non-compliance were the weapons of the new century. The latter, especially, were highly effective. More than any other form of popular protest they expressed that questioning of the established order of things which was becoming commonplace in the 1780s. The campaign mounted against the *commun de paix* tax in the Rouergue was symptomatic of this trend. Levied since the twelfth century, if not earlier, it defrayed the cost of protecting the upland villages of Guyenne from the incursions of mercenaries. That at least was the theory. By the eighteenth century most of the monies raised went straight to the royal exchequer, and although the sums involved were not large, non-payment became an issue of principle. In 1777 a royal *arrêt* successfully quashed the first signs of resistance to this iniquitous and vexatious tax. Three years later, however, a campaign of passive non-compliance began in earnest with over sixty parishes involved at its height. When the commissioners of the Provincial Assembly of Upper Guyenne arrived in the village of Trémouilles, they were mistaken for collectors of the *commun de paix* and confronted by angry peasants led by a man wielding an axe.[23] Payment of the levy soon ceased throughout much of the region leaving the authorities bemused as they pondered how to tackle the phenomenon of a tax strike. The government tried to stimulate the zeal of its subordinates, but the intendant warned that the villages were in a state of slow combustion. Any attempt to convene village assemblies would endow the movement with leaders and ignite a conflagration. In such an event, the rural police force (*maréchaussée*) would be quite unable to cope, and troops would have to be called in.

Was the burden of royal taxation increasing in the second half of the eighteenth century? This is a question that admits of no clear answer. In fact, the question itself is less clear than might appear at first sight. We need to distinguish between direct and indirect taxation; between the mid-century trend and the more sombre outlook of the last ten or fifteen years of the *ancien régime*; between economic reality and popular perceptions of that reality. If research has failed to produce instant answers, it has, however, alerted us to some of the factors which must be accommodated in future generalisations. Undertaxed Brittany cannot stand duty for the rest of France; but nor can the overtaxed Guyenne, or the Auvergne, or the vast province of Languedoc with its internally biased system of tax distribution. On the other hand, it *is* instructive to know that average per capita direct taxation differed by as much as 400 per cent between parts of Brittany and parts of Guyenne. Such a discrepancy holds out all sorts of possibilities for a deeper understanding of peasant behaviour after 1789. It is also important to bear in mind that royal fiscality had a differential impact. As we have defined them, the peasantry included sellers of grain, buyers of grain and those who realised the ideal of self-sufficiency, more or less. Poor peasants met the demands of the fisc by selling their labour, or the aleatory products of cottage industry, whereas rich peasants covered their tax obligations by selling grain. Yet Labrousse has shown that the purchasing power of wage earners declined by a quarter in the half-century after 1741. By contrast, those peasants producing a marketable surplus disposed of an appreciating asset, at least until the 1770s. Thus it is likely that many country dwellers found taxation an increasing strain on their income, even as others registered a slight easing of the burden. A picture of grimmer conditions for the majority corresponds closely to the popular perception that fiscal pressure had increased exorbitantly within the life-time of a man and, ultimately, this must be our guide. The French peasantry entered the crisis of 1788–9 with the conviction, if not the statistical evidence, that they had never been so heavily taxed.

Seigneurialism

Increasing fiscal pressure, or at least increasing sensitivity to fiscal demands, focused attention on the issue of exemptions. And the issue of exemptions brought into play the larger question of the role of seigneurial-ism. In principle, the clergy and the nobility were exempt from direct taxation and were consequently referred to as the 'privileged orders'. In practice, matters were not quite so simple: the clergy enjoyed the right to assess themselves and paid to the royal exchequer a sum known as the *don gratuit* at regular intervals, while the nobility paid the *capitation* and the *vingtième*, but not the *taille*. Moreover, a host of commoners had won exemption from the *taille* by purchasing offices, and many non-noble seigneurs (i.e. bourgeois who had acquired fiefs) contrived to escape the *taille*, too. In the South the major state taxes were geared to the land rather than to the persons who happened to own it. For example, in Languedoc about 10 per cent of the land surface was classified as 'noble' for fiscal purposes. This could give rise to a curious anomaly: a noble might own 'commoner' land on which he was required to pay the *taille*. Nevertheless, it is still a fair generalisation to say that nobles were exempt from the *taille* and paid the other direct taxes to which they were subject at much reduced rates.

Since virtually all nobles were seigneurs, even if all seigneurs were not nobles, it was perhaps inevitable that peasant hostility to the fisc should fuel hostility to the institutions of seigneurialism. Even in undertaxed Brittany, the peasantry were keenly aware that the nobles derived the main advantage from the province's fiscal immunities. In the heavily taxed, and no less heavily seigneurialised, Guyenne and Auvergne 'privilege' was a positive economic threat, however. When a landowner of Naves near Rodez purchased an exempting office, the villagers discovered that his share of the *capitation* (100 *livres*) now fell on them instead.[24] This system of quota payment of taxes prevailed throughout France and it enabled the wealthy to browbeat the rural community in all sorts of insidious ways. The *élection* assembly of St Flour complained in 1788 that exempting offices, and particularly the coveted rank of King's Secretary, changed hands frequently: 'some have been bought and sold four times in the space of five or six years in the district'.[25] This merry-go-round made the apportionment of taxes a nightmare and effectively deterred villagers from seeking the redress of long-standing fiscal abuses for fear that they would simply aggravate the problem by provoking a rush to purchase exempting offices. Ironically, therefore, we often find the rural community cast in the role of defender of the status quo, albeit a status quo congenitally biased in favour of the rich and powerful. But this role demanded a posture of vigilance rather than acquiescence, for the threat to the traditional order of village life came as much from the seigneur and the upwardly mobile bourgeois proprietor as from any other source.

These are weighty matters, however. The trend of recent research has been to play down the significance of 'privilege' and of seigneurialism as precipitants of the late *ancien régime* crisis. 'Privilege was universal', argues William Doyle, 'and the French king had few subjects who, in virtue of the province or town where they lived, or some body to which they belonged, did not enjoy the right to some sort of special treatment.'[26] The belittling of the seigneurial or feudal regime goes back to Alfred Cobban[27] and has likewise spawned a substantial literature in which cherished notions concerning the reality of seigneurialism and the extent of opposition to it before 1789 are subjected to scrutiny. What must strike even the casual student of the origins of the French Revolution is the degree to which historical writing on this subject relies on assertion rather than evidence. The predominantly English and American historians who have criticised the tendency to view the events of 1789 as a classic 'bourgeois' revolution which swept away an obsolescent feudal structure have undoubtedly dispelled many myths, but only by dint of putting into circulation new myths. Their edifice, it might be thought, rests pretty heavily on assertion, too. What is lacking is the groundwork: nobody seems to have bothered to find out how 'privilege' impinged on the population in practice; how far seigneurial authority still permeated daily life in the eighteenth century; to what extent the revolutionaries agreed on a package of agrarian reforms and how they conciliated differing notions of property rights.

On the subject of privilege enough has been said to indicate that it is quite misleading to assert that 'Privilege was universal', as though it was a known quantity evenly distributed across the realm. In this area the traditional picture brooks no reinterpretation: the clergy, nobility and the bourgeois elite within the Third Estate were grossly privileged, whereas the peasantry had no privileges that they would have recognised as such. Seigneurialism, by contrast, impinged upon the lives of all country dwellers, whether directly or indirectly. The seigneurie can be defined as a system of land tenure, as a jurisdiction of rights and as a unit of judicial administration. However, by the eighteenth century, only a minority of peasants would have been familiar with the seigneurie in this compact form. The château expressed seigneurial power in the countryside, but few seigneurs resided permanently in their châteaux and few châteaux were surrounded by demesne lands. Instead, the seigneurie had fragmented and it impinged upon the peasant chiefly as a disembodied and rather alien mechanism for rent collection and petty judicial repression – disembodied because the physical presence of the seigneurie was often vestigial, and alien because the lucrative seigneurial rights were put out to lease, whilst the non-lucrative seigneurial responsibilities were neglected. Seigneurialism, in short, was adapting to the role it performed best: that of surplus extraction.

Peasant wealth could be tapped in a number of ways: by the pre-emptive acquisition of holdings on death (*mainmorte*), by levying a tax on the purchase or transmission of property, by collecting quitrents, by taking a portion of the harvest and by fining offenders who came before seigneurial courts. The first and the last of these rights were relatively unimportant; fees chargeable on property transactions (*lods et ventes*) and harvest dues provided the bulk of non-landed seigneurial income. In addition, many seigneurs maintained mills or bread ovens which their vassals were required to use regardless of cost. The leasing of such utilities generated further income. What kind of burden these levies imposed on peasant surplus is far from clear. We have in-depth studies of seigneurial accounts which give some idea of the yield of dues paid in cash or kind, but equivalent studies of peasant household budgets are virtually non-existent. The day-to-day difficulties of life on a small holding subject to the ecclesiastical tithe, seigneurial harvest dues and the fiscal demands of state cannot be recaptured in detail; they have to be imagined. On the other hand, it *is* possible to make some reasonably sound generalisations about the incidence and relative burden of seigneurial dues across the kingdom. Three sources are invaluable in this respect: the petitions, addresses and memoranda submitted to the Feudal Committee of the Constituent and Legislative Assemblies which fill thirteen substantial boxes in the National

Archives; the monographs drawn up to mark the one hundred and fiftieth anniversary of the French Revolution in 1939; and the doctoral theses recently completed by students of Albert Soboul.

The first point to emerge from a reading of this material is that seigneurialism really did exist. It was integral to the social and economic fabric of the *ancien régime* and still significant as a political force (witness the composition of Calonne's municipal assemblies). Perhaps this is to state the obvious, but Alfred Cobban's charge that 'feudalism', as he termed it, was a reification invented to buttress the idea that the French Revolution was a 'bourgeois' revolution[28] has unleashed considerable controversy among historians. Between 1789 and 1794 'la féodalité' was a political catchphrase on everyone's lips, but it became a catchphrase precisely because it conjured up a meaningful reality for millions of French men and women. A second point follows from this: seigneurialism provoked a growing, if guarded, resentment in the second half of the eighteenth century. On the evidence of the theses and regional monographs now available, it would be difficult to sustain the view that the peasantry only became sensitive to the injustices of the seigneurial regime in the radicalising atmosphere of the meetings of the Estates-General. Finally, it could be argued, albeit not conclusively, that the growing popular resentment of seigneurialism was linked to an intensification of feudal obligations which marked out the pre-revolutionary decades.

Harvest dues constituted the most burdensome aspect of seigneurialism, so much so that their incidence provides a rough guide to the intensity of seigneurial pressure on peasant surplus. Where such dues existed the seigneurial regime continued to impinge upon the rural community in no uncertain fashion; where they did not, seigneurialism had ceased to play an important socio-economic role in the countryside. The only substantial exception to this general rule was Brittany where harvest dues were insignificant and seigneurs relied on casual taxes on property transfers (*lods et ventes* and *rachats*) and quitrents instead. However, this rough delineation of the problem does not take us very far. Harvest dues may have survived in some regions and not others, but they were not levied at a uniform rate; they were not levied on all arable land; they were not the sole tax on agricultural produce in some localities; and they were not always readily identifiable, especially when compounded with the tithe. Last, but not least, they figure in our sources under a bewildering variety of names: *champart* (Ile-de-France, Picardy, Flanders, Gâtinais, Guyenne, Lyonnais, Dauphiné); *tierce* (Burgundy); *terrage* (Champagne, Lorraine, Poitou); *tasque* (Languedoc, Provence); *agrier* (Aunis, Saintonge, Angoumois, Foix) and *cens* (Upper Auvergne). Table 1 gives some idea of the geography of harvest dues, together with rates of assessment expressed as

Table 1. *Seigneurial harvest dues on the eve of the revolution*

Region	Locality, District or Province	Due	Rate (expressed as percentage of gross production except where indicated)	Comments
Paris Basin	Beauce[1]	champart	8.3	paid jointly with tithe (16.6%)
	Orléanais[2]	champart	8.3 → 10.0	maximum rate, including *censive*
	Beauvaisis[3]	champart	4.0	*bailliage* of Nemours
	Gâtinais[4]	champart	8.3 → 12.5	
	Champagne[5]	terrage	6.7	village of Chervey (*arrondissement* of Bar-sur-Seine, Aube)
	Champagne[6]	champart	9.1	village of Valdampierre (*bailliage* of Chaumont-en-Bassigny)
North East	Hainaut–Cambrésis[7]	terrage	3.0 → 8.0	
	Argonne[8]	terrage	16.7	village of Montcheutin (Ardennes)
	Cateau-Cambrésis[9]	terrage	9.0	often paid jointly with tithe (17.0%)
	Vermandois[10]	terrage	10.0	village of St Martin-Rivière (Aisne)
Burgundy	Auxois[11]	tierce	6.25 → 7.1	villages of Verdonnay, Tanlay, Nesle (Yonne and Côte-d'Or)
	Auxois[12]	tierce	6.7 → 9.1	
	Auxois[13]	tierce	4.2 → 8.3	village of Argentenay (Yonne)
	Tonnerrois[14]	tierce	7.7 → 9.1	
	Avallonnais[15]	tierce	5.3	
South West	Plain of Niort[16]	terrage	8.3 → 16.7	paid jointly with tithe (16.6%)
	Vendée[17]	terrage	8.3	
	Saintonge[18]	agrier / champart	11.1 → 14.3	
	Ile-d'Oléron[19]	agrier	25.0	on vines
	Gironde[20]	champart	16.7	on cereals
		agrière	14.3 → 20.0	on vines
Massif Central	Limousin[21]	tierceries	33.3	
	Rouergue[22]	champart	6.25 → 25.0	
	Auvergne[23]	censive	23.3	net production
	Velay[24]	censive	13.3	net production
	Brivadois[25]	censive	24.4	net production
Midi	Lauragais[26]	tasque	11.1	vestigial
	Castrais[27]	tasque	16.7	vestigial
	Toulousain[28]	tasque	10.0	net production
South East	Lyonnais[29]	champart	20.0	maximum rate
	Dauphiné[30]	champart	5.0	

Notes to Table 1

1 A.N. DXIV 3.
2 A.N. DXIV 3.
3 P. Goubert, *Beauvais et le Beauvaisis de 1600 à 1730: contribution à l'histoire sociale de la France du XVIIe siècle* (Paris, 1960), p. 179.
4 *Archives parlementaires de 1787 à 1860. Recueil complet des débats législatifs et politiques des chambres françaises (première série, 1787–99)* (92 vols., Paris, 1862–1980), vol. iv, p. 196.
5 J.-J. Vernier (ed.), *Cahiers de doléances du bailliage de Troyes (principal et secondaire) et du bailliage de Bar-sur-Seine pour les Etats-Généraux de 1789* (3 vols., Troyes, 1909–11), vol. i, p. 611.
6 A.N. B^a32
7 G. Lefebvre, *Les Paysans du Nord pendant la Révolution française* (Bari, 1959), p. 150.
8 A.N. D*XIV 1.
9 M. Delattre, 'Le Régime seigneurial, la délinquance, les mentalités paysannes dans la Châtellenie du Cateau–Cambrésis au XVIIIe siècle' (Mémoire de maîtrise, n.p., 1970), p. 34.
10 A.N. DXIV 1.
11 A.N. DXIV 3.
12 R. Robin, *La Société française en 1789: Semur-en-Auxois* (Paris, 1970), p. 301.
13 A.N. DXIV 11.
14 F. Genreau, 'Les Paysans et l'abolition des droits féodaux dans le district de Tonnerre (Yonne), 1789 à 1793' (Diplôme d'études supérieures d'histoire du droit, University of Dijon, 1972), p. 26.
15 A.N. D*XIV 1.
16 A. Benoist, 'Les Populations rurales du "Moyen-Poitou protestant" de 1640 à 1789. Economie, religion et société dans un groupe de paroisses de l'élection de Saint Maixent' (University of Poitiers, Thèse pour le doctorat de troisième cycle, 4 vols., 1983), vol. ii, pp. 431–6.
17 A.N. DXIV 11.
18 A.N. DXIV 2.
19 A.N. DXIV 2.
20 A. Ferradou, *Le Rachat des droits féodaux dans la Gironde, 1790–1793* (Paris, 1928), p. 243.
21 A.N. DXIV 11.
22 J. Bastier, 'Droits féodaux et revenus agricoles en Rouergue à la veille de la Révolution', *Annales du Midi*, 95 (1983), 264.
23 G. Lemarchand, 'La Féodalité et la Révolution française: seigneurs et communauté paysanne (1780–1799)', *Ann. hist. Rév. fran.*, 52 (1980), 540.
24 *Ibid.*
25 *Ibid.*
26 G. Frêche, *Toulouse et la région Midi-Pyrénées au siècle des lumières (vers 1670–1789)* (Mayenne, 1974), p. 511.
27 *Ibid.*
28 Lemarchand, 'La Féodalité et la Révolution française', p. 540.
29 M. Garaud, *La Révolution et la propriété foncière* (Paris, 1958), p. 36.
30 *Ibid.*

a percentage of the total crop. All the figures relate to levies imposed on the cereal harvest, except where it is stated that they apply to the produce of the vine.

It would be unwise to place a great deal of confidence in random and unweighted data of this sort. Nevertheless, the figures reproduced above do serve to demonstrate the extreme unevenness of seigneurial surplus extraction. The rate varied from seigneurie to seigneurie, from parish to parish and from province to province. When combined with literary evidence they also provide a rudimentary map of seigneurial exactions. Dues appear to have been heaviest in the South West (Poitou, Aunis, Saintonge, Périgord, Quercy) and in the Massif Central, particularly along its western and southern escarpments (Limousin, Auvergne, Rouergue). It is noteworthy that eastern France scarcely features in our table. This may reflect only the vagaries of the available documentation, but it is more likely that harvest dues no longer burdened peasant surplus to any appreciable degree in the East. Despite appearances, the same observation holds for the Midi. Here the *tasque* could be locally burdensome, but only a tiny percentage of peasant tenures were subject to it. In Upper Languedoc, for instance, seigneurs made more money out of property transfer taxes (*lods et ventes*) than out of harvest dues. Burgundy, on the other hand, presents a problem. This was a region of powerful and inter-ventionist seigneurs whose activities provoked widespread resentment among the peasantry in the final decades of the *ancien régime*, yet harvest dues were no more onerous than on the cereal plains around Paris. Obviously, peasant resentment of seigneurialism turned on more than simply the issue of harvest dues, but these other issues are virtually impossible to quantify.

The pattern of seigneurial exactions sketched in above has one potential shortcoming. It assumes that all commoner land bearing crops paid dues. Unfortunately, this assumption is unwarranted: in some localities the peasantry had acquired allodial lands (known as *alleux*) which were exempt from seigneurial jurisdiction, in others seigneurs had abandoned or lost track of their rights, or converted them into a fixed money rent. Hence the picture of extreme incoherence which analyses of estate registers (*terriers*) reveal. Poitrineau reckons that as much as 25–30 per cent of the land surface in the plain of Lower Auvergne may have been allodial,[29] whilst detailed study of the *cadastre* of the *bourg* of Auriol in Provence reveals massive variations in the level of harvest dues from one plot of land to the next.[30] Where such dues existed, they could deprive the farmer of a sizeable portion of his income, but they were comparatively rare. Only 3 per cent of the total arable surface was still subject to harvest dues on the eve of the revolution. This must be regarded as a minimum figure unique to the Mediterranean littoral, however. In the North most holdings remained subject to seigneurial exactions, albeit at vastly differing rates. The *champart* was pretty general throughout the Beauce and the Gâtinais, while in Hainaut and the Cambrésis Lefebvre estimates that about 50 per cent of agricultural land paid the *terrage*. In the South West harvest dues seem to have been both exceedingly onerous and exceedingly extensive. The *terrage* was widely levied in those regions subject to the Custom of Poitou, usually in compound with the tithe, and in this form it could amount to a 25 per cent deduction from gross production. The same is true of the Quercy and the Rouergue: dues were medium-to-heavy and wide-spread. In 1780 the Provincial Assembly of Upper Guyenne complained that 'land subject to the right of champart is condemned to barrenness'. Out of a dozen sheaves of corn, 'the seigneur takes three, the tithe owner one, while taxes absorb two more'.[31] Or, to make the point another way, dues payable in kind or in cash constituted 71 per cent of the income of noble and bourgeois seigneurs in the Rouergue, compared with 34 per cent in Upper Auvergne, 19 per cent in the civil diocese of Toulouse and 8 per cent in the Lauragais.[32]

All allowances made, therefore, our contour map of the seigneurial regime still holds good. What is striking about it is less the variable intensity of seigneurial involvement in the social and economic life of the rural community than its very pervasiveness. Virtually all country dwellers must have come into contact with the seigneurie at some point in the agricultural calendar, and more often than not they encountered it first in the guise of surplus extractor. Rural proprietors, whether bourgeois or peasant, were liable to harvest dues and quitrents, and so were sharecroppers. Even the landless poor lived in the economic shadow of seigneurialism, for they were subject to monopolies (*banalités*) and hunting laws like anyone else. Moreover, any individual who acquired property – be it only a hut and a garden – would likely incur charges on it, whether *lods et ventes*, *rachat* or *mainmorte*. This near-ubiquity of seigneurial exactions is important, for it helps to explain both the scale and the transcendent unity of the popular movements of 1789. No doubt *gros fermiers* and rich *laboureurs* had more to gain from the liquidation of the seigneurial regime than sharecroppers, and no doubt sharecroppers stood to gain more than plot holders and agricultural labourers, but everybody had something to gain – not least bourgeois proprietors who played a highly ambiguous role during the first tumultuous summer of the revolution.

But how had that popular front come into being? In a famous article G. V. Taylor expressed astonishment at the 'docility shown by the peasants towards the seigneurial system',[33] – docility as evidenced by the parish *cahiers*, that is. Yet, even in terms of the content of the *cahiers*, this seems a perverse conclusion to reach (see pp. 58–9) and in any case it has been superseded by more recent research. Georges Lefebvre never doubted that tensions engendered by seigneurialism formed a major component of the crisis of the rural economy. By the end of the *ancien régime*, he argues, relations between seigneurs and the peasantry of Hainaut–Cambrésis had so deteriorated that 'the very principle of feudal property was being challenged'.[34] This view is endorsed by Emmanuel Le Roy Ladurie who grants that peasant–seigneur animosities were endemic, but insists that the nature of this type of conflict was beginning to change after about 1750.[35] Peasant cultural horizons were widening; privilege, whether fiscal or seigneurial, no longer commanded automatic, unquestioning respect. He admits that the change was a two-way process: as the seigneurie evolved into an ever more ruthless mechanism for the extraction of surplus and the promotion of agricultural capitalism, it lost its legitimacy in the eyes of the masses. The process was obviously uneven: less pronounced, perhaps, in Brittany and the Auvergne than in Languedoc where the volume of litigation between seigneurs and village communities began to rise from the 1730s. Ominously, the peasantry seemed as ready to join in attacks on honorific rights as on the more tangible perquisites of seigneurial power. This point has been graphically illustrated by Olwen Hufton who stresses the role of youth groups in rousing hostility to seigneurs in the Hérault plain.[36] As she shows, the pleasures of the hunt were a tailor-made opportunity for friction between seigneur and vassal, and the rituals of the poacher provided the ideal cover for inarticulate social protest. In 1773, the governor of Guyenne learned that nobles in the district of Lectoure were being victimised by bands of masked men whose forays had become known as the *chasses masquées*. The purpose of these raids, according to his informant, 'was less to kill game than to insult the seigneurs of these estates'.[37] Altogether a dozen proprietors reported attacks on their servants, sharecroppers and forest guards, gun shots fired at their châteaux, threatening posters and thefts. The Gascon nobility were seriously alarmed and blamed youth groups acting on the covert orders of the legal bourgeoisie of Lectoure. Peasants may not have been directly involved, but they maintained a wall of silence when investigating magistrates sought to identify the perpetrators of the disorders.

In Gascony the anti-seigneurial animus drew inspiration and example from long-running disputes over the tithe. With an income of 150,000 *livres* the archbishop of Auch was one of the richest prelates in the kingdom and the bulk of this wealth derived from a swingeing tithe amounting to one-eighth or 12.5 per cent of all cereal crops. Fraudulent declaration of the grain harvest had become endemic, as had trials of strength between rural communities and the clergy, but the frequency of litigation on this issue increased markedly after 1750. Attempts to extend the tithe to straw triggered a massive display of passive non-compliance between 1769 and 1773. Then resistance diversified to become a veritable anti-feudal front. *Chasses masquées* apart, the movement won a notable victory in the 1780s when the clergy and their proctors were forced to reduce the tithe to a tenth. 'Movement' is an appropriate word to use in this context, for the tithe strikes of the 1760s, 1770s and 1780s in Gascony trained a generation in the art of popular mobilisation. The resistance involved every stratum of rural society from the village bourgeoisie downwards. It was as if the 'popular front' of 1789 had already come into being.

Signs that the bourgeoisie were beginning to challenge the seigneurs for the leadership of the rural community can also be detected in Upper Guyenne. In this region of heavy harvest dues the determination of seigneurs to cash in on rising cereal prices by renewing their *terriers* (the so-called 'feudal reaction') had caused alarm since the 1760s. When seigneurs also tried to dodge their fiscal obligations communities resorted to litigation as a matter of course. This is what happened at Privezac (Rouergue) when the title to the seigneurie changed hands and the new owner (a robe noble) tried to pass off his lands as noble and therefore exempt from the *taille*.[38] The villagers resisted stoutly and in 1785 the seigneur was condemned to pay out 5,000 *livres* in arrears of *taille* to the community. He complained ruefully that the peasants had been encouraged to make a stand by the local bourgeoisie. Indeed they had, and they had learnt the lesson well. In 1789 the château of Privezac was pillaged, and then burnt out in 1792.

The emphasis of anti-seigneurialism was somewhat different in Burgundy and the border provinces of the East. Here the issue of the commons and common rights tended to pit rural communities against their seigneurs. Le Roy Ladurie sums up the problem neatly: 'the Burgundian peasantry of the eighteenth century were anti-feudal because they were anti-capitalist'.[39] That is to say, seigneurs were modernising their seigneuries reckless of the consequences for the peasantry. Modernisation presupposed enclosures which curtailed *vaine pâture* and the *droit au regain*, the fencing off of woodlands which inhibited casual grazing and scavenging for firewood, the partition of common land on terms grossly favourable to the seigneur (*triage*), the buying in of stock which was then fattened on village fallow and stubble, and so on. All this came in addition to the active enforcement of harvest dues and monopolies, of course. Symptomatic of the trend was the complaint of the villagers of Fontenay-sous-Vézelay in the heavily-wooded Nivernais. Since fuel prices had begun to rise, they alleged in a petition to the Feudal Committee of the Constituent Assembly, timber 'has become the principal object of the ambition of seigneurs; they have contrived to deprive village communities of it which, in consequence, have lost both their woods and grazing for their stock'.[40] In 1769 the inhabitants of a neighbouring hamlet had lost two-thirds of their woodland as a result of a fraudulent *triage*. Not dissimilar complaints reached the ears of the Committee from the openfield villages of eastern Champagne and Lorraine. Seigneurs had taken to maintaining huge flocks of sheep on the meagre village pastures and in so doing they undermined the viability of the common flock upon which the poor chiefly depended.

The consequence was a manifest increase in social tensions. Friction between seigneurs and their vassals seems to have reached a peak in Burgundy between 1735 and 1750; then it eased before crystallising afresh in the 1780s. To the north, on the fringes of Burgundy, the Auxois and Champagne the agitation did not begin in earnest until the 1760s, but by the 1780s it had become general in this region, too. As in the South peasant resentment tended to focus on the irritants of seigneurialism, such as hunting rights, first and then, as positions hardened, spread to other more substantial issues. On occasion, we can capture this process in detail. Thus, in the village of Larrey (Châtillonnais) violations of seigneurial hunting rights were punished with a fine of 10 *sols* until 1752.[41] This rose to 3 *livres* 5 *sols* in 1762; 20 *livres* in 1764 and 100 *livres* in 1769. By 1765 we find the inhabitants of Larrey refusing to pay the *tierce*, then they refused to undertake seigneurial *corvées* or to cook their dough in the seigneurial bread oven. How long their resistance lasted on this occasion is not recorded, but it seems unlikely that relations with the seigneur improved. In the summer of 1790 the village participated in the agitation against unredeemed harvest dues which spread eastwards from the Gâtinais (see pp. 117–20). The case of Larrey is not exceptional: by the 1780s village communities in this region were combatting the pretensions of their seigneurs with increasing skill and sophistication. The fulminations of the Parlements of Dijon and Besançon proved no deterrent; on the contrary they served only to consolidate the rural community in the face of what all sections of the peasantry came to perceive as seigneurial aggression. Encroachment on commons and the steady erosion of collective rights were not easily resisted, but it slowly dawned on communities that they possessed a whole range of sanctions which could be deployed as the need arose. All that was required was a mental revolution. When, in 1784, the inhabitants of the hamlet of Mennouveaux (Bassigny) announced to the Chapter of Langres that they would not pay their dues until they had seen the titles,[42] it was a sign that a shift in attitudes of seismic proportions had occurred.

The suggestion by Le Roy Ladurie that seigneurialism and capitalism –

in their eighteenth-century incarnations – were somehow linked cannot be allowed to pass without comment, not least because it bears upon the issue of the 'feudal reaction'. The idea, at least, is not new: long ago Lefebvre drew attention to the capitalist potential of the seigneurial relationship. He called it 'capitalism . . . under the cover of feudal dues',[43] and Pierre de Saint Jacob has since described the evolution of the Burgundian seigneurie in the latter half of the eighteenth century as 'physiocratic',[44] which amounts to the same thing. However, Le Roy Ladurie has extended and systematised this insight to such an extent that he proffers it as an alternative model of social development. Far from agrarian capitalism emerging out of the ruins of feudalism, they were 'mutually reinforcing'.[45] Feudalism or, to be more precise, the seigneurial demesne provided the prototype for modern large-scale farming. Had the revolution not intervened, the seigneur might well have done for France what the improving landlord did for England. The theory is certainly plausible and it has been widely invoked by those historians who doubt whether it is meaningful to describe 1789 as a 'bourgeois' revolution. However, two objections arise: first, the metamorphosis of the seigneurie in Burgundy and the provinces of the East seems to have been peculiar to these regions. Save, perhaps, for the grain-growing area around Toulouse, seigneurialism retained its traditional character in the rest of the kingdom. Second, Le Roy Ladurie plays down the significance of seigneurial surplus extraction and emphasises instead the role of the *réserve* or demesne in nurturing agrarian capitalism. Yet most seigneurs had long since sacrificed the coherence of their demesne land in an effort to stay solvent. Once again, the picture seems too narrowly drawn on a handful of dynamic and modernising seigneuries. The corollary that peasants automatically adopted an anti-capitalist stance towards the emanations of seigneurialism, or, indeed, towards agrarian reform in general should not pass unchallenged, either. The peasantry, as we shall see, did not speak with one voice on this issue, nor did they display consistent attitudes over time and place. A petition despatched to the Constituent Assembly by the inhabitants of the barony of Fénétrange is revealing in this respect.[46] Like many communities in Lorraine, they were inundated with sheep brought in by permission of the seigneur. The presence of these ill-policed flocks in an unenclosed agricultural landscape tended to limit the scope for agricultural modernisation 'from below'. Were it not for the sheep, complained the villagers, they could have devoted more land to the cultivation of clover.

Modernising initiatives were not restricted to seigneurs, therefore. In the East, particularly, the rural community was presiding over a quiet renovation of agricultural practices during the last quarter of the eighteenth century. Nevertheless, the tensions engendered by that process of modernisation formed a notable component of the phenomenon known to historians as the 'feudal reaction'. In its classic formulation the idea of feudal or seigneurial reaction emerged from the scholarly debates of the late nineteenth century and it proposes that the peasantry experienced an intensification of feudal obligations during the final decades of the *ancien régime*. This brilliant hypothesis has enormous explanatory potential, for it promises to unlock some of the secrets of the popular mobilisations of 1789. However, the theory of a feudal reaction has proved tantalisingly difficult to demonstrate in practice. Faced with this dilemma, historians tend to adopt one or other of the following positions: they either assert the reality of the feudal reaction in rhetorical terms arguing, in effect, that it must have existed because the revolts of 1789 were anti-feudal in character; or they subject the notion to reinterpretation. That is to say, they emphasise this or that facet of the putative feudal reaction and play down those aspects which they find uncongenial or insufficiently documented. Thus, for Emmanuel Le Roy Ladurie, the seigneurial reaction of the late eighteenth century was essentially a crisis of seigneurial management.[47] Fief owners were seeking to regain control of their possessions; the intensification of feudal dues was not directly at issue. Likewise, William Doyle acknowledges that the zeal with which seigneurs defended and clarified their prerogatives increased, but he, too, doubts whether anything more than the resurrection of old dues which had lapsed was at stake.[48] With these modifications, one might conclude that the idea of a seigneurial reaction has won general acceptance. But does such a watered-down definition retain any explanatory potential? Yes, says Doyle: it helps to explain the sense of grievance which peasants expressed in the *cahiers*. Yet he minimises the import of this revelation by then playing down the extent to which seigneurialism was challenged in the rural *cahiers*.

Georges Lefebvre never doubted that the issue of seigneurialism figured prominently in the thoughts of country dwellers as they drew up their *cahiers*, but his scrutiny of twenty-three tithe and *terrage* registers from the Cambrésis failed to provide evidence for the view that seigneurs were actually increasing harvest and pecuniary dues on the eve of the revolution.[49] An intensification of the seigneurial regime had certainly taken place, but it consisted principally of a resumption of dues which had lapsed, allied to an abusive exploitation of two long-standing seigneurial privileges: exclusive rights to fell and to plant trees on verges and public squares (*droit de plantis*) and repossession of village commons via the *droit de triage*. Subsequent research has largely vindicated this picture. Throughout the North East and the East seigneurs avidly exploited their rights of *plantis* and *triage*, to such an extent that these rights had become the symbols of seigneurial tyranny by the end of the *ancien régime*. The legislators of the Constituent Assembly acknowledged as much when they empowered communes to seek restitution of their commons in March 1790, and abolished the *droit de plantis* without compensation several months later.

Nevertheless, the impression persists that Lefebvre envisaged a more pervasive form of feudal reaction. His articles and general books certainly convey this impression, and it is significant that he proposed to mark the one hundred and fiftieth anniversary of the revolution with a special research effort devoted to the disputed issue of the feudal reaction. Embedded in the guidelines laid down on that occasion we find the following advice: 'The problem can be resolved by comparing two or more *terriers* of the same seigneurie; for example, one dating from the second half of the eighteenth century, and another from the first half, or from the seventeenth century.'[50] It is a neat solution, indeed, but one which few, if any, historians have succeeded in carrying out to the letter. Such evidence as exists is disparate and chronologically recalcitrant, in the sense that it does not always fit into the time sequence required. Abuse of the *droit de plantis* in Picardy, Artois and Hainaut *does* appear to have been a post-1750 development in the main, but seigneurial expropriation of common pasture and woodland was much less time-specific. In the district of Is-sur-Tille (Burgundy) the right of *triage* was invoked against twenty-one village communities between 1669 and 1740, and sixteen between 1750 and 1789.[51] The more long drawn out the process of feudal reaction, the more opaque does it become.

On the other hand, we should not overlook the lessons to be learned from the renewal of estate registers (*terriers*); nor can we afford to ignore the evidence contained in petitions addressed to the Constituent Assembly, or its Feudal Committee. The frequency with which the *terriers* were renewed undoubtedly increased in the second half of the eighteenth century (see plate 3). Indications that this was indeed so can be collated for most provinces. However, the motivation behind this process was not necessarily sinister. As fiefs changed hands, were divided or amalgamated, *terriers* became obsolescent and had to be redrafted. Peasants profited from periods of weak seigneurial jurisdiction to wriggle out of their obligations and then complained bitterly when a new incumbent hired feudal experts (*feudistes*) who began to call in the arrears. On the other hand, it is also true that feudal dues were the perfect answer to an investor's prayer. They were inflation-proof, low risk and low cost – never more so than when *portable*, when, that is, the peasant had to transport them from his field to the château. There is no source of income 'more solid, more assured than that of ground rent, it involves no danger and no expense', observed the municipality of Arpajon (Cantal) in a memoir addressed to the Con-

TERRIER DE LA SEIGNEURIE

de Juniville

M *Noel Menard Manouvrier a Juniville*

Doit pour les Frais de fa Déclaration audit Terrier,
fuivant les Lettres-Patentes du Roi du 20 Août 1786,
ce qui fuit.   *10 Septembre 1788*

Honoraires.	Livr.	Sols.	D.
1°. Pour le premier Article		15	
2°. Pour les autres Articles au nombre de à 7 fols 6 deniers l'un	"	"	
3°. Pour l'écriture de 1 Rôle — à 15 f. pour l'Expédition & 5 f. pour la Minute.	1		
Débourfés.			
4°. Pour le Contrôle de la Minute	4	7	6
5° Pour l'ancien Contrôle de 1 Rôles d'Expédition, à 5 f. l'un	"	5	
6°. Papier de Minute & d'Expédition	"	5	
T O T A L	2	12	6

*J'ai remis audit Menard cinquante deux fols fix D. porté y deffus
laquelle fomme il adeclaré payer comme contraint à trois ans*

= 1790 =   = Cottin l...

Plate 3. Receipted bill for the cost of renewing the *terrier* of the seigneurie of
Juniville (Ardennes), addressed to Noël Menard, day labourer

stituent Assembly.[52] Unsurprisingly, therefore, the incidence of *terrier*
renewal increased with the escalation in grain prices. This *did* lead to
abuse, even to trickery and the fabrication of phoney dues on occasions.

Regions in which seigneurs relied heavily on 'useful' rights as a source of
income, and in which grain surpluses could be easily marketed were particularly susceptible to *terrier* revision. The Périgord, Quercy, Bas
Rouergue and the Albigeois, for instance, were all linked by good roads to
the cities of the Garonne basin and the Languedoc plain and a chorus of

complaint, unequalled anywhere else in the kingdom, issued from these provinces during the last three decades of the *ancien régime*. At Meljac on the border between the Rouergue and the Albigeois the squire held down the peasantry with the aid of a local attorney who was notorious in the district for his skill in giving 'new deeds a veneer of age by smoking them in the chimney or over a candle'.[53] In 1790 the château of Meljac was pillaged by the villagers. Discontent smouldered in nearby Belmont, too, where a monastic institution enjoyed both the tithe and harvest dues.[54] After an abortive attempt by the monks to extend the tithe to straw and to levy an 'illegal' *champart*, the community lined up behind a bourgeois proprietor and resorted to law. The case was still pending when the revolution broke and settled the matter. In the years that followed the municipality of Belmont bought up the lands formerly belonging to the abbey and divided them among the inhabitants – a neat if unanticipated solution to the problem of feudal reaction.

Throughout this region, in fact, the pattern of agrarian revolt in 1789 and 1790 (see pp. 67–81) can be closely correlated to the incidence of feudal reaction. In the midst of that violence a bitter indictment of seigneurial excess reached the Constituent Assembly from the 'rent payers of the seigneurs of the Rouergue and Quercy'. It declared that 'there was not a seigneurie in the [two] provinces which, on the last renewal [of *terriers*], had not greatly increased its yield'.[55] A sweeping generalisation, no doubt, but one for which a *prima facie* case can be made. Moreover, the profiteering to which the petitioners referred relied heavily on the much discussed, if rarely documented, arbitrary extension of dues. From Hautesvignes (Agenais) we learn that harvest dues had been unilaterally increased in 1781;[56] from nearby Birac we have a similar report,[57] while the *cahier* of the town of Caussade (Quercy) alleged that seigneurs were collecting dues twice over from individuals who had failed to keep a record of the original payment.[58] The sheer weight of harvest dues (including the tithe) was no doubt part of the problem in the South West. Allowance must also be made for the growing incoherence of seigneurialism as members of the old nobility sold off fiefs, and even portions of fief, to wealthy commoners. These bourgeois seigneurs had a reputation for enforcing their rights more rigorously. For the peasantry, however, the fragmentation of seigneurial jurisdiction simply meant more visitations from the *feudiste*, more *terrier* renewals, more occasions for abuse, and less chance of judicial redress. The villagers of St Vincent-Rive-d'Olt (Quercy) summed up the problem in a sentence: 'Our community has so many charges because it is subject to a dozen seigneurs who order the verification of dues as easily as one would change a shirt.'[59]

The monolithic character of feudal reaction in parts of the South West cannot be generalised, however. Elsewhere in the kingdom seigneurial rack-renting seems to have been an episodic problem. Nevertheless, the two or three thousand items of correspondence sent in for the consideration of the Feudal Committee between August 1789 and September 1791 suggest that two other regions would repay closer investigation: the Senonais (that is to say the area around the town of Sens) and the Dauphiné. The Senonais, which in 1790 became a district of the department of the Yonne, retains our attention because of its proximity to the Gâtinais which spearheaded resistance to the continued payment of harvest dues in 1790 and 1791 (see pp. 117–20). By all accounts seigneurialism was increasing its grip in this region during the decades immediately prior to the revolution. The parishioners of Champigny on the edge of the Gâtinais complained that their seigneur had invented a hitherto unknown wine-pressing and corn-grinding right when renewing their *terrier*,[60] and an anonymous memoir provides further evidence that the abuses which we have described in the South West were common currency in the region. When a seigneur succeeded in acquiring adjacent fiefs, it aounced, 'the most burdensome *terrier* never failed to become the general rule'. As *terriers* were renewed, 'old rights were extended, often new ones were established'. *Feudistes* were not satisfied unless they managed to 'cram' into the *terriers* every prerogative listed in the feudal directory. Moreover, this determination to push up dues by fair means or foul had been manifest 'for about thirty years'.[61] In the Dauphiné it was the same story according to a printed brochure published in Grenoble several months after the anti-seigneurial uprisings of the spring of 1789 (see pp. 67–8). The unidentified memorialist gave concrete examples to demonstrate how the burden on peasant surplus had increased, and revealed that there were currently over fifty court cases pending between seigneurs and their vassals. This latter allegation was confirmed in an endorsement by a barrister at the Parlement of Grenoble who was himself acting for over twenty communities.[62]

In this context it would seem appropriate to reconsider the question of the *cahiers*. As I have mentioned, G. V. Taylor subjected the *cahiers* of the Third Estate to a searching statistical analysis which threw up a number of startling conclusions.[63] Not the least of his findings was the discovery that the proverbial hostility of the peasantry towards seigneurialism was a myth. Of the 428 parish *cahiers* which he examined, only 21 per cent demanded an end to monopoly rights (*banalités*); 11 per cent demanded the abolition of seigneurial courts; and a mere 4 per cent called for the destruction of the feudal regime completely. We are not told what proportion of his sample *cahiers* expressed hostility to harvest and ground rents, but must presume that few did. Such findings are significant in themselves, but they also contain broad hints as to how we should conceive the origins and course of the revolution and for that reason have been extremely influential. An absence of groundswell hostility to the emanations of seigneurialism implies an absence, or, at least, an attenuation of socio-economic crisis at the end of the *ancien régime*. It undermines many of the assumptions upon which this chapter is based. William Doyle puts it thus: 'Down to the spring of 1789, the forces pushing France towards revolution were almost entirely political. There was no underlying social crisis; it seems unlikely that such social discontents as surfaced in the *cahiers* would have done so without the stimulus provided by the constitutional wranglings that followed the collapse of the government.'[64]

Is it then just muddled thinking which has caused historians from the time of Georges Lefebvre to discern the lineaments of a fundamental agrarian crisis which reached critical proportions in the final quarter of the eighteenth century? To be sure we must guard against 'reading a spurious intentionality'[65] into the evidence, but we should not abandon the traditional empirical skills of the historian for all that. Quantification is no fail-safe solution to the problem of 'spurious intentionality'. The trouble with Taylor's verdict on the parish *cahiers* is that it does not correspond to the empirical reality. Indeed, one may doubt whether his statistical reality extends beyond the 428 *cahiers* subjected to analysis. Our own analysis of 389 parish *cahiers* yields quite different results: in the *bailliage* of Troyes (including four secondary seats) 40 per cent of peasant *cahiers* explicitly criticised seigneurial dues and monopoly rights; in the *bailliage* of Auxerre 36 per cent of *cahiers* did the same, while in the *bailliage* of Sens this figure was 27 per cent.[66] In each case grievances relating to hunting rights, the renewal of *terriers* and seigneurial courts have been ignored. Had they been included, the volume of complaint against the seigneurial regime would have been very much greater. These are localised examples to be sure, but seigneurialism was a localised problem in the sense that its intensity varied between widely placed extremes. The parish *cahiers* need to be studied *en bloc* as well as piecemeal, for otherwise all sense of the texture and contours of seigneurialism is lost. They also need to be decoded: there are grounds for supposing that peasants practised a degree of self-restraint when listing their grievances, but this is a matter more properly discussed in the political context of 1789.

Chapter 3

1789: between hope and fear

For students of the French Revolution the significance of the year 1789 can be simply stated. That year saw the absolute monarchy concede the arguments of its critics and call an Estates-General for the first time in one hundred and seventy-five years. However, it should be remembered that country dwellers contemplated the approach of 1789 in starker terms: it signalled a year of dearth, a year of fear. While vague and contradictory rumours of great doings in Versailles circulated in the villages, the peasantry got on with the more immediate business of staying alive in conditions of serious, if not unprecedented, harvest deficit. The extent of grain rioting, alone, suggests that 1789 would have ushered in a social explosion of some description irrespective of events being transacted in the capital. In reality, of course, it is impossible to make such a neat distinction between the internal and the external causes of peasant discontent. Almost from the start, the crisis exhibited a dual character: an old-style food crisis (*crise de subsistances*) combined with a new-style political crisis to produce a series of rural insurrections engulfing large parts of the kingdom. The violence was directed against traditional enemies and by traditional means for the most part, and it seemed patterned on the *jacquerie* model of the seventeenth century. But the hopes and fears roused by the news of the summoning of an Estates-General lifted peasant awareness of the import of their actions to an uncommon degree. Those actions, in turn, acquired a scope which the vestigial royal and seigneurial power in the countryside was incapable of opposing. Only with the founding of the municipalities in the early months of 1790 did properly constituted authority reappear.

The immediate origins of the agrarian distress which underscored the first year of the revolution can be traced back to the spring of 1788 when a prolonged drought blighted the prospect of an adequate harvest. Storms and heavy rainfall followed in July and August which destroyed what confidence remained. That autumn resistance to payments in kind mounted: the collection of seigneurial harvest dues fell into arrears while in the

Mâconnais tenant farmers began to default on their leases. Winter came early and lasted long: from November until mid-January much of the country was snowbound and subject to exceptional frosts. Casual workers felt the pinch first, then craftsmen and other non-producers of foodstuffs. Among the hardest hit were the winegrowers whose precarious livelihood was wiped out. In some regions three-quarters of the vine stock were destroyed by the cold, while in the South the decimation of chestnut and olive orchards mortgaged the future of the poor peasantry. In the towns soup kitchens opened; in the rural parishes desperate hordes besieged monastic storehouses. Vagrancy and vagabondage became a scourge of terrifying proportions for landowners and sedentary peasantry alike. But by March, even *laboureurs* and *ménagers* were having to juggle their resources in order to make ends meet.

Properly speaking, then, the crisis of 1789 began in 1788 and the symptoms of agrarian distress endured until the early months of 1790, and later still in the South West where the barely adequate harvest of 1789 succeeded in containing the situation, but little more. This is important, for it is essential to realise that the mobilisation of country dwellers did not wait upon events in Versailles or Paris. Nor can the risings be explained solely in terms of an instinctive and punitive reaction to the Great Fear, as many historians have supposed. Georges Lefebvre's painstaking reconstruction of that event make this point abundantly clear.[1] Already, in late 1788, peasants were gathering for collective action against seigneurs in the Franche-Comté. The local news-sheet reported on 5 January 1789 that 'agitation has spread from the towns to the countryside'[2] and warned of the danger of a general uprising. Nearly identical reports reached Necker, the chief minister, from the Dauphiné in February and from Provence in March. Ominous signs of the coming storm in the South West were also apparent. A projected assault on the château of St Léon-d'Issijac (Périgord) attracted no more than a handful of activists in January; three weeks later a fresh gathering drew in the majority of the parish.[3] By April the mobilisations in the South East had acquired a highly organised and explicitly anti-seigneurial character. In a scatter of communities across Provence and the Dauphiné, peasants gave notice of their intention to cease payment of harvest dues. Sometimes they even demanded the restitution of payments made on the 1788 harvest. Often these demands were accompanied by direct action to destroy enclosures and restore grazing rights, occasionally by assaults on châteaux, seigneurial mills and bread ovens. The mobilisations were not yet general, nor were they endorsed by the entire spectrum of village opinion. Many peasants teetered on the brink of outright rebellion, preferring bluff to the bravado of collective lawbreaking. Nevertheless, the classic symptoms of agrarian insurrection were unmistakeable and seigneurs began to remove their rent rolls and title deeds to places of safety. Not for nothing has Georges Lefebvre argued that the pattern of the great peasant revolts of 1789 was established during the winter and early spring.[4]

Elections to the Estates-General

The electoral statute was promulgated on 24 January and it prescribed a remarkably broad-based franchise. All adult Frenchmen registered as tax payers were qualified to attend specially convened assemblies of the community of inhabitants or parish for the purpose of drawing up lists of grievances known as *cahiers* and of selecting delegates. These delegates, usually numbering from two to four, were then required to attend a much larger electoral assembly representing the entire *bailliage* (or *sénéchaussée*). The *bailliage* assemblies brought together delegates from the villages and delegates from the towns, and they varied enormously in size. Whatever their size, though, they all had the same basic task: to hammer out a composite 'general' *cahier* from the multiple parish or 'preliminary' *cahiers* and to elect deputies who were to carry it to the Estates-General. It might be thought that this cumbersome, two-tier electoral process was designed to emasculate rural opinion, but there is no evidence that such was the government's intention. On the contrary, Necker instructed the royal officials charged with supervising the *bailliage* assemblies to stay outside the fray. All in all, the electoral regulations constituted an honest attempt to adapt existing institutions for the purpose of consulting public opinion on a scale never before imagined. In 1789 France went to the 'polls' in conditions tantamount to universal manhood suffrage.

This is not to suggest that private individuals missed the chance to bring influence to bear, however. Opportunities for abuse and undue pressure existed at each stage in the electoral process: village assemblies could be 'led'; they could be 'packed'; they could be 'invited' to endorse a model *cahier* without discussion. In the *bailliage* assemblies feuding between urban and rural delegates degenerated into violence on occasions, while the professional bourgeoisie intrigued ceaselessly to ensure that the deputies were chosen from within their ranks. The parish assemblies convened on Sundays after Mass and usually during the first fortnight of March, although the statute laid down no specific dates for the elections. More guidance was offered on the subject of leadership: the assemblies were to take place in the presence of 'the local judge, or, in his absence, some other public official'.[5] In practice this tended to mean the seigneurial judge who thus acquired a considerable say in the proceedings. Seigneurial judges, or their equivalents, presided over 53 per cent of village assemblies in the Orléanais[6] and some 50 per cent of those comprising the *bailliage* of Semur-en-Auxois where they shared the responsibility with royal judges.[7] In neither locality were village *sindics* given the chance to lead their communities. The domination of *hommes de loi* was not universal, however. Of the fifty-one communities of inhabitants composing the *bailliage* of Mirecourt in Lorraine, forty were headed by their mayors; one by its deputy mayor; two by seigneurial nominees; one by its seigneur; one by a judge and one (the principal seat) by the lieutenant-general of the *bailliage* as prescribed in the regulations.[8]

More often than not, therefore, villagers were called upon to express their grievances in the presence of one of their major adversaries, a situation which was fraught with difficulty. Usually those difficulties passed unrecorded, but occasionally communities submitted two *cahiers* which enable us to reconstruct the sequence of events. Such was the case at Pouillenay in the Auxois where the first *cahier* called for constitutional and fiscal reforms in fairly general terms, whereas a subsequent document, headed 'specific complaints', instanced a whole litany of seigneurial abuses. The suspicion arises that the first *cahier* was drafted in advance of the meeting and imposed upon the assembled peasantry by the local judge. There can be no doubt that this is what happened in the case of the parish of Frenelle-la-Grande (*bailliage* of Mirecourt), for the *cahier* was dated 8 March, that is to say a week before the electoral assembly convened. Then, on 26 March, twenty-five inhabitants signed a protest describing how they had been browbeaten during the meeting. The signatories were agricultural workers almost to a man, and their target seems to have been the rich *laboureurs* of the parish rather than the seigneur. How frequently such abuses crept into the process of consultation it is impossible to judge. Certainly, model *cahiers* circulated widely in some districts: in the Tonnerrois (Yonne), for instance. But the dissemination of preconceived *cahiers* does not necessarily imply that peasant grievances were watered down or deflected. After all, they usually made reference to specifically rural hopes and expectations, albeit in a fairly circumspect fashion. In any case there is ample evidence to show that peasants were prepared to amend the documents submitted to them when they imperfectly coincided with local needs, and this notwithstanding the baleful presence of the seigneurial judge.

The composition of the groups of delegates mandated to attend the *bailliage* assemblies also suggests that country dwellers were determined that their case should be heard. When, on 10 March, the bourgeois mayor of Flavigny (Côte-d'Or) convoked the inhabitants of the nearby hamlet of Villeberny, they duly endorsed the *cahier* which he produced and elected him their representative. Four days later they had second thoughts, drafted an amendment to 'their' *cahier* and entrusted it to two *laboureurs*. The bulk of delegates to the electoral colleges were, in fact, substantial peasant farmers. In some districts they seemed poised to dominate the proceedings effortlessly. Of the 996 spokesmen chosen by the parishes of the *bailliage* of Chaumont-en-Bassigny, 90 per cent, at least, were *laboureurs*.[9] Significantly, the next largest group consisted of agricultural wage labourers (3.6 per cent). The representatives of the towns were bourgeois to a man, but they found few allies in the countryside. Elsewhere, the urban bourgeoisie could usually count on a contingent of attorneys, notaries, barristers and rural proprietors 'living nobly', but in nearly every case that we have examined delegates drawn from the peasant strata of society predominated. Large numbers of *laboureurs*, winegrowers, village craftsmen and rural merchants attended the *bailliage* assembly of Château Thierry[10] and a similar situation prevailed in the *bailliage* of Mirecourt.[11] Of the sixty-eight (out of 108) delegates whose social status can be determined, 35 per cent were *laboureurs*; 14 per cent styled themselves 'merchants'; 13 per cent were lawyers; artisans accounted for 7 per cent, lesser peasant farmers 5 per cent, winegrowers 3 per cent and agricultural labourers 1 per cent. Analysis of the 252 delegates to the assembly of the *bailliage* of Semur-en-Auxois yields comparable results (liberal professions, i.e. bourgeois: 20 per cent; 'merchants': 29 per cent; independent peasant farmers: 25 per cent; winegrowers: 11 per cent; artisans: 9 per cent; agricultural labourers: 5 per cent; schoolmasters: 1 per cent).[12] The ubiquity of 'merchants' is apt to cause surprise, but it should be remembered that many of these individuals would have been substantial peasant farmers with trading interests.

All these examples are taken from the cereal plains of the Paris basin and Lorraine, of course. This was the natural habitat of the *coq de village* – the well-to-do peasant farmer. Few members of the bourgeoisie played an active part in village life and their mediating role was correspondingly slight. In the South, by contrast, the professional and proprietorial bourgeoisie were more firmly embedded in the fabric of rural society and we would expect to find them featuring more prominently in the electoral process. Soundings bear out this hypothesis to some degree. The delegates to the assembly of the secondary *bailliage* of Salers in the Auvergne were drawn overwhelmingly from the ranks of the rural bourgeoisie.[13] All but a handful of these spokesmen have been identified and an undifferentiated mass of legal practitioners formed the largest group (39 per cent). Then came their close relatives the notaries (22 per cent) and the barristers (13 per cent), followed by 'merchants' (13 per cent); rural proprietors 'living nobly' (10 per cent); a judge (1 per cent); a procurator (1 per cent) and a seigneur (1 per cent). It is possible that the small number of unidentified individuals were peasants and likely that the 'merchant' category contained several farmers who were part-time traders. Even so, four-fifths of the assembled delegates were drawn from the non-peasant elite of the Third Estate. On the other hand, Salers was scarcely typical of southern *bailliages*. It was small (thirty-five communities producing eighty delegates), remote and deeply impregnated with seigneurialism. These were the conditions that suited the rural bourgeoisie best.

In the event, though, it did not much matter how the *bailliage* assemblies were composed for the coteries of bourgeois patriots nearly always made the running. The first task confronting the assembled delegates of large *bailliages* was that of reducing their membership, for the electoral statute set an upper limit of 200 on the number participating in the selection of the deputies. No advice was offered as to how this slimming exercise might be conducted, but it frequently resulted in the exclusion of a sizeable proportion of the peasant delegates. A fresh weeding-out of rustics took place as commissions were appointed for the purpose of condensing the *cahiers*. Having borne their precious lists of grievances to the seat of the *bailliage*, many peasants were bitterly disillusioned by the abrupt and impatient reception accorded to them. At Chaumont-en-Bassigny town and country eyed each other suspiciously as the delegates wrestled with the task of reducing their numbers by 80 per cent. Almost inevitably, the towns emerged victorious and succeeded in packing the committees with an assortment of delegates drawn from the professional and proprietorial bourgeoisie. A last-minute attempt to redress the balance was made, but it came too late. The *grand bailli* reported that the peasant delegates had returned to their parishes 'muttering angrily'.[14]

By the spring of 1789 expectations were running so high in the countryside that it is difficult to conceive how the *bailliage* assemblies could possibly have satisfied the peasantry. Some parishes appear to have believed that by the mere fact of inscribing their grievances they had brought about a fundamental change in the order of things; others supposed that the incorporation of their demands in a general *cahier* conferred on them the force of law. Beneath the millenarianism lay anger, however: anger which the frustrating experience of the *bailliage* assemblies now brought into play. The extent of that frustration can be measured in the correspondence which showered upon Necker in the wake of the *bailliage* elections. Those historians who find the anti-seigneurial animus of the preliminary *cahiers* insufficiently proven would do well to consult this material. From all corners of the kingdom came allegations that rural opinion had been ignored or watered down. The *laboureurs* of the village of Valdampierre (Haute-Marne) wrote to complain that the general *cahier* of the *bailliage*

of Chaumont-en-Bassigny made no mention of the heavy *champart* that
burdened their parish. When their representatives had tried to raise the
issue, they had been fobbed off with the answer that it was a private
matter. This was the peremptory tone used against country members of the
bailliage assembly of Boulogne according to another source, whilst the
inhabitants of Bachivilliers (Oise) protested that their grievances against
seigneurial dues had been excluded from the general *cahier* of the *bailliage*
of Chaumont-en-Vexin. Seigneurial monopolies excited particular hostility, to judge from these petitions. Just a fortnight before the opening of
the Estates-General, the community of Castelnau-Peyralès (Aveyron) drew
up what amounted to a second *cahier* alleging that the assembly of the
sénéchaussée of Villefranche-de-Rouergue had refused to allow a complaint against milling rights to go forward. Monopolies, they were told,
were a form of property which could not be tampered with whoever might
own them. This was the line preached in the *bailliage* assembly of Péronne,
too. In a letter to Necker, the *sindic* of the village of Pressoir (Somme)
reiterated the popular demand for abolition of the seigneurial mill, adding
that the parish delegates had been overawed by the 'messieurs' of the town.

It would be wrong to suppose that the urban bourgeoisie rode rough-
shod over the peasantry, however. They, too, found the electoral
assemblies an unnerving experience. 'What is really tiresome', commented
Desmé de Dubuisson, lieutenant-general of the Saumur *bailliage*, 'is that
these assemblies that have been summoned have generally believed themselves invested with some sovereign authority and that when they came to
an end, the peasants went home with the idea that henceforward they were
free from tithes, hunting prohibitions and the payment of seigneurial
dues.'[15] Inexperience, ignorance and the draconian effect of the legislation
limiting the size of the deliberative body combined to reduce the proceedings to a shambles in several *bailliages*. A lawyer attending the sessions of
the *sénéchaussée* assembly held in Mende declared the election of deputies
to be invalid and blamed the irregularities on 'coarse' and 'superstitious'
country people.[16] He added that the delegates had been stirred up by
intriguers, and this was clearly a widespread problem. In many localities
groups of urban patriots canvassed rural voters, only to discover that the
assemblies degenerated into factional confrontations which soon spilled
into the streets. At Mâcon, incoming rural electors received slips urging
them to vote for André Merle, the popular mayor of the city.[17] Merle had
become the darling of the masses after providing the poor with relief work
during the bitter winter of 1788–9. On this occasion the patriots over-
played their hand, however, for the elections were interrupted by a riot
when a rumour circulated that the mayor was about to be dismissed.

One point to emerge strongly from the parish *cahiers*, the elections and the recriminations which they occasioned is that seigneurialism was under attack. It was under attack from below, but it was also under attack from above. Peasants criticised the general *cahiers* for failing to incorporate the grievances of each and every community, yet the fact remains that 50 per cent of the 666 or so general *cahiers* called for the abolition of seigneurial courts and 64 per cent demanded the abolition of seigneurial dues. By contrast, 85 per cent of noble *cahiers* were utterly silent on the issue of seigneurial dues.[18] We may speculate on how this conversion came about. The bourgeoisie are frequently, and correctly, portrayed by historians as co-beneficiaries of the feudal regime, although the extent to which they lived off the pickings of seigneurialism varied enormously from region to region. Were they swayed by enlightened argument? Were they bending to the wishes of peasant delegates? Both, almost certainly. The events of the winter and early spring of 1789 left the wealthy elite of the Third Estate feeling distinctly uneasy about seigneurial rights. Whilst the professional and proprietorial bourgeoisie of the *sénéchaussée* of Villefranche-de-Rouergue stolidly maintained that feudal rent was sacrosanct, the majority did not share this view. In the general *cahiers* they signalled their willingness to contemplate an orderly run-down of the seigneurial regime. But this attitude of reasonableness had well-defined limits. It applied to feudal rent, not all rent. Behind the negotiating posture lay a steely determination to defend 'correct', that is to say bourgeois, property rights. On this issue the popular alliance which launched the revolution would eventually come to grief, for the great mass of the peasantry understood the meaning of property in terms diametrically opposed to those employed by the bourgeoisie. The gulf is apparent in the parish *cahiers*, but it first became explicit during the elections. At Auxonne in Burgundy the delegates to the *bailliage* assembly voted to include in their *cahier* a condemnation of the Enclosure Edict of 1770, accompanied by a plea in favour of *vaine pâture*. An anonymous memorialist recorded that 'this proposition was passed on the advice of the country people and against the unanimous opposition of the inhabitants of the towns'.[19]

Rural revolt

Between December 1788 and March 1790 passions ran high in the countryside. Virtually every region of France was touched by insubordination, intimidation or collective violence to some degree. Nevertheless, the peasant mobilisations which took place during these months had a clear sense of direction and purpose and it is possible to identify eight principal theatres of revolt (see map 4). The flush of uprisings that occurred in the South East has already been mentioned. Sporadic guerrilla activity

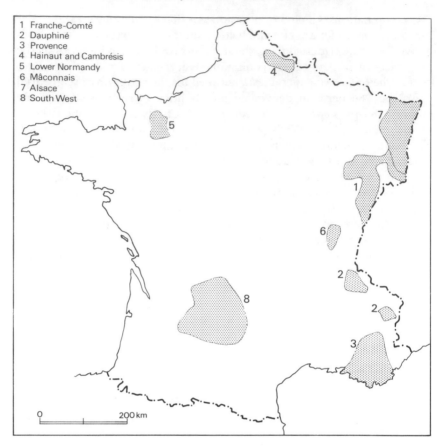

1 Franche-Comté
2 Dauphiné
3 Provence
4 Hainaut and Cambrésis
5 Lower Normandy
6 Mâconnais
7 Alsace
8 South West

0   200 km

Map 4. Epicentres of rural revolt, 1788–90
Sources: G. Lefebvre, *The Great Fear of 1789* (London, 1973); A. Ado, *The Peasant Movement in France during the Great Bourgeois Revolution at the End of the Eighteenth Century* (Moscow, 1971); J. Boutier, 'Jacqueries en pays croquant, 1789–90', *Annales E.S.C.*, 34 (1979), pp. 774–5

began in the Franche-Comté around the turn of the year; by February the Dauphiné was reported to be in a state of incipient insurrection, while rioting and expeditions against châteaux fanned out across Provence in March. Troops were moved into the region and damped down the Provençal risings in April. The Dauphiné insurrection appeared to run out of steam in May and June, only to be reactivated by the Great Fear spreading down from the North between 27 July and 9 August. As for the Franche-Comté, it exploded in a veritable paroxysm of anti-seigneurial violence between 19 and 31 July. A fourth epicentre of unrest lay to the North East in a wedge of territory stretching from St Quentin to the Brabant border and consisting mainly of the provinces of the Hainaut and the Cambrésis. Here the elections provoked bitter dissension and put the peasantry on an active footing. Bread rioting broke out in Cambrai on 6 and 7 May and swiftly spread throughout the district. With bands of insurgents trekking from monastery to monastery in search of grain, the movement soon acquired an agrarian and anti-seigneurial character. Troops poured into the Cambrésis and the peasantry fell back on the tactic of passive resistance, but the leasing of tithe collecting rights triggered a fresh outbreak of violence in July. This time, however, the disturbances were confined to the Hainaut and to Flanders.

The *bocage* district of Lower Normandy emerged as another, well-defined focus of rural revolt. Between 21 July and 3 August at least two dozen châteaux were visited by parties of armed peasants. Usually, they refrained from looting and concentrated their energy on seigneurial charters and title deeds. In this instance the impetus for the risings seems to have come from the towns of the region which were busily engaged upon their own Bastille-style revolutions. By contrast with the risings in the East, the Normandy revolt was a tame affair, however. In the Mâconnais – our sixth epicentre – an insurrection to rival that of the Franche-Comté took place between 26 and 31 July. The roots of the rebellion went deep and will be examined more closely in the pages which follow, but the immediate cause of the fermentation can be traced back to the elections of March. The campaign to secure the nomination of André Merle as deputy had cemented an alliance between the *menu peuple* of town and country. Consequently, when the townspeople of Mâcon started to hijack grain convoys on 20 July the peasantry proved only too willing to follow their example. As in the Cambrésis, their action quickly broadened into a generalised assault on the institutions of seigneurialism. Between twenty and thirty châteaux were invaded, not to mention numerous monastic foundations, presbyteries and a few bourgeois manors. Many of the châteaux were pillaged and several burned, notably that of the Talleyrand-Périgord family at Senozan.

During the last fortnight of July urban and rural revolt engulfed Alsace, too. The fermentation in the towns and cities dated back to the summer of 1787 when Calonne's local government reform (see pp. 27–9) challenged the position of noble and seigneurial oligarchies throughout the region. Faced with stiff resistance, the government backed down and restored much of the old municipal status quo, but the Paris revolution and the taking of the Bastille enabled the urban bourgeoisie to seize the initiative once more. Arthur Young, the English agricultural writer, arrived in

Strasbourg on 20 July and witnessed the beginnings of the insurrection. The populace, he noted in his diary, 'show signs of an intended revolt. They have broken the windows of some magistrates that are no favourites; and a great mob of them is at this moment assembled demanding clamorously to have meat at 5s. a pound.'[20] The countryside, meanwhile, had been in a state of incipient rebellion since the spring of 1789 and that summer the two streams of unrest converged. Even so, it is important to keep the alliance of townspeople and country dwellers in perspective, for it was not unconditional or automatic. In Alsace, particularly, the urban bourgeoisie were caught in the cross-fire between nobles and seigneurs on the one hand and a peasantry bent on effacing ancient servitudes on the other. Hardly had the municipal revolution begun in Strasbourg, than Dietrich, the leader of the patriots, learned that his own properties (he had bought a seigneurie in 1771) were under threat from insurgent peasants.[21] In Haute-Alsace, too, many Jewish merchants and moneylenders fell victim to the roaming bands.

More recent research has uncovered an eighth epicentre of agrarian revolt in the South West of France.[22] Between December 1789 and early March 1790 a little over a hundred châteaux were invaded by peasant bands drawn from at least 330 different parishes. As map 5 shows, these incursions took place along the western and south-western flanks of the Massif Central from the Limousin in the north to the Albigeois in the south. Nevertheless, the impetus for the uprisings derived from two main sources: the Vicomté of Turenne and the upland parishes around Figeac and Maurs. Both were districts in which seigneurial harvest dues bore heavily on peasant surplus, and both had a long history of peasant insurgency going back to the Croquandages of the seventeenth century. The timing of these revolts sets them apart from the mobilisations we have examined so far, however. While the Great Fear appears to have triggered a localised movement against châteaux in the neighbourhood of Cahors early in August, the bulk of parishes in the South West stayed relatively calm throughout the summer. The spur to action came later – in the autumn – as seigneurs, tithe proctors and assorted landlords turned up as usual to skim off a proportion of the far from abundant harvest. By now garbled accounts of the decree of 4–11 August apparently abolishing the feudal regime (see pp. 81–5) were circulating in the countryside and they stiffened peasant resolve to delay, if not to refuse outright, payments on the 1789 harvest. Roving emissaries stumped the parishes offering highly tendentious 'clarifications' of the new legislation. In more than one locality, the rural population were encouraged to believe that the king himself had endorsed a pre-emptive strike against the seigneurs.

Ill-advised recourse to law by impatient farmers of feudal rights seems to have triggered the conflagration which took the form of a series of parish or inter-parish raids on nearby châteaux, manors, monasteries and priories. In the Rouergue disturbances began in mid-December and climaxed in mid-February. A dozen châteaux were ransacked including that of Meljac, whose seigneur had been an accomplished practitioner of 'feudal reaction' (see p. 57). His furniture together with the entire contents of the château, were publicly auctioned by the insurgents. At Le Claux the rising was specifically aimed at a *feudiste* who was renovating the *terriers* of the local seigneur, while at Firmi the hostility of the insurgents who gathered in the courtyard of the château was focused on the *fermier* whom they accused of levying harvest dues with false weights and measures. As elsewhere, the monasteries were singled out for particular attention, either because they contained stockpiles of food, or because they were important seigneurial institutions in their own right. Thus, the monks of Bonnecombe who collected hefty *champarts* in most of the parishes of the *ségala* found themselves besieged and ransomed by successive bands of armed peasants. The frenzy gripping the Rouergue soon shifted southwards to engulf the Albigeois where a further fifteen châteaux were attacked, but, simultaneously, the revolt was fanning outwards from the Vicomté of Turenne, too. By February the Périgord was in arms, followed by the Agenais where the shock waves of insurrection encountered those coming from the west via the Rouergue and the Quercy. Then the conflagration died down as abruptly as it had started. The last recorded expeditions against the châteaux took place along the border between the Rouergue and the Albigeois early in March.

How, then, should we interpret these 'peasant wars' which marked the passing of the old regime? Their chronology, alone, is instructive for it underlines a point made many years ago by Georges Lefebvre in his pioneering analysis of the Great Fear. 'To get the peasant to rise and revolt', he wrote, 'there was no need of the Great Fear, as so many historians have suggested: when the panic came, he was already up and away.'[23] Rural panics, we now know, were far from rare occurrences in the conditions of eighteenth-century France. What *was* unusual was the socio-economic and political conjuncture of 1789 which made possible the amalgamation of at least five regionally distinct fears into one over-arching 'great' fear which travelled the length of the kingdom. Yet this Great Fear can be fairly precisely pinned down to the last fortnight in July and the first week of August. It cannot, therefore, be invoked as an all-purpose explanation of the rash of peasant uprisings which began in December 1788 and ended in March 1790. The agrarian disturbances in Provence, the Dauphiné, the Franche-Comté and the North East all broke out in the winter or spring. In the Dauphiné, it is true, there was a fresh

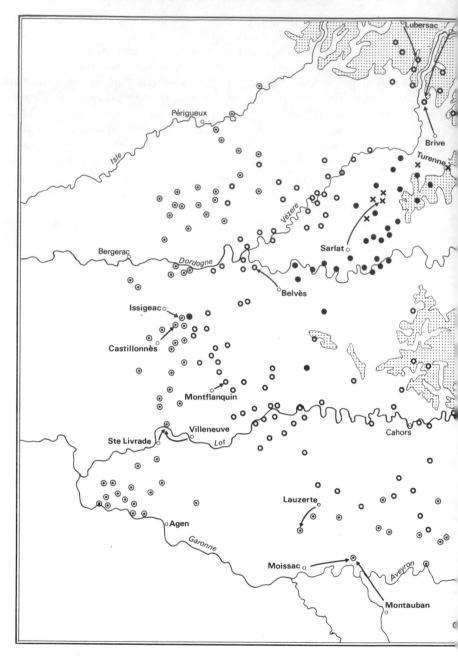

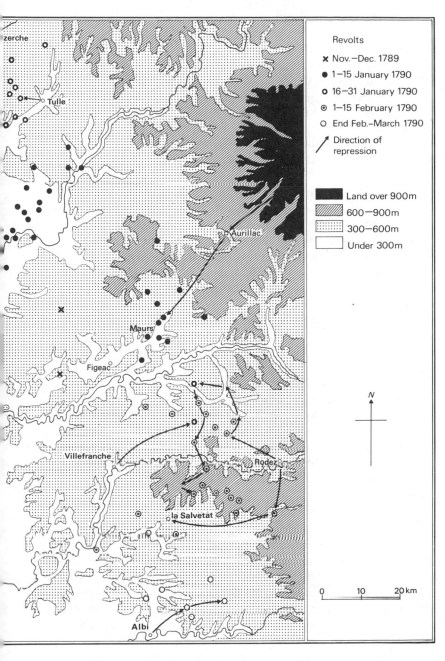

Map 5. The revolt of the South West, winter 1789–90
Source: J. Boutier, 'Jacqueries en pays croquant, 1789–90', Annales E.S.C., 34
(1979), pp. 774–5 (redrawn)

mobilisation in late July which was unleashed by a current of fear descending from the North, but the rekindling of violence in the Franche-Comté during the third week of July owed nothing to the Great Fear. On the contrary, it actually precipitated the fear which engulfed the Dauphiné a week or so later. As for Alsace and the Normand *bocage*, these regions rose in rebellion despite their isolation from the main axes of fear, while the causal link between the Great Fear and the Mâconnais insurrection is far from evident either. The South West, of course, lay astride three major currents of fear, but failed to ignite before the late autumn.

The conclusion that the spirit of revolt developed during the long and miserable winter of 1788–9 seems inescapable. Attacks on grain convoys, popular price fixing and generalised food rioting prepared the way for assaults on monastic storehouses, expeditions to the châteaux and the surreptitious restoration of collective rights over forest, fallow and common. The experience of drawing up the *cahiers* helped country dwellers to formulate their grievances, while the experience of the *bailliage* electoral assemblies taught them who their allies and their enemies were likely to be. As the year advanced the disturbances acquired an explicitly anti-feudal character: that is to say, they ceased to resemble mere food riots and took on a more organised and purposeful appearance. By the summer, hunger and desperation had ceased to be the dominant factors behind the peasant offensive. They had been replaced by an awareness that the entire social order was crumbling and by an opportunistic desire to strike while the iron was hot.

The precise circumstances which determined a posture of active defiance in some districts, passive resistance in others and continued acceptance of the dictates of seigneurialism elsewhere will never be known in detail. All we can do is to exploit the findings of case studies. In the Mâconnais, for example, it is clear that the revolt issued from a society caught in the throes of a severe agrarian crisis.[24] That crisis stemmed in large measure from the conversion to vine monoculture. By the end of the *ancien régime*, the Mâconnais resembled a vast vineyard tended by sharecroppers and day labourers whose livelihood was crucially dependent on the market for wine. Wild fluctuations in production levels and prices left many *vignerons* quite unable to meet their obligations. In 1778 the vintage failed completely, yet by the mid-1780s prices had collapsed in the face of massive over-production. Then the savage winter of 1788–9 not only wiped out the 1789 vintage, but much of the vinestock of the region, too. Poor peasants reliant on mixed farming and customary rights were faring little better, either. Most of the land belonged to absentee magnates or wealthy ecclesiastical foundations who were busily exploiting the freedom to enclose their properties enshrined in the edict of 1770. Tension mounted as peasant flocks were excluded from meadow and forest and non-resident proprietors (*forains*) introduced commercial fatstock in their place. Exasperated villagers broke down hedges and filled ditches in the time-honoured fashion, while the intendant in Dijon anxiously pondered the social implications of the rush to enclose. These fears were expressed again in the *cahier* of the Third Estate of the *bailliage* of Mâcon which called for the reinstatement of free grazing in meadows after the first haying, but the time for palliatives was past. The revolt began among the poor wine-growers of the village of Igé who had long been at loggerheads with their seigneur. The immediate subject of dispute was a spring situated in the grounds of the château to which the seigneur refused common access.

In the days that followed the revolt spread fast with the agrarian imperative never far beneath the surface. At Verzé a contingent of Igé insurgents persuaded the local population to join in by recalling to mind seigneurial usurpation of the commons; at Senozan the steward of the Talleyrand-Périgord family was likewise held to account for usurpation of the commons; at Cluny the monks tried to forestall action against their properties by conceding grazing rights in their meadows and scavenging in their forests; restrictions on access to meadows also served to focus popular anger at Lugny. These examples are all drawn from the Mâconnais, but the determination to use collective violence in order to overturn two decades of physiocrat-inspired reforms was not unique to this region. In all the epicentres of revolt, demands for an end to feudal dues were sandwiched together with demands for the restitution of common land and the resumption of *vaine pâture* in field and meadow. Acknowledging this two-pronged assault, Lefebvre was moved to make a famous judgement on the popular intervention of 1789. The stance of the peasantry during that crucial year was, he argued, both conservative and revolutionary: 'they destroyed the feudal regime, but consolidated the agrarian structure of France'.[25]

That the peasantry entered the revolutionary fray as a homogeneous social force was, for Lefebvre, axiomatic. For about a year and a half the common struggle against the seigneur and the tithe owner bound country dwellers together. Subsequently, issues came to the surface which tended to undermine the unity of the rural community (attribution of the tithe, the Civil Constitution of the Clergy, the sale of *biens nationaux*, the partition of common land etc.), but for a while, at least, the differing objectives of the various strata of the peasantry were not clearly delineated. This is a view which has much to recommend it. However, Lefebvre's arguments were refined over fifty years ago when the writing of the social and economic history of the revolution was just beginning, and they need to be reappraised. Can we be sure that the anti-feudal animus permeated all sections of the peasantry evenly? After all, landless agricultural labourers had much less to gain from an eventual abolition of harvest dues than their landed neighbours. And what about the upper echelons of the peasantry – the *laboureurs*, *ménagers* and *gros fermiers* – for whom the feudal regime could provide rich pickings?

One point seems well established. The impetus for the insurrections came from within the rural community. Contemporaries liked to depict the risings as the work of 'brigands' acting upon the peasantry from the outside, but there is little evidence to sustain this interpretation. Itinerants, vagabonds and other 'marginals' played an insignificant role. Even in the Mâconnais, which was a major crossroads, only five of the seventy-four insurgents captured by the Tournus militia hailed from outside the district. Whether we focus on the mobilisations in the East or those in the South West, the insurgents turn out to have been local villagers acting, for the most part, against local targets. They also appear to have been drawn from virtually every stratum of rural society, as Lefebvre suggested. When the Mâcon militia surprised a group of peasants preparing to attack the château of St Léger, it took eighteen prisoners, all of whom were either day labourers, farm servants, weavers or winegrowers. At nearby St Point the insurrectionaries consisted entirely of winegrowers and small cereal farmers (*grangers*) together with their wives and servants, while at St Laurent-lès-Mâcon, a port on the Bresse side of the river, a local innkeeper and a cloth merchant led a group of sailors and wharvesmen in an attack on the public weigh scales. In general, it seems that agricultural workers, *vignerons* and poor plot farmers who had been adversely affected by the curtailment of collective rights provided the rank and file of the insurrection in the Mâconnais. But the records of the investigating magistrates provide plentiful evidence of elite participation, too. A tenant farmer led the fire-raisers of the château of Senozan; a distiller of alcohol the initial insurrection against the Baron of Igé. Among those subsequently imprisoned or hanged, we also find sundry *laboureurs*, millers, craftsmen, a *greffier* and a salt and tobacco retailer who stirred up the peasantry by claiming that he had received an order from the National Assembly cancelling the payment of seigneurial dues and the tithe.

A close analysis of the social anatomy of the mobilisations in the South West by Jean Boutier yields broadly comparable results.[26] In this region of 'petite culture' rural artisans rather than landless labourers formed the single largest group among the insurgents to judge from the rather small number of individuals who were subsequently arrested (see table 2). Well-to-do peasant farmers also gave the movement substantial support, although they contrived to avoid the responsibility for leading the bands. That role tended to devolve on 'broker' groups: a miller at St Mayme-de-

Table 2. *The social bases of insurgency in the South West*

Occupation	Bas Limousin	%	Périgord	%	Haut Agenais	%
laboureurs	14	29	11	24	1	4
sharecroppers			4	8	3	11
day labourers	15	30	6	12	3	11
winegrowers	4	8	4	8	1	4
artisans	15	30	14	29	9	32
servants					3	11
sergents			2	4		
praticiens	1	2				
maîtres-chirurgiens			1	2		
unidentified			6	12	8	28
total	49		48		28	

Source: J. Boutier, 'Jacqueries en pays croquant', p. 771

Péreyol (Dordogne), a carpenter at Montignac (Dordogne) and a tavern keeper at Cendrieux (Dordogne). It is surprising that more sharecroppers are not listed among the victims of the repression: the village worthies of Cendrieux certainly considered sharecroppers to have participated in the revolts and the sharecroppers of the South West had long been campaigning for a reduction in the tithe (see pp. 50–1). Perhaps, as Boutier suggests, allowance should be made for the possibility that many *laboureurs* were, in fact, share-crop tenants.

In some instances it is clearly more helpful to conceive of the mobilisations as the revolts of entire communities. Often, the dividing line between peasants who set out for the local château and peasants who stayed at home appears to have followed the contours of habitat rather than those of social structure. Some villages (or parishes) mobilised *en masse*, others adopted a wait-and-see policy. Moreover, there is some evidence to suggest that the participants expected it to be thus: at Lugny and Vergisson in the Mâconnais the insurgents whipped in recalcitrants by threatening to burn down their houses. The norms of peasant revolt seemed to demand a communitarian response, and the calendared rituals of popular culture provided a ready-made framework for collective action. According to a contemporary account of the Mâconnais uprisings, 'the fête of the village of Crèches on 26 July spawned the terrible disturbances' which took place in neighbouring parishes in the days that followed.[27] It may not be coincidence, either, that attacks on châteaux in the Rouergue and the Albigeois peaked in February–March 1790 just as the Shrovetide festivities were reaching a climax. In the South, particularly, the youth group was the pivot on which much of village culture turned and Jean Boutier reminds us that the insurrections may also be viewed as an expression of the 'specific sociability of youth'.[28] He points out that the uprisings in the South West principally galvanised the menfolk of the villages, and the young men at that. Two-thirds of the insurgents were aged between fifteen and thirty-four if those imprisoned can be regarded as typical. Young men in their late twenties who were probably unmarried formed the largest contingent. No women were arrested, on the other hand, which raises the question of whether there were types of disorder specific to men — whatever their age — and types of disorder specific to women. Grain riots, for instance, have long been associated with women, as have religious disorders, and the events of the revolution served greatly to strengthen that identification.

The communitarian dimension of the revolts can also be pictured as a conflict between town and country. After all, the mobilisations were overwhelmingly rural in character and were often directed against the *bourgs*, if not the towns, in which seigneurs had taken refuge, in which tax and notarial records were kept, and from which a plethora of busybodying officials mounted their operations. During the winter of 1789–90 the *bourg* of Sauveterre (Rouergue) was subjected to repeated attacks by the peasantry of the *ségala* and the bourgeoisie spent over 4,000 *livres* on patrols and repairs to the walls. Events followed a similar pattern in the Périgord and the Agenais, where the conflagration was ignited by the march of fifteen parishes against the small town of Sarlat on 15 January 1790. Towns were regarded as symbols of authority, as symbols of royal and seigneurial oppression. However, this fact should not blind us to the evidence of threads of complicity between town and country. These threads existed at two main levels: ever since the *bailliage* elections of the spring urban patriots had more or less consciously stirred the pot of peasant discontent. In the case of the risings in Alsace and Lower Normandy the signal actually came from the towns. Meanwhile, and often independently, a feeling of solidarity developed between the common people of town and country. At Maurs, one of the epicentres of insurrection in the South West, the burghers complained that the town's artisan and wage-earning population was sympathetic to the peasantry 'on the pretext that the cause of the insurgents was their own'.[29] Even so, we would do well not to generalise this mutual sympathy. It evaporated as soon as urban militias were formed to put down the disorders.

By and large, recent research confirms Georges Lefebvre's contention that the struggle against feudalism mobilised the peasantry *en masse*.[30] The wealthy elite of *laboureurs* and *coqs de village* had everything to gain from collective action against harvest dues and the tithe, or so they believed, but the irritants of seigneurial lordship extended beyond questions of the *champart* and the *dîme*. Poor plot farmers, sharecroppers and landless or virtually landless day labourers lived in the economic shadow of seigneurialism like everybody else. They, too, were subject to *mainmorte*, to *lods et ventes*, to seigneurial *corvées* and fines, to onerous monopolies and to the vagaries of seigneurial justice. Yet we would not wish to confine the definition of the struggle to the issue of seigneurialism. The uprisings of 1788–90 momentarily challenged all forms of property, not merely that of the privileged orders, and they were popular for that reason. Jean Boutier has aptly described them as an egalitarian tornado which left in its wake a peasantry sensitive to every conceivable manifestation of social distance. Châteaux were ransacked and seigneurial rent rolls scattered to the four winds, but weathercocks were snatched from roof-tops and private pews dragged from churches as well. As an inhabitant of Allassac in the Bas Limousin put it, 'we don't need bourgeois or gentlemen any more'.[31]

This random, but revealing, remark raises a doubt concerning Lefebvre's notion of a united front against seigneurialism, however, for he repeatedly refers to the prosperous upper echelons of the peasantry as 'bourgeois'. One of the functions of his rather miscellaneously defined 'rural bourgeoisie' (see pp. 13–14) was to collect harvest dues on behalf of landlords and seigneurs who were either unable or unwilling to do the job themselves. Where, then, do we situate the upper echelons of the peasantry – ideologically and tactically speaking – during the crisis of 1788–90? In the Bas Limousin and the Périgord *laboureurs* identified strongly with the movement of resistance to feudalism, but harvest dues were both onerous and extensive in these regions. Elsewhere, the balance of advantage accruing from the maintenance or the destruction of seigneurialism was probably less clear-cut. Around Paris *laboureurs* and *gros fermiers* could easily market grain stocks and the job of *fermier des droits féodaux* provided rich pickings. Similarly, in Picardy and the Cambrésis, where ecclesiastical institutions owned vast estates, a proportion of peasant proprietors grew fat on the profits of tithe farming.

Perhaps the best way of deciding where to draw the line of socio-economic demarcation in 1788–90 is to take a look at the victims of the revolts. This has to be done impressionistically, for systematic analysis such as that undertaken by Boutier for the South West (see table 3) is rare. Nevertheless, two points can be made with reasonable certainty: few peasant land holders fell victim to the violence, but bourgeois proprietors occupied a highly ambiguous position. As regards peasant victims, Boutier lists just three out of a total of 119 which confirms that, in the South West at least, the well-to-do peasantry were in no doubt as to where their

Table 3. *The victims of insurgency in the South West*

Occupation	Bas Limousin		Périgord		Haut Agenais		Total	
		%		%		%		%
seigneurs	6	27	12	16	9	38	27	23
seigneurial officials	2	9	6	8	0	0	8	7
notaries	3	14	1	1	0	0	4	3
attorneys	0	0	1	1	0	0	1	1
bourgeois proprietors	2	9	22	30	5	21	29	24
merchants	3	14	6	8	1	4	10	8
royal officials	1	5	2	3	0	0	3	3
curés	3	14	9	12	6	25	18	15
doctors	0	0	0	0	1	4	1	1
laboureurs	0	0	2	3	1	4	3	3
unidentified	2	9	12	16	1	4	15	13
total	22		73		24		119	

Source: J. Boutier, 'Jacqueries en pays croquant', p. 769

interests lay. Interestingly, one of the peasant victims was a *laboureur* who owned a pew in the parish church. The rural bourgeoisie properly so-called (non-noble proprietors and professionals), by contrast, can be found in both camps. While they were rarely caught red-handed, piecemeal evidence suggests that they aided and abetted the insurrectionaries in some districts. A village notary in the Mâconnais allegedly displayed a printing plate engraved with the words: 'By order of the king: all châteaux should be burned and demolished.'[32] More telling, perhaps, was a letter despatched to the Feudal Committee from the Vendôme region early in 1790. It complained that rural proprietors had done little to damp down the recent agrarian insurrection, anxious as they were to escape the burden of seigneurial dues. Even petty seigneurs made little resistance, the letter continued, on the ground that they gained more than they lost in the conflagration.

On the other hand, non-peasant and yet non-noble proprietors were a clear target of the insurgents in some areas. Often such individuals had compromising links with the seigneurial regime. Some were bourgeois seigneurs on the way to ennoblement, some were specialists in feudal law and the drawing-up of *terriers*, others leased seigneurial privileges. Yet a number had no discernible link with seigneurialism, which serves to underline the multifaceted character of the revolts. They were, or rather they became by the summer of 1789, revolts against all forms of authority. Anti-feudalism contained within it a challenge to bourgeois property rights and as Georges Lefebvre correctly perceived, that challenge was first articulated around the issue of agrarian individualism. In the Mâconnais the anti-bourgeois animus remained implicit; few bourgeois manors and estates were pillaged. Here the offensive against common rights was linked in the popular mind with improving seigneurs and avaricious ecclesiastical foundations. In the South West, however, the rural bourgeoisie were a more conspicuous social force. They attracted attention as zealous acolytes of the seigneurial regime, but they also attracted attention as a class of *rentiers* creaming off peasant surplus on their own account. The figures provided by Boutier in table 3 confirm that the primary object of peasant hostility was the feudal system, such as it existed at the end of the *ancien régime* (seigneurs and seigneurial officials = 30 per cent of victims). Nevertheless, bourgeois proprietors made up nearly a quarter of all the victims, which comes as something of a surprise. We cannot, of course, be sure how many of these individuals were associated with the seigneurial regime, but Boutier is surely correct in discerning a concerted attack on 'the world of rent in all its rural manifestations, seigneurial, ecclesiastical, landed'.[33] Bourgeois rent, in the South West, was virtually synonymous with sharecropping, yet the status of *métayers* seems to have deteriorated markedly in the second half of the eighteenth century. In all probability, this is the social reality behind the massive assault on the rural bourgeoisie in the Périgord, while the burden of the tithe, in Gascony particularly, pro- vided ample reason for the animus against the clergy.

The August legislation

Between 4 and 11 August 1789 the deputies of the National Assembly agreed a package of reforms which purported to destroy the seigneurial regime in France. As the months went by and the real intentions of the deputies became clearer, the peasantry came to regard these reforms as a monstrous fraud. In March 1790 they learned that harvest dues had not been abolished outright after all, in April they discovered that the tithe would remain in force until 1791, and in May it finally dawned on the rural population that all the Assembly was offering was a chance to buy out dues. Non-redeemed dues were to continue in existence for the fore- seeable future. Indeed, their legitimacy as a form of property was enhanced. Finally, any lingering illusions on the subject of the tithe were shattered in December 1790 when a decree ordered tenant farmers to pay to their landowners the amount they would otherwise have disbursed for the upkeep of the church. If 1789 was a year of mingled hope and fear,

1790 turned out to be a year of crushing disappointment. A process of alienation began which would precipitate some peasants into the arms of counter-revolution, while prompting others to renew the struggle against seigneurialism, a struggle which would eventually give birth to agrarian forms of jacobinism.

The dramatic events of the night of 4 August need not detain us. More important were the sober resolutions which followed on 6, 7, 8 and 11 August. Two days later they were presented *en bloc* to the king and have been known ever since as 'the decree of 4, 6, 7, 8 and 11 August 1789'. The first article of this famous decree is worth quoting in full for it was to cause endless confusion:

The National Assembly destroys in its entirety the feudal regime and decrees that, as regards rights and duties both feudal and *censuel*,[34] those relating to *mainmorte réelle ou personnelle*,[35] those relating to personal serfdom and those which symbolise these conditions, are abolished without compensation. All the others are declared to be redeemable and the rate and method of redemption will be determined by the National Assembly. Those of the aforementioned rights which are not abolished by this decree will continue to be collected until such time as they are redeemed.[36]

There followed a lengthy catalogue of seigneurial perquisites and sundry privileges which were henceforth abolished: exclusive hunting rights (art. 3); seigneurial courts (art. 4); the tithe (art. 5); tax exemptions (art. 9); civil distinctions (art. 11); venal offices (art. 7); perpetual rents and harvest dues (art. 6); ecclesiastical pluralism (art. 14); surplice fees (art. 8); and so on. All these reforms were statements of intent and almost all of them required further legislation before they could become effective. Thus, the clause relating to seigneurial courts stipulated that existing judicial personnel should remain at their posts until replaced; the clause relating to the tithe emphasised that it should continue to be paid until further notice, and the article dealing with harvest and ground rents specifically mentioned the proviso of indemnification. But all this was so much fine print as far as the peasantry were concerned. They fastened on the opening statement of the decree: 'The National Assembly destroys in its entirety the feudal regime', and looked no further. Their dismay on learning that matters were not as they seemed is easy to understand, for the preamble to the decree *was* a model of ambiguity, if not downright contradictory. Those mocking words 'destroys in its entirety the feudal regime' resounded in the ears of the deputies during the months that followed. Merlin de Douai, the eminent jurist on whom the task of converting the decree of 4–11 August into practical politics devolved, even went so far as to describe article one as an 'embarrassing text'.[37]

News that great measures were being enacted at Versailles reached some country areas almost immediately. Notwithstanding the preliminary character of the decisions made on the night of 4 August, deputies hastened to pass on what they could recollect to their constituents. Already on 5 August, printed versions were circulating in Paris and they were promptly relayed to the provincial press. In Grenoble the *Affiches de Dauphiné* published a Paris-inspired report on 10 August and the *Courrier d'Avignon* did likewise on 12 August. On the same day Arthur Young recorded the arrival in Clermont of the news of 'the utter abolition of tythes, feudal rights, game warrens, pidgeons etc.', noting that it was joyously received by the mass of the people.[38] Naturally, these early accounts bore only a passing resemblance to the definitive statute which was not completely drafted until the 11th. Even then, it left much unsaid and allowed room for conjecture on a whole range of issues. For example, no mention was made of the irksome right of *banalité* which constrained the pesantry to use seigneurial mills, bread ovens, wine and oil presses. Yet on 8 August, a country priest in Brittany blithely informed his parishioners that *banalités* had been abolished. The Feudal Committee of the Assembly only resolved to abolish this right (without compensation) in March 1790. By then, however, peasants in many parts of the country had stopped frequenting seigneurial mills and ovens, and had begun to build facilities of their own.

Confusion – or wilful misunderstanding – seems to have been greatest in the East and South East where a whole series of insurrections broke out in the course of the summer. Right from the start the peasantry of Alsace set off on the wrong track when one of the deputies of the province despatched an inaccurate account of the reforms which was then printed and posted up throughout the region. In Lorraine the Commission Intermédiaire of the Provincial Assembly circulated to all parish priests an explanation of the decree which stated: 'In the first place, *the National Assembly destroys in its entirety the feudal regime*, but it does not abolish all the rights that derive from [that regime]; it has only declared them to be redeemable.' Since the province contained practically no serfs, that part of the decree relating to rights and duties abolished without compensation was 'barely applicable'.[39] Not so in the Franche-Comté where 400,000 country dwellers, amounting to approximately half the population, were subject to various forms of *mainmorte*, but here, too, confusion reigned: some villages interpreted the phrase 'those relating to *mainmorte réelle ou personnelle*' in one way, some another. Many argued that the dues which they owed were, in fact, symbolic of an earlier servile status.

All in all, it seems unlikely that the 'generous sacrifices' of 4 August did much to pacify the countryside in the short term. On the contrary, dissatisfaction with the legislation actually nurtured the spirit of rebellion in the South West. That dissatisfaction stemmed in part from doubts over the legality of what had been transacted. There was a feeling that the victory over the privileged orders was inconclusive and might yet prove short-lived. After all, the official promulgation of the decree waited upon the royal assent which was not forthcoming until 3 November 1789. It is true that the Assembly took steps to disseminate its measures throughout the kingdom on 13 August, but publication of an unsanctioned decree did not make it legally enforceable. When the deputies solicited the royal imprimatur for their handiwork in mid-September, the king replied evasively and made no secret of the fact that he found the proposed abolition of seigneurialism distasteful. This policy of obstructionism helped to build up the tensions which culminated in the celebrated March to Versailles. But the October Days broke the deadlock: on 20 October the Assembly ordered that the decree be officially entered on the registers of all judicial and administrative bodies and letters patent were issued two weeks later.

After three months of stonewalling by the monarch and his advisers the legislation of 4–11 August became law. It comes as no surprise, therefore, to discover that vested interests in the country at large were slow to fall into line. Once the immediate danger of agrarian insurrection had receded, seigneurs moved to retrieve what they could from the wreckage. A long period of manoeuvring began in which each side probed the defences of the other. The Breton rector who had presumed to announce the abolition of the right of *banalité* found himself caught in the cross-fire as peasants were assailed with writs for infringing seigneurial corn-grinding prerogatives. In the Franche-Comté the resistance of seigneurs was stiffened by the Parlement of Besançon which remained malevolently hostile to the work of the National Assembly. It delayed publication of the letters patent sanctioning the decree of 4–11 August until the end of November and used its waning judicial power to defend the seigneurs and slap down the pretensions of the peasantry. The issue which fixed everyone's attention was that of the dues liable on the 1789 harvest. Normally they were paid at Martinmas (11 November), more rarely on the Feast of St Remy (28 October), but most villages in the region resolved upon a policy of initial refusal followed by wait-and-see.

That autumn farmers of seigneurial rights and tithe proctors did their best to collect harvest dues as in years past. Resistance was not restricted to the Franche-Comté; in fact it was widespread across the kingdom. More often than not, however, it appears to have been centred in regions which had experienced serious peasant disturbances during the summer (the Franche-Comté, Dauphiné, Lower Normandy). To these may be added the

Périgord and the Agenais in the South West which succumbed to agrarian violence in the winter of 1789–90 and the Orléanais–Gâtinais region which emerged as a flashpoint of resistance to dues in the summer of 1791 (see pp. 117–20). Indicative of this first phase of resistance was a petition sent to the Feudal Committee of the National Assembly by Christophe Duy, village *sindic* and *laboureur* of the parish of Iville in Normandy. He complained that he was being harassed for the sum of one hundred *livres*, being the value of dues outstanding on the 1789 harvest. In a very rustic hand he justified his refusal to pay by citing article 6 of the decree of 4–11 August 'in which you order the abolition and clearing away of all rents [*sic*]'.[40] Such was the popular apprehension of the Assembly's measures, at least in the short term. A study of the seigneurie of Beaupuis in the Saintonge records that 152 vassals paid their dues as usual in 1788, but three-quarters of them refused to do so the following year.[41] Not a typical case, perhaps, but the Saintonge passed for one of the more peaceful provinces in 1789.

Nevertheless, this reflex resistance can be deceptive. If the peasantry collectively repudiated feudal obligations and the tithe in the autumn of 1789, it is far from certain that these dues were never subsequently paid. Direct, comprehensive and unflinching opposition cut against the grain of popular habit which tended to prefer arbitration to outright conflict. Between continued payment and formal renunciation were many intermediate positions which the peasantry quickly learned to exploit. On 15 November 1789 a number of vassals of the barony of Cazillac in the Quercy resolved to continue paying seigneurial dues, but on their own terms.[42] Instead of a harvest rent which was *portable* (i.e. had to be carried to the lord's granary), they offered a money rent fixed at a lower level. Transactions of this type became increasingly common in the early months of 1790. They represented a partial and grudging recognition that the feudal regime had not been destroyed 'in its entirety' after all.

Chapter 4

Dismantling the seigneurial regime

France's second year of revolution began auspiciously. The move of the National Assembly from Versailles to Paris eased tensions in the capital, while an abundant harvest brought relief from food shortages in most parts of the kingdom. Not for nothing have historians dubbed 1790 the 'année heureuse'. Yet there was a sombre side to this picture which should not be overlooked. While the deputies busily planned for the future, country dwellers found themselves re-fighting the battles of the past. Obstinately, feudalism refused to lie down and die. On the contrary, it arose from the ashes of 4 August like a phoenix, rejuvenated and with a fresh lease on life. The struggle resumed, therefore, amid cries of betrayal and backsliding as the Assembly prepared to whittle down its concessions of the previous year. Resurgent feudalism likewise served to prolong that unity of purpose which had been forged in 1789. Until the summer of 1792 all peasants could agree that the main task was to win back the concessions glimpsed on 4 August. By comparison, other issues seemed blurred. To be sure, the alliance lacked the breadth of that which had encompassed the demise of absolute monarchy. For one thing the rural bourgeoisie had defected to the party of order and now postured as vehement upholders of the decrees of the National Assembly. And in any case the alliance was not without stresses and strains. Landowning peasants stood to gain more from the abolition of the tithe and the eventual abolition of harvest dues than did tenant farmers and sharecroppers, unless, of course, these latter could broaden the struggle to embrace all forms of rent. Nevertheless, such divisions would rest implicit until 1793. The struggle remained essentially one pitting peasant against seigneur, or rather ex-seigneur, within a framework of law laid down by the National Assembly. The only relevant questions were how long that framework of law would last and how far the peasantry would be prepared to go in order to subvert it.

The feudal complex

Eighteenth-century lawyers described the prerogatives, perquisites and privileges attaching to lordship as the 'feudal complex'. In practice, they included the tithe under this heading even though it was very different in origin. The tithe, after all, was a harvest due which ecclesiastical seigneurs levied jointly with the *champart*, so much so that the two dues often became confused. Unpicking the 'feudal complex' was bound to be an arduous business, therefore, but it was made more so by the ill-considered promises enshrined in the August legislation. The first body on whom this unenviable task devolved was the Feudal Committee of the National Assembly. Established on the morrow of the August 'sacrifices', it set to work in earnest the following October and tabled a series of major legislative proposals over the next twelve months or so. The Committee was dominated by eminent feudal lawyers such as Merlin de Douai, François-Denis Tronchet and Goupil de Préfelne and these men were primarily responsible for the curious compromise with the seigneurial regime which became the hallmark of the National Assembly. The advent of a new legislature raised hopes in the countryside, but provoked no immediate change of tack. On 27 October 1791 the Legislative Assembly appointed another Feudal Committee whch proceeded to shore up the policy of its predecessor. Only in the spring of 1792 did the edifice built by the National Assembly start to crumble. The nation was preparing for war and a few deputies were beginning to question the political wisdom of a settlement which deterred country dwellers from identifying wholeheartedly with the revolution. Between March 1792 when the membership of the Committee was renewed and the end of August, the whole edifice collapsed. Significantly, the National Convention dispensed with the need for a separate Feudal Committee. Instead, business relating to the seigneurial regime was handled by the Legislation Committee. Its approach was altogether more pragmatic: support for the revolution could not be assumed; it had to be won with socially oriented legislation. But, at the same time, the victory over seigneurialism should be defined carefully in order to deter a generalised assault on property.

The dismantling of the seigneurial regime required the combined energy of three legislatures and the promulgation of well over a hundred decrees, amendments to decrees and commentaries on decrees. The science of legal drafting, it should be said, was in its infancy. The National Assembly alone produced ninety-six items of legislation on this subject. Nevertheless, the major shifts in public policy are captured in just eight measures if we reserve for separate consideration the legislation relating to the tithe. The decree of 4–11 August 1789 set the tone and became the basic reference point for jurisprudence throughout 1790 and 1791. This is not to suggest that it was adhered to in every particular, though. The Feudal Committee quickly encountered the ambiguities in that notorious first article of the decree. Operating as it was in the calmer social atmosphere of the autumn, the Committee also came to the conclusion that the spirit of the law was excessively generous towards the peasantry.

Hence the embarrassment to which Merlin de Douai alluded when introducing the Committee's detailed proposals for the implementation of the decisions taken in August. The debates began in February and issued in the passing of a comprehensive law on 15 March which was sanctioned by the monarch on 28 March 1790. Any lingering illusions that the Assembly had administered the *coup de grâce* to seigneurialism were immediately dispelled. The Committee invented a myth of the origins of seigneurial overlordship which enabled it to draw a distinction between two broad categories of rights: personal rights 'obliging persons directly, legitimate in the troubled times of the middle ages when the seigneur provided security and work for his vassals, useless and unjust ever since the lordship became nothing but an inert and injurious organism', and real rights 'obliging persons only through the intermediary of the land, due from the soil itself for the concession of which they had been established, usually overlaid with a seigneurial form, but, in reality, charges on the land'.[1] The former were objectionable in an age of liberty and consequently abolished outright, but the latter represented the price paid in return for the concession of a piece of land. No matter that the landlord happened to be a seigneur, or that the 'tenant' had once been a serf; no matter that the original deed of concession could not be produced, real rights were a legitimate investment enjoying the protection of the Declaration of the Rights of Man. As such they could only be extinguished 'on condition of a previous just indemnity'.[2] In the absence of redemption they would continue in force.

Even on paper this doctrine looked suspect; as a basis for policy it seriously underestimated the complexities of the seigneurial regime. To start with, the Assembly had already pre-empted the issue in its legislation of 4–11 August. The right of *mainmorte*, for instance, could be either 'real' or 'personal' or a mixture of the two, and yet it had been abolished outright six months earlier. This was a difficulty which stretched the casuists in the Committee to the full, but most items in the shopping basket of abolished rights (seigneurial *tailles*, *corvées*, the rights of watch and ward, *franc fief*, *triage*, *banalité*, *banvin*, etc.) posed no more than technical problems. Even so, the Assembly encouraged its Committee to reduce the scope of the concessions wherever feasible. Thus the monopolistic status of seigneurial mills and bread ovens was preserved if it could be shown to derive from a contract beneficial to both parties. All in all some sixty named rights were abolished on the pretext of a servile origin, and forty more items were added to the list the following year. Several of the concessions represented material gains and it would be wrong to condemn the decree just because the peasantry found it insufficiently far-reaching. Philippe Sagnac comments that the Assembly 'only suppresses rights which have almost everywhere disappeared',[3] but he underestimates the extent to which vassals still performed labour service in the East, still paid *taille* to their lords in the South West, and the prevalence of mill and bakehouse monopolies throughout the countryside. It is none the less true, however, that the Assembly excluded the principal lucrative dues owed to seigneurs from outright abolition. Monetary dues (*cens*) and harvest dues (*champart, terrage, tierce, tasque, agrier*, etc.) were deemed to represent the price of an original concession of land and could only be extinguished by payment of their capital value. More controversially in view of the stated principles of the legislation, casual rights received the ultimate accolade of revolutionary law, too. The imposition known as *lods et ventes* was paid by vassals when they sold land as a timely reminder of the servile origins of peasant tenures, yet it had to be redeemed alongside monetary and harvest dues. And to add confusion upon confusion, the Assembly abolished outright the quasi-servile form of land holding called *bordelage* in the Nivernais and Bourbonnais, despite the fact that *lods et ventes* constituted its most lucrative component.

All was not lost, however. The final clause of the decree referred, somewhat lamely, to the need to devise a 'method and rate for the redemption of those rights which had been maintained'.[4] Despite the unease, optimists among the peasantry continued to assume that the delay was only short-term. Surely, the surviving dues would be liquidated before the onset of the harvest. The debate began on 23 April when Tronchet submitted the first five clauses of a draft law for parliamentary approval. It continued for four days and resulted in the decree of 3 May (sanctioned 9 May 1790). What the Committee proposed and the Assembly accepted was a plan for the slow and orderly running-down of the seigneurial regime. Individuals were given the right to buy out the dues burdening their properties, but they had to find the money themselves. No state aid was offered and arrears had to be acquitted first. Partial redemption, that is to say the liquidation of some dues, but not others, was expressly forbidden and dues subscribed collectively by vassals had likewise to be paid off collectively. As for the price of redemption, it was fixed at twenty times the yearly amount of cash dues and twenty-five times the annual value of dues payable in kind. In the case of casual dues the arithmetic was more complicated: the Assembly tried to take account of the variable nature of dues such as *lods et ventes* with a sliding scale of redemption fees.

Was the decree 'a practical nullity'[5] as Sydney Herbert has argued? Yes, in the sense that few country dwellers could afford emancipation offered on these terms. But it is helpful to bear in mind that this long-awaited solution to the complex of rights which passed for feudalism was an exercise in the art of the possible. The measure represented a compromise between the aims of the peasantry and the interests of an Assembly overwhelmingly dominated by rural proprietors for whom rent, in all its forms, was the staff of life. Proprietors, too, experienced a sense of loss on reading the terms of the law and the deputies gave it a rough passage through the Assembly. One member pointed out that to vest the freedom to redeem in individuals was to deprive the seigneur of any real control over his resources. Redemption monies would arrive in dribs and drabs making reinvestment extremely difficult. However, the major stumbling block proved to be the clause specifying the 'taux de rachat' – the rates of indemnification. Several deputies thought these to be too generous (to vassals), or too rigid. Instead, they called for flexible redemption rates based on local valuations of feudal rents. This touched the Committee on the raw and revealed its disunity. Goupil de Préfelne spoke out in favour of '× 25' for monetary dues and '× 30' for harvest dues, while Tronchet admitted that the fixing of the 'taux de rachat' had been the hardest part of their labours. 'It positively racked our consciences', he is reported to have said.[6]

Be that as it may, the Committee had formulated a policy and the Assembly adhered to it gratefully for the next sixteen months. Further attempts to blur the honour-laden distinctions between seigneur and vassal were made: hereditary nobility and armorial bearings succumbed (19–25 June 1790) as did exclusive seigneurial rights to weathercocks, church benches and gibbets (13–20 April 1791). However, the economic foundations of the edifice set up in the spring of 1790 remained intact save for a modification in favour of the vassals of the church whose lands and prerogatives had become the property of the Nation. In a bid to stimulate the flow of redemption monies into the coffers of state, such vassals were allowed by a decree of 14–19 November 1790 to buy out annual dues and casual dues separately.

Evidence that the legislation of March and May 1790 had missed its mark accumulated rapidly in the files of the Feudal Committees of the National and Legislative Assemblies. In the absence of a massive buy-out of dues, the more onerous features of the seigneurial regime endured and each year collection became more difficult. Yet a shift in policy was not within the power of the peasantry alone to accomplish. It waited upon a concatenation of events which, in the spring of 1792, eroded the concept of property laid down two years earlier. On 19 February the deputy and future triumvir, Georges Couthon, urged the Assembly to take steps to retain the support of the rural masses. He had good reason: a poor harvest and the first signs of monetary inflation were causing acute distress in the countryside. A major insurrection was gathering momentum in the Beauce as the Assembly clung to its policy of free trade in grain. Even Paris succumbed to price-fixing riots in January and February, and besides, war was in the offing. The speech struck a chord in the Assembly and it was followed by another on 12 March in which Nicolas Golzart called for the concession enshrined in the decree of 14–19 November 1790 to be extended to all vassals without distinction. Golzart represented the department of the Ardennes in the North East where peasant resistance to harvest dues was intense and well organised. He went on to propose that state loans be made available to enable poor cultivators to buy out their seigneurial obligations.

The Legislative Assembly told its Committee to go away and digest these ideas. On 11 April 1792 it returned with a draft law abolishing casual dues without compensation unless title-deeds proving their validity could be produced. Casual dues had always been the weak link in the chain of logic invented by the first Feudal Committee and it came as no surprise that the fracture should occur there. More significant for the future, however, was the suggestion that the burden of proof be reversed. Merlin and Tronchet had buttressed their factitious distinction between 'personal' and 'real' rights with a virtual prohibition of litigation to test its validity. Seigneurs were exempted from the potentially embarrassing necessity of having to prove that the pecuniary rights which they claimed derived from a concession of land. Denied access to the relevant deeds and charters, peasant communities found it difficult to launch suits against their overlords. Instead they complained bitterly to the Committee, but it simply repeated more explicitly the decision reached earlier: 'the former seigneur in possession of a good and ancient right to collect a due on a piece of land needs no deed or special document to attest the legitimacy of that due'.[7] So, the proposal to abolish casual dues marked a radical break with the legal fictions that had informed public policy ever since the first summer of the revolution and the deputies contemplated the reform with obvious reluctance. It seemed a dangerously open-ended step to take, for who could foretell where pressure would be exerted next? On the other hand, the pace of events was hotting up and arguments of expediency offered breathing space to the beleaguered Assembly. 'Former seigneurs will complain', reasoned the deputy Jean-Baptiste Mailhe, 'but of what do they not complain? You will be absolved by the benedictions of ninety-nine hundredths of the present generation and those of generations to come.'[8]

On 18 June 1792 – the day on which the threatening manoeuvres of General Lafayette became known in Paris – the Assembly adopted the proposals of its Feudal Committee and voted to dispossess owners of *lods et ventes*, *acaptes* (death duties) and a host of lesser casual rights unless they derived from a concession of land, duly certified. Few owners could certify any such thing and hence another nail was driven into the coffin of feudalism. Too little and too late, as several deputies had predicted when the law had first been mooted in April. The fate of the 1791 constitution now lay in the hands of the *fédérés* and the *sectionnaires* of Paris. The Assembly bent with the wind and passed three measures in rapid succession which effectively destroyed the seigneurial regime. On 20 August those casual dues which had survived the strictures of the decree of 18 June–6 July became subject to separate redemption. As for harvest dues, they could now be converted into fixed annual payments, while dues levied collectively were abolished without further ado. But with foreign armies encamped on French soil and the Paris Commune posturing as an alternative government, such meagre concessions seemed out of step with the gravity of the situation. On 25 August a motion to have done with seigneurialism was rushed through the Assembly. Annual dues, like casual dues, were declared abolished without compensation unless it could be shown that they derived from a concession of land. All transactions emancipating from *mainmorte personnelle*, *bordelage* and *quevaise* (an onerous form of tenure common in Brittany) in return for a due paid in cash or kind were annulled, and ex-seigneurs were forbidden to collect arrears of dues which no longer had any legal standing. In short, the land of France was henceforth presumed to be free of feudal prerogatives except where these had been established by private treaty and upheld in law. The *ancien régime* maxim of 'nul terre sans seigneur' (no land without a lord) on which the National Assembly had based its jurisprudence had finally been revoked.

The decree of 25 August 1792 made good the rhetorical promises of August 1789. It was offered to the peasantry in atonement for three years of temporising on the issue of feudalism. The remark in the preamble that 'the feudal system is abolished, that nevertheless it subsists in its effects, and that nothing is more urgent than to cause to disappear from French territory those vestiges of servitude' seemed to acknowledge as much.[9] Even so, the measure passed over in silence an important dimension of seigneurial power: the appropriation of common land. The omission appears to have been deliberate, for three days later the Assembly returned to the issue of *triage* which had been tackled first in March 1790. In a draconian decree, the abolition of this right was given a retroactive effect and peasant communities were empowered to seek redress from seigneurs who had profited from the ordinance of 1669 to claim a share of common lands. A further article proved even more damaging to seigneurs; it invited villagers to lodge a claim to any land or rights of usage which they believed to have been 'despoiled by the feudal power'[10] (see p. 139).

In raising the curtain for the struggle over the commons, the legislation of August 1792 seemed to indicate that the struggle over feudal obligations was coming to an end. The decree of 25 August had outlawed unsubstantiated harvest dues and in so doing it cut the tap root of the seigneurial regime. Redemption payments ceased, to all intents and purposes. If, on paper, feudalism was not quite dead and buried, it ceased to impinge as an economic reality after the summer of 1792. The National Convention, unlike its predecessors, devoted little time to debating the issue and the famous decree of 17 July 1793 was more or less adventitious. All the signs suggest that the Legislation Committee was bounced into proposing a law which was unanticipated and poorly drafted. On 3 June an unnamed deputy called for 'a general law to complete the destruction of feudalism'[11] and the matter was referred to the Committee. The Committee sat on the proposal and a few days later another deputy proposed that all seigneurial title-deeds be ceremoniously burned. Under pressure, the Committee rushed out a draft law consisting of twelve articles which the Convention immediately passed. Article 1 declared in a somewhat rambling manner that all seigneurial dues, or rather ex-seigneurial dues, 'even those maintained by the decree of 25 August last'[12] were abolished without compensation. Article 2 excluded ordinary ground rent such as a tenant would pay to his landlord from abolition without compensation, while subsequent articles ordered the burning of all feudal deeds, non-compliance to be punished with five years in irons.

Fears that feudal rent might not be distinguishable from ordinary ground rent in the final analysis proved all too real. The first two clauses of the decree appeared to invite a number of interpretations: either feudal dues were abolished, but 'ordinary' leasehold payments retained, or both dues and leasehold payments were abolished where they were owed to a former seigneur, or dues were abolished outright, but not leasehold payments which were, however, redeemable. Unsuspectingly, the deputies had punched another hole in the fabric of property rights, for landowners faced expropriation by their tenants if leasehold payments had indeed been abolished or made subject to redemption. The Committee was greatly perturbed by these insinuations and endeavoured to put the record straight. But the problem lay at one remove, for, in large areas of western and south-western France, there was no such thing as an ordinary leasehold payment.

The leases of tenants under *domaine congéable* in Brittany, of share-croppers in the Périgord or Gascony, consisted of feudal, quasi-feudal and non-feudal payments which were exceedingly difficult to separate out (see pp. 113–14). Moreover, it seems that a few members of the Convention were not unhappy to see the decree being used as an instrument of social revolution in the countryside. This at least is what the Legislation Committee alleged in a long memoir to the Committee of Public Safety seeking to win support for a revision. All to no avail, however: the decree of 17 July 1793 remained on the statute book. The Legislation Committee did manage to push through a measure sorting out the problems posed by the burning of feudal deeds on 2 October, but the Terror had begun and the Convention refused the opportunity to carry out a more general overhaul of its handiwork.

Tithe and neo-tithe

The tithe had become an issue by the end of the *ancien régime* and it is to the credit of the revolutionaries that they realised as much. Reform had been talked about for years and resistance to the enterprises of tithe farmers had become a popular rallying-point in the 1780s. The solution seemed simple enough: liquidate the tithe and remove at one go the increment of ecclesiastical rent weighing down agriculture. But this solution did violence to the sacred, if ill-defined, rights of property which the National Assembly had sworn to uphold. The decision reached in November 1789 to take the possessions of the church into public owner-ship eased the conflict to some degree: at least the deputies could no longer be accused of giving away other people's property. Yet one important question remained: if the state bore the costs of the operation, who would enjoy the benefits? Predictably, the National Assembly ruled that the first fruits of the revolution should fall to the landowners. Mere cultivators of the land (tenant farmers, sharecroppers etc.) felt betrayed. Their dis-illusionment, as historians have begun to appreciate, resulted in a serious erosion of rural support for the new regime and the growth of antagonisms within the peasantry.

Hostility to the tithe derived from two sources: the feeling that it was being abusively levied, and abusively applied. The huge disparity in rates of assessment (see table 4) seemed to testify to the former, while the num-bers of parish clergy receiving a niggardly *portion congrue* provided ample evidence of the latter. In some regions the peasant sacrificed a full 10 per cent of his gross harvest 'for the upkeep of the church' whereas in others the tithe took no more than 2 per cent, and it comes as no surprise to dis-cover that hostility was most pronounced in Gascony, in the Franche-

Comté and in Flanders where record levels obtained. The tithe was generally reckoned at twice the burden of royal taxation in the Gascon diocese
of Auch before the revolution (see p. 50) and Lefebvre points to the fact
that dues owed to the church often constituted the heaviest burden on
peasant surplus in the Nord.[13] In this as in so much else, the *mainmortable*
villages of the Franche-Comté marked out the extremes, however, and it is
noteworthy that criticisms of the tithe were voiced in over a hundred
(nearly 25 per cent) of the parish *cahiers* of the *bailliage* of Amont.[14] Even
so, hostility to the tithe did not turn on quotients alone. In the popular
mind tithe farmers were deemed guilty of many of the sins attributed to the
feudistes: they nudged the rate upwards wherever possible, often con-
triving to conceal the increase by lumping together tithe and *terrage*; they
battened upon newly cultivated land or hitherto exempt land, and they
diligently 'modernised' the tithe to take account of the agricultural innovations and market opportunities. Thus, in 1766 the tithe was extended to
maize – the new high-yielding Spanish cereal – once it had become established in the diocese of Auch, while in December 1789 vassals of the
Templar Knights at Sainte Eulalie (Rouergue) complained that 'all the
fruits of the soil are subject to the tithe, even those whose cultivation has
only been tried in the last few years, such as sainfoin, clover and others'.[15]
On the whole the peasantry accepted the principle of paying the tithe on
traditional cereal crops (the so-called *grosses dîmes*), or on wine in vine-
growing districts, but they vigorously contested the right of *décimateurs* to
tax secondary sources of income such as the product of orchards, hay
meadows and farm animals (*menues dîmes*). The 'triple' tithe levied on
sheep (lambs, wool and cheese) in pastoral regions seemed to symbolise
this ecclesiastical reaction and it attracted a growing volume of criticism
during the final decades of the *ancien régime*. In 1775 the General
Assembly of the Clergy accused the Parlement of Toulouse of discreetly
encouraging the rural population to refuse the *menues dîmes* and the Parlement of Normandy likewise refused to endorse any but the *grosses dîmes*.
With peasant hostility mounting and enlightened opinion adopting an ever
more utilitarian attitude towards the church, tithe owners had every
reason to feel vulnerable when the revolution broke.

The long and less than heroic saga of the abolition of the tithe began on
the night of 4 August 1789 when the deputies resolved to treat it as a form
of ground rent which might be extinguished on payment of appropriate
compensation. This solution addressed the problem of infeudated tithes
(that is to say those which had become the property of private individuals)
and it held out the prospect of an independent source of income to the
parish clergy, but the notion that the great mass of tithes had come into
being as a result of a concession of land was manifestly false. As one deputy

Table 4. *The tithe on the eve of the revolution*

Region	Locality, Province or Department	Rate (expressed as percentage of gross production)	Comments
Paris Basin	Beauce[1]	8.3	
	Beauvaisis[2]	8.0	
	Orléanais[3]	3.3	
	Champagne[4]	7.7	
	Haute-Marne[5]	7.7 → 9.1	
North East	Flanders[6]	9.1	*quérable***
	Hainaut–Cambrésis[7]	under 9.1	*quérable*
	Cateau-Cambrésis[8]	8.0	*quérable*
Burgundy and the East	*bailliage* of Auxerre[9]	4.8 → 7.1	
	North Burgundy[10]	5.0 → 10.0	
	Tonnerrois[11]	4.8	
	Mâconnais[12]	4.8 → 9.1	on wine
		7.7 → 8.3	on cereals
	Franche-Comté[13]	8.3 → 16.7	*portable*
West and South West	Maine[14]	7.7	
	Upper Brittany[15]	7.7 → 9.1	
	diocese of Vannes[16]	3.0	
	Vendée[17]	8.3	
	Aunis and Saintonge[18]	7.7	
	Gascony and Comminges[19]	10.0 → 12.5	
Massif Central	Auvergne[20]	3.3	
South East	Dauphiné[21]	under 3.3	
	Provence[22]	under 3.3	
	Savoy[23]	1.7 → 2.0	

*Most tithes were *quérable*, that is to say responsibility for collection lay with the owner. In a few localities they were *portable*, i.e. the costs of transportation were borne by the peasantry.

Sources

1 A.N. DXIV 3.

2 P. Goubert, *Beauvais et le Beauvaisis de 1600 à 1730: contribution à l'histoire sociale de la France du XVIIe siècle* (Paris, 1960), p. 179.

3 J. McManners, 'Tithe in eighteenth-century France: a focus for rural anticlericalism' in D. Beales and G. Best (eds.), *History, Society and the Churches. Essays in Honour of Owen Chadwick* (Cambridge, 1985), p. 147.

4 *Ibid.*

5 J.-J. Clère, 'Les Paysans de la Haute-Marne et la Révolution française: recherches sur les structures de la communauté villageoise' (University of Dijon, Thèse pur le doctorat en droit, 2 vols., 1979), vol. i, pp. 220–1.

6 G. Lefebvre, *Les Paysans du Nord pendant la Révolution française* (Bari, 1959), p. 119.

7 *Ibid.*

8 M. Delattre, 'Le Régime seigneurial, la délinquance, les mentalités paysannes dans la Châtellenie du Cateau-Cambrésis au XVIIIe siècle' (Mémoire de maîtrise, 1970), p. 34.

9 C. Demay, *Cahiers des paroisses du bailliage d'Auxerre pour les Etats-Généraux de 1789* (Auxerre, 1885), p. 11.

10 P. de Saint Jacob, *Les Paysans de la Bourgogne du nord au dernier siècle de l'ancien régime* (Dijon, 1960), p. 132.

11 F. Genreau, 'Les Paysans et l'abolition des droits féodaux dans le district de Tonnerre (Yonne), 1789 à 1793' (Diplôme d'études supérieures du droit, Université de Dijon, 1972), p. 22.

12 F. Evrard, 'Les Paysans du Mâconnais et les brigandages de juillet 1789', *Annales de Bourgogne*, 19 (1947), 23.

13 J. Millot, *Le Régime féodal en Franche-Comté au XVIIIe siècle* (Besançon, 1937), pp. 102, 208..

14 P. Bois, *Paysans de l'Ouest: des structures économiques et sociales aux options politiques depuis l'époque révolutionnaire dans la Sarthe* (Le Mans, 1960), p. 203.

15 D. M. G. Sutherland, *The Chouans: the Social Origins of Popular Counter-Revolution in Upper Brittany, 1770–1796* (Oxford, 1982), p. 202.

16 T. J. A. Le Goff, *Vannes and its Region: a Study of Town and Country in Eighteenth-Century France* (Oxford, 1981), p. 260.

17 A.N. DXIV 11.

18 F. Julien-Labruyère, *Paysans charentais: histoire des campagnes d'Aunis, Saintonge et Bas Angoumois* (2 vols., La Rochelle, 1982), vol. ii, p. 130.

19 P. Féral, 'Le Problème de la dîme, de la coussure et de la glane au XVIIIe et au XIXe siècle dans le Lectourois', *Bulletin de la Société historique et archéologique du Gers* (1949), 238; M. Muller and S. Aberdam, 'Conflits de dîme et révolution en Gascogne gersoise, 1750–1800' (Mémoire de maîtrise sous la direction de M. Robert Mandrou, 1971–2), pp. 35, D73–D78.

20 R. Schnerb, *Les Contributions directes à l'époque de la Révolution dans le département du Puy-de-Dôme* (Paris, 1933), p. xxviii.

21 McManners, 'Tithe in eighteenth-century France: a focus for rural anticlericalism', p. 147.

22 *Ibid.*

23 S. Herbert, *The Fall of Feudalism in France* (London, 1921), p. 40.

put it, the tithe was a tax paid by the laity in return for religious services and since the Assembly was contemplating a take-over of the finances of the church there seemed no reason why this burdensome tax should not be abolished outright. Accordingly, on 11 August after an embittered debate the deputies voted in principle to outlaw the tithe. However, they took care to order its continued payment until such time as the future organisation of the church had been settled.

Then came an autumn of repentance as the implications of the legis-lation of 4–11 August began to sink in. Since the state had now shouldered the running-costs (as well as the fixed assets) of the church, it seemed not unreasonable to seek to recoup some of the additional expenditure from the beneficiaries. After all, the tithe was worth about 130 million *livres* – equivalent to twice the income from the *taille* – whereas the exchequer was virtually empty.[16] Talleyrand's famous motion to expropriate and then sell off the lands of the church included proposals to enable the state to cash in on the tithe, either by lengthening the calendar of abolition or by splitting it into redeemable and non-redeemable components. At a time when the experts were wrestling with the intricacies of the seigneurial regime, a proposal to complicate the seemingly straightforward resolution regard-ing the tithe attracted little enthusiasm, however. Instead, the Assembly put off a decision, leaving the peasantry sure of one thing only: they should have paid the tithe on the 1789 harvest, but might yet be exempted from paying it on the 1790 harvest. The Assembly did clarify one point, how-ever. Infeudated tithes were deemed a legitimate form of property which could be extinguished solely by process of indemnification. Consequently, they were listed among the dues subject to redemption in the decree of 15–28 March 1790.

With the liquidation of the seigneurial regime under way at last, the deputies turned their attention to ecclesiastical matters and appointed a committee to prepare fresh legislation. This body proposed that the abolition of the tithe should come into force on 1 January 1791. The idea of redemption was abandoned as unworkable, although owners of infeudated tithes were to be compensated by the state at a cost to the public purse of some ten million *livres*. This and much else was legislated despite the opposition of the higher clergy between 14 and 20 April 1790 and the royal assent was granted two days later. The decree immediately removed one major source of confusion: the peasantry, indeed all rural proprietors, would have to pay (to the Nation) the tithe on the forthcoming harvest. On the other hand, definitive abolition with effect from next year's harvest promised a massive alleviation of the burdens on agriculture. All over France the newly established department and district authorities hastened to promulgate the decree, urging country dwellers to fulfil their patriotic duties in the knowledge that the laden waggons of the tithe proctors would soon be a relic of the past. In the Côte-d'Or the department authorities despatched a copy of the decree of 14–22 April to every commune on 21 June, while the administrators of the Haute-Saône warned the peasantry that they should pay arrears outstanding on the 1789 harvest as well as the coming year's liabilities.

In some ways the decree was more eloquent in what it did not say, however, for the deputies were not to be drawn on how the abolition of the tithe would operate in practice. Yet, already, perspicacious landowners were drawing their own conclusions. In the Gers, the region around Auch where bitter conflicts over the tithe had raged since the 1750s, proprietors moved smartly to deny their tenants a share of the proceeds of abolition. The researches of Martine Muller and Serge Aberdam have uncovered a notarised contract signed in February – two months before the decree of 14–22 April 1790 – in which the landowner took care to stipulate that the tithe would be added to the value of the lease in the event of suppression.[17] Nor does this case appear to have been untypical, for the same authors also cite a sharecropping agreement which seems to date from the earliest period of the revolution. In it the proprietor announced that 'since the tithe is no longer paid, I shall take a tenth of the harvest irrespective of what it might consist'.[18] After a long and ominous silence, this solution became the official policy of the revolution. On 1 December 1790, that is to say a bare month before the tithe was due to lapse, the Assembly declared that 'tenants and sharecroppers of holdings whose yield was liable to the ecclesiastical or infeudated tithe shall pay to the proprietors the value of the tithe with effect from the harvest of 1791'.[19] Peasant farmers who owed the tithe to the church in 1789, to the Nation in 1790, were now required to make over a cash equivalent sum to their landlords. The 'neo-tithe', or the 'bourgeois tithe' as some historians prefer to call it, had been invented and the social basis on which the new order in the countryside rested narrowed perceptibly.

Actually, the decree of 1–12 December was a good deal more complex and its implications need to be grasped if we are to weigh the significance which some scholars attach to it.[20] The measure did not, of course, affect *laboureurs* who owned all or most of the land which they farmed. Like the rural bourgeoisie, they emerged as net gainers from the operation. Nor did it seek to saddle tenants and sharecroppers with neo-tithe payments for the foreseeable future. Only lease contracts agreed before the decree of 14–22 April 1790 were liable to the supplement. Those signed after the date of abolition were deemed to be subject to the laws of supply and demand. The parties might agree to insert into the contract a specific clause requiring the lessee to hand over a sum equivalent to the tithe, but the landowner had no right to such a payment. However, this freedom only applied to farmers in possession of written leases formally negotiated, or re-negotiated, after the due date. Sharecroppers often worked the land without the benefit of a written lease, or with a lease that was tacitly renewed on expiration. In such cases the neo-tithe could indeed become self-perpetuating.

Not surprisingly, therefore, the Assembly's solution to the tithe question caused mounting frustration in those parts of the kingdom where the tithe was onerous and sharecropping as a mode of tenure predominated (see map 6). In the Gers, for example, some 30 per cent of peasant households worked the land as sharecroppers, whereas owner-exploiters totalled barely half that number.[21] Here were gathered the classic symptoms of rural disenchantment: in 1791 the neo-tithe replaced the tithe and direct taxation escalated, while the abolition of feudalism in a region little touched by harvest dues brought few corresponding benefits. The authorities of the department trod warily, aware of the need to retain peasant support for the revolution and yet conscious, too, of the anxieties of land-owners as the 1791 Constitution began to run into difficulties. With the harvest approaching they were forced to react, however, and on 11 July 1791 the department published a vigorous statement in defence of the neo-tithe which was to be read out aloud in every commune. The share-croppers, or *bordiers* as they were known locally, were reminded that they passed for little more than agricultural labourers. Their masters owned the land and paid the appropriate taxes (in theory, not always in practice, see p. 189) and it was only right and proper, therefore, that they should pocket the proceeds of tithe abolition. The only 'concession' offered was that sharecroppers might negotiate with their employers to continue payment of the tithe in kind. This would relieve the bordier of the obligation to sell produce in order to raise cash, but it would also protect landowners from the effects of monetary inflation.

The political capital to be made by tying proprietors more firmly to the revolution at this juncture needs no emphasising. The king had fled Paris, apparently intending to join the *émigrés*, and demagogues in the capital were openly questioning the wisdom of constitutional monarchy. In every town and village, moderately inclined members of the bourgeoisie began to reassess their allegiances. Yet the firm line adopted by the authorities of the Gers, in common with many other department administrations in the South West, mortgaged the future. By the summer of 1793 they were to find themselves seriously out of step with the Paris revolution, while the sharecroppers sensed that their moment had at last arrived. The conflagration began in the southern cantons of the Gers, although it might easily have begun in the departments of the Landes, the Lot-et-Garonne or the

Map 6. Geography of tensions between sharecroppers and landowners, 1789–95
Sources: M. Muller and S. Aberdam, 'Conflits de dîme et révolution en Gascogne gersoise, 1750–1800' (Mémoire de maîtrise, 1971–2); S. Aberdam, 'La Révolution et la lutte des métayers', *Etudes rurales*, 59 (1975), pp. 73–91; G. Lefebvre, *Questions agraires au temps de la Terreur* (2nd ed., La Roche-sur-Yon, 1954), pp. 91–114

Dordogne for sharecroppers were in a mutinous mood throughout the region. On 14 July – a date charged with symbolism – some 300 *bordiers* gathered in the district capital of Mirande. They alleged that the decrees on the tithe had been misapplied, they demanded that the proceeds of abolition be shared equally between landlord and tenant, and they talked of cutting off heads in the event of refusal. Fixated with Federalism, the administrators of the department were caught unawares. Nevertheless, they reacted energetically and despatched to Mirande a miscellaneous force headed by a cannon. Prisoners were taken, and within a fortnight law and order had been restored. On 28 July the department authorities reiterated their proclamation of July 1791, but in sterner language, taking care this time to have it explained in Gascon. The pacification was helped by the fact that the sharecroppers lacked even the most rudimentary organisation and leadership. Nor did they show the least desire to instigate a counter-revolution – quite the contrary: theirs was a plea for more revolution, not less.[22]

This fact was not lost on the *représentants-en-mission* who toured the departments of the South West during the autumn of 1793. Their reports, combined with alarming signals from the cereal-growing plains of the Ile-de-France (see pp. 164–5), persuaded the Committee of Public Safety to toy with the idea of a social policy for 'les citoyens des campagnes'. In September Dartigoeyte, the Gascon-speaking deputy from the department of the Landes, arrived in the Gers and lent a sympathetic ear to the grievances of sharecroppers. His subsequent correspondence with the Committee was a model of political realism: the towns are unreliable . . . Federalism has failed thanks only to the good sense of the peasantry . . . we owe them something in return . . . 'if the law giving the tithe to the landlords could be repealed, the revolution would have the support of ten to twelve thousand families of sharecroppers in this area'.[23] Even more so, he added, if something could be done to ease the brusque escalation of taxes. What gave these observations such force was the fact that almost identical advice was reaching the Committee from other parts of the region. Roux-Fazillac, the Convention's envoy in the departments of the Dordogne and the Charente, announced that he had received an 'infinity of complaints' from sharecroppers whom he described as 'the only French citizens who had gained nothing from the revolution, even though they and their children fought to defend it like other citizens'.[24] In fact he went further and actively encouraged the peasantry to cease paying the neo-tithe and ground rents in general.

Once again, the business of refashioning the concept of property elaborated by the National Assembly had come perilously close to licensing a wholesale expropriation. The misgivings of the Legislation Committee in the face of wishful interpretations of the decree of 17 July 1793 have already been noted, but the Committee of Public Safety was subject to conflicting emotions. It wanted to do something for the sharecroppers in furtherance of the broadly social and egalitarian aims of the *montagnards*, yet its basic instincts were conservative and proprietorial. The result was to fudge the issue of tenant rights. On 1 Brumaire II (22 October 1793) the Convention decreed (article 1) that sharecroppers with verbal leases were no longer required to pay the neo-tithe, or, for that matter, seigneurial harvest dues of any kind. This seemed to answer the objections raised against the decree of 1–12 December 1790. However, subsequent stipulations in the measure tended to deprive the concession of much of its effect. Article 4 permitted landlords to attach special conditions to their leases, provided they had been mutually agreed and provided that they did not resemble the tithe or seigneurial dues. What this latter proviso meant in practice was left open to interpretation, but it strongly suggests that the Convention found itself incapable of resolving the points at issue.

Be that as it may, the sharecroppers regarded the decree of 1 Brumaire II as a victory, and, indeed, a further decree of 26 Prairial II (14 June 1794) confirmed that tenants farming under verbal leases unencumbered with special conditions were exempt from the neo-tithe. Nevertheless, that victory was controversial in law and precarious in practice. It rested, to all intents and purposes, on the climate of terror which the *représentants-en-mission* brought to all corners of France in the autumn of 1793. In these conditions, proprietors wisely refrained from vindicating their rights in the courts. But the Terror was a passing phenomenon and Thermidor opened the floodgates of a proprietorial reaction which flowed fast and furiously for the next three years (see pp. 134–7). Isolated and desperately vulnerable, the sharecroppers of the South West paid up their arrears and sued for the best terms they could obtain. Those who resisted were hauled before the courts where panels of landowning judges tested the decree of 1 Brumaire II to destruction. Such was the fate of Dominique Corne who sharecropped a holding at Ligardes in the Gers. Corne had paid the tithe, or rather the neo-tithe, in 1791, in 1792 and in 1793, but had refused to do so in 1794 and 1795, instancing the decree of 1 Brumaire II. The judges pointed to the fact that he had taken over his holding in 1780 with a three-year written lease which had been tacitly renewed thereafter, and argued that this established his liability. Article one of the decree of 1 Brumaire II did not apply because Corne *had* a written lease, even if it had been renewed verbally for the past twelve years. And in any case, article four of the same law permitted private conventions, which is how the court chose to regard the neo-tithe payments of 1791–3. The verdict reached on 26 August 1795 condemned Corne to pay a strict tenth of all crops harvested in 1794 and 1795 plus costs.[25]

Renewed agrarian unrest

The promulgation of the first of the anti-feudal statutes in March 1790 dispelled the atmosphere of relative calm which had prevailed in most parts of the kingdom throughout the winter. For the seigneurs, the new law was

not half as bad as they had feared, but the peasantry were utterly devas-
tated. The former contemplated the approach of spring in a confident,
even a bullish, mood, whereas the latter remained distrustful and unsure
whether to respond with further acts of violence against the châteaux or
with procrastination. In the event, the so-called peaceful year of the revolution witnessed both 'old' and 'new' forms of collective protest: the
peasantry resorted to set-piece mobilisations in the time-honoured
manner, but they also pioneered more sophisticated techniques of
resistance and intimidation which confused and divided the authorities
responsible for law and order.

The seigneurs made the first move, however, with a counter-offensive
designed to claw back the concessions wrung from them the year before.
During the first six months of 1790 complaints recounting all manner of
abuses poured in to the Assembly from every part of the country. Even if
only a fraction of the allegations was founded, there can be no doubt that
the seigneurs, or fief owners as they now preferred to call themselves, had
taken new heart. 'Your decree of 4 August checked the hostilities of the
seigneurs', declared a group of peasant farmers writing from the department of the Creuse, 'but as soon as they had knowledge of the last one
[March 1790], they recommenced their old vexations against the
petitioners.'[26] Arrears of dues owing on the 1789 harvest appear to have
been the principal bone of contention: complaints on this score reached the
Feudal Committee from Sainte Menehould (Meuse) in February, the
Lomagne (Tarn-et-Garonne) in April and from St Céré (Lot) in June.
Seigneurs in the latter locality were carefully timing their demands for
arrears to coincide with the peak in grain prices. As the year wore on the
seigneurial backlash broadened in scope and enthusiasm and the peasantry
began to report flagrant violations of the law. The *laboureurs* of the commune of Prémont (Aisne) discovered in August that they were still expected
to perform four days of labour service, while a number of seigneurs were
denounced for continuing work on their *terriers* despite the formal ban on
any such move contained in the decree of 15–28 March 1790. Owners of
dues showed few qualms about campaigning against the 'taux de rachat'
fixed by the decree of 3–9 May either. In the South and the South West,
feudal harvest rents were a highly prized form of property and the redemption terms laid down by the National Assembly looked unduly generous to
the peasantry. Fief owners in the Aveyron claimed that harvest dues were
normally bought and sold on the basis of forty times their annual yield,
that is nearly twice the value attributed to them in the decree. The resumption of normal judicial activity also tended to encourage the seigneurs, just
as the paralysis of royal and seigneurial courts in the autumn of 1789 had
worked in favour of the peasantry. In November 1790 new district courts

came into being and seigneurs featured prominently among the plaintiffs. They used the courts to pursue defaulting vassals and to test out the scope of their remaining rights as defined in March. Thus, in the district of Tonnerre (Yonne), fief owners contrived to obtain an injunction compelling the peasants to continue paying a *tierce* which patently derived from *mainmorte*.

But this was only one side of the coin, of course. The aggression of seigneurs against their vassals, the ingenuity with which they exploited the loopholes in the legislation dismantling the feudal regime was not entirely gratuitous. It reflected mounting frustration at the 'dumb insolence' of a peasantry which would neither pay nor redeem. In response to pressure from their former overlords, peasants resorted to a number of stratagems: they quibbled over details, they demanded access to title-deeds, they bombarded the authorities with petitions against the 'taux de rachat', and they took up arms. Often they resorted to these stratagems concurrently, but for the sake of clarity it is better to examine each in turn.

Quibbling over dues was an old tactic which won a new lease of life in 1790 and 1791. Often it signalled a readiness to pay, if not at the old rate and on the old terms. For example, many communities offered to continue paying harvest dues on condition that they were converted into a fixed and, for preference, monetary obligation. Thus the villagers of the *châtellenie* of Cateau-Cambrésis informed their seigneur, the archbishop of Cambrai, that henceforward they would only pay the tithe and *terrage* in cash. A similar call for commutation emanated from the Etampes district (Seine-et-Oise) just prior to the harvest of 1790. Refusal to transport the product of harvest dues to the lord's barn or château was another widely used expedient, as we have seen, and in the autumn of 1790 the peasantry resorted to it again. Reports to this effect reached the Feudal Committee from the Saintonge (Charente-Maritime), from the Ardennes and from Puiseaux on the western edge of the Gâtinais. This latter location is significant, for several parishes in the Gâtinais made a point of complaining about *portabilité* in their *cahiers* and the whole region was poised on the brink of serious unrest (see pp. 117–20).

On the whole resistance to the continued functioning of the seigneurial regime remained circumspect in character and patchy in effect, however. The peasantry played for time, querying the detail of the new legislation – was *portabilité* a 'personal' or a 'real' right? – and above all asking to see the contractual documents on which their obligation to carry on paying dues apparently rested. The seigneurs, it will be remembered, were under no legal obligation to produce their title-deeds or 'titres', as they were known. In much of France the *ancien régime* jurisprudence of 'nulle terre sans seigneur' prevailed and it put fief owners in a virtually unchallengeable position. Only in the southern third of the country was the land deemed free of seigneurial jurisdiction in the absence of proof to the contrary. The decree of 15–28 March 1790 did nothing to redress the balance between seigneur and vassal in this respect. On the contrary, it checkmated the moves made by the peasantry in an effort to even the score during the preceding summer. Seigneurs whose *terriers* had been destroyed were provided with the means of reinstating their rights, while those who had renounced their privileges under pressure were offered the escape route of annulment. None of this impressed the peasantry, however. Whether by accident or by design, they persisted in misunderstanding the legislation relating to the liquidation of the *ancien régime* and the demand to see title-deeds became a veritable hue and cry.

The phenomenon of seigneurial reaction had already focused attention on the issue of 'titres' in some parts of the kingdom. Apparently, Burgundian peasant communities were asking to see title-deeds as a matter of course in the later 1770s,[27] and by 1789 this reflex was fairly widespread if we are to judge from the parish *cahiers*. Early in 1790 such requests were renewed, respectfully at first and then with a growing sense of urgency as the harvest approached. In the district of Tonnerre (Yonne), for instance, the year 1789 had passed off quietly and little pressure was exerted on seigneurs to produce their title-deeds before the decree of 15–28 March 1790 became public knowledge. Thereafter, the pressure increased, but the local seigneurs seem generally to have acceded to the requests of their vassals. Where resistance was encountered, relations swiftly degenerated into open confrontation with seigneurs withholding their deeds and the peasants putting off the payment of harvest dues. In this they were often aided and abetted by the newly elected municipalities, for the suffrage legislation of the National Assembly only succeeded in excluding the poorest members of the peasantry from the bottom rung of local government. While the 'popular front' against feudalism remained in being, the municipalities proved a highly effective weapon against seigneurial pretensions.

All in all, twenty-six (36 per cent) of the seventy-three communes forming the administrative district of Tonnerre refused to continue paying harvest dues in the time-honoured fashion.[28] Ten villages founded their resistance on queries relating to title-deeds; nine argued that their liability to the *tierce* derived from *mainmorte*; three called for cash conversion; two refused to pay while suits against their seigneurs remained unsettled; one demanded a rate reduction and one village stolidly and ignorantly maintained that all dues had been abolished. The Tonnerrois enjoyed a high degree of calm and social cohesion throughout the revolution and it is tempting to regard these figures as broadly indicative of the lowest threshold of active resistance to the seigneurial regime in 1790 and 1791. Unfortunately, such a conclusion would be little more than a 'guesstimate'. Local studies of the impact of the National Assembly's anti-feudal legislation are thinly scattered and it is not yet possible to obtain an impression of the overall picture. In the old provinces of Aunis and Saintonge (Charente-Inférieure), the majority of peasants appear to have carried on paying their dues, notwithstanding complaints about *portabilité*. On the other hand, contemporary accounts suggest that the request to see deeds was often insincere. The peasantry used it as a bargaining ploy to ward off demands which they had no intention of satisfying. This was the situation encountered by commissioners Godard and Robin in the Lot (see pp. 114–17). Most villages in the district of Gourdon, they reported, would not pay the dues owing on the 1789 and 1790 harvests until the original title-deeds were produced. Nearly everyone they interviewed uttered the same refrain: 'titre primordial'. Similar reports reached the Feudal Committee from the Gâtinais, from the Metz region and, in 1791, from the Aisne and the Oise departments.

Seigneurs tried to overcome popular resistance by producing their estate registers, but only the most benighted communities were prepared to accept *terriers* and certified acknowledgements of dues (*reconnaissances*) in lieu of the original deed of concession. As a legal practitioner from near Périgueux (Dordogne) pointed out, *reconnaissances* 'are not title-deeds, but certificates representative of deeds'.[29] Various compromise solutions were mooted, but they all presupposed a modification of the law which no one in authority was prepared to contemplate before 1792. For instance, the municipal officers of Maisaincourt in the Ardennes recommended the creation of an arbitration service with legal powers to sort out differences between seigneurs and their vassals, while a feudal lawyer named Bataillard wrote to the Committee to propose that all seigneurial title-deeds be deposited with an impartial third party where tenants would be at liberty to consult them. Informal schemes of this type do seem to have come into existence as seigneurs opted for the wiser course of trying to meet their vassals half way, but they did little to diminish the growing resistance to harvest dues. Most seigneurs could not have produced the original charters justifying their rights even if they had wanted to. In July 1791 Joseph Amyot, seigneur of several villages in the neighbourhood of Château-Landon (Seine-et-Marne) and an indefatigable petitioner of the committees of government, complained that he was being pressurised to sign away his rights despite having lodged his deeds with a notary in the nearby town of Montargis. The insurgent peasantry gathered in the courtyard of the château and announced that they had checked the documents in question and had found five *terriers* compiled between 1606 and 1779, but no 'primordial title of 1200 or 1500'.[30] This is why the legislation of June and August 1792 which reversed the burden of proof effectively brought the payment of dues to an end. But the peasantry were not immediately appeased: there were many incidents of score-settling that autumn as bands raided château archives and the dwellings of public notaries in order to seize and destroy the offending documents. In the Doubs, the decree of 25 August 1792 was promulgated on 12 September and in the following days a number of localised insurrections broke out. Over the border in the Jura department, armed National Guardsmen invaded the office of the public receiver of domains at Arbois and forced him to hand over the deeds of the seigneurie of Vauvey. These were ceremonially burned in the square.

The news that the National Assembly expected peasants to buy out *champarts, cens* and *lods et ventes* at a commercial rate representing a return on capital of 4 or 5 per cent caused a ripple of indignation across the countryside. Of course, the Feudal Committee may have been correct in supposing that seigneurial investments did, on average, yield 4 or 5 per cent. In Alsace it seems that they yielded twice as much, whereas in the Rouergue anything above 2.5 per cent was quite exceptional. But this was scarcely the point: the peasantry expected a realistic not a commercial 'taux de rachat', that is to say redemption terms which took account of one if not two bad harvests and which acknowledged the opprobrium into which the institutions of seigneurialism had fallen. In short, they expected generous terms. From the earliest months of 1790, petitions making this point with varying degrees of sophistication flowed in to the Assembly. One of the most eloquent and prophetic came from the pen of a parish priest in the Ardèche who informed the deputies on 16 January that: 'the freedom to reimburse [seigneurial rents] will always be a useless facility for the common people . . . because the poor are never in a position to accumulate a large sum of money'.[31] Sooner or later, he warned, the Assembly would have to abolish all feudal dues.

Once the import of the decree of 3–9 May had sunk in, this flow became a veritable flood. The outcry was loudest in the South East and in the South West. Predictably, the Dauphiné emerged as the pole of resistance in the South East, for the province had been the theatre of a full-scale agrarian insurrection in the summer of 1789. Several villages felt sufficiently moved by the decree to spell out its implications in no uncertain terms: the municipality of Montferrat (Isère) compared the Assembly's handiwork unfavourably with redemption legislation in force in the neighbouring Duchy of Savoy. A payment of 68 *livres* sufficed to buy out a feudal rent of a *quartel* of wheat in Savoy, whereas the Assembly attached a price of 105 *livres* to the same due. The municipality of Brangues (Isère) demonstrated with facts and figures that 'The terms of the decree are infinitely to the advantage of the proprietors of rents, and much beyond anything they would themselves have demanded.'[32] These sentiments were echoed by the villagers of Thuellin (Isère), Andéol-en-Dauphiné (Isère), St Martin-La-Brasque (Vaucluse) and Lourmarin (Vaucluse). Meanwhile, in the Ardèche electors gathered together for the purpose of appointing the new department administration in May 1790, took the opportunity to protest against the 'taux de rachat' as well. Reactions were no less vehement in the South West. Once again the most trenchant criticism emanated from those departments such as the Haute-Vienne, the Corrèze, the Cantal, the Lot and the Lot-et-Garonne which had been traversed by peasant mobilisations during the winter of 1789–90. A group of *laboureurs* jointly exploiting a holding in the Lot-et-Garonne informed the luminaries of the Feudal Committee on 30 October 1790 that their farm was worth 12,000 *livres*, but to buy out the dues attached to it at the approved rate would cost 1,040 *livres*. Redemption on such terms made no economic sense, they concluded; 'no one will redeem, we will always have seigneurs, therefore, and consequently your work and the decree which is a sequel to it boils down to nothing'.[33]

Events tended to bear out this gloomy prognosis. The peasantry made little use of the redemption legislation, and so much of the economic fabric of seigneurialism survived, on paper at least, until the summer of 1792. However, it is important to bear in mind that the process of 'rachat' involved the state as much as it involved private seigneurs. In November 1789, the Assembly had assumed legal ownership of all the property and prerogatives of the church. Those prerogatives included the right to a wide range of monetary and harvest dues which the peasant was henceforth expected to pay to the government. Until November 1791 dues formerly owned by ecclesiastical seigneurs were collected by the district authorities within each department, thereafter by a body known as the Régie National de l'Enregistrement. As far as we can tell 'rachats envers la Nation', that is to say the buying out of dues owned by the state, occurred more frequently than the redemption of dues owned by individual seigneurs and there were good reasons for this. The state badly needed the money and offered vassals of ecclesiastical institutions the chance to buy out their obligations in two stages, whereas lay seigneurs viewed the whole exercise with a jaundiced eye and discouraged redemption. Ferradou[34] reckons that 'rachats envers la Nation' were yielding about 900,000 *livres* a month and still rising in May 1792, and he estimates that they were bringing in 12 millions a year. But for how long? No more than two years (June 1790–June 1792) presumably, which produces a maximum possible income of 24 millions from liquidated seigneurial dues. What proportion of the capital value of state-owned dues did this represent? Again there are too many imponderables for a really satisfactory calculation. However, contemporaries 'guesstimated' their value at between 200 and 600 millions, which suggests that the Nation only recouped 12 per cent of the rights which it had acquired at the very most.

The detailed picture seems to confirm these conclusions. In the district of Dijon (Côte-d'Or) dues owing to the Nation were paid pretty regularly until 1793, but the 'rachat' legislation attracted few takers. In the department of the Nord, on the other hand, the district authorities made little attempt to call in such dues and from 1790 they lapsed to all intents and purposes. The peasantry of the Doubs also stopped paying as soon as they realised that the responsible authorities were too preoccupied to take any notice. In none of these departments, therefore, were 'rachats envers la Nation' a significant phenomenon. It would be unwise to discount the effects of the redemption legislation entirely, however, for purchasers of church property, in particular, had every incentive to rid their new acquisitions of seigneurial encumbrances. Payments totalling 33,460 *livres* were made for this purpose in the department of the Yonne during 1791, and 44,044 *livres* were received in the first eight months of 1792. As for the district authorities of Aix-en-Provence (Bouches-du-Rhône), they netted 108,000 *livres* between October 1790 and October 1791.[35] Purchasers of national property tended not to be drawn from the ranks of the peasantry, though, and the great mass of the peasantry were quite unable to take advantage of the decree of 3–9 May 1790. While some attempt may have been made to buy out dues owing to the Nation, the redemption process was virtually stillborn as far as lay seigneurs were concerned. Local studies of the Seine-Inférieure, the Sarthe, the Haute-Vienne, the Gironde and the Charente-Inférieure departments indicate that only a tiny proportion of feudal dues was ever reimbursed. Either the peasantry could not pay the sums prescribed, or, in some cases, they refused to pay on principle. The latter motive appears to have been uppermost in the minds of the active citizens of the village of Lourmarin (Vaucluse) who announced in December 1791 that 'during the twenty-one months since the law on the feudal regime [3–9 May 1790] had been passed, not a single individual had bought out the odious dues with which he was burdened'.[36]

Flashpoints

In the late summer of 1790 the chief executive officer (*procureur général sindic*) for the department of the Haute-Saône replied to a letter he had received from a colleague bewailing the state of the nation: 'Like you', he wrote, 'I deplore the disorder which reigns in the countryside, but calm can only be restored bit by bit.'[37] This candid assessment of the situation serves to remind us that whatever the deputies may have supposed, the rural revolution was only just beginning in 1790. Galvanised by the tenacious myths of 1789 the peasantry were prepared to wage the struggle against feudalism on a broad front, using force to back up more traditional modes of bargaining if the occasion demanded. Petty violence became endemic, but the era of great set-piece mobilisations was far from over as well. Between 1790 and 1792 anti-seigneurial tensions reached flashpoint in five distinct regions: Upper Brittany, the Centre, the Quercy, the Gâtinais and the South East (see map 7).

The conflagration in Upper Brittany broke out in late January 1790, just as the mobilisations in the South West (see pp. 70–1) were beginning to run out of steam. Bands of three to five hundred peasants converged on about thirty châteaux in a triangle of parishes bounded by the three towns of Rennes, Redon and Plöermel. In most respects the resultant disturbances followed the pattern set the previous year. Whole communities appear to have been involved, with the well-to-do elite of peasant farmers playing a full and active role. They were protesting at the failure of the National Assembly to act swiftly on its decisions of 4–11 August, which had encouraged local seigneurs to press ahead with the collection of dues outstanding on the 1789 harvest. Unsurprisingly, therefore, château archives and other repositories of feudal documents were the principal objects of attack, but seigneurs were physically intimidated, too. Many were forced into signing away their rights and reimbursing fines levied years earlier. After a week of dithering, the bourgeois militia of Rennes finally reacted and marched into the countryside to put down the disorders. But the repression was scarcely convincing, for the urban bourgeoisie of the province continued to view the nobility as the principal threat to the revolution. The last serious incident took place in mid-February when the Benedictine abbey of Redon was attacked and burned.

However, almost exactly a year later fresh agrarian disturbances broke out. This time the epicentre lay to the north-west of Rennes, along the border between the departments of the Ille-et-Vilaine and the Côtes-du-Nord. Also the character of the uprisings had changed somewhat. They no longer resembled a largely spontaneous and even festive *jacquerie*, but instead bore the hallmarks of premeditation and organisation. The insurgents took pains to operate within the context of revolutionary legality; often they mobilised as National Guard detachments and they selected their targets with discrimination. The seigneur remained the principal target of popular enmity, but to his credentials as fief owner were added those of potential counter-revolutionary. As in many other parts of the country, the 'traditional' anarchic raid on the château was beginning to

Map 7. Epicentres of rural revolt, 1790–2

Sources: R. Dupuy, *La Garde Nationale et les débuts de la Révolution en Ille-et-Vilaine* (Paris, 1972), p. 186; *Rapport de messieurs J. Godard et L. Robin, commissaires civils envoyés par le Roi dans le département du Lot* (Paris, 1791); M. Vovelle, 'Les Troubles sociaux en Provence', in *Actes du 93e Congrès des Sociétés Savantes: Section d'histoire moderne et contemporaine*, vol. ii (Tours, 1968), pp. 325–72; A.N. DIV 38; DXIV 3, 8, 13

blur into the more disciplined, but no less intimidating, domiciliary visit in search of arms, gunpowder or refractory priests. Nor were the seigneurs simply innocent bystanders in this process of legitimising collective violence: they, too, began to organise. The sight of château battlements bristling with armed retainers and rumours of aristocratic plots served merely to fuel fears of counter-revolution.

Whether these fairly localised disturbances can tell us much about the

broader context of revolution and counter-revolution in Brittany is far
from clear. Donald Sutherland, whose researches have done most to clarify
our understanding of the Breton *chouannerie*, is sceptical.[38] Yet other
historians believe that the stark political geography of the region – the
division into *chouan* and non-*chouan* parishes – can be traced back to
1790. What few historians emphasise sufficiently is the political ambiva-
lence of the peasantry between 1790 and 1793. Impatience with the
Assembly's backsliding on the subject of the seigneurial regime could
kindle both ultra-revolutionary and counter-revolutionary sentiments.
Much depended upon the balance of forces at the local level and the kind
of leadership offered to, or withheld from, the peasantry. Tenant farmers
and *laboureurs* helped to incite the attacks on châteaux in Upper Brittany
in 1790 because they felt that there was something tangible to be gained.
When those hopes were frustrated their loyalties became malleable and
susceptible to manipulation by enemies of the revolution. The point may
be extended to the sharecroppers of the South West, too. Few social groups
had greater grounds for dissatisfaction with the work of the National
Assembly, yet royalist leaders missed the opportunity to focus that dissatisfaction against the revolution. Instead it was sublimated into rural
jacobinism.

But what focused the energies of Breton peasants against the seigneurial
regime? After all, the province was not heavily burdened with dues, compared with other regions. Here we come to the nub of the issue. It is argued
by Donald Sutherland and Tim Le Goff that the peculiarity of Brittany,
indeed of the West as a whole, lay in the fact that it contained a substantial
stratum of comfortably off peasant farmers who leased their holdings
under a variety of quasi-feudal tenures.[39] In Brittany, the commonest of
these was known as *domaine congéable* and it tended to blur the conven-
tional distinction between proprietor and tenant. The proprietor leased the
land to his tenant, but the buildings, crops and fruit trees situated on that
land belonged to the tenant. If the landowner wished to oust his tenant, he
had to buy out the 'edifices' situated on his land. This rarely happened and
consequently the tenant or *domanier* resembled an ordinary, if rather well-
to-do, owner-occupier to all intents and purposes. What brought such
hybrid tenures to the attention of the National Assembly was the fact that
they contained numerous feudal accretions. Indeed, some experts argued
that they were entirely feudal in character and should be considered in the
same light as *mainmorte* and *bordelage*, that is to say abolished outright.
It seems reasonable to suppose, then, that the issue of *domaine congéable*
contributed powerfully to the waves of peasant insurrectionism that
traversed Upper Brittany in 1790 and 1791. Certainly, tenant farmers
bombarded the Feudal Committee with petitions calling for the abolition

of *domaine congéable*, or at least the right to buy the freehold. Between January 1790 and March 1791 when a report was finally submitted to the Assembly, the Committee received at least forty communications on this subject. The report opted for the moderate solution of retaining *domaine congéable* suitably purged of seigneurial obligations. This decision, enshrined in the decree of 7 June–6 August 1791, dashed the hopes of tenants and there can be little doubt that it eroded support for the revolution in the Breton departments. The following year the Legislative Assembly reversed the decision (decree of 27 August 1792) and abolished *domaine congéable* outright. Tenants' prayers were answered and they became the owners of both the land and the 'edifices'. However, this concession to the skilfully orchestrated propaganda of the *domaniers* seems to have come too late to influence the political evolution of the region.

Much less, by contrast, is known about the disaffection which gripped the departments of the Nièvre and the Allier. Fashioned from the old provinces of the Nivernais and the Bourbonnais, these departments offered considerable resistance to harvest dues in 1789 and that resistance was renewed the following year. According to Jean-Baptiste Fauvre who had leased the seigneurial rights of the Prince de Condé, the peasantry adamantly refused to make any kind of payment, even of arrears.[40] However, the picture was complicated by the prevalence throughout the region of a feudal form of tenure known as *bordelage* which subjected vassals to punitive *lods et ventes* should they proceed to sell their holdings. In March 1790 the Assembly abolished *bordelage*, which upset local proprietors, but in a manner which did not fully address the grievances of the peasantry either. Not until August 1792 were the dues which many seigneurs had substituted for *bordelage* finally revoked. This source of disenchantment fused with a long-standing hostility to the *fermiers-généraux* employed by noble and bourgeois landowners (see map 8). These middlemen leased several holdings at once, thereby diminishing the supply of share-crop tenancies available to the poorer peasantry. Having failed to win the incorporation of their grievances in the general *cahiers* of the Third Estate, the sharecroppers returned to the issue the following year. In May and June 1790 disturbances broke out on the occasion of the meeting of the primary assemblies to elect the new district and department administrations. Despite serious clashes between poor peasants and the *fermiers*, the National Assembly took the view that landowners were entitled to lease their land however they pleased and refused to intervene.

After a brief and uneasy calm between March and May 1790, violence broke out afresh in the South West, too. Expectations had been raised to fever pitch by two consecutive years of dearth and the peasantry convinced themselves that all dues had been abolished for ever. The news that this

Map 8. Geography of protests against *fermiers-généraux*
Source: A. Ado, *The Peasant Movement in France during the Great Bourgeois Revolution at the End of the Eighteenth Century* (Moscow, 1971), p. 354

was not so reached villagers just as the 1790 harvest was about to be gathered in and it caused a ripple of anger to spread across the region. However, the worst of the violence was confined to the Quercy – now renamed the department of the Lot – where the newly elected authorities inflamed the situation by issuing a proclamation reminding country dwellers of their responsibilities early in August. Tension increased as vassals riposted with complaints against false grain measures and demands to see title-deeds. The following month the traditional symbols of insurrection – gibbets and maypoles – began to go up in the villages around

Cahors and in November armed expeditions against the châteaux resumed in earnest. Panic struck; the department authorities despatched desperate appeals to Paris, while the district administrators of Gourdon called in troops to sweep the countryside clear of seditious symbols. This latter decision proved ill-advised, for, on 5 December, a peasant army 5,000 strong converged on the district capital of Gourdon and systematically pillaged the houses of seigneurs and other wealthy inhabitants over a period of three days. Thereafter law and order collapsed in most of the department and that year the bishop forbade midnight Mass and the ringing of bells for fear of exacerbating the situation.

Meanwhile, rumours that over thirty châteaux had been burned in the department of the Lot finally galvanised the National Assembly into action. On 24 December the deputies appointed two of their number, Jacques Godard and Léonard Robin, to travel to Cahors with the mission of pacifying the peasantry. Their report, compiled after five weeks of meticulous enquiries in the department, provides the best account we have of popular reactions to the legislation of March–May 1790.[41] Several points emerge from this highly professional enquiry into the sources of rural disorder. Here, as elsewhere, the peasantry succeeded in winning control of the smaller municipalities and they used their hegemony to organise resistance to the continued payment of seigneurial dues. Integral to this process was the National Guard which proved as unreliable in the Lot as it had in Brittany. During the Gourdon insurrection, the National Guard defected to the side of the peasant insurgents. In consequence, the local nobility organised vigilante patrols for their own defence, which only made matters worse. One such group assembled at the château of Aucastel near the town of Lauzerte on 17 December and the following day it opened fire on a crowd in the *bourg* of Montcuq which touched off further disorders. Self-fulfilling fears of an aristocratic plot seized hold of the peasantry and fresh attacks were launched against châteaux in the district of Lauzerte during December 1790 and January 1791.

The report also sheds precious light on the nature of feudalism in this the most heavily seigneurialised region of France. 'In some localities', the commissioners recorded, 'the peasant pays to the seigneur a third of his harvest, that is to say three bushels out of every nine.' They uncovered *prima facie* evidence of a virulent seigneurial reaction, too: 'the surcharges are a half and even two-thirds of the sums specified in the original title-deeds'.[42] This, apparently, was the reason many peasants were refusing payment of non-redeemed dues, but the commissioners quickly discovered that there was no single standard of behaviour in these matters. Few communities, if any, offered explicit resistance to the concept of seigneurial dues, instead they rebelled against the manifold abuses which had accompanied their collection. In the district of Gourdon a minority of villages had settled their obligations arising from the 1789 harvest and those same villages were prepared to settle accounts for the 1790 harvest, too. However, the vast majority had, at the time of writing of the report in January 1791, made no payment in either 1789 or 1790. In the district of Figeac, by contrast, the movement of resistance was less firmly entrenched. Having received deputations from eighty-three of the ninety munici-palities, the commissioners concluded that many peasants had, in fact, paid their harvest dues in 1789 and 1790, but were very unlikely to show such forbearance in 1791. The punitively high redemption price seems to have been the focus of popular anger in this area, although many villages expressed vigorous demands for the partition of common land (see p. 144) as well. Complaints against overcharging were most heavily con-centrated in the district of Lauzerte and here scarcely anyone had paid dues either in 1789 or in 1790.

The disturbances in the Lot subsided, temporarily, in mid-January 1791 and the commissioners returned to Paris to pen their report. But already trouble was brewing in other parts of the country and most notably in the Gâtinais. This region deserves particular attention because it witnessed the most sustained and coherent resistance to the feudal legislation of the National and Legislative Assemblies. The Gâtinais is not easy to situate, for it forms a rather indistinct geographical entity straddling the southern rim of the Paris basin. In the west the town of Pithiviers marks its outer extremity, while that of Sens marks the frontier with Champagne to the east. Historically speaking, however, the Gâtinais coalesced around its two ancient capitals of Nemours and Montargis. In 1790, their status was preserved although the region as a whole was partitioned: Nemours became a district capital of the department of the Seine-et-Marne and Montargis became a district capital of the department of the Loiret (see map 9). Finally, a few villages in the eastern Gâtinais ended up in the department of the Yonne.

As a region the Gâtinais produced cereal crops which were subject to extensive harvest dues. The local nobility were not numerous, but they were powerful. Most relied heavily on seigneurial rights for their income; for example, the seigneur of the village of Gironville (Seine-et-Marne) took a harvest tax of one-twelfth on 19,000 hectares of peasant tenures.[43] Nor were they slow to maximise their rights when the opportunity arose: the *cahier* compiled by the Third Estate of the *bailliage* of Nemours com-plained that the *champart* was being extended to new land on the eve of the revolution. It also grumbled about *portabilité*, about *lods et ventes* and about the escalating burden of royal taxation. The state should organise the liquidation of seigneurial dues – a point which was echoed in the *cahier*

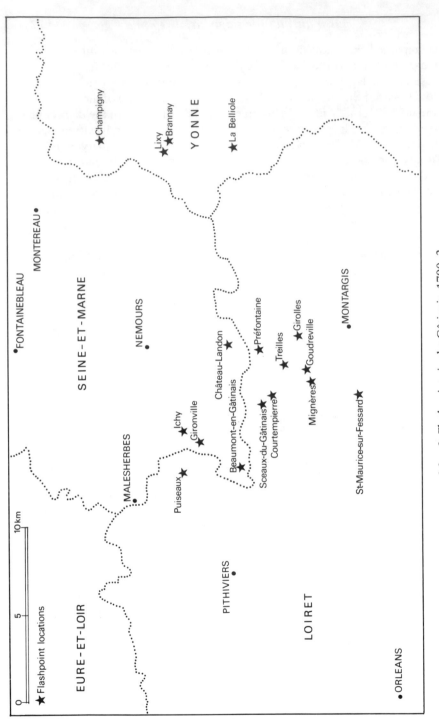

Map 9. Flashpoints in the Gâtinais, 1790–2
Sources: A.N. DIV 38; DXIV 2, 5, 10, 11, 12, 38

penned by the Third Estate of the *bailliage* of Montargis. Similar complaints were voiced by the Gâtinais parishes enclaved within the Yonne. Nearly all their arable paid a *champart* of one-twelfth, explained the villagers of Brannay, while demanding the right to commute their obligations into a cash payment. At La Belliole the parishioners grumbled that they were not permitted to remove their share of the harvest from the fields until they had transported the yield of the *champart* to the barns of the cathedral chapter of Sens. Both villages were to emerge as epicentres of rural revolt in 1790.

This, then, is the context of resentment which made the Gâtinais a flash-point. Harvest dues were not especially onerous, but they were widespread and accompanied by irritants such as *portabilité*. They seemed the more intolerable because state taxation was taking an ever-growing slice of peasant surplus, or to put it in the words addressed to the king by the Third Estate of Nemours: 'if you are going to take what remains of our income, at least relieve us of what we pay to our seigneurs, for we must have something'.[44] The news that the Assembly expected erstwhile vassals to buy out annual and casual dues virtually coincided with the start of the harvest in July 1790 and it provoked a cycle of resistance and violence which escalated steadily over the next two years. As elsewhere, the peasantry fell back on the tactic of calling for the presentation of title-deeds, but with a degree of sophistication unmatched by any other part of the kingdom at this time. In place of the atavistic violence against châteaux practised in Brittany and the South West, they carried out pre-emptive strikes against the barns of fief owners and tithe collectors. In place of the rather primitive millennial utterances which had formed the common currency of revolt in 1789, they circulated lampoons and brochures containing reasoned arguments against the persistence of the seigneurial regime: 'Should we pay the *champart* because we have always paid it?' went one; 'This is tantamount to saying that theft is permissible because it has long been tolerated.'[45]

Although the sedition was by no means universal throughout the Gâtinais during the summer of 1790, it threw the newly appointed authorities onto the defensive. In July the chief executive officer of the Yonne department warned the National Assembly that the disorders over the border in the districts of Nemours and Montargis were threatening to spread like an ink stain. Already, the district of Sens had been contaminated. Any show of force would trigger a general insurrection. This was a point which fief owners refused to accept and they railed repeatedly against the timidity of district and department administrators. Joseph Amyot of Treilles near Château-Landon (Seine-et-Marne), for instance, wrote several letters during the autumn of 1790 to complain about the studied inactivity of the local authorities. The chief culprits, he alleged, were the small rural municipalities whose peasant members simply refused to enforce the law.[46]

The following year resistance intensified. Rural legal practitioners fanned the flames of popular discontent with wilful misinterpretations of the Assembly's decrees; suits against defaulters clogged up the courts; bailiffs could not be persuaded to serve writs; and the payment of dues owing to the Nation tailed off. Former seigneurs like Amyot found themselves a prey to roaming gangs of peasants intent upon destroying the hated residue of seigneurialism (see p. 107). In the absence of the fief owners, their agents bore the brunt of popular anger. The irate villagers of Ichy drove out the local collector of feudal dues and forced him to seek refuge in the neighbouring town of Puiseaux (Loiret). By the spring of 1792 the situation had become critical. With food shortages mobilising the rural population of the Beauce, a vast crescent-shaped swathe of countryside to the south of Paris seemed on the brink of insurrection. Both the seigneurs and the insurgent peasantry redoubled their efforts to win the sympathy of the Legislative Assembly. Writing as the unofficial spokesman of the fief owners of the region, Amyot urged the deputies to revise the body of legislation pertaining to feudalism, but in a repressive direction. He proposed that seigneurs be permitted to repossess peasant tenures if liabilities outstanding from the 1790 and 1791 harvests had not been settled by May 1792. This was a preposterous idea, but at least Amyot diagnosed the essence of the problem: the legislation of March–May 1790 had failed and the Assembly's willingness to defend it was weakening. The rural population grasped as much, too. Early in May the extraparliamentary pressure on the Legislative Assembly to cut the Gordian knot of feudalism became intense. In the Loiret some thirty Gâtinais parishes jointly drafted a petition airing their grievances and nominated delegates to bear it to Paris. Invited to address the assembled deputies, the delegates vigorously denounced the terms of redemption and called for a law obliging landowners to produce their title-deeds forthwith. The episode caused a stir of anticipation throughout the region and it did much to prepare the way for the decree of 18 June 1792.

What made the implacable resistance of the peasantry of the Gâtinais even more disturbing was the fact that it seemed to fit into an unfolding pattern. The beleaguered Legislative Assembly found itself an impotent witness to a spring offensive against the trappings of seigneurialism. In January and February 1792 came reports of fresh outbreaks of château-burning in the South West. As usual the troubled department of the Lot provided the spark. In March the locus of peasant activism shifted to the adjacent department of the Cantal where political agitators (see pp. 214–15) incited the rural population to attack châteaux in the neighbourhood of Aurillac. Here as elsewhere, the peasantry used the symbols of the new order – the municipalities and the National Guard – against those of the old. Early in April, just as the Feudal Committee was tabling a draft law to abolish casual dues, further reports arrived of château-burning a little to the south in the department of the Aveyron. The Lot, the Cantal and the Aveyron formed a tight wedge of territory which had long experienced the full panoply of seigneurial excesses.

However, the major arena for agrarian violence during the spring and summer of 1792 lay not in the South West, but in the South East. Disturbances began in the Ardèche in mid-March and spread along the southern flanks of the Massif Central to the Gard. In the first few days of April two dozen châteaux were attacked in this latter department alone. Towers and dovecotes were demolished, armorial bearings disfigured and title-deeds seized for public burning. Intimidation, pillage, forced renunciations and the repayment of fines were routine. Yet the violence overflowed the narrow confines of anti-seigneurialism. The insurgents responded to shortages and spiralling prices by intervening in the market-place to fix the price of grain, they broke down enclosures, invaded the commons, punished usurpers, agitated for the partition of village pastures and wastes and called for the sale of *biens nationaux* in small parcels. In short, anti-seigneurialism became a cover under which to advance the socio-economic programme of the poor peasantry. But the risings in the South East also reflected the polarisation of political opinion in the countryside: the image of the seigneur as feudal exploiter was yielding to the image of the seigneur as counter-revolutionary plotter. In this region, at least, the anti-seigneurial instincts of the common people provided the perfect constituency for rural jacobinism (see pp. 214–16). Again, however, the equation of anti-seigneurialism and ultra-revolution should not be taken for granted. That it came about in the South East owed much to the waves of revolutionary energy pulsating from the cities of the Rhône valley and the Languedoc plain. During the spring and summer of 1792 village jacobin clubs mushroomed all over the region and their propaganda sedulously cultivated the notion that all the former seigneurs (and refractory priests) were potential counter-revolutionaries. This convenient identification, which was expanded to embrace bourgeois landowners as circumstances required, provided the political justification for renewed disorders beginning in August. The epicentre of revolt shifted eastwards to Lower Provence (the Comtat, Bouches-du-Rhône, Var) where the violence continued unabated until the autumn.

The so-called *jacquerie* of the South East poses problems of interpretation which cannot be resolved in the context of this chapter. After three years of revolution, seigneurialism had lost its primacy as the single overriding issue motivating peasant participation in the revolution. Instead, the war on feudalism had diversified to accommodate a host of objectives ranging from the destruction of enclosures to the abolition of ground rent in all its forms. The concurrent struggle to retain customary rights over the land will be explored in the following chapter, but our discussion of the dismantling of the seigneurial regime invites several concluding observations. First of all, the myth that the peasant uprisings of the summer of 1789 procured the demise of feudalism in France needs to be laid to rest. The National Assembly's 'destruction' of the feudal regime between 4 and 11 August was largely nominal. In the years that followed country dwellers tried repeatedly to abolish feudalism from below, but with negligible success. If any single event can be credited with accomplishing this feat, it was the Parisian and *fédéré* insurrection of 10 August 1792. Only then did the Legislative Assembly rush through the necessary legislation. The second point which must be emphasised is the caution which the peasantry used in their manoeuvrings against the seigneurial regime. Notwithstanding the violent episodes analysed in this section, the bulk of the rural population exhibited an ambivalent attitude towards the trappings of seigneurialism, refusing to believe that a clean break with the past was feasible. Rare were cases of outright refusal to pay dues. Rarer still were reasoned statements against the very principle of payment. In February 1791 several villages in the department of the Oise called for the abolition of *cens* and *champart* without compensation and the sale of all seigneurial property, but such demands were unprecedented and they brought a stern rebuke from the *Amis de la Constitution* of the neighbouring town of Beauvais.

A final point concerns the effectiveness of abolition. Did it make any difference in the long term? Most historians have been content to echo the opinion of Marc Bouloiseau who concludes that 'Generally speaking the peasant who worked a small plot and lived off family-run mixed farming was constantly suffering from lack of money, so that he derived no benefits from the revolution.'[47] It is true that the tithe often survived in leases, and in the small village of La Prétière (Doubs) the descendants of the original collector were still trying to call in the arrears for 1789 as late as 1805. But this verdict is far too pessimistic. It overlooks the fact that abolition seriously depleted the incomes of the nobility. The decree of 17 July 1793 on its own wiped out 100 million *livres* of feudal rents according to governmental estimates.[48] Such losses implied a corresponding gain – a gain unevenly distributed within the peasantry, to be sure. Owner-exploiters did best, but the disappointments of tenants and landless labourers should not be exaggerated. Farm rentals responded first and foremost to the laws of supply and demand and it is far from certain that they rose in strict proportion to the value of the tithe and feudal dues. In any case, the galloping inflation of 1795–7 soon enabled tenants with leases payable in cash to redress the balance. The agricultural proletariat, it is true, received meagre pickings by comparison. But in regions where *corvées* and *banalités* had remained in force up to the revolution they, too, had every reason to be thankful for the passing of the seigneurial regime.

Chapter 5

The land settlement: collective rights versus agrarian individualism

The land settlement of the French Revolution was a compromise. Contemporaries imagined that the sale of church property and the confiscated estates of *émigré* noblemen, plus the clearing of wastes and the division of common land, had brought into being a class of freehold peasant proprietors. That belief became a key component of the nineteenth-century republican myth and it was not subjected to serious historical analysis until the start of the present century. As a result, we now know that peasant land ownership was well entrenched before 1789 (see p. 7). All the revolution did was to accelerate existing trends, but the transformation was scarcely dramatic because the quantity of property changing hands represented only a small percentage of the total land surface of the country. More important, as far as the bulk of country dwellers was concerned, was the issue of collective rights over private property. Here, too, the achievements of the revolutionaries can only be described as a compromise. The royal edicts of the 1760s and 1770s limiting *vaine pâture* and promoting enclosures pointed the way, but the revolutionaries failed to capitalise on them. The storm of agrarian protest in 1789 and 1790 taught prudence, and the long-awaited laws to abolish fallow- and stubble-grazing failed to materialise. In this sphere as in that of feudal dues, the gap between rhetoric and reality remained palpable. 'The revolution imposed certain ideas of individual liberty' including 'unrestricted rights of property', argues Donald Sutherland,[1] but it must be stressed that this was an aspiration which the peasantry successfully resisted for much of the revolutionary decade.

If most historians would agree that the agrarian policies pursued by the revolutionaries smacked of compromise, there is less common ground regarding the long-term significance of those policies, however. Georges Lefebvre's singular insight of an 'autonomous' peasant revolution is predicated on the notion that the rural masses were concerned, above all else, to defend their traditional grazing, gleaning and wood-cutting rights. His implication is that the poor peasantry perceived the existence of collective rights to be more relevant to their condition than the prospect of acquiring a freehold title to microscopic plots of land. Whereas wealthy tenant farmers and *laboureurs* (Lefebvre's rural bourgeoisie) were individualistic, acquisitive and proto-capitalist in outlook, rural proletarians were collectivist, more interested in use-rights than in freehold rights, and consequently anti-capitalist in demeanour. This is the sense of his remark that the peasant revolution was 'autonomous in terms of its origins, its proceedings, its crises and its tendencies'.[2] The peasantry were profoundly ambivalent about the main capitalist thrust of the revolution, but capable of acting in concert with bourgeois revolutionaries when conditions required as much.

This interpretation satisfied a generation of scholars whose principal source for the rural revolution was *Les Paysans du Nord*. Albert Soboul criticised Lefebvre's system of social classification, but in his textbook history of the revolution published in 1962 (*Précis d'histoire de la Révolution française*) he adhered steadfastly to his mentor's anatomy of the peasantry. The poor remained attached to collective rights and hostile to advances in the direction of individual land holding. They did not share the conception of property espoused by noble or bourgeois landowners and, 'if the capitalist middle class claimed economic liberty, the popular classes within society showed a profoundly anti-capitalist prejudice'.[3] Stripped of dogmatic wrappings, this scenario has one great merit: it acknowledges the role of collective practices in the daily lives of millions of country dwellers. But it seems to underplay the extent to which the ambition to own property burgeoned in peasant hearts. The land-hungry peasantry of the cereal plains around Paris wanted two things which were probably incompatible. They wanted private property unencumbered by either servitudes or feudal dues, but at the same time they wished to retain the full range of collective rights over the lands of their well-to-do neighbours. In this they resembled the *sans-culottes* who called for price controls on foodstuffs, but expected the products of their own labours to be exempted.

The dissatisfaction with Lefebvre's formulation of the peasant revolution remained latent until a Soviet historian, Anatoli Ado, published a full-length study of the agrarian history of the revolution in 1971.[4] Ado and a younger generation of historians have concentrated their fire on Lefebvre's contention that the bourgeois and the peasant revolutions were out of step. He is right, they declare, to insist on the fact that the peasant revolution was autonomous, but wrong in supposing that it was anti-capitalist. In place of Lefebvre's pragmatism, we are offered a more ideologically coherent view of the revolution. Albert Soboul rallied to this new position during the final years of his academic career and his renewed interest in rural history encouraged a revival of reearch into the peasantry which had languished since Lefebvre's death. That research began to bear fruit in the early 1980s and it offered the first substantial revision of our understanding of the peasant revolution in over fifty years. Inspired by Ado, Soboul and his pupils have reformulated the notion of compromise which is the lynch-pin of Lefebvre's interpretation. Partial satisfaction of the land hunger of the poor peasantry turned them into a class of embryonic capitalists. The potential for the development of French agriculture in a capitalist direction lay within the bosom of the small producer, not the large landowner, be he noble, bourgeois or peasant. If agrarian capitalism showed few signs of precocity on the morrow of the revolution, this was not because of 'what the small peasantry have been able to impose on the bourgeois revolution, but because of what they have been unable to wrest from it':[5] that is to say the destruction of large property and the peculiarly anti-capitalist mentality of the *rentier*.

Advocates of this interpretation have dubbed it 'la voie paysanne' (the peasant route), in contrast to 'la voie anglaise' (the English route) in which agricultural development was pioneered by improving landlords. In truth, the theory addresses far larger issues than simply the matter of how peasants behaved during the French Revolution. Nevertheless, it raises questions which cannot be ignored. The revisionists rightly draw attention to the fact that the existence of large-scale farming was not bound to be conducive to capitalist advance. Much depended on the socio-cultural context, and in France most landlords remained incorrigibly conservative in outlook. To be sure, some proprietors had spotted the capitalist potential of the seigneurial demesne, but in general seigneurialism buttressed the *rentier* lifestyle rather than the capitalist lifestyle at the end of the *ancien régime*. Even so, serious objections can be raised against the scenario which presents the small peasantry as the economically thrusting class. To start with it simply leaves out of account the trenchant comments of Georges Lefebvre on the subject of collective rights. Perhaps the retention of customary rights over private property was not incompatible with the growth of a capitalist vocation among the lesser peasantry, after all. But the existence of this ambitious and progressive-minded lesser peasantry whose appetite for land had been whetted by the revolution has still to be demonstrated. The programme of research sponsored by Albert Soboul has uncovered clear evidence of organised movements of poor peasants seeking a share of the land in the villages of Picardy and the Ile-de-France.[6] These movements suggest that Lefebvre's profile of peasant revolution is too tightly drawn, for it can be argued that the farm hands and day labourers working the openfields of the Paris basin were petty bourgeois and capitalist in outlook. But were they typical of poor peasants in general? The pattern of the social structure on the cereal plains cannot be extended to the rest of France; nor, indeed, can that of the agitation for thoroughgoing land reform which developed in this region during the revolution. A more fundamental methodological objection arises, however. The case for 'la voie paysanne' is based on 'ifs' and 'buts'; if the poor peasantry had contrived to obtain a larger share of the land, they would surely have acquired the spirit of capitalism. As this chapter will demonstrate, egalitarian land division failed to materialise and, consequently, the scenario of peasant-led agrarian capitalism was never put to the test.

Lefebvre, of course, doubts whether the bourgeoisie and the peasant masses even spoke the same language on the subject of property and it is worth considering his view in more detail. The latter, he maintains, had a 'customary conception' of property which acknowledged the rights of the private landowner provided that they were not exercised to the detriment of the community.[7] Landowners were expected to behave responsibly: that is, to allow gleaning, stubble-grazing and if they owned forests, woodcutting. Enclosure was regarded as a hostile act, as was any attempt to exclude the common flock from meadows after the first haying. The village community also looked to its wealthier members for a steady supply of work: woe betide the landowner who hired non-local gangs of harvesters, or who engrossed the plots of his lesser neighbours. Tenants and sharecroppers did their utmost to impede the growth of a market economy in land, too. Lefebvre describes the custom of *mauvais gré* which tenant farmers in the Cambrésis used against proprietors in order to hold down the price of their leases.[8] Unable to oust his tenant without risking the wrath of the community, the landowner was forced to accept a considerable diminution of his property rights. Sharecroppers employed similar tactics, but with less success. Proprietors riposted by putting their lands in the hands of *fermiers-généraux* who sub-let to the peasantry on disadvantageous terms (see p. 12).

Nevertheless, the distinction between customary and freehold conceptions of property was not hard and fast, as Lefebvre is prepared to acknowledge. Indeed, the definition of what passed for legitimate property was being challenged on several fronts as the *ancien régime* drew to a close. In the agrarian sphere, the physiocrat-inspired edicts of the 1760s and 1770s struck the first serious blow against customary conceptions. The royal edicts on the clearing of wastes (1761–6), for instance, permitted individuals to occupy and cultivate land which had been abandoned for more than forty years. More important, the partition of commons gave the peasantry a foretaste of private property in some districts. In Flanders the allotment of marshes and common pastures into 'portions ménagères' proved immensely popular (see pp. 18–19). True, the plots were not conceded in perpetuity, but they awakened the proprietorial instinct in the poor peasantry and foreshadowed the reforms of the revolutionary legislatures. After 1789 some beneficiaries of 'portions ménagères' began to agitate for permission to bequeath them, that is to say for freehold property rights. Even so, the revolution revealed the confusion that reigned in men's minds on the subject of property rights. While the peasantry of Flanders campaigned for a secure title to their newly acquired plots of land, identical peasants in other parts of the country were busily reasserting the claims of the community over wastes and commons. Those who had cleared land at the invitation of the government in the 1760s now found themselves being treated as little better than squatters. In the Eure the poor peasantry made a determined effort to extend the frontiers of the public domain, accusing *défricheurs* of having annexed common land on the self-serving pretext that the land in question had once been subject to *vaine pâture*. But it was not just the peasantry whose perception of property showed signs of elasticity. Many members of the rural elite retained a vestigial commitment to the notion that commons and wastes formed the patrimony of the poor and should be held in trust for each succeeding generation. In the Calvados, the Agricultural Society expressed sympathy for this point of view when the wholesale division of common land reappeared on the political agenda in 1791.

Notwithstanding the criticisms directed against it, Lefebvre's contention that the rural masses clung to their collective rights and thereby forced the revolutionaries into a posture of compromise still has operative value. 'It is a mistake', he writes, 'to attribute to all eighteenth-century peasants the ideas of the rural bourgeoisie on the subject of property.'[9] His is an argument for social differentiation. The danger of the alternative 'voie paysanne' hypothesis is that, sooner or later, it elides the various fractions of the peasantry under a petty bourgeois and proto-capitalist banner.[10] Lefebvre has been taken to task for failing to allow sufficiently for the property-owning ambitions of the poor peasantry and recent research into the agrarian movements gripping the plains around Paris lends weight to this objection. But the criticism can only be one of emphasis, for a close reading of *Les Paysans du Nord* suggests that the author readily acknowledges that popular conceptions of property rights were far from static. In the conclusion to his great work, Lefebvre comments: 'the rural masses were not hostile to the principle of individual property, but they strictly limited it and remained very attached to customary conceptions'.[11]

The Rural Code

The confusion over property rights made a definitive legal statement fixing the rights and obligations of all members of the rural community a matter of top priority. That statement was voted on 28 September 1791 as one of the last acts of the National Assembly and it was sanctioned by the monarch on 6 October. Containing ninety-two articles, the decree became known, somewhat inappropriately, as the Rural Code and it provides the juridical basis for the 'historic compromise' between the bourgeoisie and the peasantry. Despite many attempts at reform, it proved one of the most durable items of revolutionary legislation. The basic provision for collective grazing remains in force to this day.

Conflict over enclosures and the commons had already alerted country dwellers to the need for some kind of 'rural code' at the end of the *ancien régime*. In 1787 controller-general Calonne ordered a fresh enquiry into the practice of *vaine pâture*, and a number of the *cahiers* expressed the wish to have the reciprocal rights and responsibilities of those who owned or worked upon the land clearly defined in a sort of rural catechism or breviary. The events of the summer and autumn of 1789 increased the sense of urgency, for the peasantry took matters into their own hands. As we have seen, they viewed the mobilisations against the châteaux as an opportunity, not only to destroy rent rolls, but to destroy hedges and ditches as well. In any case, the perpetrators of seigneurial reaction and the perpetrators of enclosures were often one and the same. But the poor peasantry, at least, were not content simply to break down fences; theirs was a plea for wholesale agrarian revolution. That revolution within a revolution displayed intermingled characteristics of individualism and collectivism. Massive, illicit, indeed anarchic, clearing of land proved its most individualistic trait. Arthur Young marvelled at the determination with which a piece of waste land belonging to the Duc de Liancourt was being prepared for cultivation: 'I saw some men very busily at work upon it, hedging it in, in small divisions; levelling, and digging, and bestowing much labour for so poor a spot.' Enquiring as to the reason for this effort, he learned that 'the poor were the nation; that the waste belonged to the nation'.[12] This encounter occurred in January 1790; in subsequent years land clearance became an obsession, and one which was pursued without thought for the future.

And yet the individualistic reflex forms only part of the picture. The poor and semi-landless peasantry were above all concerned to vindicate their traditional collective rights. In some areas this meant turning the clock back: from the earliest days of the revolution, reports Lefebvre, the enclosure edict (of 1771) became a 'dead letter' in the Nord.[13] This was not altogether surprising, for between 1789 and 1791 no one was quite sure whether the agrarian legislation of the old regime was still in force. But landowners complained that enclosures established a decade and more before the revolution were being smashed down, too. The outlook for proprietors seemed bleak and likely to become bleaker still as the 1790 hay harvest approached. Anxious administrators bombarded the committees of government with requests for advice. From the Ardennes came the warning in June that the peasantry were likely to ignore the enclosure edicts applicable to Lorraine and the Barrois (1767, 1769) and to drive their stock into meadows after the first haying. Similar fears were voiced in the Saône-et-Loire, the Yonne, the Loir-et-Cher, the Eure-et-Loir and the Calvados. The villagers of Clesles in the Marne announced on 30 May 1790 that they were going to share out the hay crop grown on the commons 'into equal portions between all the inhabitants without distinction'.[14] Hitherto, the wealthy had enforced a pro-rata division linked to taxation. In this instance, the peasantry were divided: nearly all those voting for an egalitarian distribution were *manœuvriers* save for a sprinkling of *laboureurs*, whereas the sixteen inhabitants who opposed the change were *laboureurs* to a man. This flexing of popular muscles brought other victories in its train, too. As the season for auctioning tithe-collecting rights came round, villagers in the Nord used *mauvais gré* to deter outside bidders and to win the contract for themselves. Such pressure reduced the lease for the tithe rights of the Chapter of Tournai by more than two-thirds.

It is clear, then, that the peasantry expected the revolution to usher in a series of agrarian reforms. But so did rural proprietors. The piecemeal and rather half-hearted edicts of the 1760s and 1770s had failed to satisfy either party. In those regions where the ban on enclosure had been lifted, the peasantry harboured a permanent grudge against the old regime. Yet landowners had been dismayed by the failure of the monarchy to press home the reforming initiative with laws applicable throughout the length and breadth of the kingdom. They wanted to see an end to *vaine pâture* and a privatisation of the commons, and they looked to the revolution to complete the transition to agrarian individualism. For all the popular fury against enclosures, these hopes did not immediately appear unrealistic. After all, the National Assembly was packed with rural proprietors. Nearly all the leaders of the patriot party were doctrinaire liberals with little sympathy for customary rights, and revolutionary 'liberté' seemed positively to invite the removal of servitudes burdening the land. This, at least, is how landowners interpreted the events of 1789. They argued that the legislation 'destroying' feudalism was incomplete and unbalanced without a comparable body of laws abolishing common grazing, gleaning, wood-cutting, access to meadows after hay-making and so on. If the peasantry were going to be allowed to buy out their feudal obligations, why should proprietors not be permitted to buy out the right of *vaine pâture*, asked the Comte de Lévis in a petition despatched to the Feudal

Committee in March 1790?[15] The logic was deceptively simple, as the deputies soon discovered.

Aware of the need to pacify the countryside, the Assembly wasted no time in setting up a special commission to tackle the question. It was headed by Heurtaut de Lamerville, deputy for the nobility of the Berry and a substantial landowner, and was made up of members delegated from the eight permanent committees of the legislature. Their labours resulted in a draft proposal which was submitted in August 1790. This initiative seems to have satisfied no one, for it was not until June 1791 that the parliamentary debate on the issue began. Then the discussion was interrupted by the king's flight and the subsequent crisis within the patriot party, and only in September was a text agreed and enacted. Little information is available on the reasons for this long delay, but it is not difficult to guess at the causes. To start with, the deputies disagreed on the wisdom of 'general' rural laws. Merlin de Douai, in particular, doubted whether it would be possible to frame legislation sufficiently flexible to accommodate the variety of agrarian conditions current in the kingdom, and he categorically rejected the suggestion that such legislation be given the status of a code. His position reflected that of the bureaucrats of the old monarchy who had been forced to abandon the grandiose notion of uniform and mandatory legislation two decades earlier.

While jurists like Merlin distrusted both the theory and the practice of 'universal rural laws',[16] other deputies stumbled on details such as how, when and whether to abolish collective rights. In truth, though, the issue of collective rights was more than a detail: it was crucial to the whole exercise. Virtually all the members of the National Assembly agreed that *vaine pâture* made a nonsense of the prevailing concept of freedom and impeded agricultural productivity. As an earnest of their intentions in this respect, they proclaimed that 'the territory of France is free like the persons who inhabit it'[17] – another of those utterances which was transparently false, but highly revealing of the collective state of mind. What divided the deputies was the matter of timing and tactics: over half the land of France was subject to the centuries-old custom of free grazing; never before had abolition been attempted and the tide of popular opinion was firmly opposed to any such move. Acknowledging these objections, a substantial body of parliamentarians was still prepared to brazen out the storm of protest that any curtailment of collective rights would surely provoke and the first draft proposal submitted by Heurtaut de Lamerville abolished *vaine pâture* to all intents and purposes. Wiser counsels prevailed and the report was thrown out. Not for the first time the Assembly was left with a policy which was rhetorically 'correct', but in practical terms incoherent.

Buffeted by events, it set about dealing with agrarian problems on a piece-meal basis. As the tide of popular reaction threatened to engulf the modest innovations of the 1760s and 1770s, the deputies threw their weight behind the enclosure edicts. In June 1790 the Assembly reaffirmed the legislation denying the common flock access to meadows which had been enclosed, and yet a couple of months later it urged local officials to use their authority to safeguard gleaning rights – described as the 'patrimony of the poor'.[18]

By the time discussion of agrarian reforms resumed on 2 September, the idea of a code had been abandoned and with it the enthusiasm for a total recasting of property relationships. For all its provenance, the law of 28 September–6 October 1791 was a conservative measure: the decisive liberal break-through on the issue of collective rights failed to materialise. The rights of *vaine pâture* and *parcours* were upheld, providing always that they were founded in law or custom which generally tended to be the case. It is true that the latter right was dubbed 'provisional' as though the revolutionaries intended to modify their decision as circumstances per-mitted; nevertheless, the *droit de parcours* remained in force for another century. Improbably, therefore, two key institutions of peasant farming survived virtually unscathed. On the other hand, the right to enclose and thereby remove land from the jurisdiction of *vaine pâture* was vindicated in terms which admitted of no restriction. Also, landowners won the right to grow whatever crops they pleased and the right to withdraw their stock from the common herd. However, careful limits were affixed to the right of *troupeau séparé*, while the landless poor who contributed nothing to the village stock of grazing land were none the less allowed to keep up to six sheep and a cow with calf in the *troupeau commun*.

As can be seen, the so-called Rural Code represented a compromise between the competing claims of the landowning interest and the peasantry. Far from dismantling the status quo, the revolutionaries endorsed it while making provision for piecemeal change at a future date. In effect, their pragmatism overcame their ideological loyalties. Not that the reform was billed as such, of course: on the contrary, the revolutionary bourgeoisie hailed it as a further step towards the reconquest of liberty. But nobody was deceived for long: in 1805 an anonymous official of the Ministry of the Interior passed a definitive judgement in the matter. 'The law of 6 October 1791', he noted, 'has brought little change to the old [regime] legislation.'[19]

Even the concessions enshrined in the law proved something of a dis-appointment to proprietors, for it was one thing to assert a freedom and quite another to enforce it. The peasantry were in no mood to call off their offensive against enclosures, nor did they regard the abolition of compulsory crop rotation as an unmitigated blessing. Landowners who switched from cereal cultivation to fodder crops or vines posed a dual threat to the social and economic fabric of the rural community. They diminished the supply of foodstuffs reaching the market-place and they deprived the poor of work and opportunities for gleaning. Local administrators had to be educated in the new freedoms, too, for controls and interventionism were deeply ingrained bureaucratic habits. In the Aisne, the department authorities took steps in the summer of 1793 forbidding farmers to vary the customary three-year rotation. As the dearth worsened, similar violations of the Rural Code were countenanced all over the North and East. On 9 Pluviôse II (28 January 1794), the administrators of the department of the Meurthe sought permission to uproot vine plantations which had encroached upon the arable.[20]

While the revolution continued on its radical course landowners could do little but await better days. No longer were the poor peasantry content to smash down hedges and drive their mangy stock into private meadows and fields; they began to call for a complete ban on the right to enclose at will enshrined in the Rural Code. 'This law', complained the self-styled *sans-culottes* of the village of Parly (Yonne) in the summer of 1794, 'can only have been made by the rich and for the rich, and at a time when liberty was just a word and equality a wild dream.'[21] Enclosures affected the entire community and therefore could only be sanctioned by the community speaking through the mouthpiece of its municipality. This blurring of individual rights into collective rights was a commonplace of the Year Two (1793–4), but it was not without ambiguity. In reality, the peasantry spoke with several voices, but usually we hear only one at a time. The desperately poor, that is to say the landless or virtually landless peasantry, nearly always demanded the complete restoration of collective rights, but owner-exploiters – who also availed themselves of the label *sans-culotte* – equivocated on the issue of *vaine pâture*. In some districts they threw their weight behind the calls for the maintenance of the traditional agrarian system; in others they welcomed the freedoms asserted in the Rural Code. It all depended on the balance of advantage as determined by the availability of communal grazing land, the prevalence of stock-raising, market opportunities and so forth. Nowhere is this dichotomy more clearly brought out than in a petition addressed to the Convention by the peasant farmers of the district of Brioude (Haute-Loire).[22] Writing in a hyperbolic *sans-culotte* style, the petitioners depicted a situation in which the rich protected their valuable hay fields by means of enclosures, while the poor fought to retain *vaine pâture*. Those in between, namely themselves,

wished to enclose but could not afford the expense. Few peasant cultivators farmed compact holdings, and irregular plots were more costly to
enclose than neat, square fields.

The fate of the meadows, indeed, became the issue on which all parties
put the Rural Code to the test. Traditionally, access to meadows was
denied until the proprietor had removed his hay harvest. Thereafter, common grazing of the regrowth (*regain* or *secondes herbes*) was permitted.
Occasionally, however, climatic fluctuations could deprive the landowner
of any profit from his meadows unless he reserved to himself both the first
and the second haying. In such circumstances, *vaine pâture* was temporarily curtailed and meadows were *mis en réserve*, but it happened
infrequently, required the intendant's authorisation and could only be
applied to one-third of the grassland within a community. After 1789 all
precedents evaporated and as we have seen, the issue developed into a symbol of popular revolution. Proprietors imagined that they were henceforth
free to dispose of the entire product of their meadows, even unenclosed
meadows, whereas the great mass of the peasantry drew precisely the
opposite conclusion. Neither side could fully justify its pretensions in law
and the local authorities were left to sort out the claims and counter-claims
as best they could. In the neighbourhood of Bourbonne-les-Bains (Haute-
Marne), for instance, the poor hay harvest of 1792 prompted a proprietorial offensive against the *droit au regain*, but the district administrators took their stand on the custom and insisted that only one-third of
meadowland could be reserved.

All this changed after Thermidor, although it is fair to add that signs of
agrarian reaction were evident even before the fall of Robespierre. Preoccupied with the logistical problems of keeping the armies supplied with
food and fodder, the *montagnard* Convention was already moving
towards some restriction of the *droit au regain*. Nevertheless, the new
economic and social policy was unveiled on 25 Thermidor III (12 August
1795) when the Committee of Public Safety announced that 'the right of
vaine pâture in meadows, even those which are unenclosed, shall be
suspended until after the removal of the second hay harvest by the landowners'.[23] Although the suspension was described as 'provisional', it is
clear that the measure breached both the letter and the spirit of the Rural
Code. The Thermidorians wanted to tip the balance in favour of the
moderate-minded rural proprietors who formed the political bedrock of
their regime. Hence the loaded references in the preamble to 'the livestock
of citizens without land (if any such still exist)' and to the fact that 'even
indigent inhabitants (if there are any still)' would be able to make ends
meet by working on the hay harvest as hired labourers.[24] In any case,

stubble-grazing would soon become available and the deficit could be made good by pasturing stock in the forests.

During the years that followed, this supposedly provisional *arrêté* became semi-permanent. It combined the cardinal virtues of clarifying notions of property, filling the pockets of landowners and answering the growing demand for forage. The turning point in this creeping offensive against customary rights occurred in 1796 when an exceptionally dry spring again played havoc with haymaking. Pleas from several eastern departments persuaded the Executive Directory to reactivate the ban on free grazing (*arrêté* of 19 Thermidor IV [6 August 1796]) and thereafter the *mis en réserve* of meadows became an annual event in many pastoral regions. In a letter addressed to the prefect of the Puy-de-Dôme department on 7 Messidor IX (26 June 1802), the Minister of the Interior smoothed away any lingering doubts about the legality of curtailing *vaine pâture* by arguing that the Committee of Public Safety's ban had been provisional and therefore could not possibly conflict with the Rural Code. This was casuistry of the highest order, but it enabled the minister to conclude: 'you may, therefore, suspend free grazing each year until after the second haying'.[25]

All manner of excuses were wheeled out to justify the exclusion of the common flock from hay meadows: drought, frosts, storms, floods, fodder conservation and even invasion by foreign troops. It seems, too, that the practice of *mis en réserve* varied somewhat. In 1796 the central administration of the Haute-Marne placed a ban on the entire *regain* and from the time of the Consulate onwards this became the norm throughout the department. Elsewhere, it was more usual for free grazing to be curtailed rather than denied outright. The prefects empowered municipal councils to demarcate meadow land in such a way that the proprietors retained two-thirds of the second haying, while the common flock grazed the remaining third. But even this compromise represented a serious dilution of the customary right to regrowths and it incurred the bitter resentment of the poor peasantry. That resentment flared into sporadic agrarian violence in many localities: the villagers of Allègre (Haute-Loire) invaded closed-off meadows on four separate occasions between 1796 and 1802. The first incident took place on 1 Fructidor IV (18 August 1796) when the poorer inhabitants of the commune drove nearly a hundred head of stock into meadows belonging to the justice of the peace, a district judge and the widow of a bourgeois proprietor. Troops were brought in to quell the 'anarchists' and sentences handed down (by the plaintiffs) against the ringleaders. The fines served to deter action in 1797, but the following year the meadows were again invaded as the season for the second haying approached. Further clashes occurred in 1801 and 1802 during which two carters seeking grazing and fodder for their draught animals seem to have played a prominent role. Finally, in 1808, the mayor, himself a party in the dispute, reiterated what he was pleased to call the 'law' and we hear no more of the matter.[26]

Notwithstanding the *ad hoc* measures of mayors, prefects and even the Committee of Public Safety, the law remained that which the deputies of the National Assembly had decided in 1791. Like it or not, the Thermidorians were obliged to organise their onslaught on collective rights within parameters laid down by the Rural Code. It would have been simpler, of course, to have abolished the Code and to have launched the offensive from a less vulnerable position, but this required time and a parliamentary majority. Most deputies appear to have conceded that the decree of 28 September–6 October 1791 got the balance between the bourgeoisie and the peasantry about right. And those who did not tended to share Merlin's preference for piecemeal measures. Nevertheless, reform of the Rural Code was discussed repeatedly in the 1790s, 1800s and 1810s. System-builders continued to deplore the gulf between the pronouncements of the revolutionaries and their modest achievements in the agrarian sphere and the veteran minister François de Neufchâteau spoke for this point of view when he declared: 'In vain has our Rural Code laid down the principle that the soil of France is as free as those who inhabit it, for today the French countryside still bears the traces of disorder and the marks of serfdom.'[27]

For the emerging *notable* class of the Directory, customary rights smacked of barbarism and proposals for the abolition of the *droit de parcours* were placed before the Council of Five Hundred late in 1798. Nothing came of these moves, but Bonaparte's *coup d'état* heralded a thorough review of existing legislation and in 1801 a commission was appointed with the task of examining the Rural Code. This body despatched questionnaires to all the public authorities and in 1807 it submitted a series of recommendations totalling 280 clauses. The freedom of crop rotation was reaffirmed, but in a radical break with tradition the commission proposed the abolition of *parcours* and *vaine pâture* and a series of administrative innovations affecting agricultural labourers. None of these proposals was received with much enthusiasm and in 1808 the jurist and former prefect, Joseph Verneilh Puyraseau, was given the job of revising the report. He began a further round of consultations, the results of which were published piecemeal in 1810, 1811 and 1813. Finally, in August 1814, he produced a definitive scheme comprising 960 articles which stoutly defended the proprietorial interest. By now, however, the Empire had fallen and Verneilh's proposals sank without trace. Improbably, the Rural Code of 1791 had survived and with it the uneasy compromise on the subject of collective rights.

The issue of the commons

The social and economic significance of the commons needs no emphasising. Nor does the fact that they were under attack at the end of the *ancien régime* (see pp. 17–19). The physiocrats viewed the existence of common land in the same light as they viewed the existence of customary rights: both were monuments to rural ignorance which enlightened government was duty-bound to dismantle. Meanwhile, seigneurs were engaged upon their own demolition job. Armed with the *triage* legislation of 1669, they set about annexing portions of common land reckless of the consequences for village communities. The forested commons of the East attracted particular attention: in the future department of the Haute-Marne over 150 villages were locked into struggles with their seigneurs over common land when the revolution broke.[28] Not surprisingly, then, the commons became an issue in 1789. But they have become a source of historiographical debate, too. It has been argued that the movement to divide up the commons was led by the most progressive elements within the peasantry whose acquisition of freehold plots would have nurtured the spirit of capitalism in the countryside.[29] First of all, however, we need to look at the way in which successive revolutionary legislatures tackled the problem.

After the set-piece mobilisations of 1789, no one could have been in any doubt that the peasant revolts against the châteaux were swept along on a tide of agrarian discontent. The National Assembly acknowledged as much when on 11 December it warned communities to refrain from seizing commons of which they had not been in 'physical possession on 4 August 1789'.[30] In so doing it gave notice that a root and branch alteration to the status of common land was not on the immediate political agenda. Instead, the deputies concentrated upon abuses and they added *triage* to the list of seigneurial rights abolished without compensation in March 1790. All this did was to halt seigneurial encroachments on common land; the more important question of past encroachments was left unresolved. Nevertheless, the larger issue would not go away, for educated opinion had been fixated on the debate over the commons for nearly a generation. In August 1790 Heurtaut de Lamerville introduced draft proposals for the Rural Code and they contained a recommendation that the commons be divided among those with use-rights. The principle adopted by the commission sought to conciliate the interests of all parties: in each village half the common would be divided 'par tête', while the remainder would be allocated 'au marc la livre', that is to say in proportion to taxation. The poor could expect to receive a plot, but landowners would obtain a much larger share. Whether such a scheme was actually practicable is debatable, but in any case the whole project was thrown out, as we have seen. On the pretext of the need for more information, the deputies mentally relegated the issue of the commons. A circular letter dated 30 October 1790 invited each commune to deliberate on the most appropriate means of exploiting its common land which was admirably pragmatic, but scarcely what the reformers had intended. Thus it came about that the Rural Code promulgated in October 1791 offered no clarification on the subject of communal property. The issue was still pending, or to be more precise the peasantry had yet to force it into the consciousness of their legislators.

The Legislative Assembly continued to procrastinate, but with diminishing scope for manoeuvre. On 28 November 1791 its Agriculture Committee despatched a further circular letter to all departments seeking to sound out opinion on the merits of dividing up the commons. The results were not encouraging (see table 5), or at least they confirmed the sceptics in their view that agriculture was not a fit subject for universal laws. Some department authorities declared in favour of partition and some against, while a few announced that country dwellers had already begun to divide up the commons without waiting for authorisation. Moreover, those in favour could not agree on a 'mode de partage' (method of division), and those against frequently acknowledged an amount of disagreement at the district and communal level. 'The inhabitants of the countryside have conflicting opinions on how to make the exploitation of the commons more useful to society', reported the administrators of the district of St Dizier (Haute-Marne) on 10 April 1792.[31]

But time was running out: 1792 was a make or break year for the poor peasantry. Shortages had returned and the acquisition of some land – any land – on which to grow cereals or vegetables had never seemed more urgent. In January word reached the Assembly from the Oise that villagers had begun to apportion their commons without further ado. The following month agrarian violence flared in the Lot, a department possessing substantial tracts of common land which had long kindled frictions within the rural community. Claude Duphénieux, a deputy for the Lot, urged the Agriculture Committee to bring forward its report on the 'mode de partage', but another member counselled caution, pointing out that the principle of division had not yet been decided. This exchange captured the essence of the problem. For political as well as economic reasons, nearly all the deputies agreed that continued collective exploitation was undesirable but if some wanted to see the commons sold off, others wanted to see them partitioned between residents. Yet the partisans of division were far from united and their failure to agree on three issues, in particular, served to delay the passage of a bill to alter the status of the commons: should partition be mandatory or optional? Should the plots be distributed 'by head' or 'by household'? And should these allotments be freehold or leasehold?

Late in May Jean-Baptiste Aveline, the president of the Agriculture Committee, presented a report on the commons to the Assembly and it was debated in a rather desultory fashion over the next two months. After months of reflection, the Committee had plumped for the solution of non-mandatory division on a household basis. The argument in favour of apportioning the commons in accordance with taxation was set aside but so, too, was that of the radicals who had been campaigning for a 'par tête' distribution. Moreover, the Committee laid down the requirement that a majority of inhabitants had to vote in favour before a 'partage' could take place and its definition of an inhabitant seemed to exclude tenants and sharecroppers. The response to these proposals was lukewarm at best. Aveline made clear his personal dissent from some of the major conclusions of the report and it was criticised from the floor of the Assembly by a number of deputies who remained attached to the idea of selling off the commons *en bloc*. In any case, events were now moving so fast that the report soon became an irrelevance. Four days after the popular uprising of 10 August, the deputies rushed through a bill which positively ordered village communities to divide up their common land. This measure, like the decrees of 20 and 25 August destroying feudalism and the law of 2 September ordering the sale of *émigré* lands (see p. 155), amounted to a reluctant acknowledgement that the moderate compromise of 1789–92 had come unstuck. Henceforth the revolution would be judged in terms of what it could offer the poor of town and country.

The decree of 14 August 1792 consisted of just four clauses and was quite inoperative. It made all non-wooded common land liable to sub-division into freehold plots and announced that the Agriculture Committee would propose a means of achieving this objective 'within three days'. In point of fact nearly ten months elapsed before the deputies of the Convention agreed a workable 'mode de partage'. Acknowledging that the decree of 14 August had been over-ambitious, they effectively repealed it on 11 October 1792. More important in the short term was a measure passed on 28 August which revoked the *triage* legislation of the *ancien régime* and empowered villagers to seek the restoration of any common land unjustly taken from them by their seigneurs. This was an immense concession to the peasantry and it resulted in thousands of actions to retrieve long-lost assets. In the Haute-Marne alone, scores of communes invoked the law against their former seigneurs.

The failure of the Convention to act on the decree of 14 August stemmed

Table 5. *The debate on the commons, 1791–2*

Responses to the circulars of 28 November 1791 and 18 March 1792 inviting department administrations to declare for or against the division of the commons

Department	Date of response	Reaction	'Mode de partage' favoured	Observations
Allier	18 April 1792	Favourable	by household	
Hautes-Alpes	31 March 1792	Hostile		Partition would be an ecological disaster
Ardèche	18 December 1791	Hostile		Prefer leasing and distribution of proceeds
Ardennes	2 December 1791	Hostile		Would pose difficulties for the common flock
Ariège		Hostile		Household division would be feasible in valleys
Charente	24 March 1792	Favourable		Propose different solutions for different types of communal property
Côte-d'Or	January 1792	Favourable	by household	
Creuse	20 June 1792	Favourable	⅓ by household and ⅔ on basis of property	
Drôme	27 March 1792	Lukewarm		*Conseil-général* of department could not agree on a 'mode de partage'
Gard	December 1791	Favourable	by household	
Haute-Garonne	27 March 1792	Hostile		An earlier survey showed 22% of communes favourable
Gers	31 March 1792	Favourable	sale to cover debts, followed by household partition	
Hérault	22 June 1792	Hostile		Only the Montpellier district administrators in favour
Jura	14 December 1791	Hostile		
Landes	28 July 1792	Favourable	by household and on basis of property	

Department	Date	Attitude	Mode	Comment
Loiret	13 December 1791	Favourable	by household	Reject idea of a uniform law
Lot	28 December 1791	Hostile		
Maine-et-Loire	15 December 1791			Propose different solutions for different types of communal property
Marne	28 March 1792			
Mayenne	6 April 1792	Lukewarm		
Meurthe	21 March 1792	Favourable		Temporary allotments
Morbihan	17 March 1792	Favourable		Question political expediency of *partage*
Oise	17 March 1792	Hostile		Reject idea of a uniform law
Orne	18 May 1792	Favourable	by household in inverse proportion to property	
Pas-de-Calais	21 April 1792	Hostile		Calais district administrators in favour
Basses-Pyrénées	19 March 1792	Favourable	no 'mode' proposed	
Bas-Rhin	7 April 1792	Favourable	by head	
Haut-Rhin		Favourable		No agreement on a 'mode de partage'
Haute-Saône	3 April 1792	Hostile		
Seine-Inférieure	28 December 1791	Favourable		Prefer sale and distribution of proceeds
Seine-et-Oise		Hostile		Little common land; five district administrations against, two in favour
Somme	6 March 1792	Hostile		
Var	6 April 1792	Hostile		'A dangerous example at the present time'
Vienne	4 April 1792	Hostile		Commons served poor best as pasture
Vosges	29 March 1792	Hostile		
Yonne	undated	Hostile		

Sources:

A.N. F[10]330; F[10]333[A].

G. Bourgin (ed.), *Le Partage des biens communaux: documents sur la préparation de la loi du 10 juin 1793* (Paris, 1908); J. Godechot, *La Révolution française dans le Midi Toulousain* (Toulouse, 1986), p. 139.

less from a reluctance to resort to extreme measures than from a realisation that the question of the commons was closely linked to that of food supply. Against the needs of social justice had to be balanced the needs of 'subsistances'. Hopefully, the two policies could be pursued in tandem, but government thinking increasingly dwelt on the economic advantages which would accrue to the nation-in-arms if an estimated two and a half million hectares of common land were cleared for arable cultivation. On the other hand, a blanket law which ordered the partition of land fit only for grazing might do irreparable harm to animal husbandry. Even the social objective of increasing the numbers of peasant proprietors carried risks, for might it not result in a shortage of wage labour and impair the efficiency of large-scale farming? This was a question which neither the revolutionaries, nor, subsequently, historians have been able to settle.

Clear signs of this new preoccupation can be found in the decree of 11 October which finally dashed hopes that the new legislature would authorise an all-out assault on the commons. The Agriculture Committee advised the deputies that the uncertainty over the status of the commons had brought to a halt the customary modes of exploitation in some localities. Anticipating a law on partition, communities had stopped leasing or cultivating their commons and had thereby jeopardised the supply of fodder and food. Partition remained on the agenda of government, but in the meantime the commons must be put to work. Throughout the late autumn and early winter, agrarian issues took a back seat as the deputies debated the fate of the king, but on 8 January 1793 Claude Fabre de l'Hérault tabled a fresh report on the commons. This closely reasoned document came down firmly in favour of a 'par tête' division. However, some measure of the changed social climate since August 1792 can be gained from the fact that the report gave serious consideration to the suggestion that the partition be carried out 'à raison inverse des propriétés', that is to say in inverse proportion to existing landholdings. In 1790, Heurtaut de Lamerville had proposed precisely the opposite (partition 'au marc la livre') and the idea of dividing up all common land on a per capita basis had seemed absurdly radical. Now the egalitarian principle of a 'par tête' distribution was under attack from the *partageurs* of the northern cereal plains who planned to use the chopping up of the commons and the parcelling of *émigré* land to reshape the social pyramid. Not for nothing did the Convention pass the famous Agrarian Law on 18 March (see pp. 162–3) which punished with death anyone advocating schemes for land reorganisation.

Two other points need stressing. Fabre rejected the coercive approach to the problem of the commons enshrined in the decree of 14 August 1792. Instead, he endorsed Aveline's preference for enabling legislation which left the power of decision in the hands of villagers. No one save the local inhabitants could determine whether or not a stretch of common land was suitable for enclosure and arable cultivation. Of course, it was always possible that rich flock-owners might subvert the democratic process and rig the ballot, and Aveline's requirement for a simple majority vote was vulnerable on this score. Fabre's draft decree minimised this risk by stipulating that 'if a third of the voters voted for partition, partition will be decided'.[32] Moreover, the resultant plots were to be held freehold. This was an article of faith for many deputies who took it for granted that bourgeois and peasant conceptions of property were one and the same. By 1793, the 'portion ménagère' solution favoured by *ancien régime* administrators had few takers and the only principled objection to a free-hold division came from Julien-Joseph Souhait representing the Vosges. The son of an official in the state Water and Forest Authority, Souhait had a sound grasp of rural matters and he uttered a stern and prophetic warning against this manner of proceeding. 'Since when', he asked, 'have we had the right to dispose of property belonging to future generations?'[33]

The criticisms of Souhait and several other deputies succeeded in delaying, but not in halting Fabre's draft decree. Early in April the opening clauses were adopted after several amendments. Later that month the crucial 'par tête' clause received parliamentary endorsement. Progress slowed in May as the factional struggle between Girondins and Jacobins reached a climax, but early in June the remaining clauses were swiftly endorsed. Finally, on 10 June the entire decree was read out and approved. After three years of procrastination, a legislative solution to the vexatious issue of the commons had reached the statute book.[34] The first thing to note about the new law is that it was thoroughly worked out and skilfully drafted in five sections containing a total of 99 clauses. Unlike so many items of revolutionary legislation, the measure contained few ambiguities and little bombast. If the peasantry failed to divide up their commons in consequence, it was not for want of understanding what was being proposed. Virtually all non-wooded common land could be divided provided at least a third of the inhabitants voted in favour. Absentee landowners and former seigneurs who had exercised the right of *triage* were excluded from the ballot; otherwise any adult, whether male or female, proprietor, tenant, sharecropper, farm servant or wage labourer, was entitled to participate. Once the issue of principle had been decided, the partition was to proceed on a per capita basis, irrespective of age or sex, on the condition that the village had settled outstanding debts. In theory the individual plots were freehold, but in practice the deputies acknowledged the criticism that the wealthy would simply buy out or even foreclose on the holdings of the poor and thereby defeat the social purpose of the reform. Article 12 of section two stipulated that beneficiaries would 'enjoy full property rights' over their plots, but article 13 added the rider that they could not sell their plots for ten years, nor make them over in payment of debts (article 16). Finally, a clause declared that all previous *partages* carried out according to different criteria were invalid, with the notable exception of enclosures authorised by the land clearance edicts of 1764 and 1766. As we shall see, this invitation to rake over the dormant embers of past partitions caused untold confusion and resentment.

While the deputies slowly assembled the elements of an agrarian policy, the peasantry had not been idle. The issue of the commons was a constant, if subsidiary, theme in the anti-seigneurial struggles of the early years of the revolution. From 1792 it became the dominant theme in certain well-defined parts of the country. Peasant activism rekindled the debate over the commons in several ways: manic land clearance threatened a totally anarchic privatisation of common land; popular determination to undo the effects of seigneurial *triages* likewise undermined the status quo; and everywhere long-running conflicts over the exploitation of the commons drew encouragement from the change of regime. In the department of the Lot, for instance, the villagers of Montvalent complained that they had long sought to divide up their sheep pastures and had passed a resolution to this effect on 14 February 1790. However, their seigneur and the wealthy landowners of the locality would only consent to a differential partition based on property. The 'poor inhabitants of the town of Martel'[35] just a few miles to the north gave vent to similar frustrations in a petition to the National Assembly. For over a century, they alleged, pressure to divide up the commons had been resisted by local landowners who had discreetly added bits of public land to their estates. As a result of the revolution, the poor had won a right of representation and on 10 January 1790 they pushed through a resolution to partition the commons. But that decision remained a dead letter. It should be noted that in neither case were the poor seeking a 'par tête' solution: they simply wanted the common pastures divided into equal-sized household plots.

Anecdotal evidence of mounting abuse of common land is plentiful and it is easy to suppose that *partage* was ardently desired all over France. Whether this inference is justified can be doubted, however. Many villages complained loudly of the maladministration of their commons, but many more did not. For their views we have to rely on oblique or second-hand testimony culled from the replies to government circulars (see table 5). The administrators of the department of the Hautes-Alpes contended that any clearing of common land would be ecologically dangerous, and those of the Ardèche reported in the spring of 1792 that just three communes (out of 334) had expressed an interest in partition. The department authorities of the Allier declared in favour of division, whilst conceding that local opinion was either hostile or indifferent: hostile because, as the officers of the district of Cérilly explained, the poor would be worse off as a result of partition; indifferent in the view of the district administrators of Le Donjon whose efforts to rouse the peasantry had been greeted with a 'profound silence on this matter'.[36] In Brittany, too, the issue of the commons stirred few passions: population pressure was not yet intense and heath clearance lay beyond the resources of the peasantry. 'In general the seigneurs and the rich were calling for the partition of the commons', announced a memoir despatched to the Agricultural Committee in the summer of 1792; 'the peasants, on the other hand, wanted them to remain under heath.'[37]

Nevertheless, an embryonic popular movement to partition the commons did take shape towards the end of 1791 and it received a considerable boost as news of the decree of 14 August 1792 filtered into the countryside. By no stretch of the imagination could this movement be described as a national phenomenon comparable to anti-seigneurialism; rather it needs to be studied in a regional context. Signs of peasant unrest at the inability of successive legislatures to agree a method of dividing up common land can be detected in a score of departments (see map 10), most of which form a wedge of territory to the north and east of Paris. In addition, there existed localised foyers of activism in the South East (Drôme, Gard) and in the South West (Lot, Haute-Garonne). This, then, was the geography of rural sans-culottism as revealed by petitions to the Convention demanding to know the 'mode de partage'.

The activism of the poor peasantry of the cereal plains around Paris comes as no surprise. In this region the struggle for an egalitarian partition of the commons was part and parcel of a broader campaign seeking a definitive solution to the problem of landlessness, and necessarily so, for relatively little common land remained in these departments. The Aisne made the running with reports of serious disturbances triggered by the arrest and trial of land clearers in February 1791. Allegations that the clearers were simply reclaiming land seized by the seigneurs turned the spotlight on the commons, or what passed for common land in the popular memory. Radicalisation of opinion proceeded apace and by the autumn of 1792 calls for action on the decree of 14 August had risen to a chorus. So desperate was the need for more plough land that many villages in the valley of the Aisne simply ignored the law and carried out their own *partages*. Similar action was taken in the Oise, the Somme, the Ardennes and the Meurthe. Notwithstanding the decree of 11 October, complained the administrators of this last department on 2 March 1793, many communes were busily dividing up their pastures. All such illicit partitions

Map 10. Zones of popular agitation for the division of common land, 1792–3
Sources: G. Bourgin (ed.), *Le Partage des biens communaux: documents sur la
préparation de la loi du 10 juin 1793* (Paris, 1908); A.N. $F^{10}329$, $F^{10}330$, $F^{10}332$,
$F^{10}333A$

were declared null and void, of course, but it is doubtful whether they were
actually reversed. Indeed, the whole issue had become politically as well as
emotionally charged, for in the autumn of 1792 the local authorities fell
due for renewal. From several localities came reports that dissension over
the question of *partage* had coloured the outcome of the elections. In the
Ardennes, the villagers of Givry-sur-Aisne threw out the old municipal
council in December 1792 and replaced it with one prepared to authorise
a division of common land, while the administrators of the department of
the Côte-d'Or warned that the municipal elections had brought to the fore

'the most ardent proselytes for partition'.[38] The pressure, it seems, was coming from the poor peasantry of the Morvan and Auxois uplands whose failure to secure a share of *biens nationaux* had resulted in a desperate bid to implement the decree of 14 August. Here as elsewhere, though, the poor showed little sympathy for the individualistic ethos espoused by bourgeois revolutionaries. They proceeded to divide up the commons into household strips.

On the face of it, the decree of 10 June 1793 should have been the answer to every poor peasant's prayer. Assuming that one-third of the inhabitants voted in favour, *partage* could now go ahead. No one resident was excluded and everyone from the richest landlord to the humblest agricultural labourer was treated alike. The Rights of Man, and indeed of Woman, had been vindicated. Or had they? This law, framed in the interests of plotholders and proletarians, evoked a patchy response at best. Right from the start, it was surrounded by myth-making: the revolutionaries believed, or professed to believe, that the breaking up of the commons had given two million individuals a chance of owning property.[39] Thus did the *montagnards* fulfil their commitment to that idealised species of the countryside – the village *sans-culotte*. Subsequently, historians have embroiled the law in their own polemics. With a notable lack of preconceptions, Marc Bouloiseau observes that the invitation to partition common land was 'badly received by the rural population'.[40] Albert Soboul is inclined to agree, but stresses that rural proprietors and the landed peasantry contrived to block the reform.[41] By implication, therefore, wage labourers and peasants with insufficient access to land were favourably disposed to partition. That implication becomes explicit in the work of the most recent generation of agrarian historians. On the basis of her study of the Somme, Françoise Gauthier insists that the poor peasantry wanted division and they wanted it 'par tête'. Had the *partageurs* managed to carry the day, their plots would have formed the embryo of small-scale freehold property from which capitalism would surely have developed.[42]

The objection to this 'voie paysanne' thesis is that it rests on a series of suppositions: that a significant portion of the store of common land was divided; that the poor peasantry were only deterred from taking possession of the remainder by the delaying tactics of wealthy members of the rural community; that freehold partition on a per capita basis reflected the conception of property displayed by the rural masses; and that the resultant plots provided the building blocks for agricultural capitalism. The current tendency to dwell upon the achievements of the decree of 10 June 1793 owes much to the work of Anatoli Ado, but Ado seems to exaggerate the practical achievements of this measure.[43] A definitive statement on the percentage of common land subjected to enclosure during the course of the revolution must await the completion of more local monographs, but it is highly unlikely that the public domain contracted to any appreciable degree. In most departments the majority of communes studiously avoided committing themselves one way or the other; a minority opted for *partage*, but only a handful actually carried it out. Predictably, the semi-proletarianised peasantry of the Paris basin and the plains of the East showed the greatest appetite for partition, but only in the Oise and the Seine-et-Oise did the challenge to the commons acquire the characteristics of a mass movement. Of the 410 (out of 730) communes of the Oise investigated by Guy Ikni, over 100 profited from the decree of 10 June 1793 to divide up their communal properties.[44] Many villages possessed no common land whatsoever, and consequently this figure should be regarded as something of a record. Reports filed by the district authorities of Dourdan, Corbeil and Etampes in the Seine-et-Oise indicate that only 53 (out of 208) communes in their constituency had commons. Of these 22 opted for partition. In the Somme, however, where a quarter of rural households owned no land of their own, the partition movement achieved mediocre results: only 31 communes actually divided up their commons (see table 6).

Was there a concerted attempt to block the implementation of the decree of 10 June 1793? Yes, to be sure. Dozens of examples of deliberate procrastination by municipal councils could be cited. Such bodies tended to be dominated by *laboureurs* and *ménagers* whose interests were usually best served by leaving the commons under pasture. The same was true of the rural bourgeoisie who saw the law as a challenge to their pre-eminence in the countryside. If every peasant household acquired a stake in the land, what would become of the labour market? How would the well-spring of social deference be oiled in future? The popular society of Salers in the Cantal alleged that rural proprietors were throwing their tenants off the land in order to disqualify them from a handout. Subsequently, the district officials of Mauriac (Cantal) declared all landowners who had evicted tenants without cause to be 'suspects'. Not surprisingly, historians have seized upon this *prima facie* evidence of class war in the village. Tension is always more easy to document than consensus, and for Florence Gauthier this tension derived from 'the selfishness of the class of well-to-do peasants as manifested in their refusal of a division of the commons which harmed their interests'.[45] But for their stonewalling, the rural masses would have grasped the opportunity to obtain a freehold plot of land.

The reality is altogether less complicated. By and large the commons were not partitioned because it suited *nobody's* interests to do so. Most peasants shared a customary conception of property and they found the decree of 10 June 1793 a source of frustration rather than inspiration. In the first place, it could only be enforced in districts possessing open pasture or drainable marshland, yet neither of these assets was ubiquitous. Moreover, the areas of greatest social distress tended also to be the areas with least common land. Secondly, the decision to allocate portions of common land on a per capita basis caused widespread puzzlement. In his report, Fabre assumed that families would be able to amalgamate their individual plots, but the decree laid down no machinery for achieving this reunification. Many peasants concluded that a *partage* conducted on these terms was not worth the trouble; others simply ignored the law and agreed among themselves to split up the commons into household portions. But even this solution cut against the grain of tradition in many areas, for a third objection raised against the proposed reform was that it sacrificed the interests of future generations for the short-term advantage of the present beneficiaries. The administrators of the department of the Bas-Rhin, for instance, openly wondered whether public opinion was ready to accept 'definitive, freehold partition'.[46] Allied to this point was the ecological objection: much of the national store of commonland could only be used for rough grazing or afforestation and rural communities needed no lessons from agronomists on the dangers of opening up poor soils situated at climatically vulnerable altitudes. Besides, how could the institution of the *troupeau commun* continue to function in the absence of communal pasture? In 1797 the poorer inhabitants (to judge from their signatures) of the village of Gisancourt (Eure) sought permission to reverse the partition of a marsh which they had carried out several years earlier. As a result of this ill-advised tampering with the agricultural balance, the village herd had been cut by nearly half which had reduced the supply of manure and jeopardised crops.

Not for nothing then, has Georges Lefebvre drawn attention to the shortcomings of the decree of 10 June 1793.[47] Yet the deputies warmed to their handiwork as the year went by. Objections and difficulties were brushed to one side and the *représentants-en-mission* made enforcement a matter of political etiquette. Enforcement, in this context, meant browbeating the municipalities into convening meetings at which the assembled peasantry were urged to vote for *partage*. In the Calvados, the department authorities passed a resolution on 18 Pluviôse II (6 February 1794) which made partition of the commons all but compulsory, as did the department of the Landes a few months later (see plate 4). By this time, however, the new law had lost its central egalitarian thrust, at least in so far as the government was concerned. On 27 October 1793 the Convention set up the Subsistences Commission (subsequently renamed the Commission for Commerce and Provisioning), a powerful new body to oversee all matters relating to prices and food supply, and henceforth the pressure to divide up

Table 6. *Impact of the decree of 10 June 1793*

Department	District	Total number of communes	Number of communes possessing commons	Number of communes voting for *partage*	Number of communes voting against *partage*	Number of *partages* implemented	Observations
Hautes-Alpes		182				0	as of 26 Ventôse II
Ardèche		334				5	as of 23 Germinal III
Aube	Bar-sur-Seine	64				3	as of Ventôse III
Aube	Bar-sur-Aube	92				5	
Cher		290(?)	106(?)	33	73	0(?)	
Côte-d'Or		727				50(?)	
Côte-d'Or	Arnay-sous-Arroux	82	58(?)	56*	14		*includes some hamlets
Côte-d'Or	Beaune	87	29	29	31	29(?)	as of Floréal III
Côte-d'Or	Châtillon	107		15	10	15(?)	as of 27 Floréal II
Côte-d'Or	St Jean-de-Losne	69	13	6	6	6(?)	
Haute-Garonne		737					
Haute-Garonne	Toulouse	120		15		3	
Haute-Garonne	Muret	73		4		0	
Haute-Garonne	Grenade	77		16		1	
Haute-Garonne	Villefranche	53		5		3	
Haute-Garonne	St Gaudens	250		79			as of Thermidor III
Gironde	Libourne	142	52(?)	13	37		
Landes	Tartas	71		2	30	3	as of Fructidor II
Léman		275					as of 1803
Lot	St Céré	73				4	as of 26 Brumaire III
Haute-Marne	Bourmont	70				20	as of Fructidor II with eleven more pending
Meurthe	Nancy	79				12	
Meuse	Bar-le-Duc	99					as of 18 Thermidor III
Nord		671				31(?)	as of 9 Ventôse XII

Department	Commune						
Nord	Cambrai	102		2		4	as of 24 Prairial IV
Nord	Valenciennes	88		7		17(?)	
Nord	Le Quesnoy	87		18		12	
Nord	Lille	130		17 or 18		12	
Nord	Douai	63		22	6	22(?)	based on a sample of 410 communes
Oise		730				100	as of 27 Fructidor II
Hautes-Pyrénées		546		101	147		
Saône-et-Loire	Bellevue-les-Bains	28		6	0		
Seine-et-Oise	Étampes	78	17	2	2	2	as of Ventôse II
Seine-et-Oise	Corbeil	76	28	16	5		
Seine-et-Oise	Dourdan	54	8	4		1	as of 16 Prairial II
Somme	Amiens	958	45			31	
Somme		194					
Somme	Montdidier	150		22		11	
Somme	Péronne	182		43		17	
Haute-Vienne	St Junien	32				1	as of 27 Ventôse II

Sources:

A.N. F^{10}327; F^{10}330; F^{10}332; DIV^{bis}77

A.D. Côte-d'Or L1640

P. Bozon, *La Vie rurale en Vivarais: étude géographique* (Valence, 1963), p. 152

Clère, 'Les Paysans de la Haute-Marne et la Révolution française', vol. ii, p. 425.

P. Guichonnet, 'Les Biens communaux et les partages révolutionnaires dans l'ancien département du Léman', *Etudes rurales*, 36 (1969), 28

Gauthier, *Le Voie paysanne dans la Révolution française*, pp. 62, 194

M. Henriot, *Le Partage des biens communaux en Côte-d'Or sous la Révolution* (Dijon, 1948), pp. 16–17

Ikni, 'Recherches sur la propriété foncière. Problèmes théoriques de méthode', p. 419

Lefebvre, *Paysans du Nord*, pp. 545–6, 551

M. Marion, *La Vente des biens nationaux pendant la Révolution* (Paris, 1908), p. 213 and note 1

G. Richert, 'Biens communaux et droits d'usage en Haute-Garonne pendant la Réaction thermidorienne et sous le Directoire', *Ann. hist. Rév. fran.*, 23 (1951), 274–88

ADRESSE

DES ADMINISTRATEURS

DU DÉPARTEMENT DES LANDES,

AUX Citoyens des campagnes, concernant le partage des biens Communaux.

CITOYENS,

PAR quelle fatalité funeste à vos propres intérêts et au bien public, le décret du 10 Juin 1793 (*vieux style,*) concernant le mode de partage des biens communaux, a-t-il jusqu'ici demeuré sans effet parmi vous ! Cependant la Convention nationale, dont il est l'ouvrage, ne cesse d'en provoquer l'exécution ; et nous-mêmes nous avons recommandé plusieurs fois aux Districts de l'accélérer et faciliter par tous les moyens qui sont en leur pouvoir. Nous ne mettons cette persévérance que pour votre avantage que nous désirons procurer, et pour celui de la République qui y est naturellement attaché ; nous sentons que par cette mesure votre situation doit s'améliorer ; que les Citoyens qui n'ont que des propriétés bornées, les accroîtront avec plaisir ; que beaucoup d'autres qui n'en ont pas, vont en acquérir et les ~~faire valoir d'une manière~~ plus fructueuse qu'en les laissant en commun : nous sentons qu'ils seront alors plus particulièrement attachés à la révolution, et tiendront plus à la Patrie. A quelles funestes allarmes, ou à quelle suggestion perfide cédez-vous donc en repoussant ces bienfaits ! êtes-vous insensibles au sentiment qu'inspire la propriété, aux avantages qu'elle procure ! Ah ! si vous êtes réellement patriotes et républicains, si vous aimez vos propres intérêts, ceux de vos Femmes et de vos Enfans, vous vous empresserez à réclamer le partage, à prendre toute la portion qui vous revient, à l'utiliser pour votre profit, pour celui de la République dont vous multiplierez les productions et les subsistances. Quelque fausse crainte, quelque terreur puérile des revenans, vous détourneroit-elle de cette salutaire opération ? Ah ! banissez-la : car, et l'hypocrite Clergé, et l'orgueilleuse Noblesse, et le régime féodal, et toutes ces institutions qui vexoient le pauvre Peuple, sur-tout celui des campagnes, ont disparu sans retour ; auriez-vous quelque allarme du côté des satellites des tyrans coalisés contre nous ? Mais rassurez-vous encore : toutes nos Armées sont victorieuses, les ennemis terrassés sur tous les points, et les soldats de la Liberté les chassent devant eux comme le vent chasse la poussière. Nos subsistances sont assurées. Le sol de la République se purge successivement des traîtres et des malveillans. Le supplice fait raison des uns, et la réclusion contient les autres.

Seriez-vous encore retenus par la considération des partages faits avant la loi ? Eh bien ! ils sont nuls, et vous avez le droit d'en exiger de nouveaux : peut-être des propriétaires intéressés à conserver les communaux dans l'état où ils se trouvent, à continuer de s'en servir

pour l'amélioration de leurs propres domaines, vous insinuent-ils que vous ne tirerez aucun parti de ces fonds : peut-être vous représentent-ils que vous n'avez de facultés ni pour les mettre en valeur, ni seulement pour les clorre ; mais ne les écoutez pas : car, quand réellement vos moyens ne vous permettroient pas de les faire valoir actuellement, vous pourrez les affermer, et ces propriétaires eux-mêmes seront des premiers à les prendre et à vous en payer le prix de ferme.

Formez donc au plutôt vos assemblées conformément à la loi. Appellez-y les individus de tout sexe ayant droit au partage, et âgés de vingt-un ans. Que le partage se fasse ensuite par tête d'habitant domicilié de tout âge, de tout sexe, absent ou présent ; les métayers, valets de labour, gens à gages, femmes, enfans, jeunes et vieux, tous doivent y participer. Observez seulement que les bois ne sont pas ~~sujets au partage et que la loi a réglé un autre mode de les~~ utiliser à votre profit ; à cet effet elle vous autorise à vendre les coupes ordinaires ou à les partager en nature au prorata de la portion qui vous en réviendra ; quant aux autres difficultés qui pourroient se présenter, la sagesse de la loi les a toutes prévues : ayez-la sous les yeux pendant le cours de l'opération, et ce guide assuré ne vous trompera jamais.

La source de vos allarmes ainsi tarie, vos intérêts bien connus et toutes les difficultés écartées, occupez-vous du partage de vos communaux ; la patrie, cette mère tendre, vous offre des propriétés et vous les donne gratuitement : son désir est que vous en jouissiez dès ce moment, elle vous invite à goûter la satisfaction de cultiver des fonds qui vous soient propres, après avoir tant de fois arrosé de vos sueurs ceux des autres, des fonds que vous puissiez trans-mettre à vos enfans avec la reconnoissance des utiles travaux par lesquels vous les aurez améliorés, et le souvenir de vos paisibles vertus.

Le Directoire du département des Landes, après avoir entendu la lecture de l'adresse ci-dessus, arrête qu'elle sera imprimée, et envoyée aux districts, pour être publiée et affichée dans les communes, et y être lue dans le temple de l'Etre suprême, trois décadis consécutifs, par un des officiers-municipaux.

Fait le 13 Thermidor, en séance du soir, l'an 2.me de la république Françoise, une et indivisible.

Signés SAINT-AMON, *président*; L. S. BATBEDAT, DUBOSCQ, CHAUMONT, FICOLLE, *administrateurs*; et DULAMON, *secrétaire général.*

Certifié conforme à l'original.

DULAMON, *secrétaire général.*

Plate 4. Proclamation calling for the division of common land in the Landes department

the commons came from this direction. The Commission's brief was to increase grain production by all available means and, in common with the Committee of Public Safety, it bombarded the local authorities with circulars urging the partition, leasing or even the sale of common land. The poor and dispossessed remained the nominal objectives of government concern, but the increasing preoccupation with agricultural efficiency clearly foreshadowed the policies of the Thermidorians.

There are signs that the Convention was preparing to revise the legislation authorising the partition of common land in the late summer of 1794. However, the crisis engendered by Thermidor momentarily eclipsed the on-going debate over how the commons should be managed. By the time the issue resurfaced in the spring of 1795, the political context had entirely changed: the General Maximum controlling prices and wages had been abolished and with it that omnipresent agency for economic policy, the Commission for Commerce and Provisioning. The proprietorial interest was in the ascendant once more and determined to exact retribution for its sufferings during the Terror. The controversial decree of 10 June 1793 became one of the most potent symbols of those sufferings and repeated attempts were made to remove it from the statute book. Throughout the Years Three and Four (1795–7), a petitioning campaign of such violence was waged against the law that one might easily suppose that the entire store of common land had been divided up. The reality, as we have seen, was quite different, but that was scarcely the point. Whether they cared to admit it or not, rural proprietors were protesting the very idea of social levelling which this infamous law had briefly unveiled.

On 21 Prairial IV (9 June 1796) an interim measure suspending the execution of the decree of 10 June 1793 was rushed through the Councils of the Directory. Landowners all over France responded with satisfaction in the belief that the revocation of all egalitarian *partages* would not be long in coming. According to an anxious missive from plotholders in the canton of Frasne (Doubs), counter-revolutionaries and refractory priests had rejoiced on hearing the news of suspension. That joy proved premature, however, for the neo-royalist Right never succeeded in enlarging this bridgehead. All the decree of 21 Prairial IV did was to prevent any further *partages*, and by placing a moratorium on litigation it tended to consolidate those partitions which had already been carried out. The moratorium was lifted on 9 Ventôse XII (29 February 1804), but by this time Bonaparte was about to assume supreme power and wished only to lay the legacy of the revolution to rest. All legally authenticated partitions were endorsed with the proviso that beneficiaries might now dispose of their plots as they pleased. However, many revolutionary *partages* had adhered to the stipulations of the decree of 10 June 1793 in an approximate fashion at best and these were to be scrutinised by the prefects with a view to restoring the disputed parcels to the jurisdiction of the commune. In the Nord and also in the Haute-Marne, this law enabled the local authorities to overturn a substantial number of partitions, but there is no evidence to suggest that it unleashed a generalised assault on the *partages* of the revolutionary era. In any case, such a generalised assault no longer seemed as pressing, for many *partages* had lapsed with the passing of time. And what the Thermidorian bourgeoisie had failed to achieve by legislation could always be achieved by stealth. At Lagesse in the Aube, 'la plus saine partie' (an old-regime expression which came back into fashion under Bonaparte) of the inhabitants petitioned against a partition of nearly ten years' standing in 1804 and the occasion prompted the mayor to commit some bitter reflections to paper. The *partage* law, he wrote, 'for which was claimed the specious advantage of rescuing the common people from misery and of enlisting them in the ranks of property owners, has completely missed its mark.' Within five years, the poor had begun to sell their portions to the rich; now that ten years had nearly passed, the remaining portions would soon be gobbled up: 'I can already see from my office [window] the one to whom the communal property of Lagesse will pass. Thus it is that this law which ought to have enriched the poor, has only succeeded in enriching the rich.'[48]

'Biens nationaux'

Between 1791 and 1799 the revolutionaries put up for sale a vast quantity of property which they had seized from the church and from nobles who had fled abroad. Their motives were at first financial – to meet an income deficit for 1790 which Necker admitted would rise to at least 294 million *livres*. But political and humanitarian considerations quickly clouded this otherwise straightforward calculation. By 1794 the deputies had saddled themselves with the task of using the sales of *biens nationaux* to fulfil the jacobin dream of a republic of property owners, yet the financial imperative remained as pressing as ever. This confusion of objectives left its mark on the legislation regulating the sales. Initially, the National Assembly resolved (by a decree of 14–17 May 1790) that church lands would be put on the market in large blocks with the stipulation that the sales be conducted by auction in the principal town of each district. Would-be purchasers were offered the inducement of a small down-payment followed by twelve annual instalments. The deputies resisted the suggestion that ecclesiastical estates be broken up into small parcels so as to spread the sales across a broader social spectrum, but nothing prevented speculators from buying up large holdings and reselling them in segments. Nor (until the decree of 24 April 1793) were municipalities denied the right to buy at auction for the purpose of resale to their constituents.

Sales under this first phase of revolutionary legislation commenced in November or December 1790 and they continued at a hectic pace throughout 1791 and 1792. In the Haute-Marne, for instance, nearly 39,000 hectares of church lands representing a tenth of the arable surface of the department changed hands during these years.[49] However, the popular uprising of 10 August 1792 inaugurated a second phase in the history of the revolutionary land settlement, for the deputies voted to confiscate and sell off the property of *émigrés*, too. After several false starts, the necessary legislation was formalised on 3 June 1793 and it is notable for a specific commitment to the poor which was lacking in earlier measures. *Emigré* lands were still to be sold at auction – on this point even the *montagnards* scarcely wavered – but they were to be divided up 'as far as possible, without damaging each farm or estate, into lots or portions'.[50] Furthermore, a clause in the decree made special provision for the landless. In villages where there was no common land to partition, they would receive one-*arpent* (approximately 0.5 hectare) plots in return for a modest rental payable to the Republic. Such plots could only be created in communes containing confiscated *émigré* property, of course, but in the months that followed the Convention modified this prescription in two ways. On 13 September 1793 the allocation of a plot of land was dropped, perhaps because of its financial implications. Instead, the destitute poor were offered a credit voucher worth 500 *livres* with which to bid at auction for *émigré* property situated anywhere in the district. Then, on 2 Frimaire II (22 November 1793), the injunction to split up estates, wherever possible, was extended to the remaining ecclesiastical property coming up for sale as well.

Despite the changed political environment after Thermidor, the allotments of church and *émigré* lands continued unabated until the summer of 1795 in many departments. An attempt to curtail dismemberment and to speed up the rate of sales on 12 Prairial III (31 May 1795) misfired, and it was not until the beginning of the Year Four that the deputies finally settled on a policy more in keeping with the social ethos of the times. However, this third phase in the sale of *biens nationaux* began badly, for the *assignat* had reached the point of collapse and on 30 Brumaire IV (21 November 1795) the Directory was forced to suspend the auctions. In the South, royalist reprisals against purchasers in the Aveyron and the Lozère (see pp. 240–5) had already forced the authorities into a similar course of action. With the introduction of a new currency – the *mandat territorial* – on 28 Ventôse IV (18 March 1796) dealing in national property resumed, but sale by auction was dropped in favour of a system of direct purchase which enabled bearers of *mandats* to buy on application at a fixed price. Since the *mandats territoriaux* lost four-fifths of their face value within a fortnight, purchasers made a killing, but few peasants benefited. Little publicity was given to the sales and would-be *acquéreurs* had to travel to the department capital in order to make their 'submissions'. On 16 Brumaire V (6 November 1796) the government restored sale by public auction, but in the department rather than the district capital. With inflation still unconquered, fresh difficulties followed which necessitated a further suspension of trading in *biens nationaux* in the autumn of 1798. Eventually the Directory resorted to a policy of full payment in metallic currency on 26 Vendémiaire VII (17 October 1798).

Successive revolutionary legislatures fluctuated in their expectations of the sale of *biens nationaux*. The peasantry, by contrast, remained clearsighted in their objective: they wanted access to land. Did they obtain it? This is the question to which we should address ourselves next. Contemporaries would have answered the question affirmatively, but contemporary opinion was mistaken in its conviction that the peasantry possessed little land before the revolution. By the end of the *ancien régime* the peasantry owned, on average, a third of the agricultural surface and that proportion would doubtless have increased whether or not the crisis of 1789 had supervened. For much of the nineteenth century, historians were content to accept the myth that France's uniquely stable peasantry owed its position to the sale of *biens nationaux*. Serious research into the question began late, but it produced some disturbing results: local studies indicated that the peasantry were not, after all, the principal beneficiaries of the sale of church and *émigré* lands – at least not in the short term. On the contrary, the urban and rural bourgeoisie took the lion's share of this property, for they alone possessed the capital resources, the professional skills and the leisure which buying at auction required.

Commenced in 1904, Georges Lefebvre's monumental study of the Nord department was designed with this debate in mind and twenty years later he published one of the first thorough analyses of the sales.[51] Lefebvre's findings went some way towards rehabilitating the traditional view, for in the Nord he discovered a peasantry which bid for land in considerable numbers and with considerable determination. Or, to be more precise, he discovered not one but several peasantries: the profile of the purchasers tended to reflect the profile of popular activism. In Flanders the urban bourgeoisie were omnipresent and dominated the auctions without real effort. But it is also true that the peasantry allowed themselves to be dominated in this region: they attended the auctions singly and failed to organise community action to deter 'outside' purchasers. In the south of the department, it was a different story, however. Long-standing traditions of collective action to enforce a customary conception of property (*mauvais gré*), combined with more recent traditions of anti-seigneurial violence, engendered a popular determination to seize the opportunity presented by the sales. No doubt the fact that the bourgeoisie was nowhere near as powerful in Hainaut and the Cambrésis played a part as well. By the time the first phase of the sales had drawn to a close, 1,521 peasants in the district of Cambrai had purchased 16,000 hecatres, whereas 266 bourgeois had only managed to buy up 1,600 hectares. The proportion was similar in the adjacent districts of Le Quesnoy and Valenciennes. In the department as a whole, Lefebvre calculates that 8,490 peasants bought 43,000 hectares and 2,143 bourgeois 22,000 hectares in the period up to 1793.

Some of these 'individual' peasant purchasers would, in fact, have been frontmen acting on behalf of whole communities, and we must also allow for the fact that Lefebvre's method of social classification (see pp. 13–14) is unduly favourable to the bourgeoisie. But these adjustments simply underline the point which he is making: that in the Nord, at least, the rural population greatly benefited from the sale of *biens nationaux*. During the second phase of property sales between 1793 and 1795 the peasantry continued to compete with bourgeois purchasers, which would not be surprising if it were not for the fact that the department suffered a partial occupation by Austrian troops. Less land was processed for sale; even so, the peasantry acquired a little under 12,000 hectares compared with 10,500 hectares for the bourgeoisie. Only with the modifications to the method of sale introduced by the Directory did the bourgeoisie stage a come-back: by the time of General Bonaparte's *coup d'état* they had managed to acquire a further 33,000 hectares whereas the peasantry added 16,000 hectares to their total. All in all, and leaving aside the sales of buildings, which paint a rather different picture, Lefebvre reckons that the peasantry added 71,409 hectares to their existing holdings, while the bourgeoisie acquired some 65,772 hectares. Or to put it another way, in a department where approximately 25 per cent of the land surface was sold off as *biens nationaux* between 1791 and 1799, the peasantry emerged slightly ahead, having purchased 52 per cent of the area compared with the bourgeoisie's 48 per cent.

Most of these gains were, as we have said, concentrated at the southern end of the department adjacent to the Aisne and it seems likely that this peasant preponderance extended further south still, into the Laonnais and perhaps as far as the plains of Picardy. Pockets of successful peasant bidding have also been recorded in Lower Alsace, in the districts of Is-sur-Tille (Côte-d'Or) and Neufchâtel-en-Bray (Seine-Inférieure), and in the

Sénonais (Yonne). Elsewhere, however, the Flanders model would appear to apply, that is to say the bourgeoisie took the lion's share with little, if any competition from the peasantry. In the two Charente departments the urban bourgeoisie proved the principal beneficiaries of the sales. The same was true of the area around Vitré in Brittany: the town bourgeoisie acquired 64 per cent of the surfaces put on the market between 1791 and the spring of 1793.[52] A few well-to-do peasants participated in the land-grab, but that was all. By all accounts, things were not very different in the western Sarthe and the southern Maine-et-Loire. Thanks to recent research, a more detailed picture can be drawn for the Haute-Marne.[53] Here approximately 56,400 hectares of church and *émigré* lands were sold off between 1791 and 1799, of which the bourgeoisie, properly defined, obtained 47,943 hectares (84.9 per cent) and the peasantry 8,517 hectares (15.1 per cent). Only during the second phase of the operation when estates were being offered for sale in small parcels did the peasantry manage to reverse the trend. In 1793 and 1794 they bought 1,565 hectares, compared with just 695 hectares which fell to the bourgeoisie. But this was a tiny proportion of the total volume of land sales, most of which went for auction before 1793 and after 1794.

Such statistics raise a number of interesting questions: why did the peasantry mount a successful bid to share the spoils of the revolution in the Hainaut and the Cambrésis, but allow themselves to be steamrollered in the Sarthe, the Maine-et-Loire and the Haute-Marne? What had happened to that unity of action which characterised peasant resistance to seigneur-ialism? Who were these peasants who managed, notwithstanding the dif-ficulties, to buy at auction? And what about the poor and landless? Did they get a look-in? None of these questions can be answered satisfactorily, but several points deserve to be borne in mind. The sales did not take place in isolation, but in a political context: a context clouded by the on-going struggle over seigneurialism, by the bid to extend collective rights, by a localised campaign to divide up the commons and by more generalised dis-putes over the ecclesiastical oath. It may be that the sale of *biens nationaux* became a political issue, too. In the counter-revolutionary West it is cer-tainly true that country dwellers were deterred from investing in national property for the reason alluded to by Jules Michelet, that 'the Jacobins became buyers and the buyers became Jacobins'.[54] It is worth pondering also whether a peasantry overwhelmingly imbued with a collectivist notion of property actually wanted land on the terms offered. Lefebvre's analysis appears to leave no room for doubt on this score, but he is at pains to emphasise that the approved model of land holding in the Hainaut and the Cambrésis was the 'portion ménagère'. When municipalities entered collective bids for church lands – a device frequently employed in the district of Cambrai – they did so with the intention of retaining a supervisory authority over the portions of land subsequently allocated. Moreover, the poor were endowed at the expense of the community, on the understanding that they worked their plots personally.

Not even the Convention had quite the courage of its principles. The commons *were* to be partitioned on a freehold basis (albeit with a restriction placed on the right of sale), but the decree of 3 June 1793 which formed part of the same package baulked at giving the landless poor anything more than the 'use' of *émigré* property. Untrammelled property rights, it seems, could only be acquired by purchase on the open market (decree of 13 September 1793). Even had they wanted to, few rural labourers stood the least chance of acquiring land under these conditions. Five hundred *livres* did not go very far at auction. In any case, most local authorities chose to ignore this latest frenzy of egalitarianism: district officials in the department of the Puy-de-Dôme diligently parcelled the property of *émigrés* prior to sale, but treated the additional provisions of the laws of 3 June and 13 September as a virtual irrelevance.[55] Only in the district of Riom was a list of potential beneficiaries compiled, which proved a fruitless exercise for no one turned up to claim a voucher. Perhaps this was just as well: of the 663 lots of *émigré* property auctioned by October 1794 in the district of Clermont-Ferrand, only nineteen sold for a price anywhere near 500 *livres*. It seems that the initiative also failed in the department of the Hérault: at Béziers the district administrators did issue a number of vouchers, but their use was very restricted. In the Creuse, the district of Guéret issued vouchers to at least thirteen individuals, all of whom lived in the town and none of whom strictly qualified, either because they already owned property or because the town of Guéret disposed of common land.[56] Although the evidence is sparse, the legislation may have been more fully implemented in the plains villages around Paris. Here at least, the three pre-requisites for a thoroughgoing morselisation of *biens nationaux* coincided: popular pressure, substantial *émigré* estates and a near-absence of common land. In the Seine-et-Oise some 1,546 indigent households were deemed to have satisfied the terms of the decree of 3 June 1793 and each received a one-*arpent* plot.[57] Even so, it seems that the responsible authorities must have interpreted the law in a highly unorthodox manner, for this department contained a vast army of landless and semi-landless proletarians. Bureaucratic lethargy delayed the allotment of *émigré* property in the Oise, too. Local peasants faced an uphill struggle in persuading the district authorities to market the land in units which they could afford to buy. How far they succeeded remains unclear, but the rural poor of this department appear to have evolved techniques of collective intimidation which were every bit as sophisticated as those employed in the Hainaut and the Cambrésis.

One might wonder, therefore, whether the sale of *biens nationaux* created many new proprietors. Yet Lefebvre is confident that this is indeed what happened in the Nord.[58] He argues that 30,000 peasant households purchased national property of some description and calculates that about one-third of these became first-time land owners in the process. The distribution was obviously uneven, but in the Cambrésis where 44 per cent of the land surface changed hands he contends that the revolution brought into being a new class of small peasant proprietors. The existence of such households provides bedrock support for the 'voie paysanne' interpretation outlined at the start of this chapter, allowing always that it can be shown that they behaved in a suitably capitalist manner. But the sale of *biens nationaux* in the Nord was scarcely typical of France as a whole. At the most, Lefebvre's seminal study is illustrative of certain trends affecting the frontier departments of the North East. In the Meurthe (now absorbed into the Meurthe-et-Moselle and Moselle departments), for instance, tenant farmers and a goodly number of artisans and poor peasants also gained access to land. During the Consulate the Napoleonic prefect calculated that the number of proprietors had risen by 19 per cent with substantial repercussions on the social structure of the department. In the Bas-Rhin, too, the peasantry rivalled the urban bourgeoisie in their purchases of *biens nationaux*, but here the revolutionary land settlement tended to reinforce the traditional structure of the countryside. A newly endowed class of peasant proprietors did not emerge.

In all these departments the church owned a sizeable proportion of the cultivable land surface (Nord: 19–20%; northern Aisne: 19–20%; Meurthe: 12%; Bas-Rhin: 15–20%). Consequently, the *potential* for a significant change in property relationships can be said to have existed. But elsewhere in the country this was scarcely ever the case. The church possessed approximately 11 per cent of the arable in the Sarthe and 5 per cent in the Ille-et-Vilaine: enough, that is, for the sales to make a political impact; but not enough to leave much trace on the social structure. The point holds for much of the South, too: in the district of Montpellier (Hérault) 3.2 per cent of the land surface was put up for sale as ecclesiastical property and 1.8 per cent as *émigré* property. In the adjacent district of Béziers the figures were 4 per cent and 2.2 per cent respectively. Turning to the South West, it seems that 4.51 per cent of the surface of the district of Saint Sever (Landes) was disposed of as *émigré* property and 1.69 per cent of that of Tartas (Landes). In each case the sales of church lands in the two districts amounted to 2.63 per cent and 0.33 per cent.[59] Such calculations serve to remind us that we need to keep the sale of *biens nationaux* in perspective, yet, by the same token, it is important to distinguish between short-term and long-term consequences. The bourgeoisie may have taken a disproportionate share of the property reaching the market between 1791 and 1799, but they often resold piecemeal to peasant clients. This speculative approach to the opportunity posed by the sale of *biens nationaux* was especially marked in the East where the return on land seemed meagre in comparison with investments in commerce or industry. In the Bas-Rhin, for example, the bourgeoisie cashed in many of their purchases during the Empire and the Restoration and transferred their investments elsewhere. Such moves nearly always worked to the advantage of the local peasantry, as Jean-Jacques Clère's *longue durée* study of the department of the Haute-Marne has demonstrated.[60] After 1791 the land market came alive as speculators split up their purchases and sold them off in pieces. So the peasantry got the land sooner or later. The myth that the revolution consecrated the peasantry as a land-owning class is not without an element of truth. Even if Jacques Bonhomme failed to secure a share of national property when it came up for auction, he and his like carried out a stealthy conquest of the soil in the two and three decades that followed.

A republic of property-owners?

For a few brief months in 1793 and early 1794 the creation of a property-owning democracy became an object of policy. As we have seen, the decrees of 3 June, 10 June, 13 September and 22 November 1793 were designed with this end in view, and they were followed by others, notably the notorious Laws of Ventôse. The old Enlightenment ideal of *bienfaisance* (state-supported public assistance) with its ambition to eliminate begging and vagrancy had been sublimated into a radical new panacea offering the political as well as the socio-economic improvement of mankind. Yet the transition was never as complete as the rhetoric of jacobinism, or to be more precise of sans-culottism, implied. The deputies hovered uncertainly between the redemptive qualities of small-scale property and the evident economic advantages of large-scale property. They equated poverty with virtue and wealth with vice, but offered palliatives rather than firm measures to restore the moral balance. When downtrodden sharecroppers challenged the property rights of landlords in the South West, when poor peasants campaigned for a limit on the size of farms on the plains around Paris, the Convention blustered and bluffed.

Not one of the revolutionary legislatures developed a coherent policy towards the peasantry, but this is not altogether surprising in view of the

fact that there was no single 'peasant' solution to many of the issues discussed in this chapter. The *montagnards*, however, defined the object of
their concern rather differently. In the words of Robespierre, 'The revolutions of the last three years have done everything for the other classes of
citizens, almost nothing yet for the most needy, for proletarian citizens
whose only property lies in their labour.'[61] With the Mountain's victory
over the Gironde, the poor of town and country were ceremonially ushered
into the centre of the political stage. Theirs was not to be a virtuoso performance, however. The Robespierrists innovated fearlessly in the political and religious spheres, but they set precise limits to their social reform.
Emigré lands were to be split up in order to facilitate acquisition by the
poor, but only 'as far as possible',[62] and they still had to be purchased at
auction. The commons were earmarked for partition, but purely on an
optional basis. This marked a retreat from the position adopted in August
1792. Feudal dues were definitively abolished, but bourgeois ground rents
were specifically excluded from the general anathema. The intention, it
seems clear, was to widen the property-owning base of the nation without,
at the same time, licensing an attack on all forms of property.

This was not an easy balance to achieve. From the earliest days of the
revolution, the deputies had grappled with the problem of framing legislation which condemned certain types of property, while upholding others
which were very little different in origin. There existed a constant danger
of 'slippage' as peasants tried to pass off *émigré* land as common land, or
leasehold rents as servile obligations. In the summer of 1793, the Legislation Committee was horrified to discover that a number of communes
had understood the decree of 17 July to mean that sharecroppers and
tenants of ex-seigneurs need no longer pay rent of any description (see pp.
93–4). Then there was the problem of 'agrarian socialism'. Unsurprisingly, the pressure for a more radical land reform than the Convention was
prepared to countenance was greatest on the plains around Paris and in the
villages of Picardy – the homeland of Babeuf (see p. 128). Chronic land
shortage and extremes of wealth and poverty had been the root cause
of unrest in this region since 1791. The first call for the abolition of all
feudal dues without compensation emanated from three villages in the
Oise in February 1791, and it was accompanied by a demand that the
landed property of seigneurs be put up for sale. By the winter of 1792–3
agitators were touring the villages of Picardy and the Ile-de-France in order
to gather support for the 'partage des terres' – the seizure and sub-division
of all land, irrespective of whether it was owned by members of the former
privileged orders or by bourgeois proprietors. The deputies made
advocacy of the forcible redistribution of property – stigmatised as the
'Agrarian Law' – an offence punishable by death on 18 March 1793. But

Map 11. Geography of protests against the concentration of farms
Sources: A. Ado, *The Peasant Movement in France during the Great Bourgeois Revolution at the End of the Eighteenth Century* (Moscow, 1971), p. 354; G. Lefebvre, *Questions agraires au temps de la Terreur* (2nd ed., La Roche-sur-Yon, 1954), pp. 61–80

this simply drove the agitation into different and more circumspect channels. The *partageurs* continued their campaign in the traditional guise of a bid to outlaw land engrossment (see map 11). The threat to peasant holdings posed by the activities of *gros fermiers* was not new, but it was greatly exacerbated by the sales of *biens nationaux* which disturbed the patterns of land tenure in many villages of the North and East. These land monopolists who made a living by gobbling up peasant tenures formed a 'new aristocracy' complained the mayor and villagers of Crécy-au-Mont in the Soissonnais.[63] They drove small farmers into the ranks of the agricultural proletariat, while depriving that same proletariat of wage-work on their newly enlarged estates.

The bulk of deputies in the Convention were no more sympathetic to the campaign against land engrossment than they had been to the calls for a general redistribution of property voiced earlier in the year. But then the crisis of August–September 1793 intervened and they were forced to take stock, just like their predecessors in the Legislative Assembly after the crisis of 10 August 1792. On 2 September 1793 an outline decree to limit the size of tenanted holdings was tabled, which contained a further proposal to ban the amalgamation of farms unless their total surface area amounted to less than 100 hectares. Laurent Lecointre of Versailles and Jacques Coupé of the Oise, two radical deputies whose constituents had long pressed for land reform, seem to have been behind the move, but it was thrown out. With the Committee of Public Safety yielding to *sans-culotte* pressure on all fronts, Coupé tried again some six weeks later. His draft law recommended a ceiling of between 150 and 200 hectares on holdings managed by a single tenant. This time the deputies expressed their distaste by putting off the debate until a later date. On 2 November, Coupé intervened again to get the discussion started, but with no better success. Without spokesmen in the Convention the poor peasantry could achieve nothing. Yet even with politicians willing to take up their cause they lacked the physical presence to enforce a change in the law. This was the dilemma confronting the *partageurs* in the autumn of 1793. The *sans-culottes*, to be sure, provided a substitute 'physical presence', but their interests coincided imperfectly with those of poor *haricotiers* under threat of eviction. While it is true that some of the Sections incorporated schemes for land reform in their manifestos, most *sans-culotte* energy was devoted to policing the Maximum and maintaining the food supply. Such preoccupations could all too easily engender an attitude of suspicion towards the peasantry.

To judge by their actions the *montagnards* had no coherent policy for dealing with peasant grievances. What they had was a genuine sympathy for the poor and dispossessed, an abiding respect for established property relationships once shorn of seigneurial and clerical excrescences, and a readiness to make sacrifices and to impose sacrifices on others in order to defeat their enemies at home and abroad. These commitments tended to conflict and in consequence their agrarian policy evolved in fits and starts – sometimes in response to abstract reasoning, more often in response to inescapable pressures and problems. Nevertheless, it is only fair to add that the social policy of the Mountain has been the subject of intense, even polemical, debate. Albert Mathiez insists upon the specific and audacious character of Robespierrist social policy: he maintains that it was premedi-

tated and distinguished by an attachment to real equality.[64] Not for
nothing were Robespierre and the immaculate Constitution of 1793 hailed
by Babeuf and successive generations of socialist revolutionaries. Georges
Lefebvre will have none of this: in his view neither Robespierre, nor the
other *montagnards* (nor, for that matter the *enragés*) possessed an agrarian
policy capable of appealing to the peasant masses. They were all bourgeois
individualists who distrusted radical schemes for land redistribution and
positively repudiated communism. What marked them out from other
groups of revolutionary politicians was their willingness to listen to the
ordinary people and to go *some way* towards meeting their demands. Even
so, they never felt at ease when pressing home policies of economic interventionism (allotment of *émigré* estates, partition of common lands,
enforcement of the Maximum, requisitions etc.). Their concept of equality
was not 'real', despite what nineteenth-century socialists may have chosen
to believe; it was 'liberal'. They preferred to engineer equality at the higher,
macroscopic level by means of legislation to remove civil disabilities, to
abolish primogeniture, to impose partible inheritance and to promote
education for all.[65]

Nevertheless, we should not conclude by belittling the work of the
montagnard Convention. When pushed, they achieved great things. The
property-owning base of the nation did increase as a result of the sales of
church and *émigré* lands and the chopping up of the commons, although
that increase was very unevenly distributed. Even when not pushed, the
montagnard dictatorship seemed to teeter on the brink of a more
thoroughgoing alteration to property rights on occasions. The so-called
Ventôse Laws are a case in point. On 8 Ventôse II (26 February 1794)
Robespierre's confidant, Saint-Just, read to the assembled deputies a
report on incarcerated 'suspects' whose trial the *sans-culottes* had long
been demanding. He concluded with a recommendation that the property
of those 'suspects' deemed 'enemies of the revolution' be confiscated. Five
days later, Saint-Just followed up this proposal with a draft decree containing the novel suggestion that the possessions of certified enemies of the
revolution should be used to 'indemnify' poor patriots. To this end, communes were to compile lists of their poor patriots, while the *comités de
surveillance* were to draw up statements on all the 'suspects' imprisoned in
their districts. The measure passed through the Convention, despite the
misgivings of many deputies, but it remained inoperative for want of
machinery to carry out the intended seizure of property. No 'suspect' was
ever permanently parted from his property. Nevertheless, the new laws
caused a stir of anticipation in some localities and their significance has
been hotly debated by historians. Were they premeditated, or were they
simply a legislative manoeuvre to outbid the Hébertists? Were they a sign

that jacobinism had at last transcended its bourgeois limitations, or were they accepted by the deputies as little more than a sophisticated scheme for the alleviation of pauperism? It should be noted that Saint-Just spoke of 'indemnifying' the poor, not of sharing out 'suspects'' lands on a free-for-all basis. Still, Albert Mathiez believes that a 'vast transfer of property from one political class to another' was at issue, and he makes the Ventôse Laws the pinnacle of Robespierrist social policy.[66] Georges Lefebvre, however, is a good deal more cautious in his assessment and doubts whether, in practice, the laws would have inaugurated a radical new approach to the problem of poverty.[67] In any case, the Committee of Public Safety soon confused the issue by absorbing Saint-Just's proposals into an ambitious programme for national assistance. The threat to 'suspects'' properties remained, but the prospect that they would be parcelled out to those poor in material terms, yet rich in virtue, became more and more unlikely.

Chapter 6

The administrative revolution

Between 1789 and 1792 the administrative structures of *ancien régime* France were totally, and in most cases irretrievably, altered. The process began in the spring of 1789 with municipal uprisings in the great cities and the creation of bourgeois militias, the forerunners of the National Guard. It ended in 1792 when the linear descendants of the old *parlements* – the department criminal courts – opened their doors for business. The repudiation of dynastic monarchy with the proclamation of a republic later that year served merely to top off the new edifice. Some of the reforms enacted by the National Assembly had been widely canvassed in the *cahiers*: for example, the abolition of fiscal exemptions, the removal of duties on wine and alcohol, and an end to the detestable salt tax. The *cahiers* also contained vague proposals for a reorganisation of the Gallican church and the remodelling of first-instance courts. No one, however, anticipated the scale and speed of reform as it materialised over the next two or three years. When the absolute monarchy embarked upon reform, which it not infrequently did, the initiative tended to be hesitant and the results piecemeal. Outworn institutions were not replaced; they were outflanked. When the revolutionaries embarked on reform, they did so amid a torrent of rhetoric and theorising which denied validity to any institution which was not constructed according to first principles. 'Something they must destroy, or they seem to themselves to exist for no purpose', commented Edmund Burke.[1] It was a jaundiced view no doubt, but it captures well the sense of millenarian zeal with which the fabric of the *ancien régime* was thrown into the melting-pot.

Reconstruction followed no precise blueprint: how could it when no one had anticipated the turn of events? Nevertheless, the deputies clung tenaciously to two fundamental propositions: power must be decentralised, and those who were to exercise it must be made accountable. In the context of absolute monarchy as forged by Louis XIV, the desire for decentralisation is understandable enough. Fears of 'ministerial despotism' and suspicions of 'court extravagance' had helped to launch the revolution, and to judge from the *cahiers* hostility towards the intendants was no less widespread. Beneath the surface of the unitary state seethed a mass of provincial loyalties and local particularisms which awaited but the moment for political recognition. More surprising, perhaps, was the deputies' obsession with accountability. Before 1789, comments one historian, 'there was not a single truly elected assembly in the country, only government officials; in 1790 there was no longer a single official, just elected bodies'.[2] The paradox is overstated, of course, yet it captures well the spirit of the reforms carried out in these years. With scarcely any prior experience of the functioning of representative bodies, legislators handed power to groups of private citizens chosen by ballot. The elective principle became the battering-ram of the new regime against the old, and elections its most striking constitutional innovation. Henceforth, no institution was safe from the sanction of public consent: each tier of local government consisted of elected personnel; local magistrates (*juges de paix*) were elected, as were the professional judges of the district and department courts and the court of appeal. Even the church had to yield to the principle of accountability. Under the terms of the Civil Constitution of the Clergy, episcopal and parochial vacancies were to be filled by election like any other vacancy in the public service. Many ecclesiastical deputies objected that this would enable protestants, Jews and atheists to participate in the appointment of the catholic clergy, but the majority in the Assembly brushed such scruples aside.

In retrospect it seems staggering that the deputies failed to perceive the dangers of pushing decentralisation and accountability to logical extremes. After all, they were trying to introduce the institutions and practices of liberal democracy to a country whose political reflexes were localist in outlook and feudal in nature. The safeguards against incompetence, insubordination and maladministration which they incorporated in their legislation were minimal. Even the notorious provision restricting the right to vote (see pp. 173–4) missed its mark, and in any case it was swept aside after the popular uprising of August 1792. But the deputies were not as sovereign as they liked to pretend. Whilst committees of the National Assembly debated the pros and cons of rival schemes for administrative reform, the people of France were busily filling the power vacuum with unofficial bodies, not to mention sundry militias. Sometimes these spontaneously created organs were patterned on the old Provincial Estates; more often they resembled the 'permanent committees' which had taken over town government in the spring and summer of 1789. Realistically, the deputies calculated that they could not afford to antagonise their supporters at the grass-roots, even if that support was expressed in unorthodox or inconvenient ways. Instead, they tried as far as possible to incorporate these bodies in their own schemes for reform. The famous Municipal Law enacted on 14 December 1789 is a case in point: it required every 'town, *bourg*, parish or community' to elect a municipal council even though the legislation was plainly conceived with the towns in mind. Several deputies questioned the wisdom of turning every village into a self-governing entity, but the on-going municipal revolution left little room for manoeuvre. Besides, Calonne's municipal assemblies (see pp. 27–9) of 1787 had already paved the way.

The package of fiscal, judicial, ecclesiastical and local government reforms which the National Assembly introduced between 1789 and 1792 shook rural France to its roots. For all their magnitude the Great Fear and the agrarian revolts left many localities untouched, but the pulpit announcement that every village would shortly be invited to elect a municipality brought the revolution to every peasant's doorstep. Thereafter the pace of reform became fast and furious: elections to staff the new district and department administrations followed those for the municipal councils; then the *juges de paix* and the personnel of the district courts had to be chosen. The prospect of further elections loomed in 1791 when nearly half the parish clergy refused to swear an oath of allegiance to the constitution. Meanwhile, the municipalities were busily revising the old tax rolls and laying the foundations for an entirely new system of taxation. The framework of institutions which had conditioned the lives of country dwellers for centuries was changing, and changing with a disturbing suddenness. Some historians have described this transition as an 'administrative revolution' and the phrase is apt, for the impact of these changes at the grass-roots is not to be underestimated. Issues such as fiscal reform or parish reorganisation had a powerful catalysing effect on opinions for and against the revolution. Not that this was apparent at first: until the summer of 1792 the political geography of rural France was obscured by the continuing struggle over seigneurialism. After that date, however, it became obvious that some country dwellers had done better out of the change of regime than had others.

Disintegration and reintegration

The revolution triggered off an explosion of particularism. As the cumbersome bureaucracy of the Bourbon monarchy fell apart, power shifted down the social scale and out into the countryside. The provinces were taking their revenge on Paris and the deputies could only stand and watch in awe. A gigantic centrifuge was spinning the centralised state into smithereens. In October 1789 they intervened to prevent the Provincial

Estates from emerging as an alternative source of authority, but they need not have worried. The process transcended provincial loyalties; it reached into every village and hamlet. Besides, no one was questioning the overall authority of the National Assembly; rather, French men and women were rebelling against the constriction of local freedoms by royal and seigneurial officials. This and more: beneath the hostility towards the intendants, venal corporations and busybodying seigneurial personnel lay a tangle of territorial rivalries. These had a timeless quality and there is little reason to suppose that they were any more acute in 1789 than in 1689 or, perhaps, 1889. What the revolution did was to remove the disciplines that had hitherto constricted country dwellers in the organisation of their affairs. After centuries of close administrative supervision, they suddenly discovered the freedom to act and to combine. The opportunity only lasted for a moment, but it was exploited to the full.

The chance to rearrange the contours of everyday life materialised first in the spring of 1789. By the following spring and summer it had either been seized on gleefully, or had been postponed indefinitely. There were two phases to the process: peasant communities began to flex their muscles in anticipation of the collapse of the *ancien régime*; then came a period of chaotic jostling as these self-same communities strove for administrative recognition under the new order. The first phase blurred into the second during the autumn and winter of 1789 when it became apparent that the National Assembly intended to remodel the institutions of the country starting at the bottom. With the centralised state effectively demolished, everything was up for grabs.

Intimations that the horizons of daily life might be about to change clearly reached the peasantry as early as the spring of 1789, for the rural *cahiers* contained mutterings against the administrative and ecclesiastical status quo. Territorial rivalries, it should be said, were integral to village life and could act as powerful catalysts of opinion in the countryside. For this reason alone, they deserve closer attention from historians than they have received in the past. Some villages complained about the domination of a local town or *bourg*, others bore a grudge against the ecclesiastical authorities for refusing them a parish church, many more used the opportunity to criticise the distribution of royal and seigneurial courts. Implied in all these grumbles was the conviction that village A would make a far more suitable administrative centre, parish headquarters or seat of a seigneurial jurisdiction than village B. In the province of the Rouergue and that of Roussillon villagers loudly protested against a fiscal system that sacrificed their interests to those of neighbouring *bourgs*, while in the future department of the Vendée the distribution of parishes was causing friction long before the Civil Constitution of the Clergy contrived to worsen the situation. But villages were not the only, or indeed the most important building blocks of rural life in some parts of the country. Obsessive territorialism affected hamlets, too. Whereas the villages saw each other, or local towns, as the principal threat to their independence, the hamlets lived in watchful fear of their village neighbours. Occasionally, the *cahiers* recorded their anxieties as well. In Burgundy, for instance, a number of small settlements exploited the electoral assemblies of February and March 1789 to voice their desire for administrative and fiscal autonomy.

No doubt the municipal reform introduced to the *pays d'élections* by Calonne in the late summer of 1787 played a part in the process. It alerted peasant communities to the fact that the fabric of village life was no longer sacrosanct and thereby nurtured the centrifugal pressures that were to take over two years later. Little recent research has been devoted to Calonne's ill-starred attempt to modernise local government, but it can be surmised that the idea of freedom from the pettifogging attentions of intendants and sub-delegates burgeoned in many small entities at about this time. Something of the sort appears to have happened in the Auvergne where a harsh physical environment and a loosely meshed human habitat encouraged extreme forms of parochialism. The *bourgs* and most of the villages acquired the right to elect a municipal assembly, but the hamlets were left out in the cold and viewed the whole exercise with misgivings. Some simply ignored the regulations and elected microscopic municipalities of their own. This happened at Buffières where twelve out of twenty-four illiterate taxpayers took it upon themselves to appoint a municipal assembly in August 1787. Undaunted by the hostility of the higher authorities and neighbouring villages, the hamlet defended its newly won independence until the spring of 1790.

The labours of the Constitution Committee of the National Assembly shifted this process of disintegration and reintegration into its second phase. On 14 December 1789 the deputies yielded to the overwhelming centrifugal pressure and enacted into law what had already become a practical reality. Town and village alike acquired the right to elect a municipality and in so doing to become a commune, although this term for the lowest tier of local government was not immediately adopted. With the commune replacing the old *communauté d'habitants*, the deputies reached a second historic decision a few days later: France would be divided up into departments, and the departments into districts and cantons. These units were intended to be more than simply territorial entities, for, like the commune, the departments and the districts had attached to them an administrative superstructure of elected officials. The canton was anomalous in this respect: it served merely to define an electoral constituency and the jurisdiction of the *juge de paix*. Several schemes for the organisation of the departments were discussed, but eventually the deputies resolved to adhere to existing provincial frontiers wherever possible. By mid-February 1790 eighty-three departments had been created, on paper at least. For example, it was envisioned that the old province of the Rouergue would become the new department of the Aveyron (named after an insignificant river flowing through its territory). The department was sub-divided into nine districts, eighty-one cantons and 684 communes. The Aveyron could legitimately claim to represent an ancient *pays*, but many other departments were less fortunate. Some were carved out of much larger provinces, while others were cobbled together from the bits left over.

With the promulgation of the Assembly's local government reforms, the struggle for pre-eminence began in earnest. It resembled a vast, slow-motion game of musical chairs as thousands of towns, villages and hamlets jockeyed for position in the new social order. The towns were mainly concerned to win the status of department or district capitals, and not surprisingly, for the bourgeoisie of a town like Villefranche-de-Rouergue stood to lose a great deal if the burgers of Rodez successfully petitioned for the department administration and criminal court to be set up within their walls. Throughout the land some epic battles were fought on this score: Montauban versus Cahors; Marseilles versus Aix; St Flour versus Aurillac; Saumur versus Angers – the list is long. These gladiatorial combats left the peasantry unmoved, however. Their eyes were firmly fixed upon the lower tiers of government: the cantons, the communes and, to a lesser degree, the districts. Reports that royal commissioners were allocating district and cantonal seats opened a Pandora's Box of personal animosities and territorial rivalries. The *bourgs* fought tooth and nail for the dignity of *chef-lieu de district*, and once the decision had been taken the losers competed among themselves for the consolation prize of *chef-lieu de canton*. With the territorial format of the departments barely finalised, aggrieved towns and *bourgs* sometimes managed to pilot their way across department frontiers, as it were, in the hope of securing better terms. The *bourg* of Saugues, for instance, quit the Lozère and ended up in the neighbouring department of the Haute-Loire. There was a point to this vainglorious manoeuvring, for the Assembly announced that each district capital would be equipped with a civil court, while each *chef-lieu de canton* would become the seat of a *juge de paix*. Every peasant knew that close justice dispensed by kinsmen was preferable to remote justice dispensed by 'foreigners'.

The point holds for the municipalities, too, for they were empowered to try cases of minor misdemeanour and could impose fines and even custodial sentences. Moreover, the Assembly had delegated to the municipalities the task of assessing and collecting direct taxes (see pp. 179–80): two more reasons for coveting this status. And indeed, the dignity was bitterly disputed. In regions of dispersed habitat such as the Massif Central where there existed no settled hierarchy of villages and hamlets, virtually every settlement, no matter how small, entertained illusions of municipal grandeur. Of course, the loose phrasing of the decree of 14 December 1789 did not help matters. In the department of the Aveyron hamlets consisting of no more than half a dozen households turned themselves into municipalities, while in the Ardèche the whole process of administrative renewal caused such tension that country people nearly came to blows. The royal commissioner sent out to supervise the cantonal elections for the district and department authorities reported in April 1790 that several villages were refusing to send their electors to the *chef-lieu* at Charmes in the belief that they would be molested. These were local disputes with local causes no doubt, but we cannot afford to ignore them. The territorial and administrative squabbles of 1789–90 made a lasting impression. Villagers nursed their frustrations and disappointments, and sooner or later these resurfaced in reactions to the Civil Constitution of the Clergy, to recruitment and to counter-revolution.

The new municipalities

Most country dwellers welcomed the Assembly's experiment in grassroots democracy. Ever since the summer of 1787 the reform of local government had been in the air and the calling of the Estates-General intensified speculation on this issue. The parish *cahiers* of the *bailliage* of Mirecourt in Lorraine urged that Calonne's municipal assemblies be consolidated 'by giving them surer and better defined powers'.[3] In this the deputies did not disappoint: the Municipal Law of 14 December 1789 became a pillar of the revolutionary settlement. Like most of the concessions of 1789–90 it was subjected to repeated attack in later years, but the peasantry never lost sight of this prize and defended the right to municipal self-government tenaciously.

The deputies certainly decentralised power, and on a scale undreamt of by Calonne and his predecessors, but they took care to vest that power in a political nation of 'active' citizens. All offices in the new bodies were open to election (venality and *ex officio* privileges having been abolished); however, the right to stand for election and the right to vote were confined to adult males in possession of certain qualifications. In effect, a three-tier restriction was placed upon the 'rights of man' so solemnly promulgated only six months earlier. At the lowest level citizens were sorted into two groups depending on whether they were aged twenty-five or over, had resided in the same locality for at least a year, and paid the cash equivalent of three days' labour in direct tax. Those who could meet these criteria were dubbed 'actifs' (actives) and were entitled to participate in the choosing of municipal personnel. Those who could not were described as 'passifs' (passives) and found themselves excluded from the political process until the advent of universal manhood suffrage at all levels of government in the autumn of 1792. Active citizens were divided into two more categories, however: adult males paying the value of ten days' labour in direct taxes were entitled not only to vote, but to stand for municipal office, too. Appointments to the higher echelons of local government (district and department assemblies) were made by electoral colleges consisting of 'électeurs' or delegates, and citizens whose tax payments reached the equivalent of ten days' labour were permitted to serve as electors and to take up posts in these bodies as well. To qualify for election as a deputy, however, the active citizen had to be a man of property paying a 'marc d'argent' (roughly equivalent to fifty days' wages) in direct tax.

Certain categories of adult were automatically excluded from the political nation: women, for instance, although widows were occasionally permitted to vote in municipal elections. Servants, too, were disenfranchised irrespective of whether they could muster a tax contribution equivalent to the going rate for three days' labour. Less obviously, the National Assembly contrived to deny civic rights to grown-up sons living with their parents since such individuals were not assessed separately for tax purposes. Also, the residence qualification prevented absentee landowners from interfering in the political life of the village. No wonder the peasantry greeted the reform with enthusiasm: even allowing for the qualification on the right to vote, it marked a signal advance on Calonne's scheme. Depending on the locality, the lowest tier of active citizenship (voting rights in primary assemblies) could be had for as little as 2 *livres* compared with 10 *livres* in 1787, whilst eligibility for office required a tax threshold of about 7 *livres* 10 *sols* rather than 30 *livres*.

It is true that the electoral machinery which swung into operation in 1790 marked a retreat from the conditions under which the elections to the Estates-General had been conducted, but most deputies wanted to draw a firm line beneath the anarchic liberty of 1789. Universal manhood suffrage was not a serious political option for the first two years of the revolution: it only became one when all else had failed. What strikes the historian is less the timidity of the National Assembly in this domain than its sheer audacity. Notwithstanding the active–passive divide, the French revolutionaries gave 61 per cent of adult males the right to participate in the political process, and this at a time when scarcely four Englishmen in a hundred had the vote. At the municipal level the transformation was even more dramatic, for most peasants qualified for the vote without difficulty. Indeed, many householders found that they were qualified to hold local office and to serve as electors, too. The figures suggest that 4.3 million Frenchmen satisfied the basic criteria for active citizenship at a time when the constituency of males aged twenty-five and over numbered some 7 millions.[4] If the most recent calculations of demographers can be relied upon, this would mean that about 15 per cent of the total population possessed the right to vote in primary assemblies.

But such figures scarcely express the magnitude of the transition at the grass-roots. For this we need to look at case studies which pinpoint the impact of electoral reform in human terms. By and large they show that historians have tended to exaggerate the discriminatory character of the active–passive divide. In many regions it was blurred to the point of insignificance. The department of the Sarthe is a case in point: here Paul Bois has shown that few, if any, villagers were denied the right to vote because they paid insufficient tax.[5] If the 'passive' status applied to anyone, it was to vagabonds and the mendicant poor. Indeed, he points out that most villagers were qualified to stand for office and to serve as electors, too. Perhaps the only distinct social group who paid enough tax to vote, but not enough to stand for election to the municipal council were the agricultural day labourers. Even so, a proportion still crossed the 'ten days' labour in tax' threshold. In the countryside at least, the new electoral system was genuinely democratic, he argues: it tended to mix social categories together rather than separate them out. Broadly comparable conclusions have been reached by a group of researchers working on the Burgundian department of the Côte-d'Or.[6] Their analysis of a cross-section of settlements which includes two semi-urban *bourgs* shows that passive citizens were not a negligible quantity. In every case, however, they were outnumbered by 'actives'. Moreover, the vast majority of 'actives' were not only qualified to vote, but also to hold office and to act as electors.

On the periphery of the kingdom and in some of the *pays d'états* direct taxation was lower and this may account for some of the variations in the numbers eligible to vote. Lefebvre[7] reckons that many peasant households were disenfranchised in the Nord, perhaps the majority in some villages, and this despite the fact that some municipalities deliberately fixed the price of a day's labour at below the market rate. In any case, the active–passive distinction was never properly adhered to in this region. Passive citizens loudly protested their exclusion and voted willy-nilly. By the end of 1790 most heads of household had contrived electoral registration by one means or another. Brittany was probably the most undertaxed region of France at the end of the *ancien régime* and here the proportion of active citizens does appear to have been lower than the national average. On the basis of two districts in the Ille-et-Vilaine, Donald Sutherland estimates that about 11 per cent of the total population qualified for the vote.[8] Even so, it is clear that far more adult males were enfranchised than were not. In the rural communes of the district of Vitré approximately three-quarters of householders were entitled to vote. Where Brittany seems to deviate from the norm is in the number of country dwellers qualified to take office in local government and to participate in the second stage of the electoral process. If most active citizens in the Sarthe and the Côte-d'Or could pass muster as electors, under half reached this threshold in the Ille-et-Vilaine. We are left, therefore, with a nuanced picture: the constitution of 1791 undoubtedly emancipated the great mass of the peasantry, albeit at a rudimentary level. Yet the extent to which the peasantry could capitalise upon their electoral pre-eminence varied from region to region, and probably from district to district. In the West, peasants found that they could vote, but they were rarely able to get their own kind into office.

All over France townsmen and villagers alike set about electing the new municipalities in the early months of 1790. Depending on size, each commune was entitled to a mayor, a procurator, a deputy procurator and between two and twenty councillors. Properly speaking, the municipal body simply consisted of the mayor and his councillors, but it was backed by a variable number (between six and forty-two) of *notables* or aldermen who were also elected. Close on a million individuals must have been called to public office as a result of this vast exercise in grass-roots democracy. How many actually voted can only be guessed at. In the village of Flavin (Aveyron), to take an example, the *consuls* summoned the active citizens to gather in the church at 8 a.m. on 10 March 1790. There the curate explained to the fifty-six individuals present the purpose of the meeting. After the relevant legislation had been read out loud and all those participating had sworn an oath to uphold the constitution, voting for a mayor, a procurator, five councillors and twelve *notables* got under way. The mayoral office fell to the parish priest, as not infrequently happened during the first year of the revolution. Thereafter the new council was renewed by half in the autumn of 1790 as prescribed by decree, and then at yearly intervals. When the mayor resigned on the issue of the clerical oath in February 1791, a fresh election had to be organised. All these elections were confined to active citizens, until the autumn of 1792, that is, when the Convention introduced universal manhood suffrage and reduced the voting age to twenty-one: a cosmetic exercise, in truth, for regular elections ceased to be held in 1793 and 1794, either in Flavin or elsewhere in the Republic.

The turn-out of voters in the first municipal election ever held at Flavin was low (35 per cent), but it seems that active citizens attended the polls in droves throughout the kingdom. At Le Mesnil-Théribus (Oise) 79 per cent of those entitled to vote did so; the Burgundian villages of Larrey and Ruffey recorded a turn-out of 82 per cent and 83 per cent respectively, while the *bourg* of Epoisses situated not far distant registered an attendance rate of 59 per cent.[9] In the Nord Lefebvre notes that the peasantry voted with enthusiasm.[10] Clearly, the hustings were regarded as an exciting novelty in the early months of 1790 and besides, seigneurialism had only been disarmed, not defeated. Much remained to be fought for. This excitement soon subsided, however, as country dwellers found themselves in a state of semi-permanent electoral trajectory. First the municipalities had to be chosen, then in May and June electors were invited to trek to the nearest town in order to appoint the district and department authorities. Hardly had the machinery of local government been put in place, than electors were again summoned to deliberate on the choice of candidates for judicial office. Further meetings were scheduled for the appointment of officers in the National Guard and the replacement of clergy who had refused the oath. Elections, which had always been time-consuming, became boring, financially burdensome, even offensive in the eyes of some.

Signs of exhaustion, if not yet disillusionment, were plainly evident when the first partial renewal of municipal councillors and *notables* fell due in November 1790. Electoral participation in the Côte-d'Or villages of Larrey and Ruffey plummeted to 45 per cent and 65 per cent respectively. The slide continued the following year, too. Similarly, in Le Mesnil-Théribus only 35 per cent of the commune's active citizens bothered to turn out for the municipal elections of November 1791. Abstentionism developed early in the department of the Nord as well, provoked in part by the ecclesiastical policies of the National Assembly. In theory, the resort to universal manhood suffrage in the autumn of 1792 should have arrested this slide, at least in those villages containing significant numbers of adult males who had been denied the vote. In practice, however, the political die seems to have been cast by this date: ardent supporters of the revolution continued to vote as a matter of principle, but the great mass of country dwellers had already decided against further involvement in communal affairs. The abandonment of the active–passive distinction widened the electorate by 37 per cent in the village of Larrey, but the proportion of voters attending the polls barely shifted. At Ruffey fewer peasants attended the autumn hustings of 1792 than ever before, notwithstanding a 20 per cent increase in the size of the electorate. The story was the same at Epoisses: 81 inhabitants of the *bourg* voted in the municipal election of late 1792, compared with 101 early in 1790, and this despite the inclusion of 93 former 'passives' on the electoral register.

How far did the opening up of local government challenge the authority of established elites? On paper at least 1789 offered a wonderful opportunity for the rural bourgeoisie and the wealthy apex of the peasantry to seize control of village life, while 1792 held out the prospect of power to sharecroppers, plot farmers, day labourers and the rural poor. In the South it seems that the transition from the old regime to the new was blurred by the presence of an entrenched class of bourgeois landowners who already operated the levers of local government, albeit on behalf of the seigneurs. For such individuals the reform involved little more than a change of hats (see p. 29), although they were sometimes obliged to share power with the odd *ménager* or master craftsman. The North knew little of the municipal traditions of the South, however. Here village life was more diffuse and it is likely that the introduction of elective municipalities jolted local hierarchies in a more permanent fashion. In truth, the process had already begun, for the election of parish delegates in the spring of 1789, following hard on the experience of Calonne's municipal assemblies, had brought to the fore a new elite-in-the-making. This elite consisted of well-to-do peasant farmers for the most part. In the North the professional and land owning bourgeoisie were largely urban in outlook and preferred to seek office in the towns and *bourgs*, which left the rural municipalities in the hands of *laboureurs*, small merchants and artisans.

A further instalment of democracy in the autumn of 1792 made little difference to this state of affairs – unsurprisingly, if the majority of peasant householders were already qualified to vote. Just as the newly enfranchised 'active' citizens of 1790 chose their immediate social superiors for public office, so the newly enfranchised 'passive' citizens likewise oiled the wellsprings of deference, if they voted at all. Municipal government tended to be about clienteles rather than classes. Just occasionally the convoluted politics of the rural community polarised on socio-economic lines and the alignments can be traced in election results. At St Symphorien (Côte-d'Or), for instance, the admission of 'passives' to the vote in November 1792 worked a veritable revolution in the commune. A municipality faithfully serving the interests of peasant proprietors was diluted by the inclusion of an agricultural labourer as procurator, a cooper and a navvy as councillors, and a nailer, plus another agricultural worker as *notables*. Electoral gyrations on this scale were rare, however. Usually the elite thrust into power in 1789 managed to ride out the storms of the revolution, at least until 1793. It was the very success of that elite in manipulating the electoral process that prompted the *montagnards* to dispense with the ballot box and to carry out wholesale purges of local government personnel instead.

By the spring of 1790 the foundations of a modern system of local government had been laid. Municipalities had mushroomed in every 'town, *bourg*, parish or community'. Time would tell whether the creation of some 41,000 semi-autonomous bodies was the most efficient way to run a country the size of France. The decree of 14 December 1789 conferred an enormous burden of responsibility on villagers, much more than had ever been sought in the *cahiers*. Specifically mentioned was the obligation to apportion and collect direct taxes, carry out public works, oversee the fabric of the church and maintain law and order. It had already been decided that the municipalities should control the National Guard and not vice versa, and steps were taken to prevent the two bodies from overlapping. Subsequent legislation lengthened the list of responsibilities: administration of the clerical oath; registration of births, marriages and deaths; grain censuses and requisitions; the issue of *certificats de civisme*; surveillance of suspects; and so on and so forth. Yet, the precise fashion in which these powers were to be exercised was left extraordinarily vague, at least until the law of 14 Frimaire II (4 December 1793). The most important personage was the mayor, for he was elected in a separate ballot requiring an absolute majority. But his role remained unclear: was he a figurehead or a chief executive? If the latter, did he reflect the interests of the central power or those of his local constituency? In theory, the task of representing the wider interest fell to the procurator, in practice all municipal personnel tended to identify with the home community. Exasperated, the *montagnards* created the post of *agent national* in December 1793. These national (i.e. not local) agents were attached to the department and district authorities as well as the municipalities and given special responsibility for 'enforcing the execution of the law, as well as denouncing omissions and any breaches that might have been committed'.[11] But even this draconian attempt to restore a degree of central control did little to redress the balance. For a few brief months the *montagnards* succeeded in extracting a sullen compliance from rural municipalities. That was all. On 13 Germinal II (2 April 1794) the *agent national* of the district of Murat (Cantal) complained to his subordinates in the municipalities: 'You content yourselves with reporting that everyone is behaving well. This is not enough.'[12]

Administrative muddle was not, of course, the basic problem. From the start the deputies entertained quite ludicrous ideas of what could be expected of the bottom rung of local government. Outside the towns and *bourgs* administrative talent quickly dried up. The typical municipality was not a resplendent body of civic dignitaries issuing instructions from an *hôtel de ville*, but a makeshift assembly of semi-literate peasants deliberating in the open air. With the best will in the world, many villages found it impossible to fill a council with men who knew how to read and write. A few found it impossible to nominate even one person who knew how to read and write. The language barrier complicated the problem. South of the river Loire and in parts of Brittany, the East and the North East, French was not normally spoken by the common people (see pp. 208–10). Moreover, it was very imperfectly understood and the deputies soon discovered that a gulf of incomprehension lay between them and their rural constituents. From the Pyrenees, from Gascony, from the provinces of the southern Massif Central came complaints that the peasantry seemed incapable of grasping the legislation of the National Assembly, even when it was read out aloud (see p. 209). Many of the newly elected municipalities in the Cerdagne were Catalan-speaking to a man, objected the administrators of the department of the Pyrénées-Orientales. They need not have looked so far afield: at the gates of Perpignan only the mayor, the procurator, the clerk and one *notable* in the village of St Estève could express themselves in French.

Not surprisingly, therefore, the rural municipalities tended to perform the duties thrust upon them rather badly. The setting up of the new tax system alone involved the new mayors and councillors in weeks, if not months, of to-ing and fro-ing (see pp. 183–5). Against the undoubted prestige of municipal office had to be set the fact that it was unremunerated and very time-consuming. It was also 'high profile' in the political sense: harassing seigneurs in the early months of 1790 could be fun and was enormously popular, but harassing priests who had refused the loyalty oath in the early months of 1791 was a different kettle of fish. Unable to reconcile public responsibilities with private inclinations, many mayors and councillors chose to resign instead. Already in late October 1790, the district administrators of Remiremont (Vosges) had warned: 'We must take care to give the municipalities as little work and inconvenience as possible; they are all worn out and are beginning to show considerable distaste for their duties.'[13] Some rural municipalities began to opt out within a year of their creation; others withstood the shock of the administrative revolution only to fall prey to narrow cliques of activists in 1791 and 1792. They can be roughly divided into 'accomplice' municipalities and 'authoritarian' municipalities. The former identified strongly with the local community and used their considerable institutional presence to filter the pressures of revolution at the grass-roots. Authoritarian municipalities calculated the balance of political risks rather differently and became the slavish auxiliaries of the higher authorities. Buttressed by clubs and *comités de surveillance*, they emerged in 1793 as the safe havens of republicanism in a sea of popular indifference.

Tax revolt

Underscoring all the deputies' calculations in the autumn of 1789 was the question of public finance. The events of that year had brought tax payment to a virtual standstill. Worse, this tax strike threatened to trigger a further round of agrarian uprisings aimed specifically against those entrusted with the task of collecting excise duties on items of everyday consumption. Already Picardy had become the epicentre of revolt against taxes on salt, tobacco and alcoholic drinks, and sporadic bouts of anti-fiscal insurgency had broken out in other provinces, too. The Assembly needed to move fast, yet the creation of a new tax system involved important issues of principle which could not be settled overnight. In the end a compromise was reached: for the remainder of 1789 and the whole of 1790 existing direct and indirect taxes would remain in force; then, in 1791, the new fiscal regime would begin in earnest. The advantage of this manner of proceeding was that it protected the state from the hiccough in cash-flow that a more rapid transition implied. On the other hand, it jeopardised that enormous fund of goodwill that had greeted the fall of the Bastille. As always happens when a revolution takes place, everyone expected change, and expected it *immediately*.

The peasantry had made their view of royal taxation policy clear in the parish *cahiers*. From much of rural France came calls for alleviation of the *taille* and *capitation*, removal of consumption levies, and reform of the vast bureaucracy known as the General Farm which collected most indirect taxes. The National Assembly was disposed to meet these demands in due course. Not for the first time, however, it was overtaken by events. The most sustained outbreaks of violence and civil disobedience occurred in the small towns dotting the plain of Picardy and for reasons which are not difficult to unravel. Picardy passed for one of the most heavily taxed regions of France at the end of the *ancien régime*. As a *pays de grande gabelle* the province was subject to a crushing salt tax, while winegrowers, vintners and smaller retailers complained that their trade was being stifled by a wide range of duties levied at the point of sale. Wine was not the only commodity to attract the attentions of a revenue-hungry government: in the *généralité* of Amiens the consumption of brandy and beer was inhibited by exceptionally onerous sales taxes, too. Nearly all these pettifogging duties fell within the orbit of the General Farm whose employees, or *commis*, policed every aspect of the drinks trade, not to mention the production and sale of tobacco. They also collected the *octrois* (duties payable on goods such as firewood and fatstock entering towns) and the *traites* (customs duties levied on merchandise crossing inter-

national and some internal frontiers). Stationed in every corner of the kingdom, the *commis* were among the most hated figures in French society on
the eve of the revolution.

In Picardy the news of the fall of the Bastille signalled an opportunity to
settle scores with the fiscal bureaucracy above all else. Toll gates and customs houses were demolished and many *commis* fled for their lives. The
collection of *aides* (the sales tax on alcoholic drinks) ceased temporarily,
while contraband salt and tobacco were sold openly in the markets of the
region. Whether this revolt can be compared with the mass mobilisations
against the châteaux as Barry Rose has suggested[14] is doubtful; nevertheless, the determination to act decisively against an iniquitous system of
taxation quickly spread to neighbouring provinces. By the early months of
1790 the whole of the North East was gripped by the campaign against the
drinks tax. The winegrowers and artisans of Picardy continued to make
the running, however, and by stages the movement broadened into a
general indictment of the principle of indirect taxation. Much of the
responsibility for this development can be attributed to the activism of one
man: François-Noël Babeuf. A native of the region, Babeuf worked hard to
politicise the Picard tax revolt and was arrested for his pains. But the
episode served to launch his public career: on his release from prison in
July 1790 he was greeted as something of a folk hero. Nowhere else in the
country did the tax revolt coalesce to this degree, although the repetition
of thousands of unconnected acts of violence had a cumulative impact
upon the National Assembly. Particularly serious incidents occurred in
Languedoc and Roussillon. At Béziers a crowd infuriated by confiscations
of wine drove fifty-two *commis* to seek refuge in the *hôtel de ville*, and
customs officers supervising the movement of goods between Spain and
France also fell foul of popular violence. As a result, the merchants of
Barcelona were able to flood the markets of southern France with their
draperies. Even as late as May 1792 some of the higher Pyrenean passes
remained unmanned by customs personnel. All these actions hit their
mark: receipts reaching the General Farm tailed off dramatically in the
second half of 1789. At Bourges the corporation of butchers resolved to
refuse duties on livestock bought in for slaughter, much to the dismay of
the local *directeur des aides* who complained that his agents could no
longer turn up at the slaughter houses 'without putting themselves in the
most extreme danger'.[15] Fatstock and wine admitted through the town's
Saint Privé gate between July and December 1788 had yielded receipts of
397 *livres*, but the *commis* only managed to collect 150 *livres* during the
same period in 1789. With direct taxes being withheld, with the yield of
indirect taxes flagging, something had to be done, and quickly.

Ideally, the deputies would have wished to maintain all indirect sources of revenue in order to meet the shortfall on the direct tax account, at least until a new fiscal system could be put in place. This was just not practical politics, however, and in March 1790 the *gabelle*, or salt tax, was abolished, together with duties on oils, soap, leather and iron. The demise of the royal tobacco monopoly and of the *aides*, *traites* and *octrois* followed within a year or so. An ill-advised attempt to retrieve something from the wreckage by tacking an additional sum on to the direct tax quota for 1790 completely failed. The peasantry were determined not to pay the *gabelle*, however disguised. Only a few thousand *livres* of an additional quota of some fifty-one and a half millions were ever paid. In anticipation of future difficulties, the National Assembly had decreed a special one-off tax on 6 October 1789 called the *contribution patriotique* (henceforth taxes were to be known as 'contributions' rather than 'impositions'). This levy, too, produced disappointing results. Left to their own devices by a government which refused to employ the coercive methods of the *ancien régime*, the nation's taxpayers practised systematic deception and under-assessment. In each town a handful of patriots ostentatiously paid the first instalment of this income tax, but their example was not widely followed. Even when the Assembly increased the pressure by requiring the municipalities to submit estimates of taxpayers' income, the response was lethargic at best. Five municipalities in the Cher had still not returned tax declarations in November 1791. And, of course, those declarations that did eventually reach the higher authorities were grossly inaccurate. To judge from the statements of income liable to the *contribution patriotique* in the Cher, the taxable earnings of the entire population of the department did not amount to more than two million *livres*.

Another, manifestly more popular approach was to widen the taxpaying base of the nation. Since the revolution had abolished pecuniary privileges, the National Assembly announced on 25 September 1789 that the nobility, the clergy, public functionaries and anyone else who had managed to climb aboard the bandwagon of fiscal immunity would be required to pay a proportionate share of direct taxes backdated to cover the last six months of 1789. Coupled to this decree was the stipulation that landowners should henceforth be taxed in the locality in which their property was situated; not, as happened before 1789, in the locality in which they chose to reside. Thus, members of the bourgeoisie could no longer reduce their tax liabilities by switching their place of residence from the countryside to the town. Popular though these measures were, they placed an enormous burden of work upon the newly elected municipalities whose job it was to draw up the 'supplementary' rolls. From all over the kingdom came reports of confusion and incompetence, with the result that 24,364 (out of 41,170) municipalities still had not submitted the reassessments for 1789 by the end of May 1790. In the department of the Cher over a quarter of the 'supplementary' rolls were still outstanding in November 1790, and a year later six communes still had not completed the task. What made matters worse was the fact that some municipalities regarded the operation as a heaven-sent opportunity to settle old scores. Others supposed that they could collect arrears of tax from 'les ci-devant privilégiés' which could then be set against forthcoming fiscal obligations. According to one source, parishes in the Charente-Inférieure which contained numerous members of the privileged orders 'wrongly imagined that they could freely dispose of the yield of these tax rolls in order to reduce 1790 taxes by two-fifths'.[16] All in all, the 'claw-back' of taxes from those who had been stripped of their immunity at the outset of the revolution should have produced about fourteen million *livres*, but nothing like this sum was ever collected.

Inevitably, therefore, the Assembly was forced to rely on the continued payment of *ancien régime* taxes for one more year. But how would the peasantry react when confronted with levies which resembled the *taille*, the *vingtième* and the *capitation* in all but name? Many country dwellers believed, or chose to believe, that the revolution had brought an end to state taxation in all its forms. 'If we impose taxes on taxpayers', wrote the mayor of a commune near Niort (Deux-Sèvres), 'we run the risk of being beaten to death.'[17] The fate of indirect taxes and those entrusted with their collection was scarcely encouraging, but the deputies needed time in which to organise the transition to a new fiscal regime. At least the unhappy experience of 'supplementary' rolls could be set aside: from 1 January 1790 all householders, irrespective of occupation or juridical status, were listed in the same tax register. Never again would taxation be used for the purposes of social demarcation. Removing the gross discrepancies of apportionment as between provinces, communities and individual households proved a less easy task, however. Allodial land (i.e. that which had been exempt from direct taxes before 1789) could be incorporated in assessments without undue difficulty, but no one could devise an accurate method of harmonising the incidence of taxation so that households with similar means paid similar amounts. Tax assessment in 1790, and in subsequent years, continued to be bound by precedent and the failure of the revolutionaries to resolve this problem cast a long shadow over their fiscal reforms.

In Upper Brittany the abolition of fiscal exemptions made little difference in the short term. Country dwellers in the district of Fougères (Ille-et-Vilaine) found themselves taxed for about the same amount in 1790 as they had been during the last year of the *ancien régime*. Exempt from the *taille*, Brittany would not learn the price of integration until the new tax system was unveiled in 1791. Elsewhere, however, the interim arrangements for 1790 evoked mixed reactions. In the Nord, the recourse to precedent simply perpetuated the overtaxing of the countryside and the undertaxing of towns such as Dunkirk. By contrast, the permanent officials of the Provincial Assembly of the Berry did make an effort to redress the balance between town and country. In 1790 the *taille* and *capitation* for Bourges shot up from 16,888 *livres* to 47,746 *livres*, while that of Châteauroux rose from 12,064 *livres* to 27,749*livres*.[18] Since direct taxes continued to be distributed on a quota basis, the total burden on rural parishes decreased in proportion. Even so, it seems unlikely that taxes were apportioned between householders in a more even-handed fashion. Here the municipalities were to blame, for they persisted in using the tax rolls as a weapon of vengeance. Throughout the Cher and the Indre, municipal officers imposed swingeing assessments on 'ci-devant privilégiés', while taking care to 'look after themselves',[19] their kinsmen and employees.

This was only to be expected. What is more remarkable is the fact that the municipalities chose to cooperate at all, for they had been called upon to complete three sets of tax rolls in as many months. Yet few, if any, defaulted: despite the difficulties, the decrees of the National Assembly commanded widespread support in the countryside. The problem was rather to instil a sense of urgency in taxpayers and in the local officials entrusted with collection. By August 1790 nearly three-quarters of the municipalities in the former *pays d'élections* had completed the rolls for the *taille* equivalent (known as the *imposition principale*), but receipts were slower to come in. The Assembly had hoped to raise some 180 million *livres* from the interim taxes for 1790: in the event only 33 million had been collected by September 1790. Accordingly, the deputies announced that all arrears, whether owed for 1790 or for earlier years, had to be cleared by the middle of 1791 at the latest. In the Cher this deadline was met, more or less, but in the adjacent department of the Indre a growing hostility to the tithe and the seigneurial *terrage* impeded the collection of taxes. In September 1790 the taxpayers of the district of Châteauroux still owed 26,988 *livres* for 1788 and 164,609 *livres* for 1789. Receipts for 1790 were pitifully low, too, despite all the blandishments of the higher authorities.[20] Which of these two departments was more characteristic of conditions in the country as a whole is difficult to judge in the present state of our knowledge. Nevertheless, it is worth noting the social analysis of the tax strike volunteered by the administrators of the Indre: owners of land were continuing to meet their obligations, but tenant farmers were systematically refusing to pay.

On 1 January 1791 the new fiscal regime finally came into being. Since indirect taxes had been abolished to all intents and purposes, the main thrust of the reform was to replace the *taille* and the *vingtième* with a direct tax on the income from land. Thus was the key element in Calonne's reform package vindicated after four years of debate over fiscal policy. The new tax, known henceforth as the *contribution foncière*, was calculated from the average annual yield of real estate over fifteen years, with the proviso that it should not exceed one-sixth of net income. Payable in cash, the deputies expected it to produce 240 million *livres* in the first year, that is to say about 75 per cent of total direct tax receipts. Like the *taille*, the *contribution foncière* was a quota tax ('impôt de répartition') which was fixed by decree and then shared out between the departments, districts and the communes. Buttressing the land tax was a poll or property tax (*contribution personnelle et mobilière*) and a tax on trade or commerce (*patente*) designed to provide, respectively, 20 per cent and 3.4 per cent of state revenue. The remainder would be made up from customs duties and taxes on legal deeds.

The *patente* can be left out of account because it scarcely impinged on the countryside, but the *contribution personnelle et mobilière* ensnared many peasants and calls for closer examination. In reality, this was a portmanteau tax which the National Assembly devised in an effort to tap sources of wealth which escaped the purview of the land tax. As such it had five elements: a modest poll tax; a graduated tax on servants; a tax on saddle horses and mules; a tax on moveable assets and business wealth which was assessed on leases; and a householders' tax (*taxe d'habitation*) likewise assessed on rental values. This latter element was effectively an additional tax and it was used to 'top up' the yield of the first four elements which would otherwise vary from year to year. While eighteenth-century taxpayers preferred taxes of fixed duration, eighteenth-century governments preferred taxes that produced a fixed yield and the National Assembly tried to ensure that the *contribution personnelle et mobilière* for 1791 yielded 66 million *livres*. Fixity of yield was one thing for the *contribution foncière*, however; it was quite another for the *contribution personnelle et mobilière* which, as the minister of finances candidly admitted, 'cannot have as indisputable a basis as that of the land tax'.[21] The peasantry soon had reason to complain of the *contribution personnelle et mobilière* which they likened, damningly, to the old *capitation*.

Nevertheless, all would have been well if the revolutionaries had accompanied their reforms with a systematic re-evaluation of land and property values. This they did not do, nor could they have done it in the conditions of the 1790s. At the very least, a thoroughgoing land survey required the services of a professional fiscal bureaucracy which few politicians were prepared to countenance before the advent of Napoleon.

True, many southern villages possessed land surveys (*cadastres*) of their own but as we have already had occasion to remark (see pp. 36–9), these were scarcely exempt from reproach. Besides, the *cadastres* corresponded to the territory of the community of inhabitants, not to that of the commune in which taxes were henceforth to be assessed. Inevitably, therefore, the deputies were forced to incorporate a good deal of the *ancien régime* fiscal edifice in their plans for the future. If the new taxes were to take effect promptly, they would have to be distributed according to pre-1789 reckonings of taxable capacity. Or, to be precise, they would have to be distributed in accordance with precedent attenuated by adjustments to take account of the abolition of provincial immunities and the territorial re-division of the kingdom. It goes without saying that such adjustments were bound to be highly subjective.

On 27 May 1791 the National Assembly spelled out the sums to be raised by each department. That of the Cher was assessed for 1,558,900 *livres* in *contribution foncière* and 350,200 *livres* in *contribution personnelle et mobilière*.[22] How these figures had been arrived at was left unclear; nor were the administrators of the department offered any guidance on how to distribute the burden between the districts and communes. In the event, they apportioned the *contribution foncière* in accordance with the *vingtième* rolls for 1770, even though the defects in these rolls would be such as to warrant a substantial revision the following year. The *contribution personnelle et mobilière* proved much more difficult to distribute, however. Could it be assessed on the basis of the direct tax rolls for 1790 or 1789? But how, then, to distinguish between landed and non-landed sources of income in this region of *taille personnelle*? Eventually, the directory of the department hit on a formula combining population, the *contribution foncière* and an amount of guesswork. Similar expedients were resorted to in the Indre: here the *contribution foncière* was geared to the 1790 *vingtième* rolls. As for the *contribution personnelle et mobilière*, it was apportioned solely on the basis of population except that the component known as the *taxe d'habitation* was manipulated in such a way as to increase the burden on the towns and *bourgs*. In the Indre, therefore, country dwellers had reason to be grateful to their administrators, but in other departments there are grounds for supposing that the variable character of the *taxe d'habitation* was exploited to the detriment of the peasantry.

Was the new fiscal system an improvement upon the old? In theory, yes. All property and virtually all personal income was now liable to taxation and, over a period of time, the most flagrant inequities between provinces, between town and country, between villages and between comparable households were removed. Such exemptions as remained operated in favour of the very poor rather than the very rich. Whether French men and women perceived the transition in these terms is more doubtful, however. In some parts of the country the revolution had raised expectations to such a degree that nothing short of the complete abolition of state taxation would have satisfied. Even after 1789, many country dwellers continued to pursue this aim by means of the systematic withholding of taxes. The tax strike, indeed, bedevils the whole question of what Paul Bois has termed 'the fiscal disappointment'.[23] Could the peasantry have felt let down by the new regime even as they succeeded in dodging its fiscal demands? Neither that sense of disappointment, nor the extent to which tax evasion was practised, is easily measured. On paper the burden of direct taxation in the department of the Sarthe increased by 64 per cent between 1790 and 1792, but non-payment, late payment, the pressures of monetary inflation and savings accruing from the abolition of indirect taxation would have eroded the real effect of the increase. Nevertheless, there was an undeniable popular reaction against the new taxes in this department, so much so that royalists used the issue in order to try and detach the peasantry from their support of the revolution.

Frontier provinces which had enjoyed valuable fiscal privileges until 1789 were particularly hard hit. In Brittany average per capita taxation appears to have doubled, and a similar progression occurred in some of the villages of the Vendée. The removal of provincial anomalies in the North East worked to the disadvantage of the Cambrésis, too. Georges Lefebvre estimates that direct and indirect taxes totalled some six and a half million *livres* in the future department of the Nord at the end of the *ancien régime*. On paper at least, this figure had risen to eight and a quarter million *livres* by 1792. That is to say, householders found themselves paying 11 *livres* on average under the new regime compared with 7 *livres* 10 *sols* under the old.[24] Yet this is not the whole picture, or even the major part of the picture. In many departments it is likely that there was no actual increase in the burden on peasant surplus. Announcing the quota of state taxes for 1791, the directory of the department of the Gers rejoiced in the fact that it had only risen by one-sixth compared with 1789. For owners of land whose tithe payments had just ceased, this seemed a small price to pay. Even the quotas were not bound to show an increase: average per capita taxation remained unchanged in most of the villages of the Puy-de-Dôme and the Ardèche. In the Lozère, the Aveyron and the Lot the average householder received a lower tax assessment than he had been accustomed to receiving at the end of the *ancien régime*. Nor can 1791 be dismissed as a fluke year: in the Haute-Loire average per capita taxation declined from 7 *livres* 17 *sols* in 1788 to 6 *livres* 3 *sols* in 1791 and 6 *livres* 0 *sols* 10 *deniers* in 1798.[25]

But averages give no sense of the reality of fiscal pressure for individual peasant households. Perhaps the total burden of state taxation did not increase after 1789, yet the distribution of that burden left much to be desired. Not until 1807 was a truly scientific survey of land values undertaken and several decades passed before it reached fruition. In the meantime country dwellers complained loudly about the mingled shortcomings of the old and new systems of taxation. Between February 1791 and July 1792, the *Feuille villageoise* (see p. 211) published no fewer than ten articles on the subject of taxation, but all its attempts to prove that the fiscal burden had actually diminished were brushed aside. Two new grievances exacerbated the perennial problem of uneven distribution. In some localities, but particularly in the West, rural proprietors off-loaded their responsibility for the *contribution foncière* onto their tenants. This was not illegal and something of the sort had happened during the *ancien régime*; however, it could easily work to the disadvantage of the *tenuyer* or *fermier*. The tenant was entitled to a corresponding reduction in his rent, of course, but the usual process of bargaining over leases might whittle it away to a token sum. The second grievance concerned the *contribution personnelle et mobilière* and it was more widespread. From the Côtes-du-Nord, the Orne, the Gers, the Pyrénées-Orientales, the Vienne and another half dozen departments situated to the west of a line drawn from Paris to Marseilles came reports that this new sumptuary tax was being unfairly assessed. Through their control of the department and district authorities, the urban bourgeoisie contrived to off-load its principal burden upon the countryside.

The mechanics of the process are difficult to unravel: the whole subject of revolutionary fiscal policy awaits an historian prepared to do it justice. Among the first tasks would be to establish whether the abuse of the *contribution personnelle et mobilière* was confined to the western and central sectors of the country. Nevertheless, the sheer volume of acrimony provoked by this tax cannot be ignored and to judge from petitions two points seem to have been at issue. Many peasants grumbled that their leasehold plots were being taxed at punitive rates; the villagers of Jars (Cher), for example, used the opportunity afforded by the plebiscite on the constitution of 1793 to complain that 'the *cote mobilière* paid by workmen and day labourers amounts to half, two-thirds, even the whole of the price of their leases. Unlike our hamlets, the towns are far from bearing the weight of taxation.'[26] In the case of sharecroppers, this bias could be passed off all the more readily in that the majority did not possess up-to-date written leases. The poor *bordiers* of the Gers, reported *représentant* Dartigoeyte, 'pay more in *mobilier* tax than they used to pay in *capitation*'.[27]

Apart from a number of petitions demanding to know why servants had been exempted from the prescriptions of the new tax, the other main source of bitterness was the *taxe d'habitation*. In the department of the Indre, as we have seen, this element of the *contribution personnelle et mobilière* was given a progressive twist to ensure that the commercial and industrial wealth of the towns was more effectively taxed. The more usual practice, however, was to make up the deficit in tax yield from the pockets of the peasantry, and necessarily so, since most departments were agricultural in character and lacked sizeable towns. In the Cantal, the electoral assembly of Arpajon complained that the *contribution personnelle et mobilière* only bore down 'on the cottages of farmers because those who used to be called well-to-do no longer live in the countryside'.[28] Similar complaints were voiced from as far afield as the Oise and the Puy-de-Dôme. Ironically, but inevitably, a tax which had been designed to embrace non-landed sources of income ended up hitting peasant households hardest. Incapable of reform, the *contribution personnelle et mobilière* should be abolished in the countryside, concluded the primary assembly of St Ciers-de-Canesse (Gironde): 'experience has shown that [it] only weighs down the poor; this defective tax law is quite unable to reach the rich'.[29]

These were damning words and they were spoken in the summer of 1793 when public confidence in the revolution had reached an all-time low. But does this mean that the fiscal policy of the National Assembly missed its mark altogether and became instead an argument for counter-revolution? Paul Bois stresses the sense of 'disappointment' which greeted the tax reforms, while Georges Lefebvre goes further and suggests that they constituted 'a grave setback to popular support of the revolution'.[30] In Brittany, certainly, the introduction of a universal and proportional tax on land caused major problems of adjustment, problems which were still unresolved when the stirrings which prefigured the *chouannerie* (see p. 225) occurred in March 1793. In the Sarthe, too, royalists did their utmost to catalyse peasant resentment of the new taxes into outright hostility towards the revolution. Yet Bois refuses to make a linear equation between tax revolt and counter-revolution. Taxes were simply one disappointment among several which helped to predispose country dwellers against the revolution in this part of France. Elsewhere, it is by no means certain that the fiscal disappointment *did* predispose country dwellers against the revolution: the sharecroppers of the Gers, for instance, remained doggedly loyal to the freedoms won in 1789 despite their grievances over taxes and the tithe. Disappointment there certainly was in 1791 and 1792, but it was a finely calculated disappointment as each household totted up its gains and losses. Abusive assessment of the *contribution personnelle et mobilière* notwithstanding, many peasants had good reason to be grateful for the financial reforms of the National Assembly. Land and property taxes may have increased, but indirect taxes and the tithe had been abolished and seigneurial dues were heading for extinction. It is unlikely that the majority of country dwellers were worse off as a result. The sense of alienation that split the revolutionary consensus asunder between 1791 and 1793 had other causes.

Ecclesiastical reforms and the oath of loyalty

'If there was a point at which the revolution "went wrong" ', writes Jack McManners, 'it was when the Constituent Assembly imposed the oath to the Civil Constitution of the Clergy.'[31] Yet there was nothing preordained about the religious schism or the consequences that flowed from it. On the contrary, the *cahiers* suggest a wide measure of agreement on what was needed to reform the Gallican church: the abolition of surplice fees (*casuel*); adjustments to the tithe; an increase in the *portion congrue*; the redirection of ecclesiastical income; and an end to nepotism and absenteeism. Not all these reforms would have benefited the lower clergy; nevertheless ordinary parish priests enthusiastically supported the revolution at the outset. What, then, went wrong? Obviously the promulgation of the Civil Constitution of the Clergy marked a turning point, but the reason many country dwellers should find this legislation and the accompanying oath so objectionable is not self-evident. It is helpful, rather, to view the Civil Constitution as the key element in a package of reforms and proposed reforms – a package which went far beyond anything suggested, or even hinted at, in the *cahiers*. In the late autumn of 1790 it began to dawn on the rural population that the National Assembly intended to use the opportunity afforded by the sale of church property to work a thoroughgoing reform of popular religious habits. The clergy, together with the newly appointed local authorities, were to spearhead the offensive. If the repercussions of this offensive are to be properly understood, however, it is necessary to know something about the clergy of *ancien régime* France and the nature of popular religious beliefs.

The lower clergy who came into day-to-day contact with parishioners numbered about 59,500 in 1789; that is to say there was a priest with cure of souls for every 470 inhabitants compared with every 1,462 inhabitants in 1975. They can be divided into two categories: parish incumbents (39,000) and curates (20,500). In most of the kingdom the former were called *curés* while the latter were referred to as *vicaires*, but in Brittany incumbents were known as *recteurs* and the title *curé* was reserved for the curate. Allowance must be made, too, for the non-beneficed *prêtres habitués* (called *matinaliers* in Brittany) who contrived to live from Masses sung in outlying chapels. Although their numbers had dropped markedly by the eighteenth century, they represented a considerable strengthening of the clerical presence in certain dioceses of the West and the Massif Central. Whether beneficed or unbeneficed, the parish clergy lived frugally as a rule. Many had lost control of their tithe to lay and ecclesiastical impropriators and relied instead on the *portion congrue* which had been raised to 700 *livres* just before the revolution. Even so, it represented little more than half the sum which the National Assembly would judge necessary in order to maintain the decency of the clerical estate. Brittany, several adjacent provinces and parts of the extreme South West provide the only substantial deviation from the pattern. In these regions parish incumbents seem to have been distinctly better off than their counterparts elsewhere in the country. Most had retained ownership of the tithe, and a tithe that was sometimes collected at very favourable rates. Had the *recteurs* of the diocese of Rennes been liable to state taxes, comments one historian, they would have figured among the top 10 per cent of taxpayers.[32]

Despite the variations both within and between dioceses the clergy did not, in general, form an economic elite set apart from the rural community. But were they drawn from the rural community? Again, it is impossible to provide an answer which holds good for all times and all places. In recent years sufficient evidence has been produced to challenge the notion that the clergymen of eighteenth-century France were drawn overwhelmingly from peasant stock. On the other hand, there is not yet sufficient evidence to sustain the claim that the clergy chiefly originated from 'the commercial, professional and office-holding classes'.[33] While this was undoubtedly the case in the more urbanised dioceses, especially in those which contained seats of *parlements*, many rural dioceses were staffed with priests who were solidly peasant in origin. Over 50 per cent of the clergy in the dioceses of Boulogne, Coutances, Tréguier, Vannes, Bayonne and Rodez hailed from peasant households of some description. Moreover, the trend towards peasant recruitment was growing in the second half of the eighteenth century. By the end of the *ancien régime laboureur* and *ménager* families supplied more recruits for seminary training than any other social group in the diocese of Mende, while in the diocese of Elne even humble agricultural workers occasionally managed to push their sons into the priesthood. We are left, therefore, with a picture containing sharp contrasts and divergences. In Brittany, for example, the clergy of the diocese of Vannes were drawn from the ranks of peasant proprietors and rural artisans for the most part. Their authority, a recent historian has implied, derived from the fact of their insertion in the rural community.[34] This is a model which can be applied to several of the aforementioned dioceses, most notably those of the southern Massif Central. Yet a short distance to the north-east of Vannes lay the diocese of Rennes whose priesthood issued from urban and comparatively wealthy backgrounds. Here the clergy scarcely resembled their parishioners at all: in terms of standard of living and cultural outlook they were closer to the bourgeoisie. In such conditions an alternative role-model based on deference and acknowledged social hierarchy applied. This question of the relationship between priest and parish is crucial to an understanding of how the Civil Constitution of the Clergy impinged upon the countryside, but before we go any further it is necessary to identify the missing factor in the equation: the nature of popular religious beliefs.

Notions of what constituted popular religious belief can be obtained from a number of different sources: the records of episcopal visitations; the analysis of wills; the study of pilgrimages and local cults; the iconography of death; and so forth. In the absence of church-going statistics, estimates of the 'intensity' of religious conviction can be drawn from other sources: ordination rates; measurements of the speed of baptism of new-born children; responses to missionary activity; the incidence of *prêtres habitués*; and the extent of clerical 'buttressing' in the form of confraternities and lay orders. By combining these data, it is possible to map out a rudimentary religious geography of France on the eve of the revolution. First of all, however, we need to establish what ordinary people actually believed. Most historians would sum up popular religion as an unholy mixture of paganism, peasant magic and half-baked Christian doctrine. But if this dictum underlines the hybrid character of folk religion, it misses an essential element of definition: in the countryside even more than in the towns religious worship was primarily an ostentatious social exercise. Catholicism provided the framework wherein rural households and, by extension, whole villages and parishes could affirm their collective identity. It follows, therefore, that peasants showed greater attachment to the external, public rituals of their religion than to the dogmatics of faith. Weekly church services, pilgrimages and patron saints' days enjoyed massive support because these calendared events provided an opportunity for display. The same was true of church festivals such as Shrovetide, while the feast of All Souls catered for the spiritual instincts of the peasantry (it should not be forgotten that the rural community embraced the dead as well as the living). As revolutionary Dechristianisers were to discover, the cult of the dead constituted one of the most tenacious components of rural catholicism.

By contrast, the moral and doctrinal teachings of the catholic church do not seem to have bitten deep into peasant consciousness. In this respect the theology of the Counter-Reformation had yet to permeate to the grass-roots. The church was still understood as a set of institutions to be used as vehicles for the expression of peasant sociability. Popular culture and popular religion intermingled, particularly in regions such as the West and the southern Massif Central where the bulk of the population lived in villages and hamlets beyond the reach of urban cultural stereotypes. Of course, the clergy did their best to elevate religion and to edify their flocks, but it was an uphill battle, not least because the clergy were often drawn from the same cultural milieu as their parishioners and lacked either the motivation or the intellectual capacity to formulate an alternative vision of the faith. Occasionally rigorist clerics did challenge the comfortable consensus that rural catholicism was above all a cultural religion, but the consequences could be serious – for the priest personally and for religious habits generally. When forced to choose between priest and parish or, to be more precise, between priest and the physical context of popular devotions (the church and burial ground), country dwellers were thrown into a turmoil of doubt and anxiety. This is a point which is often over-looked in discussions of the impact of the Civil Constitution of the Clergy. Loss of a familiar incumbent – the very symbol of the rural community – was bad enough, but the loss of parish status, and with it the church and churchyard was too awful to contemplate.

These comments upon the nature of popular religious beliefs should be taken as generalities, however. Research over the last four decades has shattered any notion that provincial France was uniformly pious, or, indeed, that 1789 marked a turning point in rural apprehensions of catholicism. What strikes the historian is rather the stability of religious 'temperaments' over the last two hundred and fifty years. The geography of religious belief in the last quarter of the twentieth century resembles that of the last quarter of the eighteenth century to a significant degree. Then, as now, the regions of most intensive devotion to the (external) trappings of catholicism were the West (Lower Normandy, Brittany, Anjou, Maine and Lower Poitou); the southern and south-eastern escarpments of the Massif Central (Rouergue, Gévaudan, Vivarais, Velay); the North East (Artois, Boulonnais, Flanders, Hainaut, Cambrésis), and the Basque country. By contrst, the rural population of the Charente region (Aunis, Saintonge, Angoumois); of the Paris basin; of the Centre (Orléanais, Berry, Nivernais, Auxois); and of Provence responded to the disciplines of catholicism in a more detached manner. They remained church-goers – virtually everyone went to church at the end of the *ancien régime* – but their weekly attendance at Mass owed more to duty and habit than anything else.

How these discrepancies came into being is a puzzle. Nearly all the attempts to explore the origins of pre-revolutionary 'dechristianisation' succeed only in re-stating the problem. Among the most ambitious is the analysis of Provençal wills undertaken by Michel Vovelle who points to the second quarter of the eighteenth century as the moment at which catholicism reached its zenith in this region.[35] Thereafter, to judge from the diminishing tendency to make provision for *in requiem* Masses, popular religious attitudes began to change. He cites a number of possible explanations for the transition, but they do not seem wholly convincing. Experience suggests that it is easier to tackle the problem from the other end and seek out those characteristics which distinguished the regions of intensive catholic devotion. In this field scholars such as Claude Langlois and Timothy Tackett have carried out the pioneering work.[36] Tackett, in particular, has identified a number of key variables which can usually be associated with regions of strident and festive catholicism, but which were rarer in areas of more subdued devotion. The former were more 'clericalised' in the sense that they enjoyed high levels of ecclesiastical provision (parish churches, chapels, incumbents, curates, chantry priests, lay orders, etc.). In other words, the clergy were extremely thick on the ground and occupied a dominant position in rural life. But this domination was not necessarily enforced; it could be subscribed. In regions of vibrant catholicism like the West and the southern Massif Central, the clergy tended to be locally recruited and from rural, often peasant, backgrounds. Their authority was underpinned by considerations of locality, social proximity, even kinship. It may also be suggested that such clerics adopted a fairly relaxed attitude towards the various manifestations of popular religion. Country priests who were drawn from local families and who spoke to their parishioners in dialect were too much a part of popular culture to play the role of moral and theological reformers with any conviction. By contrast, many areas of lukewarm or undemonstrative catholicism appear to have lacked this dense ecclesiastical infrastructure: priests were spread more thinly; they could call upon the services of fewer spiritual out-workers (the lay orders); and their social and geographical origins precluded any real contact with the rural community.

Whether this line of argument can provide an answer to the ultimate puzzle of the religious geography of France is doubtful. Why did some families, some villages, some provinces generate more ecclesiastical vocations than others? Is the explanation to be found in the human habitat, in the social structure or in some intemporal concept of regional culture? Luckily we need go no further, for it is the more immediate question of the response to the Civil Constitution of the Clergy which is at issue in the present section. On this point the latest research does permit a measure of generalisation: the map of clerical densities provides the best guide to the reception of the oath in the countryside. Where clerical densities were high, the ecclesiastical reforms set in motion by the National Assembly provoked serious disquiet among the rural population and the majority of the parish clergy refused to swear the oath of loyalty. Where the institutional and physical fabric of the catholic church was more threadbare, the bulk of the population (including the clergy) acquiesced in the remodelling exercise. However, this rule is not invariable: several alpine dioceses of the South East were richly endowed with priests and yet this region would be overwhelmingly 'constitutional' in 1791. So we are left with pointers, or what Timothy Tackett calls 'clusters of variables'[37] which take us some way towards an understanding of how the revolution-aries' religious policies were likely to affect the rural community. To go any further we must turn to the legislation, its reception and its enforce-ment in the countryside.

The high-water mark of clerical enthusiasm for the revolution was reached in the early months of 1790 and it was reflected in the number of parish priests who participated in municipal elections and accepted the post of mayor. Thereafter their ardour could only cool, but the process was slow and uneven. In the Vivarais the lower clergy swallowed the abolition of the tithe, the nationalisation of church property and the dismantling of monasticism without a murmur, while in the adjacent province of the Gévaudan the bishop of Mende led a vigorous campaign in defence of the tithe from the summer of 1789 onwards. It is true that the bishop of Viviers would number among the handful of prelates who took the oath. Again, in Brittany, anxieties over the tithe and the legislation divesting the church of its lands surfaced early in the diocese of Rennes, but they appear to have remained muted in the parishes of the diocese of Vannes. In so far as any single event set the alarm bells ringing before the promulgation of the Civil Constitution of the Clergy, it was the hostile response to Dom Gerle's proposal that the Assembly declare catholicism the state religion. The issue split the deputies and triggered a nervous 'religion in danger' reaction in the provinces, particularly in those southern provinces where catholic and protestant peasants lived in close proximity. Local government reforms had already rekindled inter-confessional rivalries in several parts of the kingdom, and it required little in the way of provocation to persuade southern catholics that the ecclesiastical policies of the National Assembly amounted to a protestant plot nurtured by the like of Barnave and Rabaut-Saint-Etienne. On 10 May 1790, barely a month after Dom Gerle's abortive motion, protestant blood was spilt during sectarian rioting in the town of Montauban. A few weeks later the same thing, albeit on a larger scale, occurred in Nîmes when catholic and protestant voters gathered to begin the process of electing department and district administrators.

Neither priests nor parishioners were wholly unprepared for a measure of ecclesiastical reform, therefore. Nevertheless, the Civil Constitution of the Clergy must have come as a profound shock to all but the most stalwart village patriots. Voted on 12 July and sanctioned by the king on 24 August 1790, it was, in the words of Tackett, 'amazingly radical'.[38] Henceforth, parish priests and curates were to become salaried officials of state, as were bishops whose incomes were drastically reduced in consequence. Vacancies, when they occurred, were to be filled by process of election like any other vacancy in the administration or the judiciary. Groups of electors would meet in the districts to appoint the parish clergy, while department electoral assemblies would appoint bishops. In a few crisp sentences the whole issue of canonical investiture which had bedevilled relations between the Gallican church and the papacy for centuries was set aside. Newly appointed (that is to say elected) bishops were merely enjoined to write to the pontiff informing him of their existence. And this was not all: the deputies seized the opportunity to push through a series of reforms which had long been discussed. Amid general satisfaction, absenteeism and pluralism were anathematised, but cathedral chapters, canonries, vicars-general and simple benefices without cure of souls followed the contemplative orders into oblivion as well. A substantial percentage of the personnel of the catholic church was thereby earmarked for redundancy. The need for a complete overhaul of territorial structures did not pass unnoticed, either. Over fifty bishoprics and archbishoprics were abolished outright and the remaining dioceses were remodelled so that they coincided with the departments. More ominously, the legislators gave advance notice of their intention to sweep away small parishes and to substitute larger entities. This was a reform which no one had asked for and, as we shall see, it evoked a hostile response among the peasantry.

As if this ecclesiastical *coup* did not, in itself, represent sufficient of a shock, the deputies resolved to impose it by means of an oath (decree of 27 November–26 December 1790). Each bishop and each priest with parish responsibilities was required to swear 'to be loyal to the nation, to the law and to the King, and maintain with all my power the Constitution decreed by the National Assembly and accepted by the King'.[39] The new oath was put first to the bishops and other clerical members of the Assembly, but with disappointing results. Then, in the early weeks of 1791, oath-taking ceremonies were organised in parishes throughout the length and breadth of the land. By the summer it had become plain that the clergy were hopelessly divided in their response to the challenge of ecclesiastical reform: about 55 per cent swallowed hard and swore to uphold the revolutionary settlement in matters spiritual as well as temporal. Whether motivated by personal scruples or by the papal condemnation of the Civil Constitution (4 May 1791), the remainder baulked

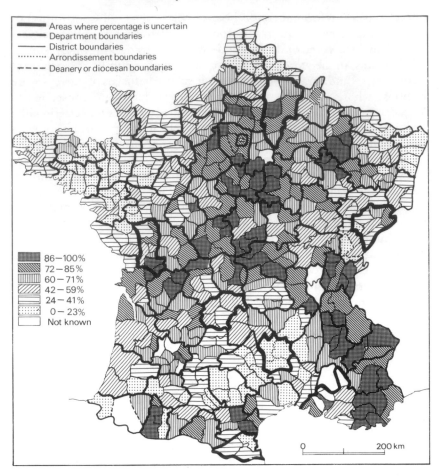

Map 12. Geographical distribution of priests swearing the oath of loyalty
(by districts, spring–summer 1791)
Source: T. Tackett, *Religion, Revolution and Regional Culture in Eighteenth-
Century France* (Princeton, 1986), p. 53 (redrawn)

at any such commitment. In effect, two churches had come into being, one
labelled 'constitutional' and one labelled 'refractory', and nothing the
revolutionaries undertook did much to disturb the balance between them.
Even as late as the autumn of 1792 the constitutional church enjoyed the
support of approximately half of the clergy. That support was very
unevenly distributed, however (see map 12). In the Basses-Alpes, the
Hautes-Alpes and the Var, for instance, over 80 per cent of the parish

clergy stayed loyal, but in the West and on the southern slopes of the Massif Central there were districts in which only a handful of clerics adhered to the oath. No more than 11 per cent of clergymen agreed to swear the oath in the Morbihan, while in the Lozère the number was probably lower still.

The reactions of the clergy cannot stand duty for those of the laity, however. For priests the oath was the crucial issue and it subsumed all others, but for ordinary parishioners the oath was significant only in so far as it threatened to deprive them of the services of a much-loved incumbent. The Civil Constitution of the Clergy challenged religious habits on a number of fronts, any one of which might kindle opposition and even resistance. For example, the proposal to alter the boundaries of parishes provoked an outcry which stretched far beyond the citadels of catholicism in the West and the Massif Central. Yet in these highly clericalised regions *every* emanation of the Assembly's religious programme seemed to pose a threat. The purging of the body politic of superfluous ecclesiastical personnel threatened to undermine clerical densities; the amalgamation of parishes in regions of dispersed settlement threatened entire communities with the loss of church services; and the introduction of lay election for bishops and priests threatened to blur the distinction between catholicism and Calvinism. Not for nothing did many villagers complain that the National Assembly was trying to change their religion. In certain parts of rural France the Civil Constitution of the Clergy threatened nothing less than a cultural revolution.

There is evidence, moreover, that it was intended as such. Embedded in the Civil Constitution was the assumption that public worship must be organised in accordance with Enlightenment norms of belief, and all over the country local administrators set out to make this assumption explicit. Much of the anguish that the church issue would shortly generate can be traced back to unsympathetic department and district officials who set out to foist their own deist principles upon a rural population whose religious convictions owed nothing whatsoever to the concept of the Clockmaker God. Nowhere was the confrontation played out more bitterly than in the West where the sense of religious despair and betrayal became a powerful incitement to counter-revolution. Historians have long been familiar with the highly clericalised piety of western country dwellers, but the researches of Timothy Tackett have uncovered the 'missing ingredient' which helps to explain the explosive impact of ecclesiastical reform in this region.[40] It was spearheaded by a vehemently anti-clerical urban bourgeoisie which, in the words of the administrators of the Ille-et-Vilaine, was bent on exploiting the Civil Constitution for the purpose of 'relegating priests to their proper place'.[41] In practice, this meant ousting the clergy from a central role in the

Plate 5. A peasant woman praying before a wayside cross, as depicted in the *terrier* of Sadournin (Gascony), 1772

life of the rural community: a potentially disastrous policy in the *bocage* country of the West where the church provided the only vehicle for peasant sociability.

Whilst the National Assembly back-pedalled with a conciliatory measure giving non-juring clergymen access to 'constitutional' churches (decree of 6–7 May 1791), the hardline officials of departments such as the Ille-et-Vilaine, the Côtes-du-Nord, Morbihan, Loire-Inférieure, Vendée,

Maine-et-Loire and the Sarthe stoked up the atmosphere of persecution. On 9 May the *Amis de la Constitution* of Nantes called for legislation forcing refractory priests to withdraw from their parishes and a few days later the administrators of the Loire-Inférieure voted an (illegal) resolution to this effect. Next the order went out to close down outlying chapels lest non-jurors should seek to hold services in them. Even regularly conducted services did not escape the all-seeing eye of secular authority: the administrators of the district of Paimbœuf intervened to curtail the burning of incense during public worship. Similar measures were enforced in neighbouring departments: the directors of the Ille-et-Vilaine ordered the expulsion of refractories on 16 June 1791 and their counterparts in the Côtes-du-Nord followed suit two days later. Exasperated, the peasantry of the St Brieuc district resorted to outlying chapels, sometimes trekking through the night in bands resembling pilgrim processions. The authorities responded by placing all rural chapels and oratories out of bounds. When this policy failed they did not shrink from using force: the news that a large procession involving fourteen parishes was converging on the town of St Brieuc prompted the district administrators to hoist the red flag of martial law on 16 July 1791.

The expulsion of non-juring clergymen from their livings and the closure of chapels hit the rural population hard. In many parts of the West it cut the umbilical between priest and parish completely. 'Constitutional' clerics were in short supply and were generally shunned in any case. After scuttling around the countryside in search of a dwindling number of acceptable (that is, refractory) priests the peasantry lapsed into a state of stupor, unable to comprehend how it had come about that there was no one to say Mass on Sundays, no one to baptise the new-born, no one to bury the dead. On 27 April 1792 the mayor of La Chapelle-Achard (Vendée) wrote to his administrative superiors in the following terms: 'Our priest being on the point of leaving, we [the municipal body] went to the presbytery in order to take possession of the registers of baptisms and marriages which we placed in a locked cupboard in the sacristy. For the present, Messieurs, we need to know how we should behave in this respect. When, as happens, there is a burial to be carried out in the parish what priest do we ask for; similarly for baptisms, who will register them?[42] In the West, it seems that the department authorities were prepared to countenance policies which are more commonly associated with the Dechristianisation campaign of late 1793.

In the southern Massif Central, by contrast, a head-on collision over the Civil Constitution of the Clergy was avoided. This was not because the texture of religious life differed markedly from that of Brittany or the Vendée, but because the urban bourgeoisie was less numerous, less cultured (in the Enlightenment sense) and consequently less anti-clerical. The lawyers and landowners who formed the backbone of the new department and district authorities were, generally speaking, sincere, if somewhat dilatory catholics. Their enthusiasm for ecclesiastical reform did not extend to meaures of coercion against refractory priests. The president of the *conseil général* of the department of the Aveyron, its secretary, the *procureur-général-syndic* and a member of the directory all chose to resign rather than have anything to do with enforcing the oath. This is not to suggest that clerical politics were conducted in an atmosphere free of tension, merely that the tensions were muted. Confrontation was tinged with complicity, most notably on the question of the expulsion of refractory priests. Whilst the administrators of the western departments repeatedly jumped the gun with draconian bye-laws inhibiting the movements of non-jurors and arbitrarily depriving villages of the use of their chapels, those of the southern Massif Central tended to drag their heels as long as possible. Municipalities and perhaps even the district authorities accepted oath statements which everyone knew to be invalid, and electoral assemblies for the selection of replacement priests were delayed time and again. Not until 31 May 1791 did the directory of the department of the Ardèche fix on a date for voting. In the Lozère the authorities managed to avoid any discussion of the oath legislation until the end of June. Throughout this region, in fact, the peasantry were spared the trauma of expulsions until 1793. No serious effort having been made to replace them, nonjuring priests in the rural parishes of the Ardèche and the Aveyron continued in office until the autumn of 1792. Only with the wholesale renewal of local government bodies in November did this complaisant attitude begin to change.

Just as the oath issue was reaching a bitter climax in many departments, the local authorities launched a fresh attack on the cultural moorings of the rural community. Articles 16–19 (chapter 1) of the Civil Constitution of the Clergy had laid down guidelines for a wholesale reorganisation of parishes with the declared objective of rooting out smaller entities. The idea was not new, indeed it had been mooted several times in the Assembly of the Clergy, but fears of an adverse popular reaction had deterred the bishops from making a move. Now the bishops were enjoined to liaise with the secular authorities in an effort to reduce the number of urban and rural parishes. Predictably, the proposal caused an uproar: even the mention of the idea produced consternation in some localities. An anonymous correspondent writing from Nérac (Lot-et-Garonne) on 22 September 1790 noted that the local peasantry were pretty indifferent to the revolution: however, 'This rounding of parishes makes them fear that church services will become less easily available; and if it is true, as has been said in the neighbourhood, that the National Assembly wants just one priest per canton, this could raise tempers and perhaps even cause a general insurrection.'[43] Their anxieties were premature but not misplaced, for once the new constitutional bishops had been elected (February–March 1791) administrators up and down the land turned their attention to the question of parish reform.

The consolidation of urban parishes passed off comparatively peacefully: the eleven parishes serving the 13,000 inhabitants of Nevers (Nièvre) were reduced to six including two annexes, while the fifteen parishes of Bourges (Cher) were reduced to four. In rural areas, however, the parish church and the graveyard provided country dwellers with a sense of cohesion. That is to say, the rural community was, in the last analysis, the community of the faithful gathered together for worship in a specific location. It follows, therefore, that disestablishment threatened to dismember the community; worse, the closure of church and cemetery threatened to cut off the living from the dead. This refrain echoes through the petitions which vulnerable parishes despatched to the authorities in their efforts to stave off abolition. 'Your intention, Messieurs', observed the inhabitants of St Doulchard in a plea addressed to the administrators of the department of the Cher, 'is surely to leave poor country dwellers in possession of the religion of their fathers. It is the most precious inheritance to have fallen to them. To take it away would be an act of atrocious barbarism'.[44] But this excessively physical concept of religion was precisely what department and district officials found most tiresome, and parish reorganisation offered an additional means of rooting it out. What could be simpler than to disestablish those small, outlying parishes which all too often served as the strongholds of the refractory clergy?

We may surmise, then, that the politics of disestablishment were soon brought to bear upon the politics of the oath. How many small parishes were disbanded, their churches closed and their cemeteries walled up is difficult to judge. Timothy Tackett argues that the reforming ambitions of local administrators 'seldom materialised outside the larger towns',[45] but this is to dismiss the issue of parish reorganisation as marginal, which it surely was not. Even if only a few hundred congregations lost the right to worship as independent entities, the fear of impending spiritual and cultural annihilation went deep. Nor was it confined to predominantly refractory zones; nor, indeed, to regions such as the West where hostile administrators gave popular religious sensibilities particularly short shrift. The Civil Constitution of the Clergy was legislated as a package, but it was not necessarily enforced as such. In the southern Massif Central departments, the authorities seem to have combined a tolerant approach towards refractory priests with a firmer stance on the issue of parish reform. The directory of the department of the Ardèche voted to 'speed up the new parish constituencies' on 17 September 1791[46] and in the months that followed the district authorities redrew the boundaries of dozens of parishes. Apprised that weighty decisions were being taken, the peasantry reacted with a mixture of anger and blind panic: in the district of the Tanargue alone some fifty parishes petitioned against the exercise. An attempt to implement the reform early in 1792 was quickly abandoned, in consequence. The peasantry were willing to hear Mass from a constitutional priest; they were even prepared to tolerate an 'intruder' priest, or so it would seem; but they refused to contemplate the closure of their churches and burial grounds under any circumstances. With public opinion already soured by the failure of the Assembly to have done with feudalism, with agrarian tensions rising once more (see pp. 121–2), the use of force to impose a settlement risked driving the rural population into the camp of counter-revolution.

By the autumn of 1792 the administrative revolution had run its course. In just three years much of the institutional fabric of daily life had been renewed and the country seemed poised to reap the benefits. A uniform system of local government had replaced the accretions of several centuries and the judiciary had been thoroughly unscrambled and firmly planted in the public domain. As a corollary, seigneurialism had lost much of its *raison d'être*. Another year of revolution and it would cease to exist altogether. The tax grievance, too, had received reasonably prompt attention: everyone was now liable to direct taxes, while the scourge of indirect taxation had been abolished, apparently for ever. All these reforms looked very impressive on paper: they addressed the problems most frequently instanced in the *cahiers* of the Third Estate, and they did so in a coherent and generous-spirited manner. Fashioned in obedience to the principles of decentralisation and accountability, this legislation constituted the legacy of the National and Legislative Assemblies.

Why then was that legacy repudiated? Much of the responsibility for the departure from these high ideals can be attributed to the other great legislative achievement of 1790–1: the Civil Constitution of the Clergy. It would be an exaggeration to say that the Civil Constitution was an unwanted reform, but for sheer all-embracing audacity the measure was virtually unsurpassed during the revolutionary epoch. Even while protesting against absenteeism, pluralism, the abuse of the tithe and surplice fees, few peasants imagined that they were giving their deputies *carte blanche* to challenge the spiritual authority of the priesthood, to amalgamate parishes and to close down redundant churches and chapels. As the implications of the clerical oath sank in, the atmosphere in the countryside became poisoned: factionalism began to erode the 'popular front' which had sustained the rural revolution at the outset. This was bad enough, but the oath issue and the threat to popular religious beliefs served to catalyse other sources of discontent as well. In Brittany, for example, dissatisfaction with the Civil Constitution combined with the disillusioning realisation that fiscal reform was going to increase the burden of taxation throughout the province. Religion *and* taxes became the new rallying cry, most explicitly in February 1791 when about 1,500 peasants invaded the town of Vannes (Morbihan). The resentment provoked by administrative meddling in matters of religion also impaired the functioning of the new local government bodies. Municipalities complaisantly registered defective oaths, and when they were challenged resorted to the tactic of resigning *en masse*. As France prepared to celebrate the beginning of a fourth year of revolution amid rumours of an impending uprising against Louis XVI, it became apparent that the work of administrative reform rested on a series of false premises. Decentralisation and public accountability were luxuries which the embattled republic would not be able to afford.

Chapter 7

Terror and Counter-Terror

The Terror started at different times for different people. The first executions on a charge of royalism pure and simple took place in Paris on the morrow of the uprising of 10 August 1792, although they were not emulated in the country at large. Refractory priests first incurred the rigours of deportation or imprisonment in the autumn of that year. Political moderates, Feuillants and Fayettists (the jetsam of constitutional monarchy for whom the label 'suspects' would shortly be invented) suffered little more than verbal threats until the spring of 1793. The Girondins, meanwhile, eluded their enemies until the summer. For their Federalist allies in the provinces the day of reckoning was delayed: not before the autumn of 1793 did they feel the cold steel of revolutionary justice. The constitutional clergy, on the other hand, managed to dodge the successive waves of persecution until the Dechristianisation campaign gathered momentum during the winter of 1793–4. But what of the peasants, the great mass of country dwellers whose involvement in revolutionary politics seemed too remote and episodic to carry with it the risk of contamination by any of the heresies listed above? When did the Terror begin for them?

The mayor of La Chapelle-Achard, whose shocked acknowledgement of the departure of the parish priest was quoted in the preceding chapter, might plausibly have argued that the Terror first visited his locality in the spring of 1792. And, indeed, there is some evidence to suggest that in several western departments busybodying district officials had stoked up an atmosphere which anticipated the Terror as early as the summer of 1791. In parts of the southern Massif Central, too, the characteristic dialectic of Terror and Counter-Terror was clearly evident by the spring of 1792. Here the root problem lay less in the enforcement of the Civil Constitution of the Clergy, than in the activities of professional counter-revolutionaries who congregated in towns such as Mende (Lozère), Ville-fort (Lozère) and Arles (Bouches-du-Rhône). The repeated encampments of opponents of the new order around the village of Jalès (Ardèche) served to underline this threat to the revolution in the South (see pp. 220–1). Neither the South nor the West can be regarded as typical, however: most country dwellers lived in ignorance of the growing pressure for stern measures until the spring of 1793. And when the Terror arrived, it came from the outside – by carriage and on horseback in the shape of roving plenipotentiaries whom the deputies despatched from their midst with instructions to travel round the departments and expedite military recruitment.

In practical terms, therefore, it was the war emergency consequent upon the formation of the First Coalition during the spring of 1793 that brought the Terror to every peasant's doorstep. March was the crucial month, for on 24 February the Convention had passed a decree calling 300,000 men to the colours. With enthusiasm for the revolution at a low ebb since the execution of the king, this recruitment drive caused tension throughout the length and breadth of the land. In many departments the tension was exacerbated by the parliamentary *commissaires* (forerunners of the *représentants-en-mission*) who used the opportunity to give provincials an elementary lesson in republican politics. This massive irruption of Paris-style jacobinism catalysed two years of growing popular disillusionment with the revolution in the West: the Vendée rebellion issued directly from the movement of resistance to recruitment. Threatening concentrations of draft-resisters developed in the departments of the southern Massif Central, too, but here the movement was less firmly rooted among the peasantry. Prompt and energetic repression retrieved the situation, at least for a time. The reflex of Counter-Terror did not materialise until the end of May when Charrier raised the standard of revolt. Unlike the forces mobilised by the Vendeans, Charrier's 'Christian Army of the Midi' was well supplies with generals but short of foot soldiers – an enduring characteristic of southern counter-revolution. Nevertheless, both can be seen as responses to the first phase of the Terror which gripped the countryside between March and June of 1793. Elsewhere the Counter-Terror took less virulent forms: in many instances it found expression in the Federalist 'revolt' which aligned about forty departments against the *montagnard* dictatorship in Paris for much of the summer.

Politicisation in the countryside

The progress of politicisation among the rural masses is not an easy matter to judge. As a result of the administrative revolution more peasants were involved in the business of (local) government than ever before, but it is far from certain that a commensurate increase in political awareness had taken place. 'It is quite evident that most artisans and peasants were not interested at all in political questions', writes Hubert Johnson,[1] yet Michel Vovelle finds plentiful signs of a precocious politicisation in the *bourgs* and villages of Provence and the Rhône valley.[2] No doubt some of the confusion can be dispelled by careful definition of meanings, for some historians measure politicisation purely in terms of an awareness of 'affairs of state',[3] whereas others adopt a two-tier approach to the problem. In recent years a number of researchers have concentrated upon the distinction between 'local' and 'national' politics, a distinction which the revolution blurred but did not altogether obliterate. Local politics consisted of what are often dismissed as parish pump issues: disputes over the firing of the village bread oven, perhaps, or the renting of church pews, or the management of common pastures. National politics, on the other hand, were more concerned with major public events: the accession of monarchs, the birthdays of heirs to the throne, the dates of battles, and so forth. This approach has several merits, not least the fact that it allows the peasantry some degree of political autonomy. But we need to bear in mind that the 'local' and the 'national' were not closed compartments. The limitations upon peasant political awareness have been compared to the plight of a man trying to survey the sky while imprisoned at the bottom of a well. Yet seismic events of the magnitude of the revolution could push back the sides of the well: squabbles over pews became part of a nation-wide campaign of anti-seigneurialism; on-going quarrels over the commons acquired strange new ideological reference points.

Nevertheless, formidable obstacles lay in the path of a full-blown peasant political consciousness. The horizons of village life could be narrowed by cultural and linguistic factors as well as by geography. At least six million country dwellers representing 21 per cent of the total population at the end of the *ancien régime* could neither understand nor speak the national language. Among this number were to be counted approximately one million Breton speakers, one million German speakers, 100,000 whose native tongue was Basque, and almost as many who spoke Catalan.[4] However, the majority of non-French-speakers lived in the hinterland to the south of the river Loire and communicated in one of several mutually intelligible dialects known collectively as patois. Here the aristocracy, the bourgeoisie, most merchants and some artisans were bilingual, but the vast majority of their peasant neighbours could only communicate through the medium of patois. For hundreds of thousands, even millions of citizens, therefore, the revolution was conducted in a foreign language. In normal times this linguistic diversity did not matter very much: *ancien régime* rulers neither addressed the peasantry, nor expected them to participate in government. But in 1789 the language of the Enlightenment became the language of liberty, the indispensable medium for the apprehension of the Rights of Man. The survival of 'barbarous' tongues could only impede the message of the revolution.

The enquiry into vernacular speech mounted by the *abbé* Grégoire in 1790 seemed to justify this point of view.[5] Writing from the Aveyron, François Chabot spoke for many when he observed that the entire population of the department spoke patois, save for a few clergymen, doctors, lawyers, old soldiers, merchants and nobles who could also communicate in French. Of the 40,000 inhabitants of his home district of St Geniez, he estimated that 10,000 could understand French, 2,000 could speak it and 3,000 were capable of reading it. Incomprehension of the national language posed a serious obstacle to the progress of politicisation among the peasantry, therefore. As a correspondent in the department of the Lot-et-Garonne (a solidly Gascon-speaking region) put it: 'The reading out of decrees bores [the peasantry] to such a degree that several respectable priests have told me that their parishioners make ready to go to sleep when one reads to them. This is because they do not understand a word, even though the decrees are read in a loud and clear voice and are explained.'[6] One solution which the revolutionaries were forced to adopt was the employment of civic missionaries well versed in 'l'idiome du pays' (the native lingo). We know, for instance, that the constitutional bishops sometimes resorted to the vernacular in an effort to get the message across. It is also likely that some of the smaller jacobin clubs conducted their business in patois, or German, or Catalan, although their minutes were always written up in French. Another solution was to translate decrees, and the Convention eventually arranged for vernacular versions of the major laws to be despatched to nearly thirty southern departments. The distribution of these departments (see map 13) gives some idea of the surviving strength of linguistic particularism in the *langue d'oc* sector of the country. Translation scarcely offered a satisfactory solution, however. Many of the patois lacked a standardised written form and few, if any, possessed a vocabulary equal to the demands of French revolutionary rhetoric. Gascon patois only has 'one term to describe each thing, consequently it lacks richness, particularly as regards intellectual matters' reported the *Société des Amis de la Constitution* of Agen.[7] A similar point was made by Barère, speaking on behalf of the Committee of Public Safety early in 1794. Breton, he alleged, employed the same word for 'religion' and 'law'; as a result Breton-speakers concluded that every change in the law brought with it a change in their religion.

This is all very well, but we should not fall into the trap of supposing that culture and language raised an insuperable barrier to politicisation. After all, peasants found out about decrees quickly enough when it suited them.

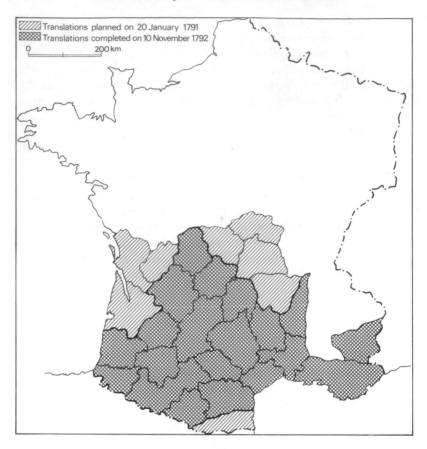

Map 13. Translation of revolutionary decrees from French to patois
Source: M. de Certeau, D. Julia and J. Revel, *Une Politique de la langue: la Révolution française et les patois* (Paris, 1975), pp. 287–8 (redrawn)

The news that the National Assembly had 'abolished' the seigneurial regime was circulating widely within days of the event. Admittedly, subsequent anti-feudal legislation took much longer to permeate. The Civil Constitution of the Clergy seems to have got through to the common people, too. Even before the decision to impose a loyalty oath turned the measure into a universal topic of conversation, it was being analysed in detail in some parishes. The Gascon peasantry may, indeed, have found the reading out of decrees boring, but they experienced no difficulty in grasping the fact that the Civil Constitution proposed a reduction in the number of parishes (see pp. 202–3). Another case in point is the decree of 7 March 1793 which brought to a head the fumbling attempts to devise an inheritance policy in line with the principles of liberty, equality and fraternity. Freedom was sacrificed in the interests of equality, and henceforth children were to enjoy equal shares of the estate of their parents. This measure, which was given a retrospective effect the following year, prompted howls of anguish from the peasantry of the South where the right of primogeniture was embedded in Roman Law. When the primary assemblies were summoned to vote on the new jacobin constitution in the summer of 1793, over one hundred used the opportunity to criticise the decree of 7 March and it is interesting to note that nearly all the protests emanated from non-French-speaking localities to the south of the river Loire.

In practice, the impediments to news transmission often assumed a more concrete character. Copies of decrees (whether couched in French or the vernacular) were always in short supply and newspapers rarely circulated outside the larger towns. Most of rural France was quite unprepared for the avalanche of printed words which the revolution precipitated. The embattled administrators of the department of the Lozère complained in August 1792 that they had had to rely on one printing press 'brought in from the outside';[8] as a result the promulgation of laws had fallen behind. Another press had just been acquired, but there remained a serious shortage of clerks. Public prints offered an alternative avenue for politicisation and the revolution triggered a massive expansion in the scale and scope of the newspaper press. Few of the new titles catered for a peasant readership, however, and only one – the *Feuille villageoise* – enjoyed a measure of success. Founded in the autumn of 1790, it appeared weekly for the next five years and may have reached as many as 250,000 readers on a regular basis. Most of its subscribers lived in the South East, the East, the Rhône valley and the Paris basin, although efforts were made to generalise the journal as an official organ for communication with the peasantry in 1793 and 1794. For example, the administrators of the department of the Gers took out a bulk subscription for 800 copies in February 1793 and despatched to the publishers a mailing list containing the names and addresses of all their municipalities.[9] Whether the *Feuille villageoise* was actually read by working peasants (as opposed to parish priests and rural notables) is a matter for debate. Melvin Edelstein argues that it was 'the first *relatively* successful political paper in French history written for the peasants',[10] but Marcel Reinhard thinks it unlikely that the paper's message reached its intended audience.[11] Less highbrow, if more restricted in circulation, was the *Manuel du laboureur et de l'artisan*, edited by Jacques Montbrion and distributed with the help of the Marseilles jacobin club. Montbrion was a veritable apostle of jacobinism and he had the idea for a journal aimed squarely at country dwellers in April 1792. Within a month or two its 'simple and instructive style' had won a following among the peasants and craftsmen of the South East.[12] Patriotic missionaries touted copies up and down the Rhône valley and we know that the *Club des antipolitiques* (see p. 214) in Aix-en-Provence used the paper in its debates. Like the *Feuille villageoise*, it was didactic, but in an earthy and more accessible manner. The most popular regular feature was a 'Conversation' in which a rustic called Anselme rubbed shoulders with the peasantry and expounded 'the fundamental points of the constitution'.[13]

Local examples apart, newspapers can be discounted as a major source of politicisation. The *Feuille villageoise* steered well clear of controversial topics such as the tithe and seigneurial dues and would only have been intelligible to the elite of the peasantry in any case. The *Manuel du laboureur* was more cleverly attuned to the interests of a rural audience, but it folded after four months. Of rather greater potential were the Societies of the Friends of the Constitution or the jacobin clubs. These bodies mushroomed all over France from the earliest years of the revolution and in each locality they gathered together the most unflinching patriots. Urban and bourgeois in inspiration, the clubs spread beyond their natural habitat and into the countryside: at the height of the Terror over 6,000 seem to have been in existence – a total which suggests that one commune in every six or seven possessed a patriotic society of some description. In reality, however, the clubs were neither as well rooted, nor as evenly distributed as these figures imply. To start with, they tended to be founded in waves and the impulse to establish village jacobin clubs came last (post-August 1793). Often these societies were no more than 'empty institutions foisted on the peasants by outsiders'[14] and Colin Lucas notes that in the Loire only seventeen out of a maximum total of fifty-nine clubs had been in existence prior to September 1793.[15] The pressure to organise country dwellers in this department came from the *représentant-en-mission* Javogues who urged that a popular society be established in every cantonal *chef-lieu*.

The club network was also extremely patchy. The highlands of the southern Massif Central and the West were 'no-go' areas for institutionalised jacobinism, either because the human habitat precluded organised expressions of political commitment, or, more likely, because the population of these regions had opted out of the revolution by 1793. In the Lozère, for instance, there were never more than a dozen functioning popular societies (6 per cent of communes) even at the zenith of the Terror. By contrast, jacobinism flourished in the departments of the South East and the Languedoc plain where the bulk of the population lived a semi-

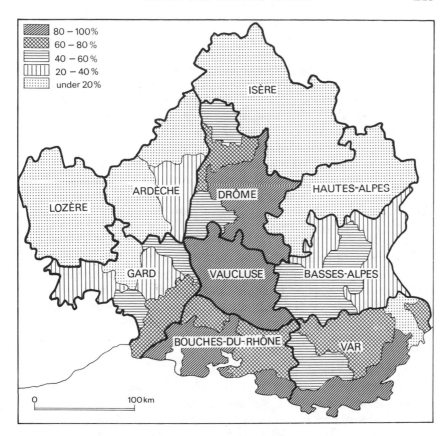

Map 14. Density of jacobin clubs in the South East, 1793–4
Source: E. Baratier, G. Duby and E. Hildesheimer, *Atlas historique: Provence, Comtat Venaissin, Principauté d'Orange, Comté de Nice, Principauté de Monaco* (Paris, 1969), map 166

urban lifestyle in *bourgs* and large villages. As early as 1792 between 75 and 90 per cent of communes in the Vaucluse, Bouches-du-Rhône and large segments of the Drôme and the Var were equipped with clubs, according to Michel Vovelle.[16] With the Gard and the Basses-Alpes boasting a penetration of 35 per cent and 45 per cent respectively, the South East could fairly claim the title of citadel of jacobinism (see map 14). The modest score of 20 per cent for the department of the Pyrénées-Orientales situated at the other extremity of the Mediterranean littoral seems paltry, until it is remembered that the jacobin presence in the rest of the country rarely attained this threshold. Even allowing for the possibility that many rustic clubs had a pretty nominal existence, Vovelle's assertion that the density of popular societies in the Midi provides 'an incontrovertible test of village politicisation'[17] seems justified.

Mapping the distribution of clubs scarcely addresses the central question of the social identity of jacobinism, however. How many jacobins were there and from what backgrounds were they drawn? Some decades ago Crane Brinton 'guesstimated' the number of club members at 500,000,[18] but the more recent research of Gérard Maintenant points towards a much lower figure of 150,000, or 0.5 per cent of the total population.[19] In the South East, of course, average enrolments per head of population were very much higher. The *bourg* of St Zacharie (Var) counted 195 clubbists among 1,500 inhabitants in 1792, for example; that of La Garde Freinet (Var) boasted a society which printed enough membership cards to equip every adult male inhabitant. But who were these home-grown activists of town and village? In the early years of the revolution it is safe to assume that the societies were dominated by an elite of middle-class landowners and professionals. The lower orders were neither expected, nor invited to share in the burden of upholding the constitution. 'Until 1791', comments Michael Kennedy, 'I detected almost no peasants in the Societies of the Friends of the Constitution, even in rural areas.'[20] Peasants and artisans, if they wished to articulate a burgeoning political consciousness, had to organise societies of their own. Several such plebeian bodies were, in fact, established, of which the *Club des Antipolitiques* of Aix-en-Provence was the most notorious. Founded in November 1790, the *Antipolitiques* provided a platform from which small shopkeepers, artisans and peasants could mount a challenge to the mercantile and professional bourgeoisie who had won control of the city. Less well known, yet indisputably peasant, was the *Société des hommes de la nature* which was set up in the small town of Arpajon (Cantal) by the Auvergnat radical, Jean-Baptiste Milhaud, in April 1791. Milhaud used the society as the springboard to a parliamentary career, but in the process he worked a durable politicisation of the peasantry in this *jacquerie*-prone sector of the Cantal. As the alternative label for the club (*Société patriotique et agricole des francs-tenanciers des campagnes*) implied, it was principally a vehicle for venting the frustrations of *laboureurs*, frustrations concerning taxation and feudal dues which, in this part of the country, took the form of town versus country conflict.

In the spring of 1792 the tempo of revolution sharply accelerated and the clubs – now more widely known as 'popular societies' – lost some of their socially exclusive flavour. Galvanised by the war effort, exasperated by grain shortages and tempted by the prospect of a division of common lands, the land-hungry peasantry of the northern plains began to toy with the politics of agrarian radicalism. In the South the still unresolved issue of seigneurialism likewise nurtured pockets of rural sans-culottism, in the Haute-Garonne, in the Lot, in the Cantal and, above all, in the South East. Country dwellers, that is to say farmers, village artisans and even a few poor plotholders were no longer refused admission to the clubs. And when the existing clubs proved inaccessible, they created their own. Thus, on 26 February 1793 the winegrowers of Marcillac (Aveyron) informed the jacobin club of Rodez that they had just established a popular society whose members were 'cultivators' almost to a man. The trend should not be exaggerated – jacobinism never embraced the rural masses – but it is unmistakeable for all that. From a reading of surviving membership lists, Brinton estimates that peasant enrolment increased from a threshold of 8 per cent achieved by 1792 to 11 per cent by 1795.[21] Even large urban clubs such as the jacobins of Marseilles acquired a token peasant membership of some 2 per cent in 1793–4.

This stealthy politicisation of the countryside was far from homogeneous, nor can it simply be equated with the growth of jacobinism. During the early years of the revolution peasant activism transmitted an ambiguous political message: anti-feudal rioting in 1789 might presage a firm commitment to the republic of 1793, but it was not bound to do so. Neither radicalism nor royalism were immutable dispositions within the body politic. Nevertheless, certain patterns of politicisation recur and the most pervasive was sharply polarised conflict between town and country. Tensions of this type were endemic, but the revolution projected them onto a broader ideological canvas. First the *bailliage* elections to the Estates-General and then the administrative and territorial in-fighting of 1790 traced out the rough contours of a party alignment which subsequently hardened into 'patriot' and 'fanatic' camps. In the West where town versus country conflict reached an intensity unmatched anywhere else in the country (see pp. 225–7), the patriot party consisted of urban officialdom, to all intents and purposes, whereas the 'fanatics' enlisted the great majority of the peasantry who deeply resented the urban-inspired assault upon their religious habits. Such an alignment was not 'given', however. In the Arpajonais and in the protestant Cévennes the peasantry passed muster as the patriots, and they launched repeated raids upon noble- and priest-riddled neighbouring towns.

Town versus country politicisation presupposed a communitarian response to the revolution. In the South East the messages of revolution tended to split or divide communities into segments. Here it would be inappropriate to think in terms of conflict between towns and their rural hinterlands; rather we should conceive of politicisation as a process of osmosis in which the towns (or their dominant factions) contaminated the surrounding countryside. Several ecological peculiarities of the region help to explain why peasant politicisation should have followed this route: the South East, unlike the West or for that matter the Massif Central, formed a highly urbanised society in which the counterweight of villages and hamlets was weak or non-existent. Instead the rural population congregated in *bourgs* where they lived cheek by jowl with a resident bourgeoisie of cultured and sophisticated landowners and professionals who played the role of a 'relay class'. By a process which Maurice Agulhon has explored in detail, these individuals disseminated the political currents emanating from cities such as Marseilles and Aix-en-Provence.[22] Their proselytising zeal evoked a ready response in a population which had been harrowed by repeated waves of anti-nobilism since March 1789.

The South East provides an example of precocious and sustained politicisation in which the *prise de conscience* of the urban and rural masses appears as the logical consequence of the structures of the region. Either extreme jacobinism or extreme royalism: no other outcome was possible. And yet the growth in political awareness was not bound to occur in a linear fashion. It may be that the average country dweller's perception of the revolution more closely approximated to the scenario unfolded by Paul Bois in his study of the department of the Sarthe.[23] The key to Bois's model of politicisation is disappointment: the peasantry participated enthusiastically during the early years of the revolution, only to turn against the new regime when it failed to deliver the goods. Fiscal disappointments (see pp. 188–9), in combination with mounting frustrations over feudal dues and the sale of *biens nationaux*, nurtured in the minds of country dwellers a sharpened perception of their interests and a growing realisation that the revolution had done little or nothing to secure those interests. From that realisation sprang a commitment to counter-revolution that was every bit as tenacious as the rural jacobinism of the South East. We should be wary about generalising this model, of course. If only on the tax front, few peasantries can have received quite such a raw deal as that of the West. But even Michel Vovelle, who pioneered research into the political orientation of the South East, considers that it may have a wider application.[24] He points to that portion of the Comtat between Avignon and Arles which became known as the 'Vendée Provençale' from 1793. Yet, prior to this date the inhabitants of the region were chiefly noted for their attachment to agrarian radicalism. How did the switch come about? Is this another case of peasant alienation in the face of bourgeois land engrossment? Something similar may have happened in the Seine-et-Marne where agitation for the division of common land was transmuted into *chouan* sympathies under the Directory.

Politicisation was not of necessity static and durable, therefore. Nor did it depend upon structural factors such as the existence of an antecedent 'relay class': it was often contingent on local personalities or local issues. We should not underestimate the role of the isolated propagandist in the countryside. Such men were usually bourgeois, but were not bound to be so (Babeuf, for example). Professionals such as doctors, notaries and land surveyors (who had a vested interest in promoting the sale of national property and the partition of common land) commonly featured in the ranks of rural jacobinism. By the same token it is not rare to discover tithe farmers nurturing hopes of a counter-revolution among the common people. In March 1797 the Directory received a letter from the depths of the Lozère denouncing one Emmanuel Panafieu, a 'sworn enemy' of the revolution, in the following terms: 'Rich on the tithe which he used to collect, he has never been able to stomach this new regime, one of the chiefs in the Charrier uprising, arraigned as such on 24 July 1793', etc. etc.[25]

In the absence of a fertile medium the parish pump orator was unlikely to contrive a genuine awakening of the rural masses, however. Single-person politicisation lacked stamina and displayed the hallmarks of immaturity: factionalism, territorialism and heavy reliance on the patron–client relationship. Single-issue politicisation avoided these pitfalls, but remained blinkered, none the less. Briefly, the issue of the neo-tithe galvanised the sharecroppers of the South West into action, but it failed to trigger a more general political awakening comparable to that experienced in the South East and they soon returned to a torpid state. The campaign against the institution of *domaine congéable* in Lower Brittany (see pp. 113–14) is a further case in point. Unlike the *bordiers* of the Gers (see pp. 100–3), the *domaniers* pressed their case with consummate skill. In fact, they fairly bombarded the National Assembly with petitions detailing the iniquities of this form of land tenure. Yet the issue does not appear to have broadened their political horizons to any measurable degree. The *domaniers* neither enlisted in the van of revolution in order to fight for abolition, nor did they express their 'disappointment' with the new order by joining the *chouannerie*. Demoralised, they simply opted out of the revolution.

Counter-revolution

In the late winter and spring of 1793 the pressures telescoping national and local politics came to a head. With the beginnings of conscription, with *commissaires* of the National Convention roaming the highways, it became increasingly difficult to stand on the sidelines. Some peasants were pulled into the orbit of revolution through the medium of jacobinism, others were enlisted under the banner of counter-revolution by their priests or former seigneurs. The majority, perhaps, tried to ignore what was taking place or paid lip-service to whichever party seemed in the ascendant – a stance fraught with danger as events would shortly demonstrate. Whether many country dwellers consciously opted for counter-revolution may be doubted: even in the West it could be argued that the peasantry were seeking redress for their grievances *within* a framework of revolution. Counter-revolution as a concept appealed most to the *émigré* princes and their agents, to backwoods noblemen who had often lost a good deal as a result of the abolition of seigneurialism, and to refractory priests. These are the kind of people whom we find plotting against the new order before March 1793, when the Vendée revolt suddenly endowed counter-revolution with a popular base.

Two regions swiftly attracted attention as potential epicentres of royalist revolt: the West and the southern Massif Central, defined generously so as to embrace the lower Rhône valley, the Comtat Venaissin and the western fringe of Provence (see map 15). In the West the first attempt to prepare the ground for a return to absolute monarchy was undertaken by the Marquis de la Rouërie during the early months of 1790. The following year he quit France and travelled to the *émigré* headquarters in Coblenz where he presented himself as the leader of a Breton Association. Endorsed by the Comte d'Artois, the Association founded committees in small towns throughout Brittany, Normandy, Anjou and Poitou and busily set about stockpiling munitions. An uprising in Brittany, initially directed against the provincial capital of Rennes, seems to have been in prospect for the summer of 1792, but on the last night of May one of La Rouërie's secretaries, together with several other conspirators and all their papers, were captured. La Rouërie himself avoided arrest only to fall victim to illness, and his death in January 1793 brought to an abrupt end the first attempt to stage a full-scale royalist revolt in the West.

To what extent La Rouërie represented the cause of the princes as opposed to the glowing embers of Breton regionalism is open to dispute. Nevertheless, his network of cadres and committees helped to pave the way for both the Vendée revolt and the Breton *chouannerie*. All over the West allegiances were crystallising inexorably and La Rouërie was not the only nobleman to spot the potentialities of the situation. The Baron de Lézardière, for example, organised a mini-conspiracy centred on his château in the *bocage* country of the Vendée in the spring of 1791. Before a call-to-arms could be issued the alarm was raised, but the episode left little doubt as to where the loyalties of country dwellers lay. On 17 August 1791 the jacobins of Angers (Maine-et-Loire) called for the pre-emptive demolition of all château fortifications, a call echoed by the jacobins of Poitiers (Vienne). The Vendée department aroused most anxiety, but the word 'Vendée' was rapidly becoming a portmanteau term to identify

Map 15. The heartlands of counter-revolution

counter-revolutionary outbreaks in a large segment of territory embracing parts of the Loire-Inférieure, the Maine-et-Loire and the Deux-Sèvres, as well as the Vendée. A few days after the fall of the monarchy, a momentarily serious insurrection took hold in the neighbourhood of Bressuire (Deux-Sèvres). Led by country noblemen who were to be involved in the Vendée revolt the following year, the conflagration spread to eighty villages before it was damped down by National Guardsmen. Arrests were made, but the ringleaders were soon released, thereby further demoralising the authorities responsible for law and order. By the spring of 1793 many National Guardsmen had concluded that it was pointless to risk their necks in defence of the republic.

At a glance, the growth of counter-revolutionary commitment in the southern Massif Central runs parallel to events in the West. The South, too, had its share of international plotters all claiming mandates from the *émigré* princes. It possessed *hobreaux* noblemen in abundance who were willing to fortify their châteaux, gather together their retainers and do battle with the revolution, and it was rather better supplied with die-hard priests prepared to lead from the front. Nevertheless, the differences are more telling than the similarities: in the southern Massif Central the threshold of peasant support for counter-revolution was much lower. In this region of intense seigneurialism and burdensome fiscality, country dwellers computed their gains and losses rather differently and the net result was far from entirely discreditable to the revolution. Moreover, the confessional divide between catholic and protestant introduced a variable which was absent from the western counter-revolutionary equation. Sectarianism cut across the town and country polarity which contoured political allegiances in the Vendée; sometimes it cut across villages, too, thereby precluding a whole-community response to the challenge of counter-revolution. The sectarian issue also tended to strait-jacket popular perceptions of counter-revolution to the point where the struggle could only be interpreted in religious terms. The agents of the princes and their recruiting sergeants in the provinces found this to be a great source of strength: they had only to play up the protestant menace in order to per-suade the catholic peasantry to stand in line. But it was a source of weak-ness, too: the southern counter-revolutionary movement never developed a broad critique of the new order and remained vulnerable to the vagaries of revolutionary religious policy. As far as the rank and file were con-cerned, they were fighting for the 'bons prêtres' (good priests) and the true religion, much less for the king and a Bourbon restoration. A final point of difference deserves mention, for it follows naturally upon the comments already made. In the southern Massif Central every counter-revolutionary stirring between 1790 and 1793 was vigorously repressed and there can be no doubt that the energy and vigilance of the local authorities had a deterrent effect. In the West the same vigour and energy was only deployed after March 1793, and by then it was too late.

The first serious signs that the revolution was losing the support of a proportion of the peasantry emerged in the Ardèche during the summer of 1790. That August between 20,000 and 40,000 catholic peasants drawn from 180 parishes gathered in the open countryside around the château of Jalès.[26] Although the encampment was instigated by local nobles who were unquestionably hostile to the revolution, the motivation was more religious than counter-revolutionary: two months earlier several hundred catholics had lost their lives in a brawl with protestants in the town of Nîmes (see p. 196) and there were calls for a punitive raid on the Calvinists of the Gard. The administrative reforms of the National Assembly came as a nasty shock to catholics after decades of institutionalised superiority (since 1685, in fact), and many of those attending the rally voiced the demand that protestants be excluded from municipal office. A fresh call to arms was issued for February 1791 (the second Camp of Jalès) and it happened to coincide with a sectarian clash in the town of Uzès (Gard) which sent another ripple of catholic fear throughout the region. This time fewer peasant detachments congregated on the plain of Jalès, but the movement bore an overtly counter-revolutionary character. Its leaders, Louis Bastide de Malbosc and the priest Claude Allier, seem to have been acting in tandem with *émigré* agents and were certainly playing for high stakes. As far as the assembled peasantry were concerned, however, the objective remained that of bringing help to their embattled co-religionaries in the Gard. Prompt repression, concerted by the department authorities of the Ardèche, brought the whole affair to an ignominious conclusion: the château of Jalès was sacked by troops and Malbosc arrested. A fortnight later he was found dead on the banks of the Rhône.

After the abortive encampments at Jalès, the focal point of southern counter-revolution moved westwards to the Lozère and the Aveyron. The agents of the princes whose task it was to coordinate the efforts of royalists at home and abroad took the view that the Ardèche was worn out. This was not strictly correct; after the fiascos of 1790 and 1791 the peasantry simply preferred to adopt a wait-and-see policy. Nevertheless, attention switched to men like Vital-Auguste de Borel and Marc-Antoine Charrier who had been building up a network of contacts spanning the Aveyron and the Lozère. Borel was the first to make a move: on 24 February 1792 the ardently aristocratic National Guard of Mende which he commanded provoked a brawl with three companies of grenadiers as they entered the town. The troops withdrew in disarray and this became the signal for wholesale counter-revolution. Local patriots were arrested, royalists smashed up the jacobin club of Mende with axes and the constitutional bishop fled his palace. His example was followed by most of the permanent officials of the department of the Lozère. Almost immediately, however, the patriots set about organising a riposte. Calls for troop reinforcements went out to all the neighbouring departments and on 7 March the activities of the Mende royalists were denounced at the bar of the Assembly. Loyal battalions of National Guardsmen and troops of the line poured into the department and the status quo was soon restored. Borel and his confederates escaped to Lyons and from there to Chambéry.

Unlike in the West, opinion was so divided in the southern Massif Central and the South East that counter-revolution never managed to get much more than a toe-hold. Energetic administrators and reliable bodies of armed men were always on hand to retrieve the situation. The month which saw the collapse of Borel's ambitions in Mende also witnessed the defeat of the Arles royalists (known as *chiffonistes*) by an armed contingent of Marseillais. With a fresh outbreak of anti-seigneurial violence about to begin (see pp. 121–2), it seemed to the royalists that they had failed to cement a durable alliance with the peasantry. Their one last hope before the Terror battened down the countryside was Charrier. The Charrier revolt took place on the confines of the Aveyron and the Lozère in May 1793 and it posed by far the most serious challenge to the revolution in the region. This was not because of the numbers involved (about 2,000), nor even because the rank and file were committed royalists (again, religion was the motivating issue), but because Charrier's 'Christian Army of the Midi' showed clear signs of combat potential. Competently generalled, the army captured the town of Marvejols (Lozère) and marched on Mende where it was welcomed with open arms. The fleeing administrators withdrew to the sanctuary of the protestant Cévennes from which they launched anguished appeals for troop reinforcements. Charrier, meanwhile, turned west and retraced his steps down the valley of the Lot only to find his passage barred by troops from the Aveyron which were the first to arrive on the scene. Two pitched battles took place (at Barjac and Chanac), after which the Aveyronnais fell back in disorder. Undefeated, yet mindful of the fact that his exploits had not ignited a general uprising of the population, Charrier resolved to conduct a guerrilla war from the mountains instead. In any case, vast numbers of seasoned troops were now converging on the Lozère: by mid-June there were 20,000 encamped in Mende alone. The end came suddenly and rather unexpectedly. Charrier went into hiding, but was betrayed, captured and guillotined in Rodez on 17 July 1793.

No one, least of all the military authorities, underestimated the potential of the Charrier revolt. In this sense, the lessons of the Vendée had been learned: National Guardsmen and raw recruits could not be relied upon to overcome well-led peasant squadrons. But the young peasants, farm servants and rural artisans who formed the rank and file of Charrier's army had also been rehearsed in the possibilities of determined collective action. In March a massive anti-recruitment insurrection had taken hold of villages along the border between the Lozère and the Aveyron, villages which would answer Charrier's call only two months later. It is to this issue, which triggered rioting throughout the country, that we must now turn.

The French war effort faced a manpower crisis during the winter 1792–3. Distrusting the notion of a permanent, professional army, the revolutionaries preferred to call upon the services of volunteers as and when the need arose. The alarums provoked by the flight to Varennes prompted a call for 100,000 recruits; the following year a further 50,000 men were enrolled in the colours. The chief objection to this manner of proceeding was that it made no allowance for forward planning: volunteers could withdraw from the armies once their stint of duty was up. This, indeed, was what happened after the victories of late 1792, and the Convention found itself faced with the prospect of beginning a fresh campaigning season with reduced effectives and a lengthened list of enemies. Previous recruitment drives had not encountered serious opposition – they were, after all, voluntary. But on 24 February 1793 the deputies voted a measure which foreshadowed the recourse to conscription just six months later. The decree laid down a target of 300,000 new recruits to be achieved by means of quotas based on the presumed population of each department. However, the local authorities were allowed considerable latitude as to the manner in which they fulfilled their quotas. Three methods were envisaged: volunteer recruitment (with or without the payment of a financial inducement); designation in a ballot (*scrutin*); and the entirely random procedure of drawing lots (*tirage au sort*) which had been used to select individuals for militia service during the *ancien régime*. The constituency of eligible citizens was defined as unmarried men and childless widowers aged between eighteen and forty, but public functionaries, National Guardsmen and constitutional priests were exempted from service *ex officio*. Finally, the practice of purchasing a replacement was permitted, subject to certain restrictions.

Few, if any, of the deputies appear to have anticipated the outcry that the *levée des 300,000* would cause. Yet by the end of the first week of March it was obvious that the draft had precipitated a major crisis of confidence in the countryside, and the Convention hastily issued a back-up decree despatching *commissaires* to supervise the business of recruitment in every corner of the country. By the end of the second week of March (the town of Cholet fell on the 14th), the true gravity of the situation in the West was beginning to dawn and the deputies rushed through a decree imposing the death penalty on anyone inciting resistance to recruitment. By the end of the month, with measures founding the Revolutionary Tribunal and the *comités de surveillance* (see pp. 237–8) on the statute book, it was plain that the revolutionaries had crossed the Rubicon. So many departments reported hostility to the recruitment decree that it is easier to begin with those that remained quiescent. Generally speaking, the urban and rural populations of the East (Meurthe, Haute-Saône, Doubs) responded admirably to this latest call upon their patriotism. In some districts enough volunteers stepped forward to fill the quota, whilst in the Haute-Saône and the Doubs young men who had served in 1791 offered to return to the colours. The recruitment commissioners encountered little more than sporadic grumbling on the plains around Paris and in the South East, either.

However, in Burgundy, in the Massif Central, in parts of the South West, in Brittany, and more generally throughout the West a mood of exasperation prevailed. It was as though the issue of whether or not to fight for the republic had brought to the boil a host of simmering discontents. All those who had done well out of the revolution should be the first to enrol, declared the young men of Beaune (Côte-d'Or) on 3 March. They meant public officials, purchasers of national property and the members of the local jacobin club. Similar sentiments were expressed at public meetings in the towns of Arnay-sur-Arroux, Autun and Dijon. At Semur-en-Auxois where jacobin influence was paramount the first summons produced just three volunteers for a quota of thirty-four. In consequence, the assembled youth of the town opted for the ballot procedure and promptly designated the sons of the richest and most moderate families. The ballot or *scrutin* gave rise to so many complaints, in fact, that the *commissaires* of the Convention insisted on *tirage au sort* throughout the district of Autun.

Fortunately for the civil authorities, the Burgundian protest movement remained an urban phenomenon. The towns joined forces, but opposition in the countryside was muted and unorganised. This was not the case in the departments of the Massif Central, however, where resistance germinated in both the towns and the villages. Attempts to drum up fifty-six recruits in the town of Rodez (Aveyron) on 17 March provoked a riot led by 400 domestic servants demanding exemption on the (incorrect) grounds that they were passive citizens. (In fact the passive–active distinction had been abolished with effect from the election of September 1792.) The mayor was slightly wounded and one of the rioters was killed by National Guardsmen. Nearly simultaneous disturbances occurred throughout the department, but the most serious gripped the villages skirting the Lozère where the royalist emissary, Claude Allier, had been canvassing the population on behalf of Charrier. On the 17th and days following, contingents of armed men from miles around converged on the village of Lapanouse. Several thousand strong, the insurgents decided to attack the town of Sévérac but were put to flight by troops and artillery. Eighteen died on the rebel side and a further twenty or so were executed. If we set aside the royalist instigation which can be detected in the Lapanouse insurrection, the grievances were nearly always the same. The exemption clauses deeply offended, for they seemed to protect those who had done best out of the change of regime. Many peasants and artisans must have wondered whether the revolution was not now setting up a new class of *privilégiés*.

Why should officials enjoy the right of exemption, especially unmarried officials? The refusal to specify a means of selecting recruits should volunteers fail to step forward in sufficient numbers also proved a bad mistake. *Tirage au sort* had its own shortcomings, but at least it was egalitarian, whereas selection via the *scrutin* positively invited recrimination and factional manoeuvring. In effect, the decree gave cliques of patriots (or royalists) the chance to remove their political enemies from the scenes. At Neulise (Loire) armed youths packed the recruitment assembly and insisted that the *scrutin* be used to fill the village quota of fifteen. They then proceeded to nominate the constitutional priest (by 107 votes out of 111) and fourteen prominent patriots.

Nowhere did recruitment provoke quite so much fury as in the West, however. Beyond Poitiers in the south and Caen in the north rioting was endemic. Within the sector bounded by the cities of Nantes, Angers, Poitiers and La Rochelle this rioting coalesced into full-scale counter-revolution (see map 16). To the north of the river Loire the Breton departments of the Morbihan and the Ille-et-Vilaine gave greatest cause for concern. Columns of rustic insurgents threatened the towns of Vannes, Pontivy and Auray and the district capitals of Rochefort-en-Terre and La Roche-Bernard actually fell into their hands for a time. In the Ille-et-Vilaine, too, the worst of the rioting took place in the countryside, and townspeople were the first to find themselves in the firing line. Rennes, the provincial capital, came under threat on 17 March and Fougères and Vitré were attacked several days later. For all their simultaneity, the Breton uprisings remained leaderless, uncoordinated and politically opaque, however. Witnesses subsequently attributed to the Rochefort insurgents a desire 'to get back their king and their priests',[27] but there is no evidence that a worked-out plan of counter-revolution was being followed. In any case, the department authorities in Rennes soon regained control of the situation. La Roche-Bernard was recaptured on 29 March and in early April the recruitment process was completed in an atmosphere of relative tranquillity. The Breton population had not turned their backs on counter-revolution, but they would not make a significant contribution to the war against the republic until the *chouannerie* (see pp. 240–2) took shape in 1794 and 1795.

Only in that compact rectangle of territory embracing the departments of the Vendée, the southerly portions of the Loire-Inférieure and the Maine-et-Loire, and the north-westerly corner of the Deux-Sèvres did the *levée des 300,000* ignite the powder keg of counter-revolution. The order to start raising men for the republic had reached most local authorities in the area by 2 March. The first rumblings of discontent surfaced the following day, which was a Sunday. Over the next fortnight the region

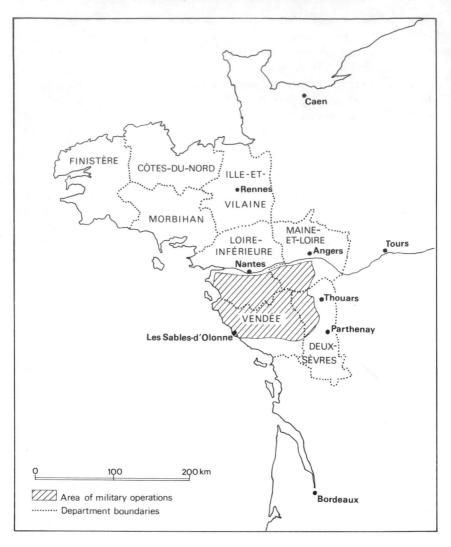

Map 16. The *Vendée militaire*

moved, in the words of Charles Tilly, 'from deep agitation to open rebellion'.[28] As elsewhere, the young men liable to conscription were incensed by what they considered the partisan character of the decree: 'Aux habits bleus de partir! Aux fonctionnaires de commencer!' (Republicans to leave, starting with the administrators!),[29] shouted the youth of Cholet (Maine-et-Loire) on the 3rd. It was scarcely an original demand in the circumstances, but what *was* unusual was the strength of feeling, the pace of the insurrection and the ease with which resistance to recruitment translated into a generalised critique of the revolution. The turning point came on 12 March when bands of country dwellers overran the strategically important town of St Florent-le-Vieil (Maine-et-Loire), a Loire crossing-point which gave communication between the Vendée and Brittany and Normandy. St Florent was also the seat of a district administration and the insurgents made a point of pillaging patriotic households and of burning official papers in a huge bonfire. The following day the first leaders emerged, a sure sign that the movement was acquiring consistency. Then, on the 14th, a counter-revolutionary army (the term is not inappropriate) converged on Cholet, the largest town in the rebel zone. Under the command of the gamekeeper and one-time soldier, Stofflet, about 10,000 rebels overwhelmed a small force of republicans leaving dead and injured numbering perhaps 300. An attempt to deepen the bridgehead by taking the town of Saumur (Maine-et-Loire) failed; nevertheless the Vendeans had won control of a slice of territory along the left bank of the river Loire from its estuary to the confluence with the Layon.

The Convention did not immediately grasp the significance of what was happening. After all, no one imagined that peasant bands could withstand the might of the regular army. That illusion was swiftly shattered: on 19 March the rebels put to flight a column commanded by General Marcé at Pont-Charrault (Vendée). The Vendée war had begun, and it had begun amid cries of treachery and treason as republicans struggled to come to terms with the concept of a popular counter-revolution. By June 30,000 troops, many of them seasoned, were committed in the West and yet the final victory was far from assured. At least the rebel bridgehead did not grow any larger: after the first few weeks the zone of operations, known as the *Vendée militaire*, stabilised. It is true that the rebels succeeded in capturing Saumur on 9 June and Angers a few days later, but they made no real effort to hold these cities and preferred to turn westwards and lay siege to Nantes at the mouth of the Loire instead. The successful defence of Nantes brought the first phase of the civil war to a climax. Thereafter, the republic organised its military effort with increasing skill and determination, whereas the Vendeans progressively lost their sense of purpose. On 1 August 1793 the Convention voted a ruthless decree declaring total war against the Vendée and reinforced its armies in the West with troops brought over from Germany. From mid-September the noose around the rebels began to tighten: columns of republican troops converged from all directions and a decisive battle was fought at Cholet on 17 October.

Defeated and deprived of some of their most able generals, the Vendeans now seized upon the only alternative which could possibly change the outcome of the war: an overland march to Granville on the Normandy coast in order to capture the port and facilitate an English landing. This ploy failed miserably. On discovering Granville to be heavily defended and with not an English sail in sight, the Vendeans fell back in disorder towards the Loire. Repeatedly worsted in battle, they were finally annihilated at Savenay (Loire-Inférieure) on 23 December, having tried and failed to recross the river Loire. A most terrible repression followed the disintegration of the Vendean army. Shortly after the engagement at Savenay, General Westermann informed the Committee of Public Safety: 'The Vendee is no more . . . It has died beneath our sabres, together with its women and children . . . I have crushed the children under my horses' hooves, massacred the women – they, at least, will not give birth to any more brigands.'[30] Terrorist rhetoric, no doubt: but there are grounds for supposing that these chilling statements should be taken at face value. From January until May 1794 columns of troops roamed the region shooting villagers, burning their farms or demolishing their houses more or less at will. The historian Reynald Secher has not hesitated to call the republican reprisals an act of genocide. He calculates that the 770-odd parishes of the *Vendée militaire* lost about 117,000 inhabitants representing nearly 15 per cent of the population during the course of the hostilities. Material losses may have been higher still: perhaps 20 per cent of dwellings demolished or rendered uninhabitable by the republic's scorched earth policy.[31] Local studies tend to underline these grim statistics. Lawrence Wylie's team of researchers discovered that the population of Chanzeaux (Maine-et-Loire) dropped from 1,800 to 1,100 between 1793 and 1795.[32] By this latter date only twenty-one out of one hundred houses in the *bourg* were left standing. The small towns of the region suffered grievously, too. The civil war left Bressuire a shadow of its former self with 80 per cent of its houses in ruins, while the population of the canton of Cholet was depleted by 38 per cent.

The social anatomy of the Vendée uprising has been left to one side so far. Most contemporary accounts simply emphasise the role of nobles and priests and refer to the rank and file as 'peasants'. One of the first reports to reach the Convention used the phrase 'almost the entire countryside, marching in battle order'.[33] Charles Tilly will have none of this and he stresses the counter-revolutionary vocation of rural artisans who were 'by no means simply peasants slightly modified'.[34] Concentrating on one area (the Mauges) in the insurrectionary zone and one category of rural artisan (the cottage weaver), he discerns an embryonic class conflict pitting textile outworkers against merchant-clothiers operating from the town of Cholet. Whether the role of weavers deserves to be highlighted in this fashion is debatable; it seems more likely that artisans simply adopted the outlook of their peasant neighbours. In the Mauges that outlook was frankly hostile to the revolution, but in the eastern Sarthe, for instance, where the social environment was favourable to the revolution, weavers remained steadfastly patriotic.

Whatever their political options, weavers formed a tiny minority of country dwellers in the West. If we want to know who rebelled and why, we have to start with the peasantry. This is the conclusion reached by Tim Le Goff and Donald Sutherland who have pioneered a major reinterpretation of the social origins of counter-revolution.[35] They address themselves to the question of land tenure and draw a distinction between owner-occupiers and tenant farmers. Even before the revolution, conditions for tenant farmers (and sharecroppers) had worsened, it appears, but the avalanche of reforming legislation after 1789 drove the wedge between well-to-do peasant proprietors and those with a precarious title to the land deeper still. The biggest bone of contention was the tithe: owners of land profited handsomely from its abolition, but tenants often found that its cash equivalent had been added to their leases. In consequence, the rural community divided under the pressures of revolutionary policies with peasant proprietors staying loyal, by and large, while tenant farmers slipped into the orbit of counter-revolution. This hypothesis seems to fit the Breton case best, where the level of support for the revolution can be correlated with the incidence of peasant proprietors. The *chouannerie* (see pp. 240–2), by contrast, flourished in districts dominated by tenant farming. Nevertheless, the scenario rests upon a worryingly large number of assumptions and imponderables: was the owner–tenant cleavage unbridgeable (most peasant households were part owners and part renters)? Was the tithe-equivalent always added to leases? Was *domaine congéable* a precarious form of tenure and were the *domaniers* clearly aligned against the revolution? Brittany, moreover, cannot stand duty for the whole of the West, and least of all for the southern counter-revolution. We have already noted, for instance, that the sharecroppers of the Gers continued to adhere to the revolution *despite* their disillusionment over the tithe. Much more research will have to be undertaken before the link between land tenure and the political options of country dwellers can be established.

If we put unproven theories to one side, there remains the expedient of counting heads. The potential of this approach has been demonstrated by Claude Petitfrère whose analysis of the pension records of over 5,000 former Vendée rebels makes for interesting reading.[36] Compiled during the Restoration, these records are not exempt from reproach; nevertheless, they enable the historian to identify the occupations of 4,715 individuals who fought against the republic. On this evidence, approximately 63 per cent of the combattants were peasants; 15 per cent were textile workers (spinners, weavers, cloth dressers, nearly all linked to the Cholet cottage industry); 19 per cent were artisans or small traders; 2 per cent could be described as bourgeois; while the remaining 1 per cent were drawn from a variety of backgrounds (priests, professional soldiers, etc.). Two points emerge clearly: the substantial craft representation in an otherwise peasant revolt, and the derisory level of bourgeois participation, which confirms the sharp town–country polarity known to have characterised counter-revolution in the West. The typical Vendean was a peasant farmer or a rural artisan or a mixture of the two, whereas the typical patriot was a merchant, a lawyer or a bourgeois landowner – many of whom would also have been local government officials and purchasers of national property. Unfortunately, the data do not permit a clear distinction to be drawn between peasants who were owner-occupiers, peasants who leased farms and peasants who were landless. Perhaps such categories exist only in the minds of historians. Petitfrère estimates that maybe two in five of the peasant insurgents could be described as well-to-do; the remainder were day labourers, farm servants and plot farmers. The prominent role played by the local nobility in the insurrection should not be forgotten, either, but they were rewarded for their services on an *ad hoc* basis and did not need to apply for pensions.

The republic in the village

The peasantry of the Vendée *bocage* country rejected the republic and all its works. As repression followed the fighting, that rejection became pathological and it marked the political outlook of the region for a century and more. Elsewhere, however, the issues were less clear-cut. In many parts of the country the revolution had brought concrete gains, even if these now had to be paid for in terms of a profound disturbance of religious habits and constant demands for men and supplies in order to press forward the war effort. Country dwellers reacted variously to the mixture of opportunities and disappointments which 1789 ushered in and it would be wrong to suppose that the violent disillusionment of the Vendeans was in any sense typical. When Georges Lefebvre analysed the role of the peasantry during the French Revolution, he omitted the counter-revolutionary dimension altogether.[37] How, then, did country dwellers react as events entered their climactic phase? Some, undoubtedly, placed their lives and fortunes in the service of counter-revolution, but they represented a tiny minority; others responded to the challenge by creating a pale imitation of the republic at village level. The majority, we suspect, did their utmost to avoid taking sides: they grasped what the revolution offered and discreetly complained about what it did not. Theirs was a strategy for survival, a strategy deeply embedded in peasant culture. This retreat from political commitment is one of the most striking features of village life during the Terror and it makes the history of ordinary country dwellers during the period very difficult to write. As the news from Paris became more and more shocking (overthrow of the monarchy; the prison massacres; execution of Louis XVI; proscription of the Girondins, etc.), municipal deliberations became less and less forthcoming. In some localities municipal councillors stopped meeting altogether for fear of compromising themselves by backing the 'wrong' side. On the day the prison massacres commenced in Paris, the municipality of Azereix in the Hautes-Pyrénées was engaged upon the seasonal task of leasing the right of *glandage* (acorn scavenging) in the surrounding forests. But then the news of the attack on the Tuileries filtered through and for a month the councillors and aldermen refused to attend meetings. Panic seized hold of the councillors again in April and May 1793 as rumours of the party conflict in the Convention reached the village. In the highly politicised *bourgs* of Provence, by contrast, the storms and stresses of the revolution produced a galvanising effect. At Lourmarin the municipal council met three or four times a week, and sometimes daily, throughout the late summer and autumn of 1792.

Provence was not France, however, any more than was the Vendée. Most villages managed to keep the pressures of national politics at arm's length until the spring of 1793. To be sure, cracks had already appeared in the united front which rural communities liked to present to the outside world. The tension between juring and non-juring clerics provided a ready-made framework for allegiances in many a locality, whilst in others it is possible to trace the contours of pro- and anti-seigneur parties which sometimes pre-dated the revolution. Agrarian tensions should not be neglected, either: the revolution gave a fresh impetus to age-old disputes over grazing and gleaning rights. In the village of St Chély-d'Aubrac (Aveyron) a disastrous court case between the inhabitants and a local land-owner over a piece of pasture in 1777 established the battle lines for a generation. Nevertheless, such animosities were generally contained and even papered over until March and April of 1793. What finally exploded the politics of consensus and precipitated the faction-based politics of village jacobinism was the arrival of the *commissaires* of the Convention. Despatched with a mandate to rescue the provincial revolution from the rising tide of 'moderation' and 'fanaticism', these men were nearly all hand-picked *montagnards* who could be relied upon not to scruple over legal forms when the survival of the revolution was at stake. Their passage through the departments brought the Terror to the doorsteps of millions of country dwellers.

Among the most notorious were François Chabot and Jean-Baptiste Bo, whose mission extended to the Aveyron and the Tarn. Such was the shock of their visitation that it was recalled with horror years later. Both of the deputies came from the Aveyron and this department bore the brunt of their buccaneering foray through the countryside. On 29 March they arrived in Rodez – just in time to preside over the execution of a young man who had led resistance to the recruitment decree – and during the next five or six weeks the apparatus of the Terror was installed in town and village alike. It is worth listing their measures, for the institutional underpinnings of jacobinism varied little from one part of the country to the next:

30 March	appointment of special delegates to supervise the task of military recruitment
6 April	imposition of a special war tax (*taxe de guerre*) on aristocrats and wealthy moderates, all sums to be paid within fifteen days
7 April	abrogation of the electoral principle: suspension of public officials lacking in civic zeal (*incivisme*)
8 April	removal of church bells
9 April	disarmament of all citizens suspected of *incivisme*; reorganisation of the National Guard
10 April	creation of a special military force to pursue refractory priests and *émigrés*
13 April	appointment of commissioners to disarm 'suspects'
14 April	*arrêté* of the department authorities setting up revolutionary committees (*comités de surveillance*) in the towns, villages and hamlets
20 April	'suspects' to be detained in the district capitals as hostages
29 April	charges against detainees to be compiled and despatched to the Committee of Public Safety
30 April	domiciliary searches authorised
5 May	householders to paint their names on front doors.

A few days after this last measure Chabot and Bo quit the department having laid the foundations for the Terror. In all the towns and most of the *bourgs* jacobin sympathisers moved swiftly to pack the newly established revolutionary committees and to round up their political enemies. The first mass arrests of 'suspects' (that is to say non-noble and non-clerical moderates) took place; local authorities were 'purged' (another new word meaning the removal of duly elected representatives and their replacement with politically reliable nominees); and discretionary tax lists were hawked from house to house by intimidating bands of village *sans-culottes*. At St Chély-d'Aubrac the inhabitants wreaked condign vengeance on the landowner who had presumed to dispute their grazing rights in 1777. She was denounced, disarmed and forced to flee as her property was laid waste. Finally, in October, she was detained as a suspect.

On leaving the Aveyron, Chabot headed for Toulouse where he caused no less havoc. An attempt to organise a congress of southern jacobin clubs earned him the suspicions of his *montagnard* colleagues and a bitter denunciation from the administrators of the department of the Haute-Garonne. Elsewhere in the provinces, other *commissaires* of the Convention embarked on a broadly similar programme of action to rekindle the dying embers of revolutionary zeal. The experiment in grass-roots democracy had failed, reported Jeanbon Saint-André from the Lot: the rural municipalities were either incapable or politically unreliable. Draconian measures were required if the poor were to be dissuaded from abandoning the revolution. Accordingly, he ordered the confiscation of *émigré* estates, the disarmament of suspects and the transfer of refractory priests to the hulks of Bordeaux. But in this region, blighted by a run of bad harvests, economic measures were required too: 'It is absolutely crucial to provide the poor with the means of survival if you want them to help you to complete the revolution.'[38] Jeanbon Saint-André's plea was echoed by many of the *commissaires*. From the Gironde, Garrau and Paganel warned that the common people blamed the revolution for the rising price of foodstuffs, while in the Jura Prost and Bourdon endorsed a decision taken by administrators to ban the movement of grain beyond the confines of the department.

This brutal (and often illegal) political and economic interventionism was not without its costs, however. In the Convention the Brissotins made capital out of the extremist activities of the eighty-two deputies touring the departments. On 16 May 1793 the *Patriote français* announced: 'We are informed that Chabot rages in the Aveyron, sending round *lettres de cachet*, the *guillotine*, and always in the midst of his pleasures.'[39] Most of the *montagnard* commissioners were back in Paris by the end of May and able to participate in the struggle to oust the Girondins, but the reaction to their passage through the departments was less easily effaced. Throughout the South West (Lot-et-Garonne, Gers, Lot, Tarn, Aveyron) the vehemence and bitterness of the Federalist rebellion owed a great deal to the fiery activism of men like François Chabot and Jeanbon Saint-André during the preceding spring. Whether the Federalist stance affected anyone other than the conservative notables and administrators who had been badly shaken by the whirlwind passage of the *commissaires* is difficult to judge. In some towns the would-be Federalists seem to have enjoyed the support of a section of the working population. This, at least, was the conclusion drawn by *commissaire* Garrau after a visit to Agen (Lot-et-Garonne) in the middle of May. Indications that the anti-Paris propaganda of the Federalists found a receptive audience among artisans and journeymen can be found in the Aveyron, too. At St Geniez-d'Olt (ironically François Chabot's home town), visiting emissaries from Federalist Lyons won many converts by linking jacobinism with food shortages: 'Paris eats cheap bread and the provinces are dying of hunger'[40] was the catchphrase that went round the town's colony of impoverished weavers.

That the towns should succumb to Federalism was, in many regions, a sufficient reason for the peasantry to stay aloof. In the southern Massif Central the rural bourgeoisie were well placed to recruit for the Federalist cause, but the sharp polarity between town and country tended to render such efforts ineffective. The peasant farmers of the plain of Forez (Loire), on the other hand, rejected Federalism because they associated it with the seigneurial regime, not unreasonably in view of the number of landlords involved in the movement. In any case, the more perspicacious members of the rural community perceived the Federalist crisis for what it was: an object-lesson in the dangers of political commitment. Only in the South East where large numbers of country dwellers had already been drawn into the orbit of revolution did Federalism make a mark. Such was the political magnetism of Marseilles that once its Sections had repudiated the authority of the Convention, a host of lesser towns, *bourgs* and villages in the Rhône valley and Lower Provence followed suit. At Lourmarin, a large village in the Lubéron hills, for instance, the pro-revolutionary faction split with a minority rallying to the Federalist interpretation of Parisian politics. Even at this level, though, it is doubtful whether we are dealing with anything more than the apex of the peasantry. Federalism may have infected the *ménager* class, but the rural poor stayed prudently aloof. According to the calculations of Thomas Sheppard, the average income (from land) of Lourmarin's putative Federalists amounted to 980 *livres* per annum, over three times the income of those local militants who remained steadfast in their support for the Mountain.[41]

After an uncertain debut in March and April 1793, the republic reached the village in earnest during the autumn of that year. With the Federalist threat removed, with armed royalism bottled up in the Vendée, in Lyons and in Toulon, village jacobinism entered a halcyon age. No two villages had an identical experience of the Terror: much depended upon the nature of pre-existing tensions, proximity to war zones and unpredictable factors such as the passage of an *armée révolutionnaire* or the visit of a *représentant-en-mission*. Nevertheless, some experiences were common to all villages. Throughout France the Terror inaugurated an intense, if short-lived, period of social levelling. The social overtones of jacobinism were often more explicit in the villages than in the towns: even the humblest country dweller could not help but take notice when his richer neighbours were taken away for detention, when their properties were put up for auction, or put out to tenants. Jacobin adaptations of popular culture drove the point home still further. In the Aveyron the delegates of *représentant* Taillefer harnessed popular millenarianism with a pro-gramme of Festivals of the Poor during which 'rich egoists' served a 'repub-lican' (that is, frugal) meal to the rustic cousins of the *sans-culottes*. For all its deficiencies the agrarian legislation of the *montagnard* Convention created a spell-binding illusion of a world turned upside-down, too. Laws providing for the egalitarian partition of common lands and the sale of *émigré* estates in small parcels (see pp. 147–61) pushed rural proprietors onto the defensive, even if they did little to ease the plight of the poor peasantry.

The massive round-up of suspects unleashed by the decree of 17 September 1793 must be accounted one of the constants of the Terror at the grass-roots, therefore. But the speedy implementation of this draconian legislation presupposed the existence of willing agents of repression at local level. These men were the remnants, or perhaps we should say the residue, of the patriot party of 1789–91. Diminished in numbers by the successive crises of the revolution, sorely tried by betrayals and defections, they now resembled a faction rather than a party and the advent of the Terror marked their apotheosis. It is easier to specify how they functioned than who they were, for there was no such thing as a typical jacobin militant of the Year Two (1793–4). Some were undoubtedly peasants, whether semi-indigent plot farmers, sharecroppers or *laboureurs*. More, perhaps, were village artisans: blacksmiths, carpenters, barrel makers, clog makers and masons. Small traders, carters and innkeepers also figured prominently among the cadres of village jacobinism, as did resident members of the rural bourgeoisie. The partici-pation of these latter can often be detected behind such professional labels as lawyer, doctor, surgeon or surveyor, but it is not unusual to find rural proprietors living off rent listed among the most enthusiastic upholders of the Terror, either. Such diversity makes a class-based interpretation of village jacobinism difficult to sustain. No doubt political alignments were sufficiently clear-cut for militants to act out a primitive form of class warfare in some localities, but it would be wrong to suppose that the poorest elements of the rural community automatically sided with the jacobins, whereas the well-to-do found themselves cast in the role of suspects. What strikes most about jacobinism and anti-jacobinism at village level, comments Colin Lucas, is the close social similarity between the two groups: 'the crucial divisions are to be found within the popular strata, and popular activism could work as easily against the revolution as for it'.[42]

Village jacobinism should be considered a 'vertical' relationship, then: one which might unite individuals of similar socio-economic status, but which usually owed more to the affinities of kinship, clientism, neighbourhood and, perhaps, temperament. Richard Cobb has stressed this latter characteristic in particular, and depicts the *sans-culotte* as a 'freak of nature, more a state of mind than a social, political or economic entity'.[43] Such a description could well be applied to the rustic allies of the Parisian *sans-culottes*, too, even if it only tells part of the story. In every locality, probably in every village, there existed individuals whose temperament predisposed them to the career of political extremism: men like Nicolas Guénot of Voutenay in the Yonne whose life history has been pieced together by Claude Hohl.[44] Guénot was born into an impoverished family of agricultural labourers and lumbermen some three and a half decades before the revolution and differed little from the scores of footloose young men who populated the villages of the Morvan uplands at the end of the *ancien régime*. Perhaps his turbulent and aggressive character marked him out more than most, but the only accomplishment which in any way foreshadowed his future career was an ability to read and write. Drawn to Paris like so many Burgundian peasants, Guénot flitted from job to job, adding to his unsavoury reputation in the process. In 1776 he enrolled in the Paris-based Gardes Françaises regiment, but was more or less thrown out seven years later and it was not until the revolution broke that he found his true *métier*. In the space of three years Guénot forged himself a career within the revolutionary police bureaucracy. First, he served as an informer and police spy, then as a clerk in one of the Paris prisons and then as a police inspector for the Section des Piques. Finally, in the autumn of 1793, his reputation for brutal diligence received ultimate recognition and he became a functionary of the Committee of General Security. Functionary or not, Guénot now postured as a man of power and influence, but the Terror which raised him up was also to cast him down. Indissolubly linked to the regime of the Year Two, he was disarmed as a terrorist after the abortive insurrection of the *faubourgs* in May 1795 and found himself at the receiving end of an arrest warrant for a change. Thirty years of neo-jacobin expiation followed, first in Paris and then back in Voutenay where he was greeted with a mixture of fear and loathing. A decade of public obloquy for each year's enjoyment of the fruits of power, this was the price that Guénot paid for his attachment to the revolution.

Few peasants rose as far or as fast as Nicolas Guénot. Nevertheless, he represents a social type whose members were probably legion. For such men the sudden curtailment of the *ancien régime* was both a fulfilment and an opportunity: a fulfilment in the sense that the revolution briefly licensed the anti-social temperament. Laws permitting domiciliary visits, forced taxes and arrest on suspicion were manna from heaven for characters like Guénot. It was an opportunity, in that the revolution unblocked the channels of advancement and launched many a country dweller on what passed for a promising career. Viewed from this angle, the republic at village level resembled a mother who suckled her numerous progeny or, to put it in modern terms, a gravy-train. During the Terror salaried posts in the revolutionary bureaucracy ramified as never before; moreover, the poor of town and country found themselves in a uniquely favourable position to exploit these opportunities. Patronage – dispensed from on high – provided the glue which held rural jacobinism together. And yet we should not neglect the ideological commitment which tempered that cohesion. Village *sans-culottes* tended to regard themselves as a race apart, as very special revolutionaries whose loyalties transcended the narrow confines of commune or parish. This, of course, is one reason they were so heartily persecuted in the aftermath of the Terror, for they seemed like unnatural sons who had placed the interests of the republic before those of their home locality – a fair criticism, in truth, for militants like Guénot exploited their links with the committees of government to devastating effect. And for every genuine agent of the governing committees there were a dozen who laid claim to this status. In February 1794 a peasant farmer from the village of Varen, which had been laid waste by the *Armée Révolutionnaire du Lot et du Cantal*, complained that he had been imprisoned and ransomed by two individuals pretending to be agents of the Committee of Public Safety. The culprits were, in fact, members of the revolutionary committee of Villefranche-de-Rouergue.

Bureaucratisation provided jobs, but it also provided security. Village republicanism rarely enjoyed mass support and was not self-sustaining. Its survival depended, instead, on good channels of communication between the centre and the periphery, on the monopolisation of all sources of local power and on fearless activism. Without the *représentants* and their delegates, without the *comités de surveillance* and the clubs, and without zealots like Guénot, it would have succumbed in most parts of the country. Even with these resources, the upholders of the republic felt desperately vulnerable in some localities. At Estaing (Aveyron), for example, the jacobin faction could muster no more than two dozen supporters out of a population of about 900. Worse, most of the trust-worthy patriots lived in outlying hamlets whereas the moderates were grouped in the *bourg*. The solution adopted by the *comité* was to install a bell which could be rung to summon help in times of danger. These surveillance committees came to symbolise the republic at village level, or perhaps we should say the Terror, for the two went hand in hand. After an uncertain start in the spring of 1793 and temporary eclipse during the Federalist crisis, they re-emerged in October and November. By the end of the year most rural communes of any substance boasted a surveillance or police committee and the law of 14 Frimaire II (4 December 1793) turned them into highly effective organs of the *montagnard* dictatorship. Their task was to mark out the frontiers of revolution, moderation and counter-revolution in the countryside using the vast arsenal of coercive power which had been entrusted to them. Not surprisingly, therefore, the *comités* evolved into the one permanent, proximate and inescapable institution of the Terror in the countryside. As such, their cadres were marked men: 'there goes a member of the *comité de surveillance* as proud as can be, but our turn will come in due course', remarked one of the suspects of Estaing as his persecutor came within earshot.[45] Jacobinism was not a career for the squeamish or the faint-hearted and many a rustic militant would pay dearly for his taste of power during the Year Two.

The *comités* also pressed forward the Dechristianisation Campaign which became an inescapable feature of village life in the winter of 1793–4. 'Dechristianisation' is, of course, a loaded term which implies a pre-existing state of Christian grace among the rural population of France, and some discussion of the nature of popular religions beliefs has already been offered (see pp. 193–4). But the term lends itself to confusion on another count, too: historians commonly refer to the gradual ebbing of public religious devotions as a process of dechristianisation, while at the same time using the term to describe the policy of forcible closure of churches and collective renunciation of public worship launched by *représentant* Fouché on mission to the Nièvre in September 1793. It is this artificial and rather brutal attempt to uproot centuries of quasi-Christian belief and practice which is at issue here: artificial in the sense that the Dechristianisation Campaign was inspired from above. Local militants seem to have rallied to the new policy under the pressure of events and powerful personalities, and not without misgivings. Early in November commissioner Lagasquie wrote (privately) from Cahors to a colleague in Rodez with the report that 'The measure prohibiting public places of worship in this department [Lot], which relegates catholics to the Daurade church, and which turns the cathedral of Cahors into a Temple of Reason has caused various disturbances which might have serious consequences.'

And he added, 'when I received this measure in Rodez, I was right to regard it as untimely and ill-considered'.[46]

The measure in question was an order from *représentant* Taillefer introducing the Dechristianisation policy to the departments under his jurisdiction. Elsewhere, too, Dechristianisation seems to have been primarily the handiwork of the *représentants-en-mission* with the more or less willing cooperation of local jacobin coteries. Michel Vovelle's geographical survey of *déprêtrisation* in the South East lays bare the forces at work.[47] He links the incidence of clerical abjurations (that is, the tendency of constitutional clerics to renounce their letters of ordination) to the passage through the countryside of the *représentants*. But not all *représentants* shared the same priorities: some were more zealous dechristianisers than others. Nor were all localities equally susceptible to atheistic propaganda. Dechristianisation followed the highways and valleys; it hopped from *bourg* to *bourg* making most progress in social milieux already detached from the disciplines of the catholic church. In the highlands, by contrast, unflinching village jacobins who were prepared to give the new policy their wholehearted support were harder to find and the fleeting Dechristianisation of envoys such as Dherbez-Latour made little impression on the peasantry. As a result, *déprêtrisation* remained a patchwork affair. The Bouches-du-Rhône and Vaucluse departments succumbed readily to *représentant* Maignet, as did the adjacent districts of the Basses-Alpes. However, the vast majority of rural parishes retained their priests in the mountain districts of Digne, Castellane and Barcelonnette and the same was true in the Var.

How did ordinary country dwellers respond to another assault upon their religious habits? The minutes of clubs and *comités* record numerous instances of communes voting overwhelmingly to cease public worship and to close down their churches. Whether these ritualised popular consultations indicated grass-roots support for the policy of Dechristianisation may be doubted, however. Most were gestures of political conformism wrung from a peasantry terrorised by roving *armées révolutionnaires* and sundry delegates armed with plenipotentiary powers. Often the renunciations were transparently insincere: on 29 Pluviôse II (17 February 1794) a delegate acting on behalf of *représentants* Paganel and Châteauneuf-Randon browbeat the inhabitants of St Saturnin (Aveyron) into giving up their weekly services in the parish church. Nevertheless, the assembled villagers insisted on adding the rider that they had no intention of changing their religion. If this is what Dechristianisation amounted to, then it could be tolerated and a *modus vivendi* of sorts established with the republic. In practice, the great majority of *représentants* and delegates carefully refrained from interfering with the more delicate aspects of folk religion such as parish organisation and the disposition of burial grounds. Fouché's summary attempt to uproot the cult of the dead in the Nièvre by emblazoning the words 'Death is an eternal sleep' on cemetery gates was not widely copied.

White Terror

The political crisis of Thermidor brought the experiment in village jacobinism to an ignominious conclusion. Those who conspired against Robespierre in the belief that the Terror would carry on as before were quickly disabused. Counter-terrorists and counter-revolutionaries (the two species were closely aligned, but not identical) moved in for the kill – literally in many cases. The result was the White Terror: a semi-organised frenzy of persecution directed against the local agents of the *montagnard* dictatorship. But the White Terror was more than simply an exercise in score-settling. In the South and also in the West it became a way of life and achieved a permanence which the party struggle had denied to the Terror. Unlike the Terror, the White Terror was fed from below. Fed initially on the politics of vengeance in small face-to-face communities, it developed into a generalised critique of the revolution. The murder gangs never lost sight of their old quarry (clubbists, village Marats, former members of the *comités de surveillance*, etc.), but they turned their attention to moderate republicans and anyone who had done well out of the change of regime, too. Purchasers of national property were blackmailed, constitutional priests harassed and government officials intimidated in a systematic attempt to destabilise the Directorial regime.

For all its longevity, the White Terror never embraced the whole of the country, however. Violence was only endemic in a score of departments grouped to the north west of the river Loire and to the south of Lyons (see map 17). Elsewhere, reactions to the policy switch inaugurated by Thermidor were muted and rarely threatened public order. Even in the West, it is questionable whether the *chouannerie* (as the White Terror was known in this region) enjoyed the active support of the mass of the rural population. Donald Sutherland has described it as 'the most extensive, persistent and durable peasant movement of the revolution',[48] but this is to forget the campaign against seigneurialism which mobilised vast armies of country dwellers between 1789 and 1793. In the South the White Terror began as an urban phenomenon in cities such as Lyons, Avignon and Aix. Thereafter, it spread into the villages, recruiting from peasant and artisan strata in the process. Returned *émigrés* and refractory priests who had emerged from hiding played a part, but not as large a part as is often suggested. In this sense the punitive reaction to the Terror was certainly

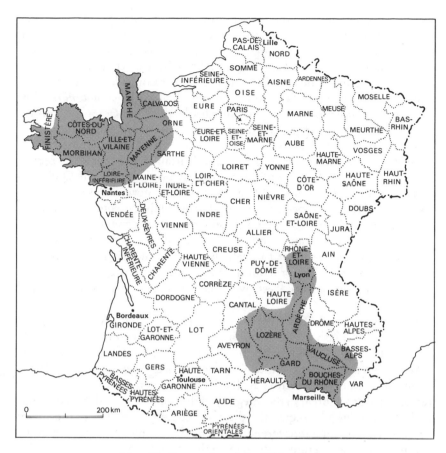

Map 17. Geography of the White Terror

popular, yet it would be wrong to suppose that the bulk of the peasantry were actively involved. Peasant support for the murder gangs had well-defined limits which excluded any action tending towards counter-revolution and the reinstatement of their former seigneurs.

Chronologically speaking, the White Terror first took shape as a movement of resistance to the military operations mounted by the republic in the West. Indeed, even before the defeat of the Vendeans at Savenay (23 December 1793), bands of *chouans* had begun to resort to guerrilla-style raids in the Breton departments across the river Loire. By the spring of 1794, these bands, numbering between fifty and a hundred, posed a serious threat to republican law and order throughout the region. They ambushed patrols, murdered government officials, intimidated tenants farming *biens nationaux* and interfered with grain convoys. In short, they pioneered all the tactics that were to serve the counter-terrorists so well over the next few years. Repeated assassination (twenty-three patriots and municipal officers died in a single fortnight in the district of Fougères [Ille-et-Vilaine]) virtually destroyed local government outside the towns, and from the summer of 1794 until the spring of 1796 the *chouannerie* controlled most of Brittany. With royalist leaders like the Comte de Puisaye actively soliciting an English landing, this situation could not be allowed to endure, however. The disembarkation of an *émigré* force in Quiberon bay in June 1795 seemed to demonstrate that Brittany had become the republic's Achilles' heel. The *émigrés* were quickly bottled up in the Quiberon peninsula and suffered a terrible military defeat; nevertheless, the Directory decided that the time had come to dispose of the *chouan* menace in the West. General Hoche was given full powers and an army of 140,000 men to sweep the region clean of counter-revolution. First the surviving bands of Vendeans were brought to heel, then scores of flying columns were unleashed upon the Breton countryside. By the summer of 1796 Hoche could report that he had destroyed the *chouannerie* to all intents and purposes.

In the West the White Terror retained a military character from start to finish. The backlash against jacobinism was subsumed into the struggle against 'les bleus' – the republican troops. In the South, by contrast, the anti-jacobin thrust to the White Terror remained paramount. Neither the Convention nor the Directory believed that the activities of the counter-terrorists posed a threat to the integrity of the republic as had the Vendeans and the *chouans*. Consequently, the murder gangs were left to their own devices with minimal interference from troops of the line. Only when the White Terror degenerated into semi-political banditry were the pleas of local officials answered with military reinforcements. The savage intra-communal violence that flared in the Midi after the collapse of the Terror was probably unavoidable. After all, the inhabitants of the region had demonstrated an early commitment to the politics of extremes and the vigorous persecution of Federalism had destroyed what middle ground existed between the parties. Even so, the complaisance of the Thermidorians greatly exacerbated the White Terror. Rather than enforce the criminal law, the deputies took the view that the witch hunt against servants of the Terror was both unstoppable and excusable. Indeed, they introduced measures which positively assisted the work of the anti-jacobin *égorgeurs* (cut-throats). The disarmament and imprisonment of 'terrorists', decreed on 21 Germinal III (10 April 1795), exposed a few real psychopaths and thousands of inoffensive clubbists and functionaries of the Year Two to public spite, injury and worse. Many of those arrested were to die in anti-jacobin prison massacres which spread like a contagion through the towns of the Rhône valley and delta during the late winter and spring of 1795. Far from halting the bloodshed, the first wave of Thermidorian *représentants-en-mission* joined in the hue and cry against the Terror. From Avignon Jean Debry instructed municipal councils to print and post up the names and addresses of disarmed 'terrorists'. Isnard, a Girondin survivor, urged fellow survivors to settle scores against the jacobins of Aix, while Cadroy helped to organise the murder squads operating in the Bouches-du-Rhône.

With the approach of spring the turbulence in the plains began to affect the hill villages of Provence and the southern Massif Central. First the institutional reminders of the Terror were effaced: after the failure of the Parisian uprisings of Germinal and Prairial municipal and district authorities concluded that it was safe to dismantle the 'holy mountains' which they had been browbeaten into erecting the year before. The enforcement of revolutionary place names lapsed, as did that of the *décadi*, *tutoiement* (the mode of republican address), and the red bonnet of liberty. Nothing escaped the reaction, not even the national cockade. At the height of the White Terror in the Aveyron on 23 Messidor III (11 July 1795), the district administrators of Rodez complained that one-third of the country people attending the market were not wearing cockades. In the villages the angelus bell could be heard again, interspersed with snatches of *Le Réveil du peuple*. From here it was but a small step to discard the human detritus of the Year Two. At Najac, a local militant subsequently complained, the mayor 'had the crier go round with a trumpet warning that all the former members of the *comité de surveillance* were forbidden to leave the commune on pain of arrest. This produced such fermentation that in two quarters of the *bourg* it was proposed that they be shot out of hand.'[49]

The retribution had to be public and sharply focused. After all, the village jacobins had not only subverted the traditional social order, they had breached the trust of the rural community. Momentarily, the locality had been placed at the mercy of an alien centralising power. The bevies of rustic *sans-culottes* who clustered around the *représentants* of the Year Two left no doubt about where their loyalties really lay. Public expiation was therefore required to restore the moral balance: 'Say your prayers, we're going to blow your brains out, you're a bloody patriot', cried the gang who burst in upon a farmer who had purchased national property in the parish of St Urcize (Cantal).[50] In another instance not far distant seven *chouans* seized Jean Raynal of Castelnau (Aveyron), dragged him to the church and forced the priest to confess him. Thereafter he was tied to the Liberty Tree and beaten, then released and forced to drink and dance. Finally the gang hauled their victim to a rocky spur, ordered him to recite the angelus and fired seven shots at his kneeling body. Ex-jacobins, former functionaries, *acquéreurs*, constitutional clerics – the counter-terrorist *égorgeurs* regarded them all as fair game. In a broad swathe of territory stretching from the Massif Central to the Alps and from Lyons to the sea, patriots raced for cover. Many fled the countryside altogether in search of safety and relative anonymity in the towns; the majority lived timorously behind tightly bolted shutters, awaiting the day when the storm would blow itself out. Purchasers of *biens nationaux* could ransom themselves by handing back their ill-gotten gains to the original owners (or their agents), and transactions of this type were common in the Lozère and the southern Ardèche. But for those more deeply implicated in the *montagnard* dictatorship there could be no escape. They survived, if they survived at all, by a combination of vigilance, cunning and an amount of luck. 'I cannot carry out my duties as *juge de paix* of the canton of Gabriac [Aveyron]', reported Jean-Antoine Aldias in April 1796, 'without risk to my life. The brigands follow me everywhere I go.'[51] Aldias had occupied the post of *agent national* of the District of St Geniez in the Year Two and he never travelled without 'a shotgun, pistols and often a sword-stick, without which I would be forced to expatriate myself'.[52] Armed to the teeth and refusing to submit, this die-hard jacobin lived to see his persecutors put behind bars, but there were a few upholders of the new order who had placed themselves so far beyond the pale that even death brought no respite. Such was the plight of the constitutional clergy. Two days after the demise of Guillaume Pie, a juror of St Chély-d'Apcher (Lozère), his corpse was disinterred and dragged round the streets with a rope round its neck. A similar fate befell Etienne Nogaret, constitutional bishop of the Lozère.

By the summer of 1795 the White Terror was in full flood and for the next two years the tide of reaction flowed fast and furious. *Emigrés* returned in droves and the targets of the murder gangs increased to include all officials of the republic, even those appointed after Thermidor. Intimidation, reinforced with spectacular acts of bloodshed, brought local government to a virtual standstill in large parts of the southern Massif Central. After a ghastly multiple assassination of patriots in the village of Laissac (Aveyron) during the night of 17–18 Messidor III (5–6 July 1795), the district administrators of Sévérac lost their nerve completely and sought refuge in the château which dominated the town. The arrival of *représentant* Musset towards the end of the summer eased the situation in the Aveyron, but local mayors and councillors had clearly had enough and inundated the higher authorities with letters of resignation. From the safe haven of Rodez, the district officers reminded the fainthearted that they had taken an oath 'to die at their posts'[53] – a reference to the rhetoric of the Year Two which now seemed like an invitation to collective suicide. East

of the Aveyron, in the Lozère, the Ardèche and the Gard, the killing continued unabated throughout 1796 and for much of 1797. Rather than alert
the higher authorities, local officials simply took to their heels. When a
republican detachment stumbled upon a royalist hideout in April 1796
they discovered 4,000 loaded cartridges, plus an equivalent number
unfilled and constructed from copies of the *Bulletin des Lois* despatched
to the municipality of Blandas (Gard).

The *coup* of 18 Fructidor V (4 September 1797) arrested the slide into
anarchy, albeit only temporarily. By ousting royalists from local office and
by reactivating the penal laws against *émigrés* and refractory priests, the
Directory gave the embattled patriots of the South fresh heart. As a result
the Year Six (1797–8) became the long-awaited moment of neo-jacobin
revival. In villages and small towns across the country the petty
functionaries of the Terror emerged from obscurity and made ready to
contest the elections scheduled for March 1798. Pale imitations of the
jacobin clubs, known as Constitutional Circles, sprang up and analysis of
their membership shows that provincial jacobinism had lost none of its
eclectic appeal. That of Limoux (Aude) marshalled shopkeepers, artisans
and farmers alongside merchant-manufacturers, former soldiers and
members of the professions. Nor had jacobinism lost its crusading
mentality: every *décadi* the Constitutional Circle of Le Mans (Sarthe)
mounted a procession to a neighbouring town or village where a Liberty
Tree would be planted and an offshoot club organised. In the South, however, the purge of elected officials could only intensify the factional confrontation. All too often it removed moderate republicans as well as
royalists and enabled the cadres of the Year Two to regain power, including erstwhile members of the *comités de surveillance*. At Villecomtal
(Aveyron), for example, the neo-jacobin faction mobilised by the impending elections was a carbon copy of the clique which had dominated the
commune in 1793–4. It numbered no fewer than ten members of the
revolutionary committee. The *coup* also appeared to justify counter-
royalist violence of a type not witnessed since Thermidor: squads of village
sans-culottes set off in pursuit of those who had persecuted them during
the preceding three years.

Jacobin hopes of a come-back crumbled when the Directory counter-
balanced the Fructidor *coup* against royalists with a further purge of
freshly elected extreme republicans (law of 22 Floréal VI/11 May 1798).
This spelled a return to business as usual for the murder gangs of the South.
In the Ardèche, for instance, the news that a government commission had
rejected the slate of neo-jacobin candidates chosen by the departmental
electoral assembly exploded with all the impact of a second Thermidor. By
the end of the year the White Terror had once more engulfed the region.

Yet, for all the efforts of royalist conspirators (whose own hopes would be dashed by the abortive insurrection of the Year Seven in the Toulousain), the White Terror was losing its sharpness of vision. In short, it was degenerating into what the authorities termed 'brigandage', that is to say semi-politicised banditry. As such, the socio-economic impulse behind the White Terror, which had never been entirely absent, became paramount. So called *chouan* gangs continued to prey on purchasers of national property, but more from motives of pillage than of chastisement for past political sins. Whilst five 'brigands' ransacked the house of Joseph Cayrac of La Boulette (Aveyron), they railed against rich landowners who did not need to work for a living whereas the poor died of hunger. Similarly, the movement of travellers and of convoys bearing tax receipts offered richer pickings than forays against village *sans-culottes* or constitutional clerics. Entire villages lived off the fruits of highway robbery (Boyne in the Aveyron; Bollène in the Vaucluse) disguised beneath the thinnest veneer of counter-revolutionary rhetoric. Yet the White Terror was not over; far from it. In the interval between the frustration of neo-jacobin hopes and the advent of Napoleon, the violence and general lawlessness reached levels unsurpassed in the Lozère, the Vaucluse and the Ardèche. The Bonapartist *coup d'état* of 18 Brumaire VIII (9 November 1799) found the latter department in a state of virtual civil war: government *commissaires* were being killed as fast as they could be replaced, tax collectors robbed before they could deposit their receipts, and *acquéreurs* hounded into selling their properties or paying reparations. So bad had the situation become that the *commissaire du Directoire-Exécutif* finally resorted to a policy of summary arrest and execution.

'You have no idea what it is like down there; it is an area unlike any other. Everyone is either a terrorist or a royalist. There is no middle ground. At Dijon or Poitiers they will reason and argue; at Marseilles they immediately resort to the dagger'. This admonition was addressed by Carnot to the long-serving parliamentarian Thibaudeau who subsequently became prefect of the Bouches-du-Rhône,[54] and it sums up the problem of the Midi.[55] Here the Terror bit deep and so, in consequence, did the Counter-Terror. Richard Cobb, who was the first historian to appreciate the scale and significance of the White Terror, points out that the courts of the Bouches-du-Rhône handled cases involving no fewer than 800 political assassinations between the autumn of 1795 and that of 1800.[56] Approximately half of the victims died in the Bouches-du-Rhône; the remainder died in the Basses-Alpes, Rhône, Loire, Haute-Loire, Ardèche and the Lozère. About forty-five patriots are known to have been murdered in the Aveyron during the same period. Yet these figures only relate to documented and identifiable cases. How many old revolutionaries must have perished in reality? Perhaps as many as two thousand, says Cobb, which puts the White Terror in the same homicidal category as the Terror itself. But the White Terror was not a national phenomenon. The disarmament of 'terrorists' assuaged calls for vengeance against the pillars of *montagnard* dictatorship in most parts of the country. Only in the West and the Mediterranean South did the Thermidorian Reaction find sufficient combustible material to ignite a major conflagration. Yet the situation in the West differed from that which we have described in the South in several important respects. The Breton *chouans* drew their inspiration from the Vendée revolt: theirs was an overtly military and counter-revolutionary challenge and the republic responded in kind. Eventually, the danger of a seaborne intervention by English and *émigré* forces prompted the Directory to embark upon a complete pacification of the region. For all its virulence, the southern White Terror was never forced to the top of the political and diplomatic agenda in this fashion, largely because counter-revolutionaries and counter-terrorists never succeeded in putting their act together. The peasantry gave conditional support to the murder gangs, but were not prepared to countenance a return to the *ancien régime*.

Chapter 8

The balance-sheet

In May 1800 François-René de Chateaubriand returned to France after an absence of eight years. The experience left an indelible impression upon the budding author and many years later he penned an unforgettable account of his journey from Calais to Paris:

From the road scarcely any men were visible; the fields were being ploughed by women, barefoot, their faces suntanned, heads unprotected unless wrapped in a kerchief: they could have been taken for slaves . . . as for the villages, one would have thought that they had been razed by fire: miserable, half-demolished and with mud or dust, manure or rubbish everywhere . . . on either side of the road stood ruined châteaux, little remaining of their plantations beyond a few squared-off trunks on which children were playing. Crumbling garden walls could be seen, abandoned churches from which the dead had been banished, bell towers without bells, cemeteries without crosses, headless saints in their niches. Walls were daubed with worn-out republican slogans: LIBERTY, EQUALITY, FRATERNITY or DEATH. Sometimes the word DEATH had been obliterated, but the letters painted in black or red were beginning to show through the whitewash.[1]

Unforgettable, but also tendentious. Chateaubriand's lyricism combined all the prejudices of a returned *émigré* with a veneer of English contempt for the state of agriculture in France. Even as his boat neared the port of Calais, he 'was struck by the impoverished air of the country',[2] or so we are told.

Parts of rural France did present a dilapidated appearance after a decade of civil turmoil, of that there is no doubt. But Chateaubriand's incognito return is a pastiche like so many of the travellers' sketches drawn up on the morrow of Bonaparte's *coup d'état*. For a reliable portrait of post-revolutionary France we need to find someone who witnessed the change of regime from the inside, without for all that having identified with either the ultra-revolutionary or the counter-revolutionary camp. Amans-Alexis Monteil was such a man. In 1802 he published a social history of the department of the Aveyron, a work which signalled the arrival on the scene of one of France's most talented early nineteenth-century historians.[3] Despite its narrow focus, Monteil's *Description du département de l'Aveiron* offers one enormous advantage: it depicts the habits and practices of daily life before and after the revolution. Casting himself in the role of a migrant who had quit his native heath before the revolution only to return in 1800, Monteil asks the question 'How had things changed in the meantime?' Like Chateaubriand he notes a decline in the number of towers and *donjons* dotting the landscape, but the villages conveyed an impression of well-being, even affluence. The returning migrant would find whitewashed houses with their thatches in good repair. As if in explanation, Monteil reminds us that the years of monetary inflation between 1794 and 1797 were a golden age for the peasantry. The homeward-bound traveller would notice other changes, too: fewer beggars cluttered the highways, although fewer hospitals existed to care for the sick and destitute; monastic bells no longer tolled from dawn to dusk; and the pleasures of the hunt had become the birthright of every country dweller. 'One would think that every rusty gun in Provence is at work, killing all sorts of birds; the shot has fallen five or six times in my chaise and about my ears', wrote Arthur Young in August 1789,[4] and since that date the freedom to hunt had hardened into one of the most powerful symbols of the new political order. Every farm could now muster one, if not two, shotguns, reported Monteil.

As a result armourers and gunsmiths had prospered as never before: one of the handful of skilled crafts to have directly benefited from the revolution. Few artisans could afford to regard 1789 as an unmixed blessing, however, for the closure of the monasteries and the emigration of wealthy clients threw the luxury trades into confusion. Under-employment was the lot of many urban craftsmen during the revolutionary decade. The artisan population of Le Mans (Sarthe) declined by a quarter, in Rodez the revolution virtually wiped out the precious-metal working and jewellery crafts and imposed serious privations on several others. Candle manufacturers suffered from the brusque loss of the ecclesiastical market: demand for waxen altar and processional candles dropped away and ordinary people no longer lit candles to accompany the rites of burial. Indeed, workmen and peasants in the Aveyron increasingly used walnut-oil lamps rather than tallow candles for lighting. The textile and dyeing industries also felt the chill of the revolution's religious policies. After 1790 the bottom fell out of the market for deep-dyed black fabrics such as had been traditionally used for monastic habits and clerical cassocks. This spelled economic stagnation for villages that specialised in the weaving of heavy serges for urban merchant-clothiers. Orders for troop uniforms averted the impending disaster in the hinterland of textile *bourgs* such as St Geniez-d'Olt

(Aveyron), but dyers could only look on powerlessly as their staple market dwindled, hastened by a switch away from public mourning garb. Nor were the professions exempt from dislocation: the closure of seminaries, theological colleges and law schools provoked a crisis of social promotion within the bourgeoisie. One result was a dramatic boost in the supply of qualified doctors; Monteil estimates that their numbers tripled in little over a decade.[5] Another was an increase in the number of unqualified persons setting themselves up as notaries.

Priests, by contrast, were desperately thin on the ground. Between 1790 and 1795 the revolutionaries effectively declericalised religion and, as Monteil testifies, the process left a mark on popular consciousness. Even if Dechristianisation won few converts, the ceremonial aspect of catholic worship took a severe battering in these years. Rural communities responded with alarm to the loss of their priests, but once the sense of panic had receded, a feeling of confidence, even liberation, intervened. Heaven had not fallen in: perhaps the deity did not require propitiation with large candles and gestures of atonement after all; perhaps the act of worship did not require the presence of a priest of any description. The erosion of ecclesiastical discipline culminating in the total separation of church and state after 1795 seems, in short, to have enabled country dwellers to concentrate on the kind of religious experience which they liked best, that is to say the collective and festive dimensions of catholicism. From many parts of the country came reports that parishioners were organising their own church services, sometimes using a municipal officer as a stand-in for the priest. Napoleon's 'domesday survey' of the state of the nation in 1801 makes for interesting reading in this respect: his commissioner in the First Military Division noted that church attendance was widespread in the countryside around Paris, but the peasantry came for the Mass and would have nothing to do with the rites of Holy Communion and Confession. More pithily, he observed that country folk 'would rather have bells without priests, than priests without bells'.[6]

The signing of the Concordat in 1801 curbed the drift towards a lay take-over of the church. Reclericalisation commenced and the 'prescribed' religion of throne and altar soon obliterated the revolutionary experience. Some things could not be changed, however, and they served as reminders that the events of 1789 would never be expunged entirely from the popular memory. Monteil draws attention to a quiet revolution in family names, for instance. Whereas a small stock of Apostles' and saints' names had formerly been handed on from one generation to the next, eldest sons now rejoiced in such epithets as 'Adolphe', 'Auguste', 'Henri' and 'Hercule'. Mothers bearing the traditional Christian names hastened to call their daughters 'Sophie', 'Amélie', 'Sylvie', 'Clarisse' and 'Adèle'. The mental revolution continued on other fronts, too. The diffusion of printed materials, acting in conjunction with a measure of politicisation, meant that a proportion of households whose literary diet had once consisted of popular almanacs now ruminated on peace treaties. Thanks to conscription, young peasants barely capable of remembering the names of their parishes before the revolution could now discourse on Italy, Bavaria, the Tyrol, even Egypt and Syria. Many had acquired a smattering of French during their travels and the role of the wars of the revolution and the Empire in eroding the insular world of the peasantry should not be underestimated. Army life taught the homesick peasant new loyalties as well as a new language. The transfer of loyalties to that nebulous entity called the Nation is another of the processes to which Monteil alludes. Deference – the product of centuries of seigneurial domination – no longer mediated relations between the peasantry and other social groups. Country folk refused to be browbeaten by their supposed superiors. Revolutionary 'liberty' and the experience of municipal self-government, says Monteil, had given them a sense of dignity, even pride.[7]

That dawning realisation among the peasantry that they could control their destiny, in part at least, also helps us to understand the anomalies of post-revolutionary demographic history. It will be remembered that the population of France stood at 28 millions – near enough – in 1789. The vast majority of these people lived in the countryside and a little over two-thirds (see p. 4) made a living from agriculture. The peasant character of late *ancien régime* society is therefore beyond question. Until the onset of the pre-revolutionary crisis the birth rate remained buoyant at an annual rate of about 39 live births per thousand inhabitants, but then a fundamental shift in reproductive behaviour occurred. In less than a generation the birth rate dropped from 39 per thousand to under 33 per thousand. Statistically speaking, the crucial moment of transition only becomes visible at the turn of the century, for the revolution initially boosted the marriage rate and restored reproductivity. Yet, by the second decade of the nineteenth century, the trend becomes unmistakeable: despite continuing high levels of marrying, couples were having fewer children. Even before the revolution contraceptive practices appear to have made some headway in the countryside, but it is difficult to resist the conclusion that the strong doses of 'liberty' and 'equality' administered in the 1790s affected family relationships and household strategies as well. Culturally, the French peasant emerged from this turbulent decade a rather different being. In the words of Jacques Dupâquier, the revolution made him 'egoistic and calculating'.[8]

'Calculating' – not least because revolutionary and Napoleonic inheritance legislation posed an insidious threat to the landed peasantry in many parts of the country. The first clear signals that the principles of 'liberty' and 'equality' were to be applied to the business of property transmission emerged in 1790 and 1791. Ostensibly, the aim was to reduce the power of the aristocracy (the right of noble primogeniture succumbed on 15 March 1790 along with part of the feudal regime), but the proposals aroused anxiety among the peasantry as well. Alarm was greatest in the South where the latitude afforded the testator under Roman Law had enabled a form of commoner primogeniture to develop. Initially, the National Assembly compromised on the issue and it was not until 7 March 1793 that the freedom to dispose of property by testament was abolished. Then, on 17 Nivôse II (6 January 1794), the egalitarian offensive was pushed a stage further with a law placing a retrospective restriction on the transmission of property by testament or contract. Any peasant *aîné* (eldest son) who had been nominated heir to the family possessions in a contract signed after 13 July 1793 now found himself in a difficult position. Excluded brothers and sisters clamoured for a share of the patrimony, unleashing thousands of petitions to the committees of government in the process. Throughout the South civil suits between siblings and between collaterals brought the courts to a virtual standstill. Thermidor triggered a reaction against the extremes of egalitarianism in this sphere as in others, and the following year the retroactive principle was repudiated. Nevertheless, the Directory refused to tamper with the essence of the Convention's inheritance legislation and it was not until the advent of Napoleon Bonaparte that a modicum of testamentary freedom was restored. A law of 4 Germinal VIII (25 March 1800) introduced the 'disposable portion' which might be used by a parent to enhance a favoured child's share of the inheritance and this provision was subsequently enshrined in the Civil Code.

Notwithstanding Bonaparte's retreat from a strictly egalitarian inheritance regime, the peasantry had had a nasty shock. Partible inheritance not only challenged paternal authority, it threatened to undermine an entire way of life. In regions of low soil fertility such as the Pyrenees and the Massif Central sub-division of holdings spelt economic disaster. Peasant farming on barren heaths and uplands positively demanded a concentration of resources; 'surplus' younger sons and daughters were expected to sacrifice their marriage and inheritance prospects in the interests of the long-term survival of the household. Roman Law legitimised this strategy and the attack on it by northerners anxious to inculcate an individualist concept of liberty and equality was bitterly resented. Unable to gainsay the law, householders resorted to low funning instead: cadet members of families were induced to renounce their portions in favour of their *aînés*; complaisant attorneys provided phoney valuations of assets so that the

eldest son might still inherit the land and buildings intact, and arrangements were made for junior offspring to receive their entitlements by
instalment and without interest. If all else failed (and the more obvious
loopholes in the law were soon plugged), the paterfamilias played his
biological trump card: family limitation. The Civil Code permitted couples
who produced three offspring to dispose freely of one-quarter of their
estate; couples with just two children recovered the right to do as they
pleased with one-third of their assets; but in the case of couples who contrived to have only one child the 'disposable portion' rose to one-half.
Hence the conviction, widespread in the nineteenth century, that the
revolution invented a 'machine for chopping up the land'.[9] In so doing it
provided the incentive for a major shift in reproductive behaviour.

Beyond this point it is difficult to probe the cultural and psychological
repercussions of a decade of turmoil on country dwellers, for the evidence
is mostly anecdotal or inferential. The material impact of the revolution
does offer scope for a more rigorous analysis, however, if only because a
number of local monographs have addressed this very issue. Even so, large
gaps in our knowledge remain and it is worth repeating Georges Lefebvre's
remark that the changes ushered in by the events of 1789 left the great mass
of peasantry dissatisfied: 'What they gained is harder to specify than what
they did not.'[10] Yet his dictum should not be taken as an entirely negative
judgement on the course of the revolution in the countryside. The poor
peasantry formulated demands which even the most forthright jacobins
refused to countenance, it is true. Nevertheless they, too, registered gains
in common with other sections of the rural population.

First, the question of landholding. By the end of the *ancien régime* the
peasantry owned about a third of the cultivable surface of the kingdom, as
we have seen. This figure is an average and it masks huge variations from
region to region. Nevertheless, it can no longer be argued that the
peasantry won their stake in the land *as a result* of the revolution. The
stealthy peasant conquest of the soil of France began long before the events
of 1789 supervened and would continue throughout the following century. Undeniably, however, there was a crisis of land supply during the
final decades of the *ancien régime* and it arose because population growth
momentarily outstripped the rate at which fresh land could be brought
into cultivation. Hence the paradox of 1789: the peasantry as a whole
owned a sizeable and expanding portion of the arable surface, but the
landless and semi-landless rural proletariat had never seemed more
numerous, nor more threatening. In this situation the revolution acted as
an accelerator: legislators roused the land market from its feudal torpor
and then flooded it with the property of the church and *émigré* nobles. No
less important, they presided helplessly over a massive 'land grab' which

took the form of illicit land clearance by would-be squatters. If the sales of *biens nationaux* primarily benefited the bourgeoisie and those households located at the apex of the peasantry, *défrichement* was usually the handiwork of plebeian wage earners and plot farmers. Yet, it would be wrong to imagine that ordinary peasants were systematically excluded from the fruits of the revolutionary land settlement. Much depended on time and place, as Lefebvre has demonstrated (see pp. 156–7). Wielding an array of community sanctions, the peasantry of the Hainaut and the Cambrésis managed to secure the bulk of ecclesiastical property despite the purchasing power of the urban bourgeoisie. And what slipped beyond the grasp of country dwellers in the 1790s was sometimes retrieved by the rural community in the 1800s and 1810s as speculative purchasers sold up and moved their capital elsewhere.

'Since the division of properties disposed of by the nation everyone has become a *laboureur*', commented the sub-prefect of Toul (Meurthe) in 1804.[11] A palpable exaggeration no doubt, but one which captures the degree of change as perceived by contemporaries. But the eastern departments are precisely where we might expect the sales of *biens nationaux* to have left a mark on the social structure. Elsewhere, church property was much less extensive and it was the obsessive clearance of wastes that attracted most attention. In Normandy the church nowhere owned more than a tenth of the land surface and little noble property was confiscated. Instead, the sub-prefect of Vire (Calvados) emphasised the role of *défrichement* and egalitarian inheritance legislation in bringing more land under the plough. One consequence of the land settlement was an expansion in the numbers of owner-exploiters. Most, to be sure, could scarcely be regarded as self-sufficient *laboureurs*, but the mere fact that many more peasants had access to a plot of land than hitherto was bound to have implications for the market – the market, that is, for wage labour, and also for foodstuffs. In short, it seems that the revolution strengthened the subsistence sector of the rural economy. Far from nudging French agriculture in a capitalist direction, petty producers practised auto-consumption as far as possible. So, too, did a goodly number of bourgeois proprietors for whom the *rentier* lifestyle had lost its attraction since the galloping inflation of 1795–7. 'Before 1789 landowners with several estates and even those with only one did not bother to exploit them personally', reported the department authorities of the Aveyron in 1796, 'but since foodstuffs have been in short supply and have increased in price, all those whose leases have expired since the revolution are farming their possessions personally.'[12]

The nearly effortless return of the nobility to a position of social and economic pre-eminence also testifies to the conservative character of the revolutionary land settlement. It is true that most *émigrés'* lands were put up for auction, often piecemeal, but nobles who refrained from emigrating and yet avoided proscription during the Terror never suffered confiscation. Perhaps as much as half of the noble patrimony survived the revolution unscathed, in consequence: more in regions such as the West, the Sologne and the southern Massif Central. Of course, the revolutionaries liked nothing better than to proclaim the destruction of the nobility and historians have been content to follow in their wake, but the truth of the matter is not difficult to discover. It may be found in Napoleonic tax lists which accurately record the contours of post-revolutionary society. Almost invariably the old names of noble (or *anobli*) families appear among the biggest taxpayers. In some departments, indeed, it is difficult to detect social mobility of any description, whether up or down the scale. Twenty-six of the thirty biggest taxpayers of the Lozère were *ancien régime* nobles in 1811, for instance. Moreover, the trend tended unmistakeably towards a reconstitution of the noble estate. Once Napoleon Bonaparte was firmly ensconced as First Consul, *émigré* nobles returned to France in droves. All tried to put their affairs in order and many proved remarkably adept at piecing together their erstwhile possessions. The White Terror helped in this respect, as did the various stratagems employed in the 1790s to prevent the definitive alienation of noble estates. But when all else failed, returned *émigrés* set about repurchasing their property morsel by morsel. In the Ardèche the de Vogüé family bought back their feudal seat at Vogüé, while in the Aveyron Count Crusy de Marcillac, whom Napoleon appointed sub-prefect of Villefranche-de-Rouergue, began the uphill task of treating with the two hundred purchasers of his ancestral properties. Once Napoleon's fall from grace had been consummated at Waterloo, the great majority of *acquéreurs* offered to redeem the Count's properties in return for the purchase price. The transaction was completed by 1822 and may be regarded as typical of many. During the Empire alone it has been estimated that despoiled nobles managed to retrieve a quarter of their landed property.[13] What they could not retrieve were their seigneurial perquisites which left many illustrious lineages in straitened circumstances, especially in the South.

Here lay an opportunity for agricultural modernisation, an opportunity to switch from the *rentier* lifestyle to that of the improving landlord. The fact that it was not seized raises a second question, related to that of landholding: what were the economic repercussions of the revolution? Georges Lefebvre's judgement in the matter is unequivocal and it is worth repeating. 1789, he argues, revealed a peasantry subject to twin impulses: a 'revolutionary' desire to have done with seigneurialism in all its forms, and a 'conservative' desire to resist the encroachments of individualism in the agricultural sphere. Hence his famous dictum, 'they destroyed the feudal regime, but consolidated the agrarian structure of France' (see p. 75). Yet Lefebvre subscribed to the commonplace conviction among historians of his generation that events in France between 1789 and 1799 could be described meaningfully as a 'bourgeois revolution'. Challenges to this interpretation with its explicit ideological reference points issued in the 1960s and they provoked fresh research into the nature of the peasant revolution. Such challenges also brought the admission that it might be better to conceive of the French Revolution as a long-term bourgeois revolution.

This seems sensible, for the more we learn about the short-term consequences of the revolution, the more problematic does the link with capitalism become. As one historian remarked recently, the combined effects of revolution and war brought about 'a complete disorganisation of economic activity'[14] from which it took the country between two and three decades to recover. Applied to commerce and industry, 'disorganisation' is probably not too strong a word to use. After 1793 France lost virtually all her colonial trade – perhaps the most dynamic sector of her economy at the end of the *ancien régime* – and the port cities suffered grievously in consequence. But it was not only the ports which suffered, but also the agricultural hinterlands which supplied textiles and provisions for overseas markets. In 1806 Napoleon introduced the Continental Blockade which made matters worse, on balance. By 1812–14 the annual volume of French external trade amounted to only half that registered in 1784–8. Industry was already experiencing a recession when the revolution broke, but the impact of subsequent events was not uniformly negative. If the woollen and linen industries slipped into terminal decline in many districts, the cotton-manufacturing centres profited from the absence of English competition in the market-place and enjoyed real periods of growth during the Empire. Nearly incessant warfare stimulated the production of coal and iron, too, although the growth in this sector of the economy occurred chiefly in Belgium, beyond the historic borders of France. The obvious comparison is with Britain, which was registering a quickening of industrial growth in this period. But comparisons can be misleading: Britain's Industrial Revolution was unique. More telling was the failure of post-revolutionary France to fulfil the promise of the late *ancien régime*. Industrial growth continued through these years, but at a sluggish rate.

The agricultural economy is our principal concern, however. In this sphere the 'disorganisation of economic activity' was largely superficial. The war effort removed young peasants from the land, it is true, but in most areas there existed an over-supply of manpower anyway. Requisitions deprived farmers of their draught animals at intervals and caused shortages of metals for implements, but these were irritants which scarcely impinged upon agricultural productivity. On the cereal plains around Paris the imposition of the Maximum had seriously disrupted market networks and landowners were still complaining of the losses they had sustained during the early years of the Consulate. But, again, the difficulties encountered by grain exporters were not symptomatic of the pressures operating on agriculture as a whole. Most farms and most farmers were attuned to the task of providing for basic needs, neither more nor less, and intrusions such as the Maximum or monetary inflation simply reinforced the subsistence orientation of the rural economy. The greatest challenge confronting peasant society – that of feeding more mouths – was met by the traditional expedient of opening up more land and not by means of progressive improvements in agricultural efficiency.

Unsurprisingly, therefore, agriculture stagnated throughout the revolutionary and Imperial epoch. In broad terms production just about kept pace with population growth, but productivity may have declined slightly. The terrible dearths of the 1790s did something to generalise potato cultivation, even though the crop was difficult to fit into the cycles of polyculture. Nevertheless, the peasantry treated the new crop with suspicion, preferring, whenever possible, to treat it as fodder rather than as a food substitute. Natural fodder was in short supply in any case, partly because of the constant demands of the armies but also because land clearance had reduced the stock of rough grazing. This brought the late *ancien régime* stock-raising crisis to a head in many parts of the country. Around Paris sheep flocks declined sharply in size, while in the East and the North East the shortage encouraged experimentation with artificial fodder crops. Such experiments made the fallow period redundant and marked out the regions which would pioneer agrarian and industrial change in the nineteenth century. None of this promise for the future was foreshadowed in the rest of the country, however. Attitudes (of rural proprietors as well as peasants) remained pre-capitalist; for want of investment in improvements, yields remained low, and techniques appeared rooted in the Middle Ages. Even in Normandy oxen were still used for ploughing at the end of the Empire and harvesters cut the ripening corn with sickles rather than scythes.

Sluggish and backward-looking: these words sum up the condition of the agricultural sector of the economy on the morrow of the revolution. Indeed, it has been argued by Michel Morineau that productivity – the barometer of agricultural modernisation – marked time until the 1840s.[15] An obvious question therefore arises: did the revolution distort the agrarian history of modern France? The answer is not clear-cut and it leaves ample room for debate among historians. For instance, Emmanuel Le Roy Ladurie has drawn attention to the role of the seigneurie as the forcing house of agrarian capitalism, and Georges Lefebvre likewise acknowledges the commercial zeal with which seigneurs exploited their forests at the end of the *ancien régime* (see pp. 52–5). Did the destruction of seigneurialism thereby arrest the development of agrarian capitalism? It is undeniable that the revolution set back commercial forest management by a generation and more. Yet many historians would take the opposite tack and argue that the seigneurial regime – no more, no less – constituted the fundamental impediment to agricultural modernisation. The feudal system of surplus extraction impoverished the peasantry, nurtured a *rentier* style of life among the wealthy, and sustained a rural community which tended to block new initiatives and to prop up the status quo.

But was the rural community a by-product of seigneurialism? On this historians seem unable to agree. Some assert that the revolution encompassed its demise. Others, on the contrary, argue that villagers emerged from the revolutionary climacteric with their internal solidarities strengthened, not weakened. Certainly, it has to be allowed that the dismantling of seigneurialism removed one of the forces which gave shape and meaning to the rural community. Yet other pressures remained. Collective rights continued to bind country dwellers together in a complex web of relationships which none of the revolutionary legislatures had succeeded in unpicking. In no other sphere was the gap between the revolutionaries' words and their deeds more palpable. After ten years of parliamentary theorising on the issue, there were probably more peasants relying on collective rights than there had been at the end of the *ancien régime* – proportionally as well as numerically, for the land settlement of the revolution had the effect of swelling the category of micro-proprietors for whom *vaine pâture* and related rights were a cushion against destitution. This, ultimately, must explain the lacklustre performance of French agriculture during the early decades of the nineteenth century. The revolution boosted the 'dead weight' or subsistence sector of the rural economy. Advocates of the 'peasant route' towards agricultural modernity (see pp. 125–8) have countered with a vision of capitalist-minded peasants producers doing battle with a *rente*-obsessed class of rural proprietors. The latter seem familiar enough, but the former have yet to be identified.

The survival of the rural community in some shape or form implies that the peasantry experienced the revolution as a coherent entity, and in so far as peasant participation was subsumed into the struggle against seigneurialism this inference is surely justified. Yet we should be wary of assuming that all revolutionary policies evoked an even response from all country dwellers, as though differences in family status, socio-economic condition or gender counted for nothing. The divisive effects of egalitarian inheritance legislation have already been mentioned, and much could be made of the fact that women played a larger role in crowd actions against merchants and shop-keepers (and intruder priests) than did men. Nevertheless, it is the socio-economic variable which has attracted most attention in recent years. Georges Lefebvre performed a singular service in putting the peasant revolution on the historical map, but now scholars are asking whether there was not, perhaps, more than one peasant revolution: a revolution of peasant proprietors? A revolution of sharecroppers and tenants? A revolution of agricultural wage earners?

This is the third question that requires consideration and the best place to begin is with the issue of seigneurialism. To judge from the character of the popular rebellions or *jacqueries* which launched the revolution in the countryside, all peasants of whatever station harboured a deep resentment of the seigneurial regime (see table 2). In fact that resentment was not confined to the peasantry, for bourgeois proprietors were sometimes involved in the attacks on the châteaux as well. Whether all peasant households in a given locality bore a similar burden of feudal exactions is much less certain, yet it would be wrong to suppose that the countryside contained a class of peasants (the owner-exploiters) who shouldered the entire weight of the seigneurial regime and a class of peasants (the landless or semi-landless poor) who escaped feudal obligations, to all intents and purposes. Owners of land under cereal cultivation benefited handsomely from the abolition of harvest dues; of that there is no doubt. But seigneurial *lods et ventes*, *banalités*, *péages* and *corvées* bore down on country dwellers indiscriminately, irrespective of status. As for seigneurial justice, it held few terrors for the comfortable *laboureur* (who sometimes helped to run the system in any case), but woe betide the poor peasant caught infringing his lord's *droit de chasse*. The insurgent bands of 1789 were not only bent on destroying the records of feudal obligations; they took elaborate steps to force seigneurs to repay the fines imposed by their courts as well. On this issue, then, the argument for a differential impact remains unproven. The rural revolution gathered momentum precisely because the ramifications of seigneurialism reached into every peasant cottage.

In the absence of up to date research, it is difficult to specify the impact of the revolution's tax reforms on the rural community. Nevertheless, it seems unlikely that fiscal policy provoked a schism within the peasantry. The major tasks confronting legislators were to sort out the problem of exemptions and to devise a method of assessment which distributed the burden of taxation fairly between town and country, between departments and between village communities. In this latter aim they were only partially successful, yet peasant criticism of the new tax structures remained muted – probably because the intensity of fiscal pressure eased for a time in the 1790s. The *contribution personnelle et mobilière* proved the most difficult tax to assess and soon acquired a reputation for bearing heavily upon the poor. This was because it presumed a connection between affluence and rental values. But, as the administrators of the district of Mamers (Sarthe) pointed out, 'The tenant of an estate worth 1,000 *livres* has a dwelling which is no different from that of a plot farmer with a property worth 80 *livres*. Yet, according to the law, they are required to pay the same amount of tax.'[16] Worse, the agricultural labourer who profited from the revolution to clear a few square metres of soil on which to grow vegetables suddenly found himself being taxed as though he were an established landowner. The revolutionaries responded to such criticisms in the only way possible: by reducing global assessments. Seventeen departments won the right to a rebate in 1791 and 1792. The following year the anticipated yield of the *contribution personnelle et mobilière* was cut by half and in 1794 it was not levied at all.

Prompt remedial action (albeit at serious cost to the exchequer) ensured that popular dissatisfaction with the new fiscal regime remained diffuse. As a result it is difficult to distinguish those peasants who responded positively to the tax reforms of the National Assembly from those who did not. Such discontent as there was peaked in the early months of 1793: warnings of impending disturbances reached the Convention from several different parts of the country. In the event, however, the crisis passed, or perhaps it was subsumed into the campaign against recruitment. Only in the Vienne did peasants mobilise against the *contribution personnelle et mobilière*, although it is true that fiscal disappointment played a part in the revolt of the *bordiers* of the Gers in July 1793. The case of the Gers (see pp. 100–2) suggests that sharecroppers may have been the principal losers following the change in tax regime, but in the current state of our knowledge it is impossible to generalise. More likely, the revolution achieved a reduction in the total burden of direct and indirect taxation, the benefits of which were unevenly distributed between town and country, between departments and between rich and poor. Sharecroppers may have felt cheated, but so did servants, land clearers and small-scale owner-exploiters.

By contrast, there are good grounds for supposing that the fumbling manner in which the revolutionaries liquidated the tithe exacerbated relations between sharecroppers, tenant farmers and landlords. Peasant proprietors and bourgeois landowners profited nicely from the legislation pushed through the National Assembly in the course of 1790: the former retained that portion of the harvest which used to be devoted to the upkeep of the church and did so without any corresponding pecuniary obligation to support the new state church, whereas the latter were authorised to add the value of the tithe to the leases of their tenants and the terms of their sharecroppers (see pp. 98–100). Manifestly, the revolutionaries intended that liquidation should benefit the owners of the land rather than those who merely worked it. On the face of the matter, therefore, the issue of the tithe drove a wedge between the independent peasant proprietors who had good reason to support the new regime and the mass of tenant farmers (and sharecroppers) whose expectation of an even-handed approach from the National Assembly had been cruelly abused. Whether this divergence went deep is a matter for debate, but several historians take the view that the frictions engendered by the attribution of the tithe to landowners helped to polarise rural society on political lines. Peasant (and bourgeois) proprietors adhered to the patriot party in the confident belief that the National Assembly was serving their interests, whereas tenants and share-croppers fell prey to disillusionment and royalist propaganda stressing the shortcomings of revolutionary policy on the tithe, taxes and seigneur-ialism.

Evidence of disillusionment with the handiwork of the National Assembly certainly exists and much of it has been cited in preceding chap-ters. The difficulty, as always, lies in measuring its impact on the various fractions of the rural community. In 1798 Lecointe-Puyraveau, the government commissioner in the Deux-Sèvres, observed trenchantly that country dwellers' grasp of the revolution extended to little beyond the abolition of the tithe and feudal dues. Even then, 'he has paid both the tithe and the dues to the landlord'.[17] Paul Bois reaches a similar conclusion with regard to the Sarthe department,[18] as does Georges Lefebvre for the Flanders region. And yet it is worth noting that Lefebvre hesitates over the issue. He acknowledges that landlords endeavoured to recoup the benefits of tithe abolition by adding its value to leases, but admits that the rental value of farm land scarcely rose as a result: 'in the Year XII [1803–4] it was roughly the same as it had been in 1789'.[19] Perhaps there is a danger in con-centrating narrowly on legislative texts and the stated intentions of proprietors. In the real world of the late eighteenth-century countryside the price of leases was determined by the laws of supply and demand, and it may be that the issue of the tithe is less important than it seems.

Nevertheless, Tim Le Goff and Donald Sutherland insist that tenants 'whether small or large, can safely be said to have got no direct concrete benefit from the social policy of the revolution'.[20] Such a statement is far too categoric, for the reasons already given. But it also leaves out of account the effects of rampant inflation which worked massively to the advantage of the tenantry. Any proprietor still reliant on cash rentals in 1795 was in dire straits indeed. From all over the country came demands that the Convention pass a law permitting the cancellation and renegotiation of fixed-term leases. Landowners were facing ruin, warned a petition from Chirac in the Lozère on 13 May 1795: at current prices the value of their *rentes* had dwindled by 93 per cent. In the Ardèche a cash rent worth 100 *setiers* of rye in 1790 would only purchase two *setiers* five years later. If *rentiers* contemplated the future with mounting apprehension, tenants exploited the inexorable collapse of the money economy with grim satisfaction. The killings they made during these years more than expunged the insult of the neo-tithe, festering differences over feudal dues and disappointment with the new tax regime. Debts could be paid off with nearly worthless *assignats*; a farm could be had for the price of a plough-team.

Such strictures tend to undermine the notion that the freehold–tenure divide provides the key to the political geography of rural France. Indeed, the whole argument appears to rest upon a premise which is suspect: that freeholders and renters were marshalled into hard-and-fast categories. No doubt every rural community boasted a number of self-sufficient *laboureur* households, and most would have contained households living solely from land leased on a tenancy or share-crop basis. Yet the vast majority of peasant households fell into neither of these categories: they survived by working freehold plots, by renting additional plots and by selling their surplus labour. For every peasant proprietor able to tot up his gains with little, if anything, to place in the debit column, there must have been dozens of peasants for whom the revolution represented a mixture of gains and losses. In short, the argument advanced by Le Goff and Sutherland simplifies the patterns of landholding in the countryside to an unacceptable degree. Moreover, the contrast observed in the political behaviour of peasant freeholders compared with that of tenants and share-croppers seems decidedly opaque. In Brittany the evidence may indicate that self-sufficient farmers stayed loyal to the revolution, whereas tenant farmers displayed a greater sympathy for the *chouannerie*, but it is doubtful whether this conclusion bears more than regional significance. Share-croppers in the South West resisted the temptation to abandon the revolution, despite fiscal disappointments and a running battle with proprietors over the tithe. Tenant farmers baulked at counter-revolution in the eastern Sarthe, too. In the Charente-Inférieure they rallied massively to the Civil Constitution of the Clergy, while in the southern portion of the Deux-Sèvres sharecroppers bought *biens nationaux* and prospered as never before.

So much for the landed peasantry. What about the agricultural day labourers, the plot farmers, the squatters on heath and common and the mendicant poor whose numbers had risen substantially in the final decades of the *ancien régime*? Wage earners had watched their purchasing power decline by a quarter between 1741 and 1789 (see p. 32) and the unfavourable conjuncture forced many rural households into a dangerous over-reliance on cottage industry, collective rights and ecclesiastical alms. How had the lowest tiers of the peasantry fared during the revolution? Georges Lefebvre drew up a largely negative balance-sheet as far as these social categories were concerned.[21] The agricultural proletariat, as he defines it, must be accounted among the victims of the revolution. Notwithstanding the formation of a new class of small peasant proprietors in the Cambrésis, the symptoms of agrarian crisis persisted. Beggars were more numerous in the Nord after the revolution than they had been before. Yet Monteil, writing of the Aveyron during the early years of the Consulate, was struck by how the late *ancien régime* agrarian crisis had eased, at least in so far as the hordes of beggars were concerned. Clearly, the plight of the rural poor varied in its intensity and it is worth looking at the ways in which the revolution affected them in more detail.

The retreat from indirect taxation for a time (consumption taxes were gradually reintroduced under the Consulate and the Empire) undoubtedly created a breathing space for the urban and rural poor. Nor should the benefits accruing from the abolition of seigneurialism be discounted. More significant, perhaps, the wage–price conjuncture was reversed during the revolution. By the end of the decade real wages registered a net improvement on rates prevailing at the end of the *ancien régime*. On the debit side, however, we need to bear in mind the vicissitudes of cottage textile production which was a crucial input to many a poor peasant's household budget. In the Ardèche, for instance, the collapse of the market for raw silk brought whole communities to the brink of destitution. The revolutionary land settlement cut both ways, but on balance it is probably fair to say that it left the poor more vulnerable to economic adversity than before. Certainly the revolutionaries put up for sale an immense quantity of land and buildings and Lefebvre has demonstrated (see p. 160) that agricultural labourers and tenant farmers were not entirely excluded from the exercise. More important, the revolutionaries facilitated (if they did not condone) an illicit ploughing up of heath and waste which must have benefited the poor peasantry for the most part. On the other hand, the jacobin-inspired attempt to found a property-owning democracy failed miserably. Egalitarian partition of common land evoked a patchy response at best, while the scheme to help the landless purchase *émigré* property proved a nonstarter. On the plains around Paris poor peasants demanded action against engrossers, but fainthearted legislators refused to impose a 'maximum' on the size of holdings. More seriously, the policy of selling off church lands as *biens nationaux* had a disastrous effect upon the provision of charitable relief. Country dwellers grumbled about having to pay the tithe and dues to ecclesiastical seigneurs, but much of this income was injected back into the rural economy in the form of alms doled out at the gates of abbeys and monasteries. Now the great foundations were earmarked for extinction, leaving the poor of surrounding parishes stripped of a resource on which they had come to rely. And if destitution and disease resulted, the poor could scarcely look to the hospitals. In 1794 their lands were put up for sale, too. As wealthy bourgeois purchasers swooped on institutions which, for all their faults, had given shape and meaning to rural life for centuries, the humblest level of country dwellers must have wondered whether it had all been worthwhile. In the economic sense, almost certainly not, although variations of population pressure, land supply and agricultural balance make generalisation difficult. The poor peasantry of the Paris grain belt and of the North East appear to have gained least from the revolution, for in these regions there existed little spare land for ploughing or rough grazing at the end of the *ancien régime*. In the South and South East, however, the land surface remained under-exploited and the poor were often able to attenuate the hardships of the revolutionary years by hacking fields out of the heath and by increasing their livestock.

But revolutions are not to be measured in economic terms alone. Even the most hard-pressed peasant would have been conscious of the political dimension. This is the fourth and final issue that needs to be addressed. Perhaps the most obvious point to emerge from the preceding chapters is that none of the revolutionary legislatures evolved a 'peasant programme'. The *montagnard* Convention came closest with its attachment to the interests of society's 'malheureux', but even the *montagnards* persisted in viewing the peasantry as stereotyped 'citizens of the countryside'. *Civisme* rather than social origins defined the preoccupations of the jacobin republic and only the relentless pressure of counter-revolution and foreign invasion forced an awareness that there did exist specifically peasant problems. Even so, that awareness was fitful at best: sharecroppers eventually won concessions on the issue of the neo-tithe, and the landless poor were invited to apply for vouchers which could be used to purchase national property. Neither measure had much impact, however, and the suspicion remains that, even at the radical zenith of the revolution, agrarian legislation was designed more for rhetorical than for practical effect.

Could it have been otherwise? Perhaps not. The French peasantry were a massive and yet diverse phenomenon. There was no such thing as an average eighteenth-century peasant, comments Pierre Goubert.[22] Instead, he discerns at least a dozen types and a 'peasant programme' would have been required for each. Nevertheless, certain issues motivated all peasants in 1789 and foremost among these was seigneurialism. Contrary to received wisdom, the revolutionaries did not destroy the feudal regime on the night of 4 August. What happened was that the deputies panicked in the face of mounting agrarian violence. As a result, a number of concessions were rushed into print, including the statement 'The National Assembly destroys in its entirety the feudal regime' (see p. 82). Then the tide of peasant insurrectionism ebbed and on recovering their composure, the deputies tried to minimise their undertakings. The most that can be said in favour of the first generation of revolutionary legislators is that they provided a contractual means of extinguishing seigneurialism. This was not what the peasantry wanted, of course, but for two and a half years their petitions gathered dust in the archives of the Feudal Committee. In the end, the feudal regime was destroyed from below with the endorsement of a shamefaced and discredited Legislative Assembly.

Arrogance and insensitivity also characterised the handling of such issues as the tithe and the disposal of church lands. Peasant resentment of the tithe went hand in hand with hostility to feudal dues. Both were harvest taxes, both were proportional and often they were paid cumulatively to the same lord. The August legislation promised immediate relief on this front, too, but then there followed a long period of tergiversation during which the confidence of country dwellers in the National Assembly was sorely tried. First it seemed that the tithe had ceased with the payment due on the 1789 harvest, then it transpired that the state would replace the church as beneficiary for one year only in 1790. This was disappointing, but the prospect of abolition without prior indemnification offered some consolation. Imagine the dismay of tenants and sharecroppers, however, when the legislators intervened to ensure that the proceeds of abolition ended up in the pockets of landowners. Few decisions did more to underline the proprietorial character of the revolution at this juncture. The same may be said of the terms laid down for the sales of *biens nationaux*. 'Would it not be appropriate to divide up the various properties into small lots?', asked Regnault, deputy for the *sénéchaussée* of Saint Jean-d'Angély, during the parliamentary debates on the issue.[23] The Duc de La Rochefoucault-Liancourt also demurred on behalf of the poor, but the mass of the deputies swept such scruples aside. Occasionally, plot holders overcame the obstacles placed in their path and bid collectively for land. Yet the process of buying at auction under the hostile eye of district officials was fraught with difficulties and it is scarcely surprising that the peasantry came to view the exercise with a degree of cynicism.

By contrast, the peasantry successfully resisted the doctrinaire enthusiasms of bourgeois revolutionaries on the subject of collective rights. By the end of the decade customary grazing of unenclosed meadows (*droit au regain*) had been curtailed, but that was all. This was a far cry from the hopes entertained by an Assembly packed with rural proprietors at the start of the revolution – hopes which found expression in Hertaut de Lamerville's initial proposal to do away with *vaine pâture*. When it came to the crunch, issues such as free grazing, gleaning and scavenging affected the immediate livelihood of many more country dwellers than did the attribution of the tithe, or the sale of church and *émigré* estates. Accordingly, the National Assembly backed off and the long-gestated Rural Code turned out to be a rather timid document. It offered landowners a (largely unenforceable) right to enclose, while allowing peasants an (eminently enforceable) right to graze their stock as tradition dictated. In effect, therefore, agrarian *liberté* was postponed indefinitely. All attempts to revise the Rural Code in a direction favourable to landowners stumbled against the political argument: the great majority of peasants relied on collective rights and would not be parted from them without resistance.

Even though legislators failed to implement a package of reforms geared to peasant needs, it would be wrong to conclude that country dwellers emerged from the revolution empty-handed. The commitment to individual political freedom shared by all the revolutionary assemblies produced measurable benefits, particularly in the realm of local government. As we have seen, the devolution of power down the social scale began under Calonne, but the revolutionaries effectively relaunched the process with their justly famous Municipal Law of 14 December 1789. This reform was accompanied by an invidious restriction on the right to vote, it is true. Not until the autumn of 1792 did the revolutionaries bring their political practice into line with their principles as laid down in the Declaration of the Rights of Man. Nevertheless, the active–passive distinction scarcely detracts from the magnitude of their achievement: the enthronement of the electoral principle in 1789 resulted in a massive extension of the political rights of the peasantry (see pp. 173–6). And with that extension came a right to self-government. The new municipal bodies were not only elected by peasants and filled with peasant councillors (for the most part); they were entrusted with an assortment of executive, judicial and fiscal responsibilities. Freed from the interference of the seigneur or his representative, freed from the tutelage of the absentee landowner: no wonder country dwellers defended municipal self-government as one of the finest fruits of the revolution.

The long-term significance of the National Assembly's local government reforms should not be overlooked, either. In effect, the municipalities provided a training-ground for a new rural elite. Perhaps a million country dwellers were introduced to the business of village government in 1790 and the turn-over of personnel increased that number as the revolution proceeded. Not all were peasants, of course. In the South, particularly, the political vacuum caused by the retreat of royal and seigneurial power was filled by a rural bourgeoisie of leisured landowners, professionals such as notaries and doctors, innkeepers and small merchants. Yet there are good grounds for supposing that the majority of new initiates to political office were, in fact, peasants, albeit peasants of the more substantial kind. In the North and the East the Municipal Law consolidated the position of the *gros fermiers* who now acquired political power commensurate with their economic standing in the community. Municipal office also helped to compensate for the loss of all the 'collecting functions' which big farmers used to perform on behalf of seigneurs. In Poitou, by contrast, the reform of local government brought to the fore an elite of millers, substantial tenants of share-crop holdings and *laboureurs*, all of whom had grown rich on the sale of wheat and young mules. The sharecroppers, in particular, accomplished an astonishing social transformation which serves to remind us that the balance of gains and losses accruing from the revolution should not be interpreted too rigidly. Many bought out their landlords after 1789, thereby reaching the apex of the peasantry in one easy move.

The other major sphere in which the revolution brought tangible gains to all country dwellers was that of judicial administration. Accessible, inexpensive and impartial justice was a rare commodity at the end of the *ancien régime*. Just how rare is revealed by a reading of the preliminary *cahiers de doléances* drawn up in the parishes during the winter of 1789. From nearly all parts of the kingdom there issued a litany of complaints condemning, among other things, seigneurial neglect of 'police'; overlapping or incoherent jurisdictions; incompetent or vengeful judges; and inadequate facilities for the arrest and detention of offenders. Much of this public indignation with the functioning of the lower reaches of the judicial machine was expressed in the general *cahiers* of the Third Estate as well, 50 per cent of which demanded the abolition of seigneurial courts. The revolutionaries needed no reminding of what was expected of them, therefore, and on this issue at least they answered every country dweller's prayer. Between 1789 and 1792 an entirely new system of civil and criminal justice was put in place. For the peasantry the most attractive feature of the new system was the provision for a *juge de paix* in each canton. This individual was elected by the constituency of active citizens and empowered to handle much of the business formerly transacted by seigneurial courts. His primary task was to operate a conciliation service or, in the event of failure, an arbitration service; but he could also judge minor cases without appeal. More serious litigation went before the district courts. Country dwellers loved the new first-instance courts precisely because they were accessible, inexpensive and relatively impartial. Governments, on the other hand, found the system generous to a fault and came to regret the loss of control that the electoral principle presupposed. Under the Directory the number of cantons (and therefore the number of *juges de paix*) was steadily reduced, but Bonaparte's decision in 1801 to slim down the complement of *juges de paix* by nearly half provoked an outcry. The department of the Aveyron saw its contingent drop from eighty-four in 1791 to forty-two. Justice, remarked Monteil gloomily, was becoming distant and expensive once more.[24] It was also losing its democratic flavour, for the First Consul soon broke with the tradition of direct election and introduced instead a system combining election with co-option.

Municipal democracy did not long survive Napoleon's distrust of representative institutions, either. Yet it would be wrong to suggest that Napoleon destroyed the administrative and judicial achievements of the revolution. The self-governing commune and the *juge de paix* survived as institutions and were restored to vigour under subsequent regimes. Nor did Napoleon succeed in rooting up the ideas of equality and accountability which had been nurtured by such institutions in the 1790s. During the Empire peasant jacobinism sublimated into peasant Bonapartism, but the Bonapartism of the rural masses (as opposed to that of the notables) retained a left-wing flavour. When Martin Nadaud, the Limousin worker who became a radical parliamentarian in 1848, sat down to write his memoirs, he penned a classic account of political osmosis.[25] His father, a poor peasant who migrated seasonally to Paris, had formerly worked for one of Napoleon's companions-in-exile and he used to bring home copies of the *Bulletins de la Grande Armée*, although quite unable to read. For this reason the young Martin was sent to school where he was taught the basic skills by a retired officer of the Empire. The whole family swiftly became ardent Bonapartists and Martin recalls how the long winter nights of 1829–30 were spent intoning the freedom-loving songs of Béranger with his father and uncle (who had been wounded at Waterloo) bellowing out the chorus lines. Following in his father's tracks as a migrant mason, Nadaud *fils* used Bonapartism as a stepping-stone to utopian socialism and republicanism.

The fate of peasant royalism is less easy to specify if only because royalism had been a matter of habit rather than conviction for the majority of country dwellers. Convinced royalists reacted to the news of General Bonaparte's *coup d'état* on 18 Brumaire VIII (9 November 1799) with a degree of optimism. It was anticipated that the First Consul would prepare the way for some form of Bourbon restoration and *émigrés* began to return to France in the knowledge that Louis XVIII was sounding out the ground. Napoleon, however, would have none of this. He was pursuing hereditary ruling ambitions of his own and warned Louis that he 'would have to walk over one hundred thousand corpses' in order to return to France.[26] By 1803 the prospect of a rapprochement had clearly evaporated and the case for political and military resistance to the regime was being voiced once more. But the *chouannerie* was dead: neither the leaders nor the peasantry possessed the stamina for renewed guerrilla warfare and the reprisals which inevitably followed. Besides, the First Consul had resolved some of the grievances which had precipitated the conflagration in the West in the first place. On 15 July 1801 a Concordat was signed with the Vatican which restored the catholic church to a powerful position in the state. The Pope reluctantly assented to the confiscation and the sale of ecclesiastical property as *biens nationaux*, but Napoleon effectively washed his hands of the constitutional church and allowed the refractory clergy to fill most of the vacant posts in the parishes. In the South, too, the Empire had a soothing effect on political passions. Savage repression brought the White Terror to heel by 1802 and for about a decade calm descended upon the countryside. Time softened the contours of village factionalism and epithets such as 'jacobin' or 'royalist' lost their emotive appeal. Not so in localities divided by religion, however. Here the battle-lines between catholic and protestant remained tightly drawn, as the bloody score-settling in the Gard which greeted the news of Napoleon's defeat at Waterloo in 1815 would testify.

Few peasants felt anything but impatience with the revolution on the eve of Bonaparte's *coup* against the Directory. It had gone on for too long; it had interrupted too many routines. Even those who had benefited materially from the change of regime tended only to count the attendant costs. Yet benefits there had been, and they should not be overlooked. For the majority of country dwellers the ending of seigneurial obligations and the tithe marked the watershed; for the minority it was access to land. The issue of seigneurialism – or feudalism as the revolutionaries preferred to call it – posed the single greatest barrier to a return to the *ancien régime*. Decades after the revolution, mere mention of the subject of seigneurial power was capable of sending a *frisson* of fear coursing through the peasantry. In regions such as the Morvan, the Mâconnais and the southern Massif Central anxiety on this score was almost pathological. The land constituted the other great windfall – a slightly paradoxical windfall to be sure, since few peasants succeeded in buying *biens nationaux* at auction. But it can be assumed that plot farmers and sharecroppers often obtained a share of the spoils at one remove. Agricultural wage earners, meanwhile, were sometimes able to establish a precarious title to fields hacked out of the heath or common. Overall, then, the revolutionaries did little to alter the prevailing agrarian balance, but they did enough to seed the political myth that the revolution gave the land to the peasants.

No single statement can ever hope to capture the total experience of the peasantry during the revolution. Nevertheless, the balanced verdict of Lecointe-Puyraveau, government commissioner in the Deux-Sèvres, does not fall too short of the mark. Writing in 1798, he acknowledged that the issue of the tithe, military conscription and constant requisitions had tested enthusiasm for the revolution. The peasant farmer

might well have complained, but he has sold his remaining foodstuffs at extraordinary prices and for three years has been able to settle his lease with the modest production of the farmyard; to such an extent that he seems to have kept all the wealth in his hands, while the landowner is forced to beg his help and to cancel rental payments which have not yet fallen due in order to survive . . . As for the more intelligent kind of cultivator knowing how to read and write, he has been called to municipal office. This has flattered him and the satisfaction derived from issuing orders has given him a taste for the new regime and he has attached himself to it.[27]

Notes

Preface

1 Reprinted in G. Lefebvre, *Etudes sur la Révolution française* (Paris, 1954), pp. 246–68.
2 G. Lefebvre, *Questions agraires au temps de la Terreur* (Strasbourg, 1932). Reprinted in a revised and augmented edition in 1954.
3 E. Soreau, *Ouvriers et paysans de 1789 à 1792* (Paris, 1936).
4 A. Ado, *The Peasant Movement in France during the Great Bourgeois Revolution of the End of the Eighteenth Century* (Moscow, 1971); in Russian.

1: Rural France in the eighteenth century

1 P. Goubert, *Beauvais et le Beauvaisis de 1600 à 1730: contribution à l'histoire sociale de la France du XVIIe siècle* (Paris, 1960), pp. 51, 75.
2 J. Dupâquier, *La Population française aux XVIIe et XVIIIe siècles* (Paris [Que sais-je?], 1979), p. 68.
3 *Ibid.*, pp. 42–3, 67–8.
4 B. Derouet, 'Une Démographie différentielle: les populations rurales d'Ancien Régime', *Annales E.S.C.*, 35 (1980), 3–41.
5 *Ibid.*, p. 23.
6 In J. Molinier, 'L'Evolution de la population agricole du XVIIIe siècle à nos jours', *Economie et statistique*, 91 (1977), p. 81.
7 Dupâquier, *La Population française*, pp. 114–16.
8 In G. Duby and A. Wallon (eds.), *Histoire de la France rurale* (4 vols., Paris, 1975–6), vol. ii, pp. 359, 370.
9 Derouet, 'Une Démographie différentielle', p. 18.
10 J. Dupâquier and C. Berg-Hamon, 'Voies nouvelles pour l'histoire démographique de la Révolution française: le mouvement de la population de 1785 à 1800', *Ann. hist. Rév. fran.*, 47 (1975), 3–29.
11 Dupâquier, *La Population française*, p. 116.
12 A.-A. Monteil, *Description du département de l'Aveiron* (2 vols., Paris, *an* X), vol. ii, p. 53.

13 G. Lefebvre, *The Great Fear of 1789: Rural Panic in Revolutionary France* (London, 1973), p. 7; Lefebvre, 'La Révolution française et les paysans', p. 250.

14 Lefebvre, *Les Paysans du Nord pendant la Révolution française* (condensed version, Bari, 1959).

15 G. Lefebvre, 'Répartition de la propriété et de l'exploitation foncière à la fin de l'ancien régime', in his *Etudes sur la Révolution française*, p. 209.

16 F. Gauthier, *La Voie paysanne dans la Révolution française: l'exemple de la Picardie* (Paris, 1977), p. 30.

17 Lefebvre, *Paysans du Nord*, p. 321.

18 Goubert, *Beauvais et le Beauvaisis*, p. 158.

19 G. Lefebvre, *Questions agraires au temps de la Terreur* (2nd ed., La Roche-sur-Yon, 1954), p. 61.

20 Lefebvre, *Paysans du Nord*, p. 108.

21 *Ibid.*, p. 351.

22 R. Redfield, *Peasant Society and Culture* (Chicago, 1956), p. 25.

23 P. Goubert, *Beauvais et le Beauvaisis*, pp. 93–4.

24 J.-C. Toutain, 'Le Produit de l'agriculture française de 1700 à 1958: II, La Croissance', in *Cahiers de l'Institut de science économique appliquée*, supplement to 115 (1961), 276.

25 In Duby and Wallon, *Histoire de la France rurale*, vol. ii, pp. 395, 417.

26 A. Zink, *Azereix: la vie d'une communauté rurale à la fin du XVIIIᵉ siècle* (Paris, 1969), pp. 93–109.

27 Duby and Wallon, *Histoire de la France rurale*, vol. ii, p. 408.

28 Lefebvre, *Paysans du Nord*, p. 89.

29 J.-M. Sallmann, 'Le Partage des biens communaux en Artois, 1770–1789', *Etudes rurales*, 67 (1977), 76.

30 G. Lefebvre, 'The Place of the Revolution in the Agrarian History of France', in R. Forster and O. Ranum (eds.), *Rural Society in France: Selections from the Annales, Economies, Sociétés, Civilisations* (Baltimore, 1977), p. 36.

31 Gauthier, *La Voie paysanne dans la Révolution française*.

32 C. Demay (ed.), *Cahiers des paroisses du bailliage d'Auxerre pour les Etats-Généraux de 1789* (Auxerre, 1885), p. 448.

33 P. Sagnac and P. Caron (eds.), *Les Comités des droits féodaux et de législation et l'abolition du régime seigneurial, 1789–1793* (Paris, 1907), p. 169.

34 H. L. Root, 'En Bourgogne: l'état et la communauté rurale, 1661–1789', *Annales E.S.C.*, 37 (1982), 288–302.

35 Lefebvre, *Paysans du Nord*, p. 333.

36 See M. Bordes, *L'Administration provinciale et municipale en France au XVIIIᵉ siècle* (Paris, 1972), p. 337; J.-P. Gutton, *La Sociabilité villageoise dans l'ancienne France. Solidarités et voisinage du XVIᵉ au XVIIIᵉ siècle* (Paris, 1979), pp. 90–1; P. M. Jones, *Politics and Rural Society: the Southern Massif Central, c. 1750–1880* (Cambridge, 1985), p. 182.

37 In Jones, *Politics and Rural Society: the Southern Massif Central*, p. 182.

2: *The crisis of the late* ancien régime

1 Lefebvre, *Paysans du Nord*, Part One; Lefebvre, *Etudes Orléanaises* (2 vols., Paris, 1962–3), vol. ii, p. 5.

2 C. E. Labrousse, *Esquisse du mouvement des prix et des revenus en France au XVIIIe siècle* (2 vols., Paris, 1933). See also Labrousse, *La Crise de l'économie française à la fin de l'Ancien Régime et au début de la Révolution* (Paris, 1944).

3 G. V. Taylor, 'Noncapitalist Wealth and the Origins of the French Revolution', *Amer. Hist. Rev.*, 72 (1967), 491.

4 W. Doyle, *Origins of the French Revolution* (Oxford, 1980), p. 31.

5 For a summary, see G. Lefebvre, 'Le Mouvement des prix et des origines de la Révolution française', in his *Etudes sur la Révolution française*, 154–63.

6 *Ibid.*, p. 33.

7 Lefebvre, *Paysans du Nord*, p. 193.

8 A. Poitrineau, *La Vie rurale en Basse Auvergne au XVIIIe siècle* (Paris, 1965).

9 In Duby and Wallon, *Histoire de la France rurale*, vol. ii, p. 428.

10 D. M. G. Sutherland, *The Chouans: the Social Origins of Popular Counter-Revolution in Upper Brittany, 1770–1796* (Oxford, 1982), p. 70.

11 G. Frêche, *Toulouse et la région Midi-Pyrénées au siècle des lumières (vers 1670–1789)* (Mayenne, 1974), pp. 497–505.

12 Jones, *Politics and Rural Society: the Southern Massif Central*, p. 158.

13 See H. Guilhamon (ed.), *Journal des voyages en Haute-Guienne de J. F. Henry de Richeprey* (2 vols., Rodez, 1952–67).

14 Sutherland, *The Chouans*, p. 136.

15 Guilhamon (ed.), *Journal des voyages*, vol. i, pp. 292, 293 and 294–5, n. 1.

16 *Ibid.*, vol. ii, pp. 308–9.⅔

17 *Ibid.*, vol. i, pp. 261–2.

18 Archives Départementales [henceforth A.D.] du Puy-de-Dôme C7373.

19 A.D. Puy-de-Dôme C7361.

20 Richeprey, *Journal des voyages*, ed. Guilhamon, vol. i, p. 259, n. 1.

21 E. Le Roy Ladurie, 'Révoltes et contestations rurales en France de 1675 à 1788', *Annales E.S.C.*, 29 (1974), 9.

22 'It was said, at present, that *something was to be done by some great folks for such poor ones, but she did not know who nor how*, but God send us better, *car les tailles et les droits nous ecrasent*' (A. Young, *Travels in France during the Years 1787, 1788, 1789* [London, 1900], 12 July 1789 [Young's italics]).

23 Richeprey, *Journal des voyages*, ed. Guilhamon, vol. i, pp. 106–7.

24 *Ibid.*, vol. ii, p. 311.

25 A.D. Puy-de-Dôme C7373.

26 Doyle, *Origins*, p. 117.

27 See A. Cobban, *The Myth of the French Revolution* (London, 1955), also reprinted in his *Aspects of the French Revolution* (London, 1973), pp. 90–112.

28 Cobban, *The Myth of the French Revolution*, in *Aspects of the French Revolution*, pp. 95–7.

29 See Duby and Wallon, *Histoire de la France rurale*, vol. ii, p. 423.

30 R. Baehrel, 'L'Exploitation seigneuriale au XVIIIe siècle', in *Commission de recherche et de publication des documents relatifs à la vie économique de la Révolution. Assemblée Générale de la Commission Centrale et des Comités Départementaux, 1939*, vol. I: *La Bourgeoisie française, de la fin de l'ancien régime à la Révolution, l'exploitation seigneuriale au XVIIIe siècle d'après les terriers, la condition des ouvriers* (Besançon, 1942), pp. 251–302.

31 A.D. Aveyron C1530.

32 See J. Bastier, 'Droits féodaux et revenus agricoles en Rouergue à la veille de la Révolution', *Annales du Midi*, 95 (1983), 282; J. Dalby, 'The French Revolution in a Rural Environment: the Example of the Department of the Cantal, 1789–1794' (University of Manchester, D.Phil. thesis, 1981), p. 46; J. Bastier, *La Féodalité au siècle des lumières dans la région de Toulouse (1730–1790)* (Paris, 1975), p. 260; Frêche, *Toulouse et la région Midi-Pyrénées*, p. 508.

33 G. V. Taylor, 'Revolutionary and Nonrevolutionary Content in the *Cahiers* of 1789: an Interim Report', *French Historical Studies* 7 (1972), 495.

34 Lefebvre, *Paysans du Nord*, p. 169.

35 In Duby and Wallon, *Histoire de la France rurale*, vol. ii, p. 563.

36 O. H. Hufton, 'Attitudes towards Authority in Eighteenth-century Languedoc', *Social History*, 3 (1978), 281–302.

37 D. Foucault, 'Lectoure pendant la Révolution, 1789–1794' (University of Toulouse, Mémoire de maîtrise, 1980), p. 140.

38 Jones, *Politics and Rural Society: the Southern Massif Central*, pp. 159–60, 173–4, 176.

39 In Duby and Wallon, *Histoire de la France rurale*, vol. ii, p. 562.

40 Archives Nationales (henceforth A.N.) DXIV 11.

41 'La Communauté rurale dans la France de Centre-Est au XVIIIe siècle', in *Les Communautés rurales/Rural Communities: recueil de la Société Jean Bodin pour l'histoire comparative des institutions*, vol. 43 (Paris, 1984), pp. 540, 549–50.

42 *Ibid.*, p. 540.

43 Lefebvre, 'La Révolution française et les paysans', p. 256.

44 P. de Saint Jacob, *Les Paysans de la Bourgogne du nord au dernier siècle de l'ancien régime* (Dijon, 1960), pp. 241–50, 405–34.

45 In Duby and Wallon, *Histoire de la France rurale*, vol. ii, p. 583.

46 A.N. DXIV 6.

47 In Duby and Wallon, *Histoire de la France rurale*, vol. ii, pp. 423, 435–6, 583.

48 Doyle, *Origins*, pp. 197–8.

49 Lefebvre, *Paysans du Nord*, pp. 157–64.

50 See *Commission de recherche et de publication des documents relatifs à la vie économique de la Révolution. Assemblée Générale de la Commission Centrale et des Comités Départementaux, 1939*, vol. i: *La Bourgeoisie française, de la fin de l'ancien régime à la Révolution, l'exploitation seigneuriale au XVIIIe siècle d'après les terriers, la condition des ouvriers* (Besançon, 1942), p. 17.

51 'La Communauté rurale dans la France de Centre-Est au XVIIIe siècle', p. 543.

52 In Jones, *Politics and Rural Society: the Southern Massif Central*, p. 165.
53 See N. Castan, 'Crime et justice en Languedoc, 1750–1790', (University of Toulouse, Thèse de doctorat d'état, 2 vols., 1978), vol. ii, p. 580.
54 *Ibid.*, p. 591.
55 A.N. DXIV 13.
56 A.N. DXIV 5.
57 *Ibid.*
58 V. Malrieu (ed.), *Cahiers de doléances de la sénéchaussée de Montauban et du pays et jugerie de Rivière-Verdun pour les Etats Généraux de 1789* (Montauban, 1925), p. 6.
59 See J. M. Roberts and J. Hardman (eds.), *French Revolution Documents*, vol. i (Oxford, 1966), p. 77.
60 A.N. DXIV 11.
61 This memoir can also be found in A.N. DXIV 11.
62 A.N. DXIV 13.
63 Taylor, 'Revolutionary and Nonrevolutionary Content in the *Cahiers* of 1789', pp. 479–502.
64 Doyle, *Origins*, p. 158.
65 Taylor, 'Revolutionary and Nonrevolutionary Content in the *Cahiers* of 1789', p. 482.
66 J.-J.Vernier (ed.), *Cahiers de doléances du bailliage de Troyes (principal et secondaire) et du bailliage de Bar-sur-Seine pour les Etats-Généraux de 1789* (3 vols., Troyes, 1909–11); G. Demay (ed.), *Cahiers des paroisses du bailliage d'Auxerre pour les Etats-Généraux de 1789*; C. Porée (ed.), *Cahiers de doléances du bailliage de Sens pour les Etats-Généraux de 1789* (Auxerre, 1908).

3: 1789: between hope and fear

1   Lefebvre, *The Great Fear of 1789*.
2   *Ibid.*, p. 45.
3   J. Boutier, 'Jacqueries en pays croquant. Les révoltes paysannes en Aquitaine (décembre 1789–mars 1790)', *Annales E.S.C.*, 34 (1979), 765.
4   Lefebvre, *The Great Fear of 1789*, pp. 45–6.
5   In P. Kessel, *La Nuit de 4 août 1789* (Paris, 1969), p. 68.
6   G. Lefebvre, *Etudes Orléanaises*, vol. i, p. 62.
7   R. Robin, *La Société française en 1789: Semur-en-Auxois* (Paris, 1970), p. 348.
8   J.-M. Ory, 'Sociétés et mentalités vosgiennes à la veille de la Révolution d'après les cahiers de doléances des communautés du bailliage de Mirecourt en Lorraine (mars 1789)', *Bulletin de la Société philomatique vosgienne*, 84 (1981), 95–6.
9   A.N. B^{a}32.
10 *Ibid.*
11 Ory, 'Sociétés et mentalités vosgiennes à la veille de la Révolution', pp. 101–2.

12 Robin, *La Société française en 1789: Semur-en-Auxois*, pp. 349–50.

13 A. Poitrineau, 'Les Assemblées primaires du bailliage de Salers en 1789', *Rev. d'hist. mod. et contemp.*, 25 (1978), 421.

14 Kessel, *La Nuit de 4 août 1789*, p. 73.

15 Lefebvre, *The Great Fear of 1789*, p. 39.

16 A.N. B^{a}51.

17 F. Evrard, 'Les Paysans du Mâconnais et les brigandages de juillet 1789', *Annales de Bourgogne*, 19 (1947), 38–9.

18 S. R. Weitman, 'Bureaucracy, Democracy and the French Revolution' (unpublished Ph.D. thesis, Washington University, 1968), pp. 354–5. G. Chaussinand-Nogaret offers an alternative computation: noble *cahiers* supporting retention of dues (17 per cent); proposing abolition (13 per cent); making no mention of the subject (70 per cent), in *The French Nobility in the Eighteenth Century: from Feudalism to Enlightenment* (Cambridge, 1985), p. 162.

19 A.N. B^{a}37.

20 A. Young, *Travels in France*, p. 206.

21 Lefebvre, *The Great Fear of 1789*, p. 110.

22 See Boutier, 'Jacqueries en pays croquant'.

23 Lefebvre, *The Great Fear of 1789*, p. 121.

24 See Evrard, 'Les Paysans du Mâconnais et les brigandages de juillet 1789', pp. 9–32.

25 Lefebvre, 'La Révolution française et les paysans', p. 257.

26 Boutier, 'Jacqueries en pays croquant', pp. 769–73.

27 In Evrard, 'Les Paysans du Mâconnais et les brigandages de juillet 1789', p. 107.

28 Boutier, 'Jacqueries en pays croquant', p. 772.

29 *Ibid.*, p. 769.

30 Lefebvre, *Paysans du Nord*, pp. 794–8.

31 Boutier, 'Jacqueries en pays croquant', p. 761.

32 Evrard, 'Les Paysans du Mâconnais et les brigandages de juillet 1789', p. 98.

33 Boutier, 'Jacqueries en pays croquant', pp. 770–1.

34 Deriving from the seigneurial obligation known as the *cens*.

35 A condition of semi-serfdom surviving in parts of eastern France at the end of the *ancien régime*. *Mainmorte personnelle* applied to individuals and restricted their right to leave the seigneurie. *Mainmorte réelle* applied to land and it prevented a vassal from disposing of his holding to anyone other than kith and kin living communally with him. A third permutation, known as *mainmorte mixte*, was widespread in the Franche-Comté. The abolition of *mainmorte* was one of the most complex issues tackled by the National Assembly.

36 *Lois et actes du gouvernement: tome premier, août 1789 à septembre 1790* (Paris, 1834).

37 *Suite du rapport fait à l'Assemblée nationale au nom du comité de féodalité le 8 février par M. Merlin, député de Douay. Imprimé par ordre de l'Assemblée* (Paris, n.d. [1790]), p. 5, n. 1.

38 Young, *Travels in France*, p. 235.
39 A.N. DXIV 6 Meurthe.
40 A.N. DXIV 3 Eure.
41 F. Julien-Labruyère, *Paysans charentais: histoire des campagnes d'Aunis, Saintonge et Bas Angoumois* (2 vols., La Rochelle, 1982), vol. i, p. 58.
42 A.N. DXIV 3 Dordogne.

4: Dismantling the seigneurial regime

1 S. Herbert, *The Fall of Feudalism in France* (London, 1921), p. 129.
2 *Declaration of the Rights of Man and of Citizens*, article 17.
3 P. Sagnac, *La Législation civile de la Révolution française, 1789–1804* (Paris, 1898), p. 100.
4 *Collection générale des loix* (24 vols., Paris, 1786–1800), vol. i, p. 642.
5 Herbert, *The Fall of Feudalism in France*, p. 139.
6 *Réimpression de l'Ancien Moniteur* (32 vols., Paris, 1847), vol. iv, 25 April 1790.
7 A.N. DXIV 13.
8 Herbert, *The Fall of Feudalism in France*, p. 189.
9 In *ibid.*, p. 191.
10 G. Bourgin (ed.), *Le Partage des biens communaux: documents sur la préparation de la loi du 10 juin 1793* (Paris, 1908), p. 398.
11 Herbert, *The Fall of Feudalism in France*, p. 196.
12 In J. Millot, *L'Abolition des droits seigneuriaux dans le département du Doubs et la région Comtoise* (Besançon, 1941), p. 211.
13 Lefebvre, *Paysans du Nord*, p. 148.
14 J. Girardot, *Le Département de la Haute-Saône pendant la Révolution* (3 vols., Vesoul, 1973), vol. i, pp. 98, 149.
15 In P. Sagnac and P. Caron (eds.), *Les Comités des droits féodaux et de législation et l'abolition du régime seigneurial, 1789–1793* (Paris, 1907), p. 60.
16 Sagnac, *La Législation civile de la Révolution française*, p. 155 and note 1; G. T. Matthews, *The Royal General Farms in Eighteenth-Century France* (New York, 1958), p. 25, n. 26.
17 M. Muller and S. Aberdam, 'Conflits de dîme et révolution en Gascogne gersoise, 1750–1800' (Mémoire de maîtrise sous la direction de M. Robert Mandrou, 1971–2), p. E41.
18 *Ibid.*, pp. E50–E51.
19 In J. B. Duvergier (ed.), *Collection complète des lois, decrets, ordonnances, reglemens et avis du conseil d'état* (78 vols., Paris, 1824–78), vol. ii, p. 75.
20 See T. J. A. Le Goff and D. M. G. Sutherland, 'Religion and Rural Revolt in the French Revolution: an Overview', in J. M. Bak and G. Benecke (eds.), *Religion and Rural Revolt: Papers presented to the Fourth Interdisciplinary Workshop on Peasant Studies, University of British Columbia, 1982* (Manchester, 1984), pp. 123–45.

21 Muller and Aberdam, 'Conflits de dîme et révolution en Gascogne gersoise, 1750–1800', pp. A12–A17.

22 A.D. Gers L116.

23 Muller and Aberdam, 'Conflits de dîme et révolution en Gascogne gersoise, 1750–1800', p. F26.

24 *Ibid.*, pp. F28–F29.

25 A.N. DIII 96.

26 Herbert, *The Fall of Feudalism in France*, pp. 156–7.

27 H. L. Root, 'Challenging the Seigneurie: Community and Contention on the Eve of the French Revolution', *The Journal of Modern History*, 57 (1985), 660.

28 F. Genreau, 'Les Paysans et l'abolition des droits féodaux dans le district de Tonnerre (Yonne), 1789 à 1793' (University of Dijon, Diplôme d'études supérieures d'histoire du droit, 1972), p. 139.

29 A.N. DXIV 3.

30 A.N. DIV 38.

31 In Sagnac and Caron (eds.), *Les Comités de droits féodaux et de législation*, p. 78.

32 In Herbert, *The Fall of Feudalism in France*, p. 151.

33 A.N. DXIV 5.

34 A. Ferradou, *Le Rachat des droits féodaux dans la Gironde, 1790–1793* (Paris, 1928), pp. 197–8.

35 Herbert, *The Fall of Feudalism in France*, p. 176.

36 In Sagnac and Caron (eds.), *Les Comités des droits féodaux et de législation*, p. 280.

37 Girardot, *Le Département de la Haute-Saône pendant la Révolution*, vol. ii, p. 105.

38 Sutherland, *The Chouans*, p. 140, n. 21.

39 See Le Goff and Sutherland, 'Religion and Rural Revolt in the French Revolution: an Overview', pp. 130–1.

40 A.N. DXIV 13.

41 *Rapport de messieurs J. Godard et L. Robin, commissaires civils envoyés par le Roi dans le département du Lot, en exécution du décret de l'Assemblée Nationale du 13 décembre 1790* (Paris, 1791).

42 *Ibid.*, p. 25.

43 J. Dupâquier, *La Propriété et l'exploitation foncières à la fin de l'Ancien Régime dans le Gâtinais septentrional* (Paris 1956), p. 173.

44 *Archives parlementaires de 1787 à 1860. Recueil complet des débats législatifs et politiques des chambres françaises (première série, 1787–99)* (92 vols., Paris, 1862–1980), vol. iv, p. 196.

45 A.N. DXIV 5.

46 A.N. DXIV 38.

47 M. Bouloiseau, *The Jacobin Republic, 1792–1794* (Cambridge and Paris, 1983), p. 159.

48 A.N. DIII 359.

5: The land settlement: collective rights versus agrarian individualism

1 D. M. G. Sutherland, *France 1789–1815: Revolution and Counter-Revolution* (London, 1985), p. 13.
2 Lefebvre, 'La Révolution française et les paysans', p. 249.
3 In the English translation, A. Soboul, *The French Revolution, 1787–1799* (London, 1974), p. 186.
4 A. Ado, *The Peasant Movement in France during the Great Bourgeois Revolution.*
5 A. Soboul, 'A propos d'une thèse récente: sur le mouvement paysan dans la Révolution française', *Ann. hist. Rév. fran.*, 45 (1973), 97.
6 See F. Gauthier, *La Voie paysanne dans la Révolution française* and 'Formes d'évolution du système agraire communautaire en Picardie (fin XVIIIᵉ, début XIXᵉ siècle)', *Ann. hist. Rév. fran.*, 52 (1980), 181–204; G.-R. Ikni, 'Recherches sur la propriété foncière. Problèmes théoriques et de méthode', *Ann. hist. Rév. fran.*, 52 (1980), 390–424, and 'Documents: sur la loi agraire dans l'Oise pendant la Révolution française', *Annales historiques compiégnoises*, 5 (1982), 18–26.
7 Lefebvre, *Paysans du Nord*, p. 70.
8 *Ibid.*, pp. 103–7.
9 *Ibid.*, p. 70.
10 See Gauthier, *La Voie paysanne dans la Révolution française*, p. 213.
11 Lefebvre, *Paysans du Nord*, p. 908.
12 Young, *Travels in France*, p. 291.
13 lefebvre, *Paysans du Nord*, p. 425.
14 A.N. F^{10}332.
15 A.N. DXIV 13.
16 In S. Aberdam, *Aux origines du code rural, 1789–1900: un siècle de débat* (Paris, 1982), p. 10.
17 Decree of 5–12 June 1791.
18 Decree of 12–20 August 1790. See Duvergier (ed.), *Collection complète des lois*, vol. i, p. 302.
19 A.N. F^{10}337.
20 O. Festy, *L'Agriculture pendant la Révolution française: les conditions de production et de récolte des céréales. Etude d'histoire économique, 1789–1795* (Paris, 1947), pp. 109–10 and notes.
21 G. Lefebvre, *Questions agraires au temps de la Terreur*, p. 117, n. 2.
22 A.N. F^{10}329.
23 A.N. F^{10}336.
24 *Ibid.*
25 *Ibid.*
26 M. Saby, *Allègre et sa région au fil des siècles* (Le Puy, 1976), pp. 167, 274–7.
27 N. François de Neufchâteau, *Voyages agronomiques dans la sénatorerie de Dijon* (Paris, 1806), p. 16.

28 J.-J. Clère, 'Les Paysans de la Haute-Marne et la Révolution française: recherches sur les structures de la communauté villageoise' (University of Dijon, Thèse pour le doctorat en droit, 2 vols., 1979), vol. i, p. 157.

29 See discussion in D. Hunt, 'Peasant Politics in the French Revolution', *Social History*, 9 (1984), 294.

30 Decree of 11 December 1789.

31 In Clère, 'Les Paysans de la Haute-Marne et la Révolution française', vol. ii, p. 416.

32 In Bourgin (ed.), *Le Partage des biens communaux*, p. 693.

33 *Ibid.*, p. 706.

34 For the text of the law of 10 June 1793, see Bourgin (ed.), *Le Partage des biens communaux*, pp. 728–39.

35 A.N. DXIV 5.

36 A.N. $F^{10}330$.

37 A.N. $F^{10}333^A$.

38 In Bourgin (ed.), *Le Partage des biens communaux*, p. 55.

39 A.N. $F^{10}329$.

40 Bouloiseau, *The Jacobin Republic*, p. 184.

41 A. Soboul, *Problèmes paysannes de la Révolution, 1789–1848* (Paris, 1976), pp. 206–7.

42 Gauthier, *La Voie paysanne dans la Révolution française*, chapter 9, and Hunt, 'Peasant Politics in the French Revolution', p. 294.

43 Ado, *The Peasant Movement in France during the Great Bourgeois Revolution*.

44 G. Ikni, 'Recherches sur la propriété foncière', p. 419.

45 Gauthier, *La Voie paysanne dans la Révolution française*, p. 202.

46 A.N. $F^{10}330$.

47 Lefebvre, *Paysans du Nord*, pp. 549–51.

48 A.D. Aube 2 0 1778.

49 See Clère, 'Les Paysans de la Haute-Marne et la Révolution française', vol. ii, p. 458.

50 *Loi relative à la vente des immeubles des émigrés du 3 juin 1793*, article 5, in *Lois et actes du gouvernement* (Paris, 1834), vol. vii, pp. 96–103.

51 Lefebvre, *Paysans du Nord*, pp. 431–525.

52 Sutherland, *The Chouans*, p. 213.

53 See Clère, 'Les Paysans de la Haute-Marne et la Révolution française', vol. ii, pp. 456–561.

54 J. Michelet, *Histoire de la Révolution française* (9 vols., Paris, n.d. [1847–53]), vol. iii, p. 280.

55 D. Martin, 'La Vente des biens des émigrés dans le district de Clermont-Ferrand, 1792–1830', in G. Gerbaud, A. Lamadon, D. Martin and J. Petelet, *La Révolution dans le Puy-de-Dôme* (Paris, 1972), pp. 160–3.

56 P. Pageot, 'La Vente des biens des émigrés dans le district de Guéret', *Mémoires de la Société des sciences naturelles et archéologiques de la Creuse*, 40 (1980), 600–3.

57 Lefebvre, *Questions agraires au temps de la Terreur*, pp. 29–30 and n. 1.
58 Lefebvre, *Paysans du Nord*, pp. 514–21.
59 For these figures see: R. Marx, *La Révolution et les classes sociales en Basse-Alsace. Structures agraires et vente des biens nationaux* (Paris, 1974), p. 533; Bois, *Paysans de l'Ouest*, p. 305; Sutherland, *The Chouans*, p. 77; G. Lefebvre, 'La Vente des biens nationaux', in *Etudes sur la Révolution française*, pp. 223–45; A. Le Boterf, 'La Vente des biens nationaux dans le district de St. Sever, 1791–an X. Etude sociale et économique' (University of Paris, Mémoire de maîtrise, 1971), p. 30; D. Larroque, 'La Vente des biens nationaux dans le district de Tartas' (University of Paris, Mémoire de maîtrise, 1971), p. 24.
60 Clère, 'Les Paysans de la Haute-Marne et la Révolution française', vol. ii, pp. 562–612.
61 *Œuvres de Maximilien Robespierre*, ed. M. Bouloiseau and A. Soboul (10 vols., Paris, 1903–1967), vol. x, p. 32.
62 See above, note 50.
63 A.N. F^{10}332.
64 A. Mathiez, 'La Politique sociale de Robespierre', *Annales révolutionnaires*, 6 (1913), 551–63.
65 G. Lefebvre, *The French Revolution* (2 vols., London and New York, 1965–7), vol. ii, p. 114.
66 A. Mathiez, *La Révolution française* (3 vols., Paris, 1932–3), vol. iii, p. 148.
67 Lefebvre, *The French Revolution*, vol. ii, p. 113.

6: The administrative revolution

1 E. Burke, *Reflections on the Revolution in France* (Harmondsworth, 1973), p. 147.
2 A. Métin, *La Révolution et l'autonomie locale* (Toulouse, 1904), p. 19.
3 *Cahier* of Vicheray; see Ory, 'Sociétés et mentalités vosgiennes à la veille de la Révolution', p. 92.
4 See J.-R. Suratteau, 'Heurs et malheurs de la "sociologie électorale" pour l'époque de la Révolution française', *Annales E.S.C.*, 23 (1968), 558.
5 P. Bois, *Paysans de l'Ouest: des structures économiques et sociales aux options politiques depuis l'époque révolutionnaire dans la Sarthe* (Le Mans, 1960), pp. 224–37.
6 F. Fortunet, M. Fossier, N. Kozlowski and S. Vienne, *Pouvoir municipal et communauté rurale à l'époque révolutionnaire en Côte-d'Or, 1789–an IV* (Dijon, 1981), pp. 4–20.
7 Lefebvre, *Paysans du Nord*, p. 766.
8 Sutherland, *The Chouans*, p. 155.
9 See A.N. F^{1c} III Aveyron 1; M. Edelstein, 'Vers une "sociologie électorale" de la Révolution française: la participation des citadins et compagnards (1789–1793)', *Rev. d'hist. mod. et contemp.*, 22 (1975), 513; Fortunet *et al.*, *Pouvoir municipal et communauté rurale à l'époque révolutionnaire en Côte-d'Or*, p. 17.

10 Lefebvre, *Paysans du Nord*, p. 768.

11 Law of 14 Frimaire II, section 2, article 14.

12 In J. Dalby, 'L'Influence de la Révolution sur la société paysanne dans le Cantal, 1789–1794', *Revue de la Haute-Auvergne*, 49 (1983), 120.

13 In M. Marion, 'Le Recouvrement des impôts en 1790', *Revue historique*, 121 (1916), 13, n. 2.

14 R. B. Rose, 'Tax Revolt and Popular Organization in Picardy, 1789–91', *Past and Present*, 43 (1969), 92.

15 In M. Bruneau, *Les Débuts de la Révolution dans les départements du Cher et de l'Indre, 1789–1791* (Paris, 1902), p. 96.

16 Marion, 'Le Recouvrement des impôts en 1790', p. 27.

17 In *ibid.*, p. 14.

18 Bruneau, *Les Débuts de la Révolution*, p. 231.

19 *Ibid.*, p. 234.

20 *Ibid.*

21 A.D. Pyrénées-Orientales L802 Printed circular despatched by Minister of Finances.

22 Bruneau, *Les Débuts de la Révolution*, pp. 236–8.

23 Bois, *Paysans de l'Ouest*, p. 629.

24 Lefebvre, *Paysans du Nord*, pp. 604–5.

25 J. Merley, *La Haute-Loire de la fin de l'ancien régime aux débuts de la Troisième République* (2 vols., Le Puy, 1974), vol. i, p. 266.

26 In C. Riffaterre, 'Les Revendications économiques et sociales des assemblées primaires de juillet 1793', *Commission de recherche et de publication des documents relatifs à la vie économique de la Révolution, Bulletin trimestriel* (1906), p. 356.

27 In Muller and Aberdam, 'Conflits de dîme et révolution en Gascogne gersoise, 1750–1800', p. F26.

28 In Riffaterre, 'Les Revendications économiques et sociales', p. 355.

29 In *ibid.*, pp. 355–6.

30 Bois, *Paysans de l'Ouest*, pp. 629–34; Lefebvre, *The French Revolution*, vol. i, p. 158.

31 J. McManners, *The French Revolution and the Church* (London, 1969), p. 38.

32 Sutherland, *The Chouans*, pp. 201–2.

33 T. Tackett, *Religion, Revolution, and Regional Culture in Eighteenth-Century France: The Ecclesiastical Oath of 1791* (Princeton, 1986), p. 86.

34 T. J. A. Le Goff, *Vannes and its Region: a Study of Town and Country in Eighteenth-Century France* (Oxford, 1981), pp. 250–64.

35 M. Vovelle, *Piété baroque et déchristianisation en Provence au XVIIIe siècle: les attitudes devant la mort d'après les clauses des testaments* (Paris, 1973).

36 See T. Tackett, 'L'Histoire sociale du clergé diocésain de la France du XVIIIe siècle'. *Rev. d'hist. mod. et contemp.*, 27 (1979), 198–234, and T. Tackett and C. Langlois, 'Ecclesiastical Structures and Clerical Geography on the Eve of the French Revolution', *French Historical Studies*, 11 (1980), 352–70.

37 Tackett, *Religion, Revolution, and Regional Culture in Eighteenth-Century France*, pp. 249, 299.
38 *Ibid.*, p. 12.
39 McManners, *The French Revolution and the Church*, p. 50.
40 T. Tackett, 'The West in France in 1789: the Religious Factor in the Origins of the Counter-Revolution', *The Journal of Modern History*, 54 (1982), 715–45; see also his *Religion, Revolution, and Regional Culture in Eighteenth-Century France*, pp. 251–83.
41 Tackett, *Religion, Revolution, and Regional Culture in Eighteenth-Century France*, p. 275.
42 In R. Secher, *Le Génocide franco-français, la Vendée-Vengé* (Paris, 1986), p. 85.
43 In F. Mombet, 'Langue, mœurs et coutumes: une enquête historique', *Revue de l'Agenais*, 108 (1981), 42.
44 In Bruneau, *Les Débuts de la Révolution*, p. 392.
45 Tackett, *Religion, Revolution and Regional Culture in Eighteenth-Century France*, p. 199.
46 C. Jolivet, *La Révolution dans l'Ardèche, 1788–1795* (Largentière, 1930), p. 295, n. 1.

7: Terror and Counter-Terror

1 H. C. Johnson, *The Midi in Revolution: A Study of Regional and Political Diversity, 1789–1793* (Princeton, 1986), pp. 259–60.
2 See M. Vovelle, 'Formes de politisation de la société rurale en Provence sous la Révolution française: entre Jacobinisme et contre-révolution au village', *Annales de Bretagne*, 89 (1982), 185–204.
3 P. Burke, *Popular Culture in Early Modern Europe* (London, 1978), p. 259.
4 M. Lyons, 'Politics and Patois: the linguistic policy of the French Revolution', *Australian Journal of French Studies*, 18 (1981), 264.
5 See A. Gazier, *Lettres à Grégoire sur les patois de France, 1790–1794. Documents inédits sur la langue, les mœurs et l'état des esprits dans les diverses régions de la France au début de la Révolution* (Paris, 1880).
6 In Mombet, 'Langue, mœurs et coutumes: une enquête historique', p. 42.
7 *Ibid.*, p. 39.
8 A.N. F^{1c} III Lozère 8.
9 A.D. Gers L.181*.
10 M. Edelstein, '*La Feuille Villageoise*, the Revolutionary Press and the Question of Rural Political Participation', *French Historical Studies*, 7 (1971), 176–7.
11 In M. Edelstein, *La Feuille Villageoise: communication et modernisation dans les régions rurales pendant la Révolution* (Paris, 1977), p. 11.
12 Comment on the journal made by the clubbists of Buis (Drôme), quoted in M. L. Kennedy, *The Jacobin Club of Marseilles, 1790–94* (Ithaca, N.Y., 1973), p. 65.

13 Kennedy, *The Jacobin Club of Marseilles*, pp. 65–6.
14 C. C. Brinton, *The Jacobins: an Essay in the New History* (New York, 1961), p. 39.
15 C. Lucas, *The Structure of the Terror: the Example of Javogues and the Loire* (Oxford, 1973), p. 96.
16 Vovelle, 'Formes de politisation de la société rurale en Provence', p. 193.
17 *Ibid.*, p. 193.
18 Brinton, *The Jacobins*, p. 42.
19 G. Maintenant, *Les Jacobins* (Paris, 1984), p. 66.
20 M. L. Kennedy, *The Jacobin Clubs in the French Revolution* (Princeton, 1982), p. 82.
21 Brinton, *The Jacobins*, pp. 50–1.
22 M. Agulhon, *La Vie sociale en Provence intérieure au lendemain de la Révolution* (Paris, 1970), pp. 114–22, 267–84.
23 Bois, *Paysans de l'Ouest*, pp. 626–66.
24 Vovelle, 'Formes de politisation de la société rurale en Provence', pp. 195–6.
25 A.N. F^{1c} III Lozère 1.
26 Jones, *Politics and Rural Society: the Southern Massif Central*, p. 198.
27 See Sutherland, *The Chouans*, p. 260.
28 C. Tilly, *The Vendée* (Cambridge, Mass., 1976), p. 311.
29 J. Richard, 'La Levée de 300,000 hommes et les troubles de mars 1793 en Bourgogne', *Annales de Bourgogne*, 33 (1961), 248.
30 In Secher, *Le Génocide franco-français*, p. 150.
31 *Ibid.*, p. 300.
32 L. Wylie (ed.), *Chanzeaux: a Village in Anjou* (Cambridge, Mass., 1966), p. 17.
33 In Tilly, *The Vendée*, p. 322.
34 *Ibid.*, p. 329.
35 See T. J. A. Le Goff and D. M. G. Sutherland, 'The Social Origins of Counter-Revolution in Western France', *Past and Present*, 99 (1983), 65–87; see also their 'Religion and Rural Revolt in the French Revolution: an Overview', 123–45.
36 C. Petitfrère, 'Les Grandes Composantes sociales des armées Vendéennes d'Anjou', *Ann. hist. Rév. fran.*, 45 (1973), 1–20.
37 Lefebvre, 'La Révolution française et les paysans'.
38 Quoted in J. M. Roberts and J. Hardman (eds.), *French Revolution Documents*, vol. i, p. 89.
39 In J. Jaurès, *Histoire socialiste de la Révolution française* (8 vols., Paris, 1929–39), vol. vii, p. 312.
40 In J.-L. Rigal (ed.), *Comité de surveillance de Saint Geniez-d'Olt. Procès-verbaux et arrêtés* (Rodez, 1942), pp. 427–8.
41 T. S. Sheppard, *Lourmarin in the Eighteenth Century: a Study of a French Village* (Baltimore, 1971), p. 199.
42 C. Lucas, 'Résistances populaires à la Révolution dans le sud-est', in *Mouve-*

ments populaires et conscience sociale. Colloque de l'Université de Paris VII, Paris, 24–26 mai 1984 (Paris, 1985), p. 478.

43 R. C. Cobb, *The Police and the People: French Popular Protest, 1789–1820* (Oxford, 1970), p. 200.

44 C. Hohl, *Un Agent du Comité de Sûreté Générale: Nicolas Guénot* (Paris, 1968).

45 A.D. Aveyron 57L.

46 A.D. Aveyron L173 *bis*.

47 M. Vovelle, 'Prêtres abdicataires et déchristianisation en Provence', in *Actes du Quatre-Vingt-Neuvième Congrès National des Sociétés Savantes, Lyon 1964. Section d'histoire moderne et contemporaine* (vol. i, Paris, 1964), pp. 63–97.

48 Sutherland, *France 1789–1815*, p. 257.

49 A.N. F^{1b}II Aveyron 11.

50 A.D. Aveyron 67L (7).

51 A.D. Aveyron L699.

52 *Ibid.*

53 A.D. Aveyron L697.

54 In A. C. Thibaudeau, *Mémoires sur la Convention et le Directoire* (2 vols., Paris, 1824), vol. ii, p. 143.

55 See C. Lucas, 'The Problem of the Midi in the French Revolution', *Transactions of the Royal Historical Society*, 28 (1978), 1–25.

56 See R. C. Cobb, *The Police and the People*, pp. 131–50; and his *Reactions to the French Revolution* (London, 1972), pp. 19–62.

8: The balance-sheet

1 F.-R. de Chateaubriand, *Mémoires d'outre-tombe* (4 vols., Paris, 1948), vol. ii, p. 12.

2 *Ibid.*

3 A.-A. Monteil, *Description du département de l'Aveiron* (2 vols., Paris, *an* X). See also his *Histoire des Français des divers états aux cinq derniers siècles* (10 vols., Paris, 1828–44).

4 Young, *Travels in France*, p. 256.

5 *Description du département de l'Aveiron*, vol. ii, pp. 266–70.

6 In F. Rocquain (ed.), *L'Etat de la France au 18 Brumaire d'après les rapports des conseillers d'état chargés d'une enquête sur la situation de la République* (Paris, 1874), p. 254.

7 *Description du département de l'Aveiron*, vol. ii, pp. 281–2.

8 Dupâquier, *La Population française*, p. 118.

9 The phrase is attributed to Alexis de Tocqueville.

10 Lefebvre, 'La Révolution française et les paysans', p. 250.

11 In J.-L. Thiry, *Le Département de la Meurthe sous le Consulat* (Nancy, 1958), p. 145.

12 In J.-M. Tisseyre and M. Baudot (eds.), 'Rapport de Pierre-Joseph Bonnaterre

sur l'état du département de l'Aveyron et l'an IV de la République', in *Bulletin de la Section d'histoire moderne et contemporaine du Comité des Travaux historiques et scientifiques* (Paris, 1977), p. 156.

13 G. Chaussinand-Nogaret, *Une Histoire des élites, 1700–1848* (Paris – The Hague, 1975), p. 220.

14 J.-C. Asselain, *Histoire économique de la France du XVIIIe siècle à nos jours*, vol. I: *De l'Ancien Régime à la Première Guerre mondiale* (Paris, 1984), p. 114.

15 M. Morineau, *Les Faux-semblants d'un démarrage économique: agriculture et démographie en France au XVIIIe siècle* (*Cahier des Annales*, 30; Paris, 1971).

16 In M. Minoret, *La Contribution personnelle et mobilière pendant la Révolution* (Paris, 1900), p. 326.

17 In A. Benoist, 'Les Populations rurales du "Moyen-Poitou protestant" de 1640 à 1789' (University of Poitiers, Thèse pour le doctorat de troisième cycle, 4 vols., 1983), vol. i, p. 65.

18 Bois, *Paysans de l'Ouest*, p. 389.

19 Lefebvre, *Paysans du Nord*, p. 423.

20 Le Goff and Sutherland, 'Religion and Rural Revolt in the French Revolution: an Overview', p. 142.

21 Lefebvre, *Paysans du Nord*, pp. 758–64.

22 P. Goubert, 'Sociétés rurales françaises du XVIIIe siècle: vingt paysanneries contrastées, quelques problèmes', in *Conjoncture économique, structures sociales. Hommage à Ernest Labrousse* (Paris–The Hague, 1974), p. 378.

23 *Réimpression de l'Ancien Moniteur* (32 vols., Paris, 1847), vol. iv, p. 334.

24 Monteil, *Description du département de l'Aveiron*, vol. ii, p. 243.

25 M. Nadaud, *Mémoires de Léonard, ancien garçon maçon* (Paris, 1976), pp. 68–80.

26 In J. Godechot, *The Counter-Revolution. Doctrine and Action, 1789–1804* (London, 1972), p. 364.

27 In Benoist, 'Les Populations rurales du "Moyen-Poitou protestant" de 1640 à 1789', vol. iv, pp. 779–80.

Bibliography

MANUSCRIPT SOURCES

Archives Nationales, Paris

B^a5 *Elections aux Etats Généraux*: miscellaneous papers
B^a32 *Elections aux Etats-Généraux*: Chaumont-en-Bassigny
B^a37 *Elections aux Etats Généraux: Dijon*
B^a51 *Elections aux Etats Généraux: Mende*
B^a85 *Elections aux Etats Généraux: Villefranche-du-Rouergue*
DIII 96 *Comité de Législation: Gers*
DIII 97 *Comité de Législation: Gers*
DIII 177 *Comité de Législation: Nièvre*
DIII 359 *Comité de Législation*: papers relating to feudal dues
DIV 38 *Comité de Constitution: Loiret*
DIV 45 *Comité de Constitution: Allier*
DIV^{bis} 77 *Comité de division du territoire*
D*XIV 1 *Comité des Droits Féodaux*: register of correspondence received, 1789–90
D*XIV 2 *Comité des Droits Féodaux*: register of correspondence received, 1790–1
DXIV 1 *Comité des Droits Féodaux: Aisne, Ardennes, Allier*
DXIV 2 *Comité des Droits Féodaux: Charente, Charente-Inférieure, Cantal*
DXIV 3 *Comité des Droits Féodaux: Côte-d'Or, Côtes-du-Nord, Dordogne, Eure, Finistère*
DXIV 5 *Comité des Droits Féodaux: Loiret, Lot, Lot-et-Garonne, Maine-et Loire*
DXIV 6 *Comité des Droits Féodaux: Marne, Haute-Marne, Meurthe*
DXIV 8 *Comité des Droits Féodaux: Nièvre*
DXIV 10 *Comité des Droits Féodaux: Seine-et-Marne*
DXIV 11 *Comité des Droits Féodaux: Vendée, Vienne, Haute-Vienne, Vosges, Yonne*
DXIV 12 *Comité des Droits Féodaux: Seine-et-Marne, Seine-et-Oise*
DXIV 13 *Comité des Droits Féodaux*: miscellaneous papers

F^{10} 212^{A-B} *Agriculture: pétitions et mémoires, 1789–an III*
F^{10} 326   *Agriculture: pétitions et mémoires, 1754–an IV*
F^{10} 327   *Agriculture: correspondance concernant les communaux, an II–an IV*
F^{10} 328   *Agriculture: correspondance concernant les communaux, an II–an IV*
F^{10} 329   *Agriculture: communaux, Aisne–Yonne, 1792–an III*
F^{10} 330   *Agriculture: communaux, Ain–Yonne, 1792–3*
F^{10} 332   *Agriculture: partage des communaux, Ain–Yonne, 1790–an VII*
F^{10} 333^{A} *Agriculture: partage des communaux, Aisne–Yonne, 1790–an VII*
F^{10} 333^{B} *Agriculture: partage des communaux, Ain–Yonne, an II–an IV*
F^{10} 334   *Agriculture: partage des communaux, Ain–Tarn, 1790–an IV–an VIII*
F^{10} 336   *Agriculture: parcours et vaine pâture, 1791–1816*
F^{10} 337   *Agriculture: parcours et vaine pâture, Hautes-Alpes–Vendée, an X–1816*
F^{1b}II Aveyron 11   *Personnel administratif*
F^{1c}III Aveyron 1   *Esprit public et élections, 1790–2*
F^{1c}III Lozère 1   *Esprit public*
F^{1c}III Lozère 8   *Esprit public*

Archives Départementales de l'Aube, Troyes
2 0 1778   *Administration communale*

Archives Départementales de l'Aveyron, Rodez
C1530   *Administrations provinciales*
L173 *bis*   *Révolution: commission-civile-révolutionnaire*
L697   *Révolution: administration du département, troubles, an III*
L699   *Révolution: administration du département, brigandages, an IV*
57L   *Révolution: comité de surveillance d'Estaing*
67L(7)   *Révolution: comité de surveillance de Rodez, correspondance reçue an III*

Archives Départementales de la Côte-d'Or, Dijon
L640   *Révolution: biens et revenus communaux*

Archives Départementales du Gers, Auch
L116   *Révolution: administration du département, procès-verbal des séances, 1793*
L181   *Département: correspondance extérieure, 23 juillet 1791–14 août 1793*

Archives Départementales du Puy-de-Dôme, Clermont-Ferrand
C7361   *Administration générale: procès-verbal des séances de l'Assemblée préliminaire d'élection de St Flour, 1787*
C7373   *Administration générale: procès-verbal de l'Assemblée d'élection de St Flour, 1788*

Archives Départementales des Hautes-Pyrénées, Tarbes
Cadastre: terrier compoix de la baronnie d'Esparros, 1758–73

Archives Départementales des Pyrénées-Orientales, Perpignan
L802 *Révolution*: correspondence between Minister of Finances and the directory of the department

PRINTED PRIMARY SOURCES

Archives parlementaires de 1787 à 1860. Recueil complet des débats législatifs et politiques des chambres françaises (première série, 1787–99), 92 vols., Paris, 1862–1980
Bourgin, G. (ed.) *Le Partage des biens communaux: documents sur la préparation de la loi du 10 juin 1793*. Paris, 1908
Collection générale des loix, 24 vols., Paris, 1786–1800
Declaration of the Rights of Man and of Citizens [1789]. English translation in T. Paine's *The Rights of Man*. London, 1791
Duvergier, J. B. *Collection complète des lois, décrets, ordonnances, réglements et avis du conseil d'état*, 78 vols., Paris, 1824–78
Gerbaux, F. and Schmidt, C. (eds.). *Procès-verbaux des comités d'agriculture et de commerce de la Constituante, de la Législative et de la Convention*, 4 vols. + 1 vol. index, Paris, 1906–10, 1937
Lois et actes du gouvernement: tome premier, août 1789 à septembre 1790; tome septième, mars 1793 à ventôse, an II. Paris, 1834.
Rapport de messieurs J. Godard et L. Robin, commissaires civils envoyés par le Roi dans le département du Lot, en exécution du décret de l'Assemblée Nationale du 13 décembre 1790. Paris, 1791
Réimpression de l'Ancien Moniteur, 32 vols., Paris, 1847
Roberts, J. M. and Hardman, J. (eds.) *French Revolution Documents*, 2 vols., Oxford, 1966; 1973
Sagnac, P. and Caron, P. (eds.) *Les Comités des droits féodaux et de législation et l'abolition du régime seigneurial, 1789–1793*. Paris, 1907
Suite du rapport fait à l'Assemblée nationale au nom du comité de féodalité le 8 février par M. Merlin, député de Douay. Imprimé par ordre de l'Assemblée. Paris, n.d. [1790]

SECONDARY SOURCES

Aberdam, S. 'La Révolution et la lutte des métayers', *Études rurales*, 59 (1975), 73–91
Aux origines du code rural, 1789–1900: une siècle de débat. 1982
Ado, A. *The Peasant Movement in France during the Great Bourgeois Revolution of the End of the Eighteenth Century*. Moscow, 1971. (In Russian)
Agulhon, M. *La Vie sociale en Provence intérieure au lendemain de la Révolution*. Paris, 1970

Asselain, J.-C. *Histoire économique de la France du XVIIIe siècle à nos jours*, vol. i: *De l'Ancien Régime à la Première Guerre mondiale*. Paris, 1984

Baehrel, R. 'L'Exploitation seigneuriale au XVIIIe siècle', in *Commission de recherche et de publication des documents relatifs à la vie économique de la Révolution. Assemblée Générale de la Commission Centrale et des Comités Départementaux, 1939* (Vol. 1, *La Bourgeoisie française, de la fin de l'ancien régime à la Révolution, l'exploitation seigneuriale au XVIIIe siècle d'après les terriers, la condition des ouvriers*). Besançon, 1942, pp. 251–302

Bastier, J. *La Féodalité au siècle des lumières dans la région de Toulouse (1730–1790)*. Paris, 1975

  'Droits féodaux et revenus agricoles en Rouergue à la veille de la Révolution', *Annales du Midi*, 95 (1983), 261–87

Benoist, A. 'Les Populations rurales du "Moyen-Poitou protestant" de 1640 à 1789' (University of Poitiers, Thèse pour le doctorat de troisième cycle, 4 vols., 1983)

Bois, P. *Paysans de l'Ouest: des structures économiques et sociales aux options politiques depuis l'époque révolutionnaire dans la Sarthe*. Le Mans, 1960

Bordes, M. *L'Administration provinciale et municipale en France au XVIIIe siècle*. Paris, 1972

Bouloiseau, M. *The Jacobin Republic, 1792–1794*. Cambridge and Paris, 1983

Bouloiseau, M. and Soboul, A. (eds.) *Œuvres de Maximilien Robespierre*, 10 vols., Paris, 1903–67.

Boutier, J. 'Jacqueries en pays croquant. Les révoltes paysannes en Aquitaine (décembre 1789–mars 1790)', *Annales E.S.C.*, 34 (1979), 760–86

Bozon, P. *La Vie rurale en Vivarais: étude géographique*. Valence, 1963

Brinton, C. C. *The Jacobins: an Essay in the New History*. New York, 1961

Bruneau, M. *Les Débuts de la Révolution dans les départements du Cher et de l'Indre, 1789–1791*. Paris, 1901

Burke, E. *Reflections on the Revolution in France*. Harmondsworth, 1973

Burke, P. *Popular Culture in Early Modern Europe*. London, 1978

Castan, N. 'Crime et justice en Languedoc, 1750–1790' (University of Toulouse, Thèse de doctorat d'état, 2 vols., 1978)

Certeau, M. de, D. Julia and J. Revel, *Une Politique de la langue: la Révolution française et les patois*. Paris, 1975

Chateaubriand, F.-R. de *Mémoires d'outre-tombe*, 4 vols., Paris, 1948

Chaussinand-Nogaret, G. *Une Histoire des élites, 1700–1848*. Paris – The Hague, 1975

  The French Nobility in the Eighteenth Century: from Feudalism to Enlightenment. Cambridge, 1985

Clère, J.-J. 'Les Paysans de la Haute-Marne et la Révolution française: recherches sur les structures de la communauté villageoise' (University of Dijon, Thèse pour le doctorat en droit, 2 vols., 1979)

Cobb, R. C. *The Police and the People: French Popular Protest, 1789–1820*. Oxford, 1970

  Reactions to the French Revolution. London, 1972

Cobban, A. *The Myth of the French Revolution*. London, 1955

'Local Government During the French Revolution', in A. Cobban, *Aspects of the French Revolution*. St Albans, 1973, pp. 113–31

'La Communauté rurale dans la France de Centre-Est au XVIIIe siècle', in *Les Communautés rurales/Rural Communities: recueil de la Société Jean Bodin pour l'histoire comparative*, vol. 43, Paris, 1984

Dalby, J. 'The French Revolution in a Rural Environment: the Example of the Department of the Cantal, 1789–1794' (University of Manchester, D.Phil. thesis, 1981)

'L'Influence de la Révolution sur la société paysanne dans le Cantal, 1789–1794', *Revue de la Haute-Auvergne*, 49 (1983), 113–33

Delattre, M. 'Le Régime seigneurial, la délinquance, les mentalités paysannes dans la Châtellenie du Catcau-Cambrésis au XVIIIe siècle' (n.p., Mémoire de maîtrise, 1970)

Demay, C. *Cahiers des paroisses du bailliage d'Auxerre pour les Etats-Généraux de 1789*. Auxerre, 1885

Derouet, B. 'Une Démographie différentielle: les populations rurales d'Ancien Régime', *Annales E.S.C.*, 35 (1980), 3–41

Doyle, W. *Origins of the French Revolution*. Oxford, 1980

Duby, G. and Wallon, A. (eds.) *Histoire de la France rurale*, 4 vols., Paris, 1975–6

Dupâquier, J. *La Propriété et l'exploitation foncières à la fin de l'Ancien Régime dans le Gâtinais septentrional*. Paris, 1956

La Population française au XVIIe et XVIIIe siècles. Paris (Que sais-je?), 1979

Dupâquier, J. and Berg-Hamon, C. 'Voies nouvelles pour l'histoire démographique de la Révolution française: le mouvement de la population de 1785 à 1800', *Ann. hist. Rév. fran.*, 47 (1975), 3–29.

Edelstein, M. '*La Feuille Villageoise*, the Revolutionary Press and the Question of Rural Political Participation', *French Historical Studies*, 7 (1971), 175–203

La Feuille Villageoise: communication et modernisation dans les régions rurales pendant la Révolution. Paris, 1977

Evrard, F. 'Les Paysans du Mâconnais et les brigandages de juillet 1789', *Annales de Bourgogne*, 19 (1947), 7–39; 97–121

Féral, P. 'Le Problème de la dîme, de la coussure et de la glane au XVIIIe et au XIXe siècle dans le Lectourois', *Bulletin de la Société historique et archéologique du Gers* (1949), 238–54

Ferradou, A. *Le Rachat des droits féodaux dans la Gironde, 1790–1793*. Paris, 1928

Festy, O. *L'Agriculture pendant la Révolution française: les conditions de production et de récolte des céréales. Etude d'histoire economique, 1789–1795*. Paris, 1947

Fortunet, F., Fossier, M., Kozlowski, N. and Vienne, S. *Pouvoir municipal et communauté rurale à l'époque révolutionnaire en Côte-d'Or, 1789–an IV*. Dijon, 1981

Foucault, D. 'Lectoure pendant la Révolution, 1789–1794' (University of Toulouse, Mémoire de maîtrise, 1980)

François de Neufchâteau, N. *Voyages agronomiques dans la sénatorerie de Dijon*. Paris, 1806

Frêche, G. *Toulouse et la région Midi-Pyrénées au siècle des lumières (vers 1670– 1789)*. Mayenne, 1974

Garaud, M. *La Révolution et la propriété foncière*. Paris, 1958

Gauthier, F. *La Voie paysanne dans la Révolution française: l'exemple de la Picardie*. Paris, 1977

'Formes d'évolution du système agraire communautaire en Picardie (fin XVIIIe, début XIXe siècle)', *Ann. hist. Rév. fran.*, 52 (1980), 181–204

Gazier, A. *Lettres à Grégoire sur les patois de France, 1790–1794. Documents inédits sur la langue, les mœurs et l'état des esprits dans les diverses régions de la France au début de la Révolution*. Paris, 1880

Genreau, F. 'Les Paysans et l'abolition des droits féodaux dans le district de Tonnerre (Yonne), 1789 à 1793' (University of Dijon, Diplôme d'études supérieures d'histoire du droit, 1972)

Girardot, J. *Le Département de la Haute-Saône pendant la Révolution*, 3 vols., Vesoul, 1973

Godechot, J. *The Counter-Revolution. Doctrine and Action, 1789–1804*. London, 1972

La Révolution française dans le Midi Toulousain. Toulouse, 1986

Goubert, P. *Beauvais et le Beauvaisis de 1600 à 1730: contribution à l'histoire sociale de la France du XVIIe siècle*. Paris, 1960

'Sociétés rurales françaises du XVIIIe siècle: vingt paysanneries contrastées, quelques problèmes', in *Conjoncture économique, structures sociales. Hommage à Ernest Labrousse*. Paris–The Hague, 1974, pp. 375–87

Guichonnet, P. 'Les Biens communaux et les partages révolutionnaires dans l'ancien département du Léman', *Etudes rurales*, 36 (1969), 7–36

Guilhamon, H. (ed.) *Journal des voyages en Haute-Guienne de J. F. Henry de Richeprey*, 2 vols., Rodez, 1952–67

Gutton, J.-P. *La Sociabilité villageoise dans l'ancienne France. Solidarités et voisinage du XVIe au XVIIIe siècle*. Paris, 1979

Henriot, M. *Le Partage des biens communaux en Côte-d'Or sous la Révolution*. Dijon, 1948

Herbert, S. *The Fall of Feudalism in France*. London, 1921

Hohl, C. *Un Agent du Comité de Sûreté Générale: Nicolas Guénot*. Paris, 1968

Hufton, O. H. 'Attitudes towards Authority in Eighteenth-century Languedoc', *Social History*, 3 (1978), 281–302

Hunt, D. 'Peasant Politics in the French Revolution', *Social History*, 9 (1984), 277–97

Ikni, G.-R. 'Recherches sur la propriété foncière. Problèmes théoriques et de méthode', *Ann. his. Rév. fran.*, 52 (1980), 390–424

'Documents: sur la loi agraire dans l'Oise pendant la Révolution française', *Annales historiques compiégnoises*, 5 (1982), 18–26

Jaurès, J. *Histoire socialiste de la Révolution française*, 8 vols., Paris, 1923–39

Johnson, H. C. *The Midi in Revolution: A Study of Regional and Political Diversity, 1789–1793*. Princeton, 1986

Jolivet, C. *La Révolution dans l'Ardèche, 1788–1795.* Largentière, 1930

Jones, P. M. *Politics and Rural Society: the Southern Massif Central, c. 1750–1800.* Cambridge, 1985

Julien-Labruyère, F. *Paysans charentais: histoire des campagnes d'Aunis, Saintonge et Bas Angoumois,* 2 vols., La Rochelle, 1982

Kennedy, M. L. *The Jacobin Club of Marseilles, 1790–94.* Ithaca, N.Y., 1973
The Jacobin Clubs in the French Revolution. Princeton, 1982

Kessel, P. *La Nuit du 4 août 1789.* Paris, 1969

Labrousse, C. E. *Esquisse du mouvement des prix et des revenus en France au XVIIIe siècle,* 2 vols., Paris, 1933
La Crise de l'économie française à la fin de l'Ancien Régime et au début de la Révolution. Paris, 1944

Larroque, D. 'La Vente des biens nationaux dans le district de Tartas' (University of Paris, Mémoire de maîtrise, 1971)

Le Boterf, A. 'La Vente des biens nationaux dans le district de St. Sever, 1791–an X. Etude sociale et économique' (University of Paris, Mémoire de maîtrise, 1971)

Lefebvre, G. *Etudes sur la Révolution française.* Paris, 1954
Questions agraires au temps de la Terreur. 2nd ed., La Roche-sur-Yon, 1954
Les Paysans du Nord pendant la Révolution française. Condensed version, Bari, 1959
Etudes Orléanaises, 2 vols., Paris, 1962–3
The French Revolution, 2 vols., London and New York, 1965–7
The Great Fear of 1789: Rural Panic in Revolutionary France. London, 1973
'The Place of the Revolution in the Agrarian History of France', in R. Forster and O. Rannum (eds.), *Rural Society in France: Selections from the Annales, Economies, Sociétés, Civilisations.* Baltimore, 1977, pp. 31–49

Le Goff, T. J. A. *Vannes and its Region: a Study of Town and Country in Eighteenth-Century France.* Oxford, 1981

Le Goff, T. J. A. and Sutherland, D. M. G. 'The Social Origins of Counter-Revolution in Western France', *Past and Present,* 99 (1983), 65–87
'Religion and Rural Revolt in the French Revolution: an Overview', in J. M. Bak and G. Benecke (eds.), *Religion and Rural Revolt: Papers presented to the Fourth Interdisciplinary Workshop on Peasant Studies, University of British Columbia, 1982.* Manchester, 1984, pp. 123–45

Lemarchand, G. 'La Féodalité et la Révolution française: seigneurs et communauté paysanne (1780–1799)', *Ann. hist. Rév. fran.,* 52 (1980), 536–58

Le Roy Ladurie, E. 'Révoltes et contestations rurales en France de 1675 à 1788', *Annales E.S.C.,* 29 (1974), 6–22

Lucas, C. *The Structure of the Terror: the Example of Javogues and the Loire.* Oxford, 1973
'The Problem of the Midi in the French Revolution', *Transactions of the Royal Historical Society,* 28 (1978), 1–25
'Résistances populaires à la Révolution dans le sud-est', in *Mouvements populaires et conscience sociale. Colloque de l'Université de Paris VII, Paris, 24–26 mai 1984.* Paris, 1985, pp. 473–85

Lyons, M. 'Politics and Patois: the linguistic policy of the French Revolution', *Australian Journal of French Studies*, 18 (1981), 264–81

Maintenant, G. *Les Jacobins*. Paris, 1984

Malrieu, V. *Cahiers de doléances de la sénéchaussée de Montauban et du pays et jugerie de Rivière-Verdun pour les Etats Généraux de 1789*. Montauban, 1925

Marion, M. *La Vente des biens nationaux pendant la Révolution avec étude spéciale des ventes dans les départements de la Gironde et du Cher*. Paris, 1908

'Le Recouvrement des impôts en 1790', *Revue historique*, 121 (1916), 1–47

Martin, D. 'La Vente des biens des émigrés dans le district de Clermont-Ferrand, 1792–1830', in G. Gerbaud, A. Lamadon, D. Martin and J. Petelet, *La Révolution dans le Puy-de-Dôme*. Paris, 1972, pp. 146–216

Marx, R. *La Révolution et les classes sociales en Basse-Alsace. Structures agraires et vente des biens nationaux*. Paris, 1974

Mathiez, A. 'La Politique sociale de Robespierre', *Annales révolutionnaires*, 6 (1913), 551–63

La Révolution française, 3 vols., Paris, 1932–3

Matthews, G. T. *The Royal General Farms in Eighteenth-Century France*. New York, 1958

McManners, J. *The French Revolution and the Church*. London, 1969

'Tithe in Eighteenth-Century France: a Focus for Rural Anticlericalism', in D. Beales and G. Best (eds.), *History, Society and the Churches, Essays in Honour of Owen Chadwick*. Cambridge, 1985, pp. 147–68

Merley, J. *La Haute-Loire de la fin de l'ancien régime aux débuts de la Troisième République*, 2 vols., Le Puy, 1974

Métin, A. *La Révolution et autonomie locale*. Toulouse, 1904

Michelet, J. *Histoire de la Révolution française*, 9 vols., Paris, n.d.

Millot, J. *Le Régime féodal en Franche-Comté au XVIIIe siècle*. Besançon, 1937

L'Abolition des droits seigneuriaux dans le département du Doubs et la région Comtoise. Besançon, 1941

Minoret, M. *La Contribution personnelle et mobilière pendant la Révolution*. Paris, 1900

Molinier, J. 'L'Evolution de la population agricole du XVIIIe siècle à nos jours', *Economie et statistique*, 91 (1977), 79–84

Mombet, F. 'Langue, mœurs et coutumes: une enquête historique', *Revue de l'Agenais*, 108 (1981), 29–45

Monteil, A.-A. *Description du département de l'Aveiron*, 2 vols., Paris, *an* X

Histoire des Français des divers états aux cinq derniers siècles, 10 vols., Paris, 1828–44

Morineau, M. *Les Faux-semblants d'un démarrage économique: agriculture et démographie en France au XVIIIe siècle (Cahier des Annales*, 30). Paris, 1971

Muller, M. and Aberdam, S. 'Conflits de dîme et révolution en Gascogne gersoise, 1750–1800' (n.p., Mémoire de maîtrise sous la direction de M. Robert Mandrou, 1971–2)

Nadaud, M. *Mémoires de Léonard, ancien garçon maçon*. Paris, 1976

Ory, J.-M. 'Sociétés et mentalités vosgiennes à la veille de la Révolution d'après les cahiers de doléances des communautés du bailliage de Mirecourt en Lorraine (mars 1789)', *Bulletin de la Société philomatique vosgienne*, 84 (1981), 71–103; 85 (1981), 49–100

Pageot, P. 'La Vente des biens des émigrés dans le district de Guéret', *Mémoires de la Société des sciences naturelles et archéologiques de la Creuse*, 40 (1980), 594–611

Petitfrère, C. 'Les Grandes Composantes sociales des armées Vendéennes d'Anjou', *Ann. hist. Rév. fran.*, 45 (1973), 1–20

Poitrineau, A. *La Vie rurale en Basse Auvergne au XVIIIe siècle*. Paris, 1965
'Les Assemblées primaires du bailliage de Salers en 1789', *Rev. d'hist. mod. et contemp.*, 25 (1978), 419–42

Porée, C. (ed.) *Cahiers de doléances du bailliage de Sens pour les Etats-Généraux de 1789*. Auxerre, 1908

Redfield, R. *Peasant Society and Culture*. Chicago, 1956

Richard, J. 'La Levée de 300,000 hommes et les troubles de mars 1793 en Bourgogne', *Annales de Bourgogne*, 33 (1961), 213–51

Richeprey, J. F. Henry de, *see* Guilhamon, H. (ed.)

Richert, G. 'Biens communaux et droits d'usage en Haute-Garonne pendant la Réaction thermidorienne et sous le Directoire', *Ann. hist. Rév. fran.*, 23 (1951), 274–88

Riffaterre, C. 'Les Revendications économiques et sociales des assemblées primaires de juillet 1793', *Commission de recherche et de publication des documents relatifs à la vie économique de la Révolution, Bulletin trimestriel* (1906), 321–80

Rigal, J.-L. (ed.) *Comité de surveillance de Saint Geniez-d'Olt. Procès-verbaux et arrêtés*. Rodez, 1942

Robespierre, M., *see* Bouloiseau, M. and Soboul, A. (eds.)

Robin, R. *La Société française en 1789: Semur-en-Auxois*. Paris, 1970

Rocquain, F. (ed.) *L'Etat de la France au 18 Brumaire d'après les rapports des conseillers d'état chargés d'une enquête sur la situation de la République*. Paris, 1874

Root, H. L. 'En Bourgogne: l'état et la communauté rurale, 1661–1789', *Annales E.S.C.*, 37 (1982), 288–302
'Challenging the Seigneurie: Community and Contention on the Eve of the French Revolution', *The Journal of Modern History*, 57 (1985), 652–81

Rose, R. B. 'Tax Revolt and Popular Organization in Picardy, 1789–91', *Past and Present*, 43 (1969), 92–108

Saby, M. *Allègre et sa région au fil des siècles*. Le Puy, 1976

Sagnac, P. *La Législation civile de la Révolution française, 1789–1804*. Paris, 1898

Saint Jacob, P. de *Les Paysans de la Bourgogne du nord au dernier siècle de l'ancien régime*. Dijon, 1960

Sallmann, J.-M. 'Le Partage des biens communaux en Artois, 1770–1789', *Etudes rurales*, 67 (1977), 209–23

Schnerb, R. *Les Contributions directes à l'époque de la Révolution dans le département du Puy-de-Dôme*. Paris, 1933

Secher, R. *Le Génocide franco-français, la Vendée-Vengé*. Paris, 1986

Sheppard, T. S. *Lourmarin in the Eighteenth Century: a Study of a French Village*. Baltimore, 1971

Soboul, A. 'A propos d'une thèse récente: sur le mouvement paysan dans la Révolution française', *Ann. hist. Rév. fran.*, 45 (1973), 85–101
   The French Revolution, 1787–1799. London, 1974
   Problèmes paysannes de la Révolution, 1789–1848. Paris, 1976

Soreau, E. *Ouvriers et paysans de 1789 à 1792*. Paris, 1936

Suratteau, J.-R. 'Heurs et malheurs de la "sociologie électorale" pour l'époque de la Révolution française', *Annales E.S.C.*, 23 (1968), 556–80

Sutherland, D. M. G. *The Chouans: the Social Origins of Popular Counter-Revolution in Upper Brittany, 1770–1796*. Oxford, 1982
   France 1789–1815: Revolution and Counter-Revolution. London, 1985

Tackett, T. 'L'Histoire sociale du clergé diocésain dans la France du XVIIIᵉ siècle', *Rev. d'hist. mod. et contemp.*, 27 (1979), 198–234
   'The West in France in 1789: the Religious Factor in the Origins of the Counter-Revolution', *The Journal of Modern History*, 54 (1982), 715–45
   Religion, Revolution, and Regional Culture in Eighteenth-Century France: The Ecclesiastical Oath of 1791. Princeton, 1986

Tackett, T. and Langlois, C. 'Ecclesiastical Structures and Clerical Geography on the Eve of the French Revolution', *French Historical Studies*, 11 (1980), 352–70

Taylor, G. V. 'Noncapitalist Wealth and the Origins of the French Revolution', *Amer. Hist. Rev.*, 72 (1967), 469–96
   'Revolutionary and Nonrevolutionary Content in the *Cahiers* of 1789: an Interim Report', *French Historical Studies*, 7 (1972), 479–502

Thibaudeau, A. C. *Mémoires sur la Convention et le Directoire*, 2 vols., Paris, 1824

Thiry, J.-L. *Le Département de la Meurthe sous le Consulat*. Nancy, 1958

Tilly, C. *The Vendée*. Cambridge, Mass., 1976

Tisseyre, J.-M. and Baudot, M. (eds.) 'Rapport de Pierre-Joseph Bonnaterre sur l'état du département de l'Aveyron en l'an IV de la République', in *Bulletin de la Section d'histoire moderne et contemporaine du Comité des Travaux historiques et scientifiques*. Paris, 1977, pp. 135–201

Toutain, J.-C. 'Le Produit de l'agriculture française de 1700 à 1958: II, La Croissance', in *Cahiers de l'Institut de science économique appliquée*, supplement to 115 (1961), pp. 1–287

Vernier, J.-J. (ed.) *Cahiers de doléances du bailliage de Troyes (principal et secondaire) et du bailliage de Bar-sur-Seine pour les Etats-Généraux de 1789*. 3 vols. Troyes, 1909–11

Vovelle, M. 'Prêtres abdicataires et déchristianisation en Provence', in *Actes du Quatre-Vingt-Neuvième Congrès National des Sociétés Savantes, Lyon 1964. Section d'histoire moderne et contemporaine* (vol. i, Paris, 1964), pp. 63–97
   'Les Troubles sociaux en Provence (1750–1792)', in *Actes du 93ᵉ Congrès des*

Sociétés Savantes, Section d'histoire moderne et contemporaine, vol. ii (Tours, 1968), pp. 325–72

Piété baroque et déchristianisation en Provence au XVIIIᵉ siècle: les attitudes devant la mort d'après les clauses des testaments. Paris, 1973

'Formes de politisation de la société rurale en Provence sous la Révolution française: entre Jacobinisme et contre-révolution au village', *Annales de Bretagne*, 89 (1982), 185–204

Weitman, S. R. 'Bureaucracy, Democracy and the French Revolution' (unpublished Ph.D. thesis, Washington University, 1968)

Wylie, L. (ed.) *Chanzeaux: a Village in Anjou.* Cambridge, Mass., 1966

Young, A. *Travels in France during the Years 1787, 1788, 1789.* London, 1900

Zink, A. *Azereix: la vie d'une communauté rurale à la fin du XVIIIᵉ siècle.* Paris, 1969

Index

Aberdam, Serge, historian, 99
acaptes, 92
active–passive distinction, 29, 174, 175, 177, 261
Ado, Anatoli, historian, 125, 126, 147
Affiches de Dauphiné, 83
affouages, 19, 21
Agen, 234
Agenais, 71, 78
agrarian capitalism, 127, 137
agrarian disturbances, 8, 61, 67–81, 104, 111–21, 259
'Agrarian Law', 31, 142, 162
agrier, 45
Agulhon, Maurice, historian, 216
aides, 182, 183
Aisne, 107, 133, 145, 160
Aix-en-Provence, 172, 212, 214; district of, 110
Albigeois, 56, 57, 71, 77
Aldias, Jean-Antoine, 244
Alençon, 17
Allassac, 79
Allègre, 135, 136
alleux, 48, 184
Allier, 114, 145
Allier, Claude, 221, 224
Alsace, 4, 17, 18, 69, 70, 74, 78, 83, 108; *biens nationaux* in, 157
Amiens, 9; *généralité* of, 181
Amont, *bailliage* of, 95
Amyot, Joseph, 107, 119, 120
Andéol-en-Dauphiné, 109
Angers, 172; jacobin club of, 218
Angoumois, religion in, 194
Anjou, 5, 218; religion in, 194
Arbois, receiver of domains, 108
Ardèche, 108, 109, 121, 144, 173, 202, 204, 220, 254, 262, 263; taxes in, 188;

biens nationaux in, 244; White Terror in, 245, 246
Ardennes, 91, 105, 130, 145
Arles, 206; *chiffonistes* of, 222
armée révolutionnaire, 235, 239
Armée révolutionnaire du Lot et du Cantal, 237
Arnay-sur-Arroux, 224
Arpajon, 55, 190, 214; district of, 215
Artois, 18, 19, 25, 55; religion in, 194
Artois, Comte de, 218
Assembly of Notables, 27
Aucastel, château of, 116
Auch, archbishop of, 50
Auch, diocese of, 95
Aunis, 48, 107; religion in, 194
Auray, 225
Auriac-L'Eglise, 39
Aurillac, 18, 172
Auriol, 48
Autun, 224
Auvergne, 8, 28, 40, 43, 48, 49, 50, 171; taxes in, 34
Auxerre, *bailliage* of, 59
Auxois, 52, 147, 194
Auxonne, *bailliage* of, 67
Aveline, Jean-Baptiste, 139
Aveyron, 104, 121, 172, 173, 202, 232, 248, 249, 254, 263, 268; *biens nationaux* in, 155; taxes in, 188; patois in, 209; counter-revolution in, 221, 222; White Terror in, 243, 244–5, 246
Azereix, 17, 231

Babeuf, François-Noël, 162, 165, 182, 217
Bachivilliers, 66
bailliage assemblies, 62, 63, 64, 65, 66, 67, 74, 215

298